A HIGHLAND LEGACY

The Maitlands of Tain, their Work and their World

HAMISH MACKENZIE

Grosvenor House
Publishing Limited

This book is published by
Grosvenor House Publishing Ltd
Link House
140 The Broadway, Tolworth, Surrey, KT6 7HT.
www.grosvenorhousepublishing.co.uk

A CIP record for this book
is available from the British Library

ISBN 978-1-83975-346-6

In Loving Memory of
Jacqueline Roberta Mackenzie, 1951-2007

CONTENTS

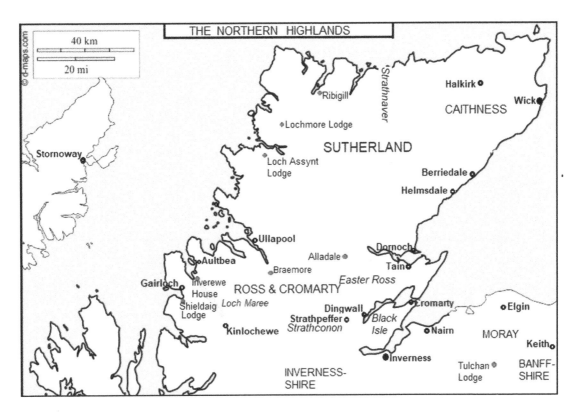

THE NORTHERN HIGHLANDS

40 km
20 mi

Stornoway

Ribigill
Lochmore Lodge
SUTHERLAND
Loch Assynt Lodge

Halkirk
Wick
CAITHNESS

Berriedale
Helmsdale

Ullapool
Aultbea
Alladale
Dornoch
Tain
Braemore
Easter Ross

Gairloch
Inverewe House
ROSS & CROMARTY
Shieldaig Lodge
Loch Maree
Kinlochewe
Strathpeffer
Strathconon
Black Isle
Cromarty
Elgin
Nairn
MORAY
Keith

Dingwall

Inverness
Tulchan Lodge
BANFF-SHIRE
INVERNESS-SHIRE

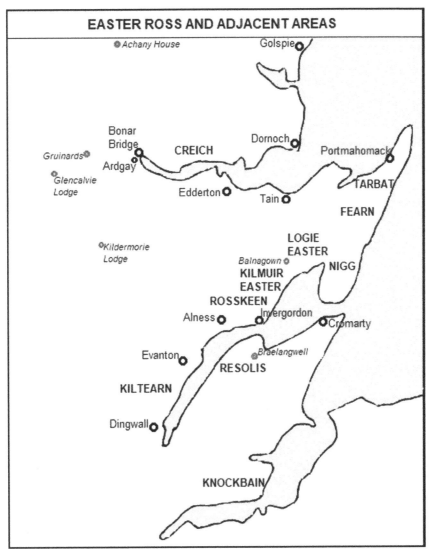

EASTER ROSS AND ADJACENT AREAS

Achany House
Golspie

Bonar Bridge
CREICH
Dornoch
Portmahomack
Gruinards
Ardgay
TARBAT
Glencalvie Lodge
Edderton
Tain
FEARN

Kildermorie Lodge
LOGIE EASTER
Balnagown
NIGG
KILMUIR EASTER
ROSSKEEN
Alness
Invergordon
Cromarty
Evanton
Braelangwell
RESOLIS
KILTEARN
Dingwall

KNOCKBAIN

v i i

INTRODUCTION

About this book

If you are looking for an architectural guide you will be disappointed by this book.

If, on the other hand, you feel that the story of a dynasty of architects, the mark they left both on their home town of Tain and the wider Northern Highland scene, and their involvement in some of the great themes of the history of the Highlands in Victorian and Edwardian times might appeal to you then please do read on. For my interest is in the people for whom the Maitland buildings were constructed, and in why they were built. This book is about the Maitlands themselves, the clients for whom they were designing buildings, and the economic and social factors that influenced their demand, and it ventures into some of the main highways, and also some of the intriguing byways, of the history of Tain and the Highlands.

The years during which the Maitland family operated were ones which saw technological and social changes at a faster pace than at any time in previous history, changes taking place in tandem with significant religious and political developments. The Highlands saw 'Improvement' and then 'High Farming', patterns of agriculture which gave us much of the rural landscape we see to-day in the rich agricultural areas of Easter Ross and the Black Isle; further north and west the controversial 'Highland Clearances' of the glens and straths for sheep farming, and later the replacement of sheep farms by deer forests which became a playground for the aristocracy and the newly rich of the Victorian and Edwardian eras; two major and dramatic religious schisms which produced the Free Church and the United Free Church; political reforms that led away from the 'parish state', with its twin pillars of heritors (landowners) and a church with important civil and judicial functions, and towards central oversight of provision for matters such as the poor law and education; the coming of the railways, with huge benefits to tourism, commerce and agriculture; the increasing wealth and power of the middle classes, which allowed them to employ architects not only to design villas but also to finance public halls and bigger and better churches; a burgeoning civic pride which left its mark on the infrastructure of Highland burghs (not least Tain); and the transformation of the malt whisky industry from a farmhouse operation into the largest manufacturing industry in the Highlands.

Each of these developments led to a demand for new buildings or the improvement of existing ones. The Maitlands earned their living by trying to satisfy those demands. And in so doing they rubbed shoulders with a wide variety of people, some of them well known to Highland, and often national, history, others long since forgotten but still interesting in their historical context.

Tain and the Maitlands

The ancient Royal Burgh of Tain in Easter Ross, some forty miles north of Inverness, is one of the gems of the Scottish Highlands - not least because of its numerous attractive buildings.

There are several approaches to Tain. Most of these present an enticing prospect - a prospect which remains hauntingly in the memory of those who love Tain but live far away. My own usual approach is from the east, driving along the long straight road from Portmahomack. You see Tain set on an ancient raised beach, with the coastal plain below and the Hill of Tain rising above it and forming a scenic backdrop. As you get nearer the image of Tain increases in size like that in a zoom lens. The roofline comes ever more sharply into focus and is dominated by two complementary towers, the steeple, with its attendant bartizans, of the early eighteenth century Tolbooth and the tall campanile of A. Maitland & Sons' Parish Church of 1891-92.

There is perhaps something symbolic about this apparent juxtaposition of a building which symbolised the burghal status of the ancient Royal Burgh and of the most prominent work of the architects who designed so much of the Tain we know to-day.

When you arrive in Tain you see more of this juxtaposition. At the heart of Tain, close to the Tolbooth, is the historic Collegiate Church, one of the most important centres of pilgrimage in medieval Scotland. Around the centre of the town are Victorian and early twentieth century Maitland buildings in a variety of styles. Joined to the Tolbooth is the Sheriff Court, in Scottish Baronial style - designed, as we will see, by Andrew Maitland, but bizarrely ascribed by all the experts to an architect whose plans were rejected. At a right angle to it, and closing off the end of the High Street, is the French Gothic Royal Hotel; behind the hotel the Renaissance Town Hall in Tower Street; a few doors along from the Tolbooth Flemish Renaissance shops; and uphill from the Tolbooth the Italianate Parish Church. The Post Office, the Library and the Masons' Lodge are all Maitland buildings. Not far away from the centre there are elegant Maitland-designed houses built for the late Victorian and Edwardian middle classes, including three built for the Maitlands themselves and two (Mansfield House and Morangie House) now operated as hotels. One and a half miles to the west is the Glenmorangie distillery, Maitland-designed and once run by the Maitlands themselves, a business which put Tain on the world stage.

Few Scottish burghs - indeed few British towns - reflect to such a degree the work of one family over such a long period. In the course of this work the Maitlands gave Tain an exuberant variety of styles befitting a vibrant time in its history, but they also gave it an essential harmony which remains to-day - a harmony of proportion, a harmony enhanced by the frequent use in their time, as in earlier ages, of the sand coloured stone from the quarry on the Hill of Tain.

Across the Northern Highlands

The Maitlands also left their mark beyond Tain and across the Northern Highlands. Their influence is particularly marked in the rich agricultural land of the eastern coastal plain, whose landscape, full of Maitland-designed farm houses, farm cottages and steadings, they helped to transform into the one we know to-day. Most of the steadings and cottages are functional and unpretentious rather than architectural treasures, but they are a living testament to the 'High Farming' of the Victorian and Edwardian period. The area also has numerous mansion houses that the Maitlands designed or renovated for landowners, including notable ones at Kincraig and Delny, and even castles such as Tulloch at Dingwall. Many of these are today used as hotels.

Venture into more remote parts of the Highlands and you find many sporting lodges, some still in use and others now converted to hotels - lodges that were built, extended or adapted for the social gatherings that so attracted the Victorian and Edwardian social élite, Glencalvie, Gruinards, Shieldaig and Flowerdale among them.

And in most of the towns and villages on the Maitlands' patch, not least Dornoch (whose skyline is dominated by the Maitland-designed Burghfield), Invergordon, Cromarty and those around the Kyle of Sutherland, there are Maitland buildings - churches, schools, public halls, villas, police stations, libraries, banks and other commercial buildings - albeit often converted to new uses.

Further afield, the parish of Gairloch on the west coast has a number of Maitland-designed or Maitland-extended buildings, including the Loch Maree Hotel, where Queen Victoria stayed, the Gairloch Hotel and Flowerdale. And among the most important Maitland buildings to the south are St Ninian's Church in Nairn and Tulchan Lodge on Speyside.

The Maitland story ...

The Maitland story begins with Andrew Maitland, who was born in 1802. He could be said to have been a late developer, since he did not set himself up as an architect in Tain until the early 1840s. For the next quarter of a century he worked as a sole practitioner with a mainly rural practice. In Part I of this book we see him building up a practice and working for many of the great estates of the Highlands, including those of the 2nd Duke of Sutherland, the opium trader Sir Alexander Matheson, Osgood Mackenzie of Inverewe and Sir John Fowler of Forth Bridge fame.

In the early 1870s Andrew was joined in his practice by two of his sons, James (born in 1845) and Andrew Junior (born in 1847). He himself continued to work until he was about 90. Andrew Junior, very much an entrepreneur, was the guiding force in the establishment of the Glenmorangie Distillery Company. For two decades he was one of the civic leaders of Tain and for six months until his premature death in 1898 Provost of Tain.[1] The years between 1870 and 1898 were the golden years of the Maitlands' business. They saw an explosion of demand for new buildings for civic and commercial purposes, hotels, schools, distilleries, mansion houses for landlords and farm houses for their tenants, shooting lodges, bigger and better churches, and villas for the middle classes. In order to try to explain the diverse factors that led to this demand the chapters in Part II of this book are mainly thematic, albeit broadly chronological within each of the themes.

From 1898 James Maitland was sole proprietor of the Maitland business, and in 1903 he took into partnership a fourth member of the family, Andrew Junior's son Gordon. Their story is told in Part III. The years up to 1914 saw a continuation of many of the themes of the previous century, though on a reduced scale. They also saw some new or enhanced sources of demand for buildings, including better cottages for farm workers, Free Libraries financed by Andrew Carnegie, a robber baron turned philanthropist, and United Free Churches (many today used as parish churches). James followed his younger brother as Managing Director of Glenmorangie and also into local government, serving as Provost of Tain from 1910 to 1921. James Maitland retired from the partnership in 1921, and Gordon, who had suffered in the Great War, in 1922.

... and who commissioned the Maitlands ? ... and why?

In 2005, having just joined the Tain & Easter Ross Civic Trust, I ventured to suggest that as part of *Highland 2007*, a celebration of Highland culture, the Trust should organise an exhibition to commemorate the Maitlands' contribution to the architectural heritage of Tain. Muggins was hoist with his own petard: it fell to me to organise this exhibition. Lachie Stewart, Chairman of the Trust and himself one of the leading Scottish architects of his generation, suggested that it would be of interest to address two questions - who were the people who engaged the Maitlands to design these buildings? and why did they do so? As I looked for the answers to these questions I found myself delving ever more deeply into the social and economic history of Victorian and Edwardian Tain, its hinterland in Easter Ross, and the wider areas of the Northern Highlands in which they received commissions - the backdrop to their lives and work. I found myself researching, too, the people with whom the Maitlands rubbed shoulders professionally, socially and in local affairs, and especially those who engaged their services. As I accumulated more and more material I found that I was writing a book.

My aim became to cast light both on the private individuals and on the civic authorities, school boards, church congregations and other bodies in Tain and the Northern Highlands who commissioned their work in the nineteenth and early twentieth centuries, and also on the factors, particularly social and economic, that led them to do so.

I learnt that if you look at a building simply as part of the built environment you are observing only one dimension, but that if you consider who it was built for and the factors behind why it was built you can see it in three dimensions.

Hunting for information

Fortunately the Northern Highlands is well served by two outstanding architectural guides. John Gifford's *Highland and Islands* in the *Buildings of Scotland* series, a product of years of painstaking research, is a tour de force.[2] Elizabeth Beaton's *Ross & Cromarty: An Illustrated Architectural Guide* and the companion volumes on *Sutherland* and *Caithness* together constitute a wonderful and well illustrated guide and companion to the best of the built environment in the Northern Highlands.[3] I have relied heavily on both these authors. To anyone interested in the buildings of the area I very enthusiastically recommend them both.

During the long gestation period of this book Historic Scotland published *Historic Tain - Archaeology and Development*, a survey in their Scottish Burgh series of the history and archaeology of Tain.[4] This provides a useful insight into the growth of Tain from its medieval origins as a place of pilgrimage, through the centuries, including the Maitland era, and into the present - though my own researches, as the astute reader may perhaps note, have led me to differing conclusions on certain matters. Also during this period the Highland Council commissioned Alan Marshall to produce a *Tain Conservation Area Appraisal*.[5] This is a perceptive study of the buildings in the historic centre of Tain and their context, and it has both informed my own writing and suggested areas for me to investigate.

This being the age of the internet, architectural information is, moreover, also readily available online. *The Dictionary of Scottish Architects* provides information about architects who practiced in Scotland between 1840 and 1980 and about the buildings they designed.[6] The information about the Maitlands themselves, reflecting the absence to date of any biographies is brief, but nevertheless provided several useful leads. The information on Maitland buildings is extremely valuable, being based on press coverage, particularly invitations to tender advertised in local newspapers. The *Highland Historic Environment Record (HER)* contains records of historic buildings, often very informative, in the Highland Council region.[7]

There is thus a wealth of information, albeit somewhat dispersed, on the architecture of many of the surviving Maitland buildings. I became aware from very early in my quest, however, that there were significant gaps in the existing knowledge of the main objectives of my study, the Maitlands themselves and for whom and why they designed these buildings.

First, I found that there was surprisingly little biographical information about the Maitlands. Fortunately the personal information available, though brief, was of excellent quality. Newspaper obituaries were easy to find, and I also came across a useful article on 'The Maitlands of Tain', written when James Maitland became Provost of Tain in 1910.[8] Rosemary Mackenzie (no relation of mine, but a pupil and later a close friend of my own Mackenzie aunts) and Jane Durham produced, moreover, in 1984 an A4 brochure for a Maitland Exhibition. The Tain & District Museum (founded by Rosemary Mackenzie) was able to provide fuller typescript notes, which could have been either an early draft or a later expansion of the brochure.[9]

These were invaluable in giving personal information, and in suggesting several lines of research into the Maitlands, many of which I might well have overlooked.

It was, moreover, disappointing to find a shortage of published information about Tain in Victorian and Edwardian times. The three standard histories of Tain have little or nothing to say about the social or economic history of the period. The Rev. William Taylor, whose *Researches into the History of Tain* was published in 1882, saw events of the nineteenth century as 'too close to be able to proceed further with ease'.[10] R.W. and Jean Munro only devoted 12 of the 131 pages in their otherwise admirable *Tain through the Centuries* (published in 1966) to events after 1837.[11] And Alan Robertson in his entertaining *The Lowland Highlanders* (published three years later) gave a mere 2 of his 110 pages to history after 1837.[12] Tain needs a work - comparable to those published in recent years on Cromarty, Wick, and Victorian Elgin - which gives the nineteenth and twentieth centuries the same attention as earlier periods.

Histories of the wider Highland scene in the years during which the Maitlands were active have for my purposes been something like the proverbial curate's egg. Many eminent historians have written, often movingly, about the Highland Clearances, and their accounts have informed the sections of my book that touch on the Clearances. But in looking at the later Victorian and the Edwardian Highlands historians have tended to concentrate more on the hardships endured by crofters than on the relatively more prosperous practitioners of 'High Farming' or on the growth and increasing power of the rural and urban middle classes. One exception, a work that does cover wider social and economic issues, is Marinell Ash's history of the Cromarty Firth,[13] a book full of useful insights on the Firth and the communities surrounding it.

These gaps have meant that I have had to research the history of the area in the Victorian and Edwardian ages almost from scratch, making particular use of council and other minutes and newspaper archives.[14] Fortunately local newspapers of the period were able to employ reporters on a scale which their successors must envy, and they thus contain a wealth of information.

My researches have sometimes led me to conclude that some widely stated bits of information do not accord with the records of the Maitlands' time. Thus I had to read the Minutes of Tain Burgh Council half a dozen times before I realised that they were telling me that the Tain Court House was not designed, as all the literature recounts, by Thomas Brown but by Andrew Maitland - a realisation I found supported by a mass of contemporary newspaper articles. I am, however, very conscious of the fact that some of my own interpretations may have to be revised when a more modern history of Tain or a wider social and economic history of the Highlands is written. I am aware too that what I have written deals, often for the first time, with significant numbers of buildings and of men and women who commissioned them. This means that, notwithstanding the efforts of those who have been kind enough to read this book, or parts of it, in draft, there is plenty of scope for errors of fact. I would welcome any suggestions for incorporation in any later editions of this book that may be published.

Hamish Mackenzie
Portmahomack
October 2020

References and Notes

[1] Several published works refer to Andrew Junior as having been Provost from 1879 to 1898 - a misunderstanding which appears to derive from the date "1897" having been rendered as "1879" in a list of Provosts in one of the main histories of Tain.

[2] John Gifford, *Highlands and Islands*, Pevsner Architectural Guides, The Buildings of Scotland, Penguin Books, 1992 - referred to hereinafter as Gifford, *Highlands and Islands*.

[3] Elizabeth Beaton, *Ross & Cromarty, An Illustrated Architectural Guide*, Royal Incorporation of Architects in Scotland, 1992; and *Sutherland,* 1995 and *Caithness,* 1996, both in the same series - referred to hereinafter as Beaton, *Ross & Cromarty*, Beaton, *Sutherland* and Beaton, *Caithness.*

[4] R.D. Oram, P.F. Martin, C.A. McKean, T. Neighbour and A. Cathcart, *Historic Tain - Archaeology and Development*, Historic Scotland, 2009.

[5] Highland Council, 2016.

[6] *Dictionary of Scottish Architects*, www.scottisharchitects.org.uk.

[7] *Highland Historic Environmental Record (HER)*, www.her.highland.gov.uk.

[8] Obituaries: Andrew Maitland - *Inverness Courier*, 29th May, 1894 and *Banffshire Journal and General Advertiser*, 5th June, 1894; Andrew Junior - *Inverness Courier*, 6th May, 1898, *Ross-shire Journal*, 6th May, 1898, *North Star and Farmers' Chronicle*, 5th May, 1898; James - *Inverness Courier*, 16th April, 1929, *Ross-shire Journal*, 19th April, 1929. Article 'The Maitlands of Tain', *Ross-shire Journal*, 18th November, 1910.

[9] Mackenzie and Durham, *The Maitland Family, Tain, 1840s to 1930s*, Tain & District Museum, 1984.

[10] The Rev. William Taylor, *Researches into the History of Tain: Earlier and Later*, John Menzies & Co., 1882. He did, however, make an exception for the restoration of the Collegiate Church.

[11] R.W. and Jean Munro, *Tain through the Centuries*, Tain Town Council, 1966.

[12] Alan G.R. Robertson, *The Lowland Highlanders*: *The Story True and Traditional of Tain and District*, Tower Bookshop, Tain, 1969.

[13] Marinell Ash, *This Noble Harbour - A History of the Cromarty Firth*, Cromarty Firth Port Authority, 1991.

[14] The *Am Baile* Searchable Newspaper Index (www.ambaile.org.uk) and the British Newspaper Archive (www. britishnewspaperarchive.co.uk) were particularly useful, the latter containing invaluable archives of the *Inverness Courier*, the *Ross-shire Journal* and the *North Star and Farmers' Chronicle*.

ACKNOWLEDGEMENTS

Jacqueline, my late wife, inspired me to write this book, and it is dedicated to her treasured memory.

The proceeds of the initial print run and all future royalties will go to the Tain & District Museum, which needs funds at a time when supporting museums ranks low amongst official priorities. The help of Margaret Urquhart, former Manager of the museum and the leading expert of our day on the history of Tain, has been crucial. She read the whole of my first draft, made numerous helpful suggestions and answered all the questions I put to her. She also produced the two fine maps. Her successor Morag Bremner gave valuable help in the early stages of my researches and later took photographs to my demanding specifications. I have also received valuable practical assistance from the present incumbent, Sheila Munro.

Mindful of the observation of George W. Bush, 43rd President of the United States, that 'one of the great things about books is sometimes there are some fantastic pictures', and concerned that those wading through 130,000 words of my turgid prose deserve some light relief, I have been keen to assemble enlightening illustrations. I am particularly grateful to the Tain & District Museum which has allowed me to dig deeply into its collection and to Jason Ubych for significant help in supplying images.

For one who dabbles in history but knows little about architecture to write about a dynasty of architects and their buildings is inherently risky. When I started my researches the noted architectural historian the late John Gifford MBE kindly sent me a copy of a groundbreaking article he wrote on Highland architects in the nineteenth century, and I have also relied heavily on his architectural guide to the Highlands in the Buildings of Scotland series and contributions to the *Dictionary of Scottish Architects*. As my labours drew towards a close the distinguished architect Alan Marshall very generously took time to read my entire text in draft and to put me right where necessary.

The help of Pauline Butler, author of a fine book on the Maitlands' client Osgood Mackenzie of Inverewe, has been invaluable. She read first drafts of a chapter and several sections of other chapters on Maitland works in Gairloch, made useful corrections and helped with illustrations. She also proof-read my complete final draft diligently and made numerous constructive suggestions.

Iain Russell, Brands Heritage Manager of The Glenmorangie Distillery Company Ltd and an expert on the history of the whisky industry, kindly read a chapter on the Maitland distilleries and provided images. Dr Jim Mackay, the guiding spirit behind the Kirkmichael Trust, vetted the chapter on Andrew Maitland's time in Resolis and provided helpful material. Douglas Gordon, from a farming dynasty which rubbed shoulders with the Maitlands, has kindly read chapters on buildings of the land and churches and helped in sourcing images. Iona Evans, granddaughter of the Count de Serra Largo of Tarlogie, has commented on sections on her larger than life grandfather and provided useful information.

I am grateful to the following for providing information, images, practical help or encouragement: Dr John Anderson, Hilary Andexer, Jane Armstrong, Helen Campbell, Colin and June Dingley, Graham Eunson, Gordon Forbes, Justine Golesworthy, Rachel Graham, Richard Littlewood, the Rev. John MacLeod, David McAllister, Bill McDougall, Meryl Marshall, Andrew Munro, Arlene Petrie, Jenny Reid, Jack, Vivianne and Douglas Reid, Ross Robertson, Jim Ritchie, Lachie Stewart, the late Susannah Stone and Dr Tilda Watson.

The staff of the National Records of Scotland, Historic Environment Scotland, the Highland Archive Centre, the Highland Council's Inverness and Dingwall Libraries and its *Am Baile* Newspaper Index and Photographic Collection have all been particularly helpful; and I am also indebted to volunteers and staff at the other bodies listed in the Illustration Credits.

Finally, my thanks are due to Becky Banning, who has steered a technophobic novice through the complexities of publication, and to her colleagues at Grosvenor House Publishing.

ILLUSTRATION CREDITS

Am Baile: 7.2, 7.3, 7.5, 17.1, 18.3, 18.6, 19.2, 19.4, and 24.3.

Morag Bremner: 18.8, 20.1, 23.1.

Crown Copyright, National Records of Scotland (RHP21795): 5.2.

Colin Dingley: 18.7.

Iona Evans: 18.5.

Mary Evans/Peter Higginbotham Collection: 7.1.

Flickr, under Creative Commons Licence CC BY-SA 2.0: 8.2 (Dave Conner).

Gairloch Museum: 14.1 and 14.3.

Geograph.org.uk, under Creative Commons Licences CC BY-SA 2.0: 1.1 (Anne Burgess), 3.2 (Richard Dorrell), 11.1 (Valenta), 12.9 (John Lord), 15.2 (Michael Shepherd), 23.2 (Trevor Littlewood), 19.3 (Sylvia Duckworth), 25.5 (Richard Sutcliffe).

The Glenmorangie Co. Ltd: 16.1 and 16.3.

Justine Golesworthy: 6.3.

Google Art Project: 1.2.

Graham & Sibbald: 18.2.

Highland Archive Centre: 3.3, 5.3.

Highland Historic Buildings Trust: 13.2.

Historic Environment Scotland: 12.6 (from the Tain & District Museum Collection), 17.2, and (copied by HES from a 1904 *Guide to the Royal Burgh of Tain and Surrounding District*) 21.1, 25.2 and 25.4.

History of Tain Royal Academy Project: 3.1.

Inverewe House Archives, courtesy of the National Trust for Scotland: 7.6 and 23.3.

The Invergordon Archive: 26.1.

Bill McDougall: 8.1.

Andrew Munro: 18.1.

Private collection: 20.3.

Royal Collection Trust/© Her Majesty Queen Elizabeth II 2020: 14.2.

Tain & District Museum Trust: 2.1, 2.2, 4.1, 5.1, 6.1, 6.2, 9.1, 9.2, 10.1, 12.1, 12.2, 12.3, 12.4, 12.5, 12.7, 12.8, 13.1, 13.3, 15.3, 17.3, 20.2, 21.2, 21.3, 22.1, 22.2, 22.3, 24.1, 25.1, 25.3, 26.2 and 26.3.

Tarbat Discovery Centre: 15.1, 17.4, 24.2.

Tulloch Castle Hotel (Arlene Petrie): 18.4.

Wikimedia Commons, public domain: 7.4, 16.2.

Wikipedia, public domain: 19.1.

PART I

ANDREW MAITLAND IN THE YEARS TO 1870

1. ANDREW MAITLAND - THE EARLY YEARS

The shoemaker's son

Andrew Maitland was born on 25th October, 1802, and was baptised on 8th November, in the parish of Keith, Banffshire, midway between Inverness and Aberdeen. He was the fourth of five children born to Alexander Maitland and Christian Gordon, who both lived at the time of their marriage on 9th July, 1793 in what the Old Statistical Account called the 'large, regular and tolerably thriving' village of New Keith. The birth of their first child, William, five months and one day later may have occasioned some remark amongst those who knew them, and perhaps admonitions from the Minister.

An article published in the *Ross-shire Journal* in 1910[1] tells us that Andrew was educated at the Parochial School in Keith under John Law, 'a dominie still remembered in Banffshire for his rare talent in handling lads o' pregnant pairts'. In later life Andrew recalled the rejoicing in Keith at the news of the victory at Waterloo.

1.1 Keith Parish Church.

William and Andrew did not follow the trade of their father, a shoemaker. William became a mason and plied his trade in Keith until his death in 1863. Andrew was, we are told, 'meant for the Church', but 'his tastes lay otherwise and he had his own way'. He had an artistic bent, but although Banffshire was soon to produce some prominent painters he decided on leaving school to enter the building trade. He is said to have been stimulated in this ambition by observing the architectural plans prepared in 1816 by James Gillespie Graham, then well known as a church architect, for a new parish church in Keith. The church, now known as St Rufus Church, was built in the Neo-Perpendicular Gothic style. It has tall and distinctive hoodmoulded, traceried windows and a tower with ornate stonework.

Learning his craft

In the early nineteenth century architecture was by no means the structured profession we would recognise to-day. In the north of Scotland most architectural work, both for landed estates and for public buildings, had, for hundreds of years, been done mainly by masons or building contractors who doubled as architects. Where the need arose architects from further afield might be used. Only the very large estates such as the Sutherland and Macdonald estates employed resident architects.[2]

It was in the building trade rather than in an architect's office that Andrew Maitland began to acquire the skills that would enable him to set himself up as an architect.

After leaving school he worked for a couple of years for a builder in Keith. He then travelled extensively, working in the early part of his career in Aberdeen, Newcastle, Edinburgh and London. Whilst he learnt about the technicalities of building, Andrew's ambition to be an architect would have been nurtured by the designs he saw around him.

In the years after the Napoleonic Wars Aberdeen was in an expansionary phase, with significant economic and population growth and building activity. The period saw the centre of Aberdeen transformed, under the aegis of its civic leaders, by a series of bold schemes whose dominant architectural feature was neo-Greek classicism. Axial streets were provided with new public buildings and were flanked by residential areas - all built in the characteristic local grey granite. By great good fortune Aberdeen could boast at this time two extremely talented architects. The elder of these was John Smith, born in 1781, who came from a family of builder-architects with useful connections. He had become Superintendent to the New Streets' Trustees in 1807, an appointment which developed in the 1820s into that of City Architect. In this capacity he designed a succession of public and ecclesiastical buildings in the Grecian style. His younger rival was Archibald Simpson, born in 1790. Simpson's parents had died young and he was supported by a builder-architect uncle, who probably encouraged him to serve an apprenticeship as a mason. Simpson went on to design a series of mainly Grecian public buildings which made a distinguished contribution to the shaping of classical Aberdeen. One of his finest works was the majestic North of Scotland Bank on the corner of Union Street and King Street - now a pub called the Archibald Simpson.

Andrew Maitland's craftsmanship attracted the attention of George Rainnie, 'a large builder and contractor', under whom, it was said, 'he had exceptional facilities for qualifying himself in the principles of building'. He would have worked in a stimulating environment, and he could well have taken part in the building of some of the masterpieces of the two great Aberdeen architects.

Andrew next spent some time in Edinburgh, where he is reputed to have assisted a fellow lodger to set the type for Sir Walter Scott's manuscripts. Among Andrew's reminiscences in later life was the 'unique privilege' of reading the proof-sheets of Scott's *Life of Napoleon Buonaparte, Emperor of the French* (published in June 1827) before they were sent to Sir Walter for correction. He also retained fond memories of William Laidlaw, Scott's amanuensis, steward and trusted friend.[3] It is not clear, however, whether his first meeting with Laidlaw took place whilst he was in Edinburgh or whether they first became acquainted in Ross-shire early in the next decade, when, as we will see in the next chapter, their paths certainly crossed.

1.2 *Princes Street with the Commencement of the Building of the Scottish National Gallery*, by Alexander Nasmyth, 1825.

What building work Andrew did in Edinburgh is not recorded, but he could not have failed to be influenced by the architecture he saw around him. The second half of the eighteenth century had seen the start of the development of the New Town as an up-market residential suburb to the north of the Old Town, with row houses behind classical facades, impressive squares such as Charlotte Square with Robert Adam's unifying 'palace front' design, and grand public buildings such as his General Register House and University College. The neo-classical style still flourished when Andrew came to Edinburgh, and there were still architectural giants at work. He would have been able to observe at first hand their work on realising the dream of completing a Modern Athens. One of these giants was W.H. Playfair, who designed the Royal Institution, now the National Gallery of Scotland (1822-35), and worked - until the money ran out in 1829 - on the transformation of Calton Hill into a new Acropolis. Another was Thomas Hamilton, the architect of the Royal High School. Perhaps the most interesting was William Burn, born in 1789, who combined a prestigious urban practice with an equally prestigious rural one.

Andrew would have been very aware, however, that neo-classicism was by no means the only style in fashion in Edinburgh, let alone in Scotland generally. From the middle of the eighteenth century 'Gothic Revival', reflecting the growth of romanticism and increasing interest in the Middle Ages, had become increasingly popular in many parts of Europe. Scotland found its own national version. In architecture, as in ballads, in novels of the romantic past, and in the cult of tartan, it was Sir Walter Scott who was a pioneer of the new 'Scottish Baronial' style. At Abbotsford in the Borders he had an old farmhouse transformed

4

between 1816 and 1823 into a castellated mansion, and he implemented a scheme of internal decoration designed to look old and specifically Scottish. Scott's son-in-law and biographer, J.G. Lockhart, records that when he returned to Abbotsford to die Sir Walter desired to be wheeled around the house in a bathchair: 'I have seen much', he kept murmuring, 'but nothing like my ain hoose; give me one turn more'.

The Scottish Baronial style of castellated architecture, with features such as crowsteps and bartizans, became popular for secular buildings. It was was enthusiastically endorsed by landowners and architects, notably William Burn himself, who designed numerous country houses in this style and encouraged the publication of R.W. Billings's influential source book *Baronial and Ecclesiastical Antiquities of Scotland*. Andrew Maitland's first work of note was to be in the Scottish Baronial style, and later in the century Andrew and his sons were to produce numerous examples of the style.

Andrew spent some years in London, where he was said to have been employed by 'several of the best known contractors', including Cubitts, a firm founded by the master builder Thomas Cubitt and one of the first to employ all trades in house. He was probably still in London in June 1837, as he is said to have recalled hearing the bell tolling on the death of William IV. Soon thereafter, however, he returned north, 'owing to his health giving way'. Ironically his two architect sons were both to go south for health reasons and to die in southern England.

Working for William Robertson

Our first specific sighting of Andrew as a budding architect is as an assistant to William Robertson, one of the best known early nineteenth century architects in the north of Scotland. Robertson was clearly a considerable influence on Andrew.

Robertson had been born in north east Aberdeenshire in 1786.[4] From around 1814 to 1823 he worked mainly around Cullen in Banffshire, probably from the estate office of the Earl of Seafield, chief of the Clan Grant. The reminiscences of the distinguished civil engineer Joseph Mitchell cast an entertaining light on the affairs of the Grants of Seafield. Before Sir Lewis Alexander Grant succeeded to the earldom in 1811 he had been 'afflicted with mental disorder, from which he never recovered, although he was never violent, nor required to be confined. ... Being thus imbecile and unfit to manage his estates his next brother and heir, Colonel Francis William Grant, was appointed curator-at-law'. Curators were not then obliged to lodge accounts with the Court and 'improvements were made, money borrowed, and the management was conducted very much as if the colonel had been absolute proprietor'.[5] The Colonel's management led to an extensive programme of building works and lengthy litigation. Astonishingly the works included demolishing the whole of the ancient Royal Burgh of Cullen (with the exception of the parish kirk) because it was deemed too close to Cullen House and replacing it with a symmetrically planned successor. Robertson was responsible for the design of the Town Hall, a post office and an hotel (still flourishing as the Seafield Arms Hotel) and stables, a key element in the new town.

By 1823 Robertson had set himself up in practice as an architect in Elgin, Moray (then known as Elginshire). His patrons included the Grants of Seafield and various related Grant families around Speyside. One of these commissioned him to design Aberlour House, a classical mansion built in 1838 'of architectural merit by British as well as Scottish standards, a really major house emanating from provincial Elgin rather than from Archibald Simpson in Aberdeen or from a design by an Edinburgh architect'.[6] It has since been used as the preparatory school for Gordonstoun and more recently as the headquarters of one of Scotland's iconic brands, Walkers Shortbread Ltd.

From the mid 1830s Robertson extended his practice beyond its base in Moray and Banffshire and won business further to the west and north, particularly in Inverness-shire and the twin counties of Ross-shire and Cromartyshire. One major commission was Dochfour House (1839-40), where he converted an eighteenth century laird's house overlooking Loch Ness, belonging to Evan Baillie of Dochfour, into a grand Italianate villa. Another elegant building, well known not least because it now faces the biggest and most used bus station in the Highlands, was the elegant Greek Doric Dr Bell's Academy in Farraline Park, Inverness, built in 1839-41 and today used as a public library.[7]

Such an extension of the practice clearly needed additional skilled assistance. It is known that Andrew Maitland assisted Robertson with work on the National Bank of Scotland in Dingwall. This was designed around 1835 and completed around 1838. It was to be used in the next century as offices for the Hydro Board, and it now serves, its austere Greek lines not improved by a large glazed extension which somehow passed the scrutiny of the planning authority, as the Highland Theological College. As well as working in Dingwall Andrew also did supervisory work for Robertson in the nearby Black Isle - not an island but the southern of two peninsulas with fertile farming land which constitute the east coast of of Ross-shire.

The census taken on 6th June, 1841, the first ever detailed one for the United Kingdom, shows Andrew in the parish of Resolis, on the north of the Black Isle. He was sharing accommodation on the Braelangwell estate with three painters. The eighteenth century mansion of Braelangwell was at that time being remodelled by William Robertson in a neo-classical style for a new owner, Lieutenant General Sir Hugh Hastings Fraser. Obituaries of Andrew record that he superintended the reconstruction. The census, however, describes Andrew as a 'wright', rather than a superintendent of works or an architect. Did the census enumerator's accuracy perhaps suffer from the considerable size of the workforce he had to record on the site in the short time allowed for the census?

Andrew would have learnt much from his experience of working for Robertson - not least the critical dependence of a provincial architect on the patronage of local heritors (landowners), the need to cover the whole range of their requirements from alterations to their farm steadings to the design of a new mansion house, and the improved chances of commissions for more important work from being able to design in a variety of styles and to inject originality into the designs. As he approached the age of 40, however, he must have asked himself what he had achieved. He had plenty of experience of the supervision of building works, experience that would stand him in good stead as an architect; but any architectural designs he had produced could only have been ancillary or minor - hardly fodder for the creative talents that Andrew was later to show. He was, moreover, junior in the hierarchy to Robertson's principal assistant, the 27 year old Thomas Mackenzie, who had joined Robertson in 1839 after training as an architect with his father and elder brother in Perth and had worked for both the great Aberdeen architects John Smith and Archibald Simpson.

Any thoughts Andrew may have had about the future were soon to be thrown into sharp focus. On 12th June, 1841 William Robertson died at Elgin at the age of only 55. Within a fortnight his nephews Alexander and William Reid advertised in the local newspaper that 'having been for several years in his employment as Draughtsmen and Assistants, [they] respectfully intimate that they intend carrying on their late Uncle's business as ARCHITECTS, and solicit the support of Mr Robertson's numerous patrons, in this and the neighbouring counties and of the public generally ... They trust to be favoured with a continuance of the patronage so liberally experienced, for many years, by their late Uncle'.[8] Alexander Reid was 24 or 25 and William only 16 years old, and they went on to re-assure prospective clients that they would be 'professionally assisted both by an experienced House Carpenter and Mason, each of whom had also for some years been in Mr Robertson's employment as superintendent of works'. The latter reference was presumably to Andrew, who could hardly have relished the prospect of assisting a boy of 16.

The death of Robertson was the catalyst for the development of no less than three different architectural practices. Robertson's nephews, based in Elgin and for a period in Inverness, practised, mainly as A. & W. Reid and sometimes with third partners, for half a century after their uncle's death. A. & W. Reid left their mark on nineteenth century Elgin in much the same way as Andrew and his sons did in Tain. Thomas Mackenzie also soon began practice on his own account, producing designs in classical and Italianate styles developed from those of Archibald Simpson. He joined forces with James Matthews, and in the years up to his death in 1854 Mackenzie & Matthews executed several important commissions. These included the splendidly ornate Caledonian Bank (now a pub) in Inverness High Street and the Free (later St Columba) High Church beside the river Ness.

The third new practice was that of Andrew Maitland, based in Tain. But his move to Tain did not happen immediately, Andrew apparently continuing to live on the Braelangwell estate until at least late 1843. Between Robertson's death in 1841 and 1845 the remodelling of Braelangwell was completed not by the young Reids but by James Ross, a former clerk of works for Archibald Simpson. It is thus quite likely that Andrew continued in a supervisory role, working for James Ross.[9] The likelihood of this being so is enhanced by the fact that one of the first commissions Andrew received after moving to Tain was one to work alongside James Ross. James Ross himself had moved to Inverness in 1842 and was building up an architectural practice which was later joined by his son Alexander, who was to become the best known and most prolific Highland architect of the second half of the nineteenth century and the early twentieth century. Before Andrew established his practice in Tain, however, two significant events were to occur.

Henrietta, the distiller's daughter

The first of these was his marriage. His bride was Henrietta Andrews, the daughter of George Andrews and his wife Henrietta Cumming. At 24 she was 15 years younger than Andrew.

George Andrews had been born around 1777 in Banff. His career appears to have been a varied one - albeit with the sale of alcoholic beverages as a connecting thread. At the time of the baptism of the younger Henrietta on 17th May, 1816 he was described as a vintner. On 18th May, 1825 ground and 'the substantial dwelling houses, offices and others built thereon' at the Ness of Cromarty, which later formed part of the Royal Hotel, were exposed to a judicial sale. The tenants were James Taylor, a fish curer, and George Andrews, innkeeper.[10] George later became a farmer and distiller at Braelangwell, where a distillery was opened in 1826. An incident in 1830 attracted publicity. 'George Andrews, distiller, Braelangwell' appeared before a Justice of the Peace Court in Cromarty to answer two informations laid against him by the Excise. 'It appeared clear from the evidence that Mr Andrews did not intentionally contravene the Revenue Law, indeed the Officer was present on one occasion and saw done, without taking the smallest notice of it, what he afterwards reported to be a fraud. So satisfied were the Justices of Mr Andrews having acted in ignorance, that they unanimously restricted the penalty to the lowest sum allowed by the statute, and at the same time recommended to the Board of Excise further to remit the sum, or to remit it altogether.'[11] By 1836 the distillery had three brewers, a maltman and a resident exciseman. The section on Resolis in the *New Statistical Account*, written by the Minister, the Rev. Donald Sage, in September 1836, noted that 'There is a distillery in the parish, at the place of Braelangwell, famed for excellent whisky'.[12]

But the distillery had financial problems. There was a meeting of the creditors of the bankrupt George Andrews, 'Distiller at Braelangwell', in 1831, and a notice of sequestration in 1843, by which time the distillery had probably been closed.[13] The 1851 census shows George as a 'Retired Distiller'. Despite the failure of their grandfather's venture, Andrew Maitland's sons Andrew Junior and James were to become distillers later in the century when they became involved with a distillery, Glenmorangie, which claims - incorrectly, as we shall see - to have been founded in the same year as their grandfather's sequestration.

The wedding of Andrew and Henrietta took place on 28th July, 1841. Andrew was described in the parish records as 'Architect, Braelangwell'.

If the wedding venue was Resolis Church it would have been a particularly appropriate one. The church, a plain rectangular one built in 1767, had been substantially altered by William Robertson in 1838-40, and it is entirely possible that Andrew himself, then working for Robertson in the Black Isle, had assisted with supervisory work.[14] The service was almost certainly conducted by the Minister, the Rev. Donald Sage. Sage had the previous year completed the manuscript of *Memorabilia Domestica, or Parish Life in the North of Scotland* based on his father's Ministry in Kildonan, in Sutherland, and his own career up to 1827. This was to be edited by his son and published in 1889. It provides a detailed and revealing insight into this period of history.

The first child of Andrew and Henrietta, George, was born on 26th May, 1842 and was baptised on 13th June. But great events were impending in ecclesiastical affairs, events which would have a profound influence not just on the history of nineteenth century Scotland, but also directly on the personal and professional life of Andrew Maitland and his family.

The Disruption ... and what it did for Andrew

Throughout their history the Presbyterian churches of Scotland have shown a remarkable propensity to fragment. The Disruption of 1843 was as spectacular a bust-up as any. It raised passions which we in a more secular age struggle fully to comprehend.

In 1843 the established Church of Scotland occupied a pre-eminent position not just in the organisation of worship but also in the guardianship of morals, in education and in the care of the poor. Heritors in each parish were responsible for the maintenance of a church, a manse and a school and were expected to contribute to poor relief. The ministers were chosen by patrons - sometimes the Crown, more often heritors (some of them members of the nobility) who had inherited rights of patronage. The presentation by the patron had then to be accompanied by a 'call' from the congregation. Whilst the Moderates (the party of the ecclesiastical and political establishment) held sway there had been sufficient accommodation between patrons and congregations for this system to work. But after the Napoleonic wars the rival Evangelical movement gained strength and by 1833 it had a majority in the General Assembly. The Evangelicals had widespread support amongst the emerging middle classes, but were seen by the land owning classes as challenging the established social order. They were characterised by a zealous piety and a commitment to making the church more popular, particularly by bringing in the working classes. Opposition to patronage, which they saw as interference by the state in church matters, was a key issue, and in 1843 it became the *casus belli*. When the Evangelicals were frustrated by decisions of the Court of Session and the House of Lords which upheld the right of patronage they felt a need for a church which was free from the state.

High drama followed. At about three o'clock in the afternoon of 18th May, 1843 the leader of the Evangelicals, the Rev. Thomas Chalmers, led 190 of the clergy out the General Assembly to form the Free Church of Scotland. In due course a third of the clergy, 474 out of 1,203, joined the new church. Nearly half the laity followed them. In the Highlands the proportions were much higher, particularly in the synod of Ross, where 23 out of 29 ministers (including the Rev. Donald Sage in Resolis and the Rev. Charles Calder Mackintosh in Tain), and in the synod of Sutherland, where 22 out of 29 ministers 'came out'.

Further drama ensued in many parts of Scotland. Ministers vacated their churches, manses and glebes and lost the financial support of the heritors. We read of congregations worshipping in a wood, in a gravel-pit and even on a ship. But Chalmers and his colleagues had a massive plan - nothing less than a new religious infrastructure for Scotland. Whatever one's views on the issues involved, it is difficult to avoid admiration for the energy deployed. Significant funds were raised, particularly from the middle classes.

By 1847 at least 750 churches had been provided, together with 400 manses and schools for 513 teachers. A 'Sustentation Fund' set up to pay ministers an annual dividend was paying a minimum stipend of £122 per year.

Andrew and Henrietta, along with almost the entire congregation of Resolis other than the heritors and larger farmers, followed the Rev. Donald Sage into the Free Church. Until a new church could be built services took place in the open air, or in bad weather in the upper floor of the Storehouse of Newhall.[15]

Free Church records contain minutes of a series of meetings (the first taking place as early as eight weeks before the Disruption) aimed at collecting funds for a new church and securing a site.[16] Andrew's father-in-law George Andrews played a prominent role, and was unanimously chosen as 'Preses' at one meeting. Unlike the other heritors, Sir George Gun Munro of Poyntzfield was 'most willing to grant a site … on his property at Jamimaville [the then preferred spelling]. The offer was, notwithstanding the obvious inconvenience of the locality to the great majority of the people, and after considerable discussion, finally accepted'. On 15th August, 1843 'Mr Maitland, Architect, Tain, who had furnished the committee with a Plan, Specifications and a general estimate of the building, being present, opened the sealed offers' and the meeting proceeded to award contracts to various tradesmen. Their work was completed by 26th January, 1844 when a meeting was held at Jemimaville 'for the purpose of finally settling with the contractors … and also of having the work inspected and taken of[f] the hands of the workmen by Mr Maitland, the architect. Mr Maitland, after minutely inspecting the whole, reported that, with a few trifling deficiencies, the work was executed in a proper, efficient and workmanlike manner. The meeting then proceeded to settle with the workmen'.

Elizabeth Beaton notes that the Free Church manse built for Donald Sage in Jemimaville 'c.1843 … with bowed outer bays linked above the main door by oversailing piended roof supported by two slender columns [is] reminiscent of the work of William Robertson, who built his own home, Ivy Cottage in Elgin, in this style'.[17] In 1843 Robertson had been dead for two years. One can reasonably surmise that Andrew Maitland, using his former employer's design, was responsible for the new manse.

We can be certain, however, of the longer term effects of the Disruption on Andrew and his family. Andrew himself was deeply religious and the Tain Free Church records show his personal commitment to that church until the end of his life. And on a professional level, it is noteworthy that most of the new churches were constructed in haste, and that as time passed many of them did not meet the aspirations and levels of comfort of the increasingly wealthy middle class who were so influential in Free Church affairs. Andrew and his sons were thus to be engaged, particularly in the last three decades of the nineteenth century, to design numerous replacement churches both in and beyond Ross-shire. The Disruption was to lead, moreover, to changes in the poor law which were to provide commissions for Andrew, and indirectly to educational reforms which necessitated new schools which provided numerous opportunities for Andrew and his sons in the 1870s.

The Resolis Riot

Meanwhile in September 1843 Resolis was the scene of what became known as the Resolis Riot. Two local authors, Dr David Alston and Dr Jim Mackay, have given vivid accounts of the riot, a response to the induction of a new minister as a replacement for Donald Sage in the established church.[18] Ministers and gentry, including the Frasers of Braelangwell, had been assaulted at the induction of a minister at Rosskeen in Easter Ross on 19th September. Nine days later a mob, the men with sticks and the women with stones, tried to prevent an induction at Resolis. The Sheriff's carriage was stoned, the Lord Lieutenant was struck, the Riot Act was read, and people, including Donald Sage's dairymaid, Margaret Cameron, were arrested. Next day a mob marched to Cromarty and released Margaret Cameron. Order was restored only when the 87th Royal Irish Fusiliers were sent to Invergordon, made arrests in Resolis and took up quarters at Fort George. Many of those involved in the riot, who included a mason and three quarriers, would certainly have been known to Andrew Maitland.

Sir Hugh Fraser of Braelangwell seems to have taken a vindictive approach to the new Free Church. After his death in 1851 a massive granite monument was erected within the nave of the ancient church of Kirkmichael, superseded as a place of worship when the parish of Kirkmichael was incorporated into Resolis in 1759 but still used for burials. The memorial later toppled over. Dr Jim Mackay, the prime mover in the fine restoration of Kirkmichael, wonders whether the collapse was aided by those not willing to forget Sir Hugh's role in attempting to suppress the riot. Andrew Maitland's active involvement with the Free Church would not have led to an easy relationship with the proprietor of Braelangwell, and this may been one of the factors that led him to prefer working in Tain.

References and Notes

[1] *Ross-shire Journal*, 18th November, 1910, the source (along with Mackenzie and Durham, *op. cit.*) of much of the biographical information in the first two sections of this chapter. The phrase 'lad o' pregnant pairts' seems to have been popular in educational literature.

[2] John Gifford, *Architects of the Highlands in the Nineteenth Century - a Sketch*, in *The Scottish Georgian Society, Bulletin no. 7*, 1980, gives an excellent account of the development of architectural practice in the Highlands.

[3] Mackenzie and Durham, *op. cit.*

[4] A booklet, *William Robertson 1786-1841, Architect in Elgin*, written by Elizabeth Beaton as a contribution to the 1984 Festival of Architecture set up by the Royal Institute of British Architects, has provided much useful information on Robertson.

[5] Joseph Mitchell, *Reminiscences of My Life in the Highlands*, vol. two (1884), reprinted David & Charles, 1971, p.46.

[6] Beaton, *William Robertson*, p.22.

[7] One plaque, to the left of the door, ascribes the design to William Robertson. Another plaque, to the right, ascribes it, however, to 'Archibald Simpson or Robertson'. One of the two modern biographies of Simpson includes Dr Bell's Academy as 'showing his mannerisms' but cannot give a positive ascription, whilst the other does not mention it.

[8] *Elgin Courant*, 25th June, 1841, quoted in Beaton, *William Robertson*.

[9] *The Dictionary of Scottish Architects* ascribes the remodelled design of Braelangwell to James Ross, 'possibly completing work for Archibald Simpson', so implying that William Robertson was not involved. It is clear, however, that Andrew Maitland worked for William Robertson in the Black Isle, and the 1841 Census shows that Andrew was at Braelangwell, during William Robertson's lifetime, whilst the re-modelling was taking place. A well-researched biography of Archibald Simpson by David Miller, *Archibald Simpson, Architect - His Life and Times*, Librario Publishing Ltd, 2006, does not list Braelangwell amongst either Simpson's commissions or those attributed to him. The account given by Beaton, *Ross & Cromarty*, pp.36 and 77, which is consistent with that of Gifford, *Highlands & Islands*, p.390 has therefore been preferred.

[10] *Inverness Journal*, 1st April, 1825.

[11] *Inverness Journal*, 5th March, 1830.

[12] *New Statistical Account*, Cullicudden and Kirkmichael (the parishes out of which Resolis was formed).

[13] *Aberdeen Journal*, 19th January, 1831 and *Morning Post*, 15th April, 1843.

[14] Gifford, *Highlands & Islands*, p.447 ascribes to William Robertson the Tudor-chimneyed vestry, big lancet windows, and bellcote, and, inside, the rectangular gallery round three sides, with a panelled front and Roman Doric columns, and the pulpit with Tudor Gothic sounding board. This work would certainly have merited some supervision. The church is no longer in use.

[15] *Resolis, 'Slope of Light', Guide to a Black Isle Parish*, written and published by Dr Jim Mackay, Cullicudden, 2009, p.28.

[16] At the time of writing the records of Resolis Free Church other than the baptismal record were privately held, but Dr Jim Mackay was able to furnish the author with extracts which he had been allowed to make.

[17] Beaton, *Ross & Cromarty*, p.35.

[18] David Alston, *My Little Town of Cromarty*, Birlinn Ltd, 2006, pp.237-242; Jim Mackay, *Tales from Kirkmichael*, published by Jim Mackay, 2018, pp.54-64.

2. FROM RESOLIS TO TAIN, VIA BALNAGOWN

Two puzzles

Almost all accounts of the Maitland family seem to start by referring to the date and circumstances of Andrew's arrival in Tain. Some confidently assert that he settled in Tain in 1842. Others, with equal assurance, give the date as 1844. The proponents of both 1842 and 1844 usually go on to say that he came to the area as a result of an important commission from Sir Charles Ross for work at Balnagown Castle, in the parish of Kilmuir Easter and some five miles south of Tain - but this leads to another puzzle, for none of them tell us what Andrew Maitland actually did at Balnagown.

This confusion is not new. Thus an obituary of Andrew in 1894 says 'Mr Maitland's duties naturally brought him before the attention of the public, and eventually he was invited by the late Sir Charles Ross of Balnagown to undertake large additions and alterations to Balnagown Castle. Shortly thereafter, in the year 1842, he settled down in Tain, and began practice on his own account in that town'. Another obituary says that 'in 1844 he started business as an architect in Tain upon his own account', and likewise an obituary of James Maitland in 1929 states that James 'was born in Tain in 1845, the year after his father settled in St. Duthus'.

Records of the period throw some light on these questions.

Balnagown in the early 1840s

2.1 Balnagown Castle, photographed by William Smith of Tain.

Sir Charles Ross, 8th Baronet, had succeeded to the Balnagown estate in 1814 when he was only two. His mother, Lady Mary Ross, had taken over the management of the estate. Because of the weak character and eccentric behaviour of her son she remained in charge until her death in September 1842. A history of Balnagown relates that during dinner Sir Charles 'would go into a corner of the dining room and stand on his head. He enjoyed playing pranks. Often he would retreat up an oak tree in the castle grounds and have his food taken out to him there, earning him the soubriquet "the Jackdaw".'[1]

The development of Balnagown as we know it had been started by Lady Mary's father-in-law, Admiral Sir John Lockhart Ross. Sir John is best remembered by posterity for his introduction of Cheviot sheep into Ross-shire and as one of the initiators of the Clearances in the county. Between the two wings of an L-shaped medieval tower house Sir John had built an elegant extension. This transformation was carried several stages further by Lady Mary, an inveterate builder with a penchant for the Gothic style. The Balnagown history mentioned above is full of information on Lady Mary's projects. The years 1818 to 1821 saw a Gothic loggia and conservatory built at the western end, and in the period 1832 to 1835 a Gothic portico was added to create an entrance at the south side. Her major project was the construction in the next few years of a whole new castellated Gothic wing at the eastern end overlooking the Balnagown River. The gallery, the dining room and other rooms in the new wing were decorated with magnificent Gothic vaulting and tracery. 'While ... the style of this wing', the history continues, 'is reminiscent of the architect Sir James Gillespie Graham, one of Scotland's leading exponents of the early Gothic Revival, there is no evidence that he designed any of the additions to Balnagown. ... There are certain oddities in the planning of the Balnagown wing - the alignment of the doorways in the Gallery for instance - which suggest that a professional architect was not employed. While the inspiration may well have come from Gillespie Graham, the design itself is probably the work of a gifted amateur, no doubt Lady Mary herself, working with a local builder'. Lady Mary also laid out gardens and riverside walks, complemented by an Italian Garden which was completed by her daughter-in-law in 1847.[2] One author speculates that Andrew may have worked on the Italian Garden.[3]

But there is a far more likely explanation of what Andrew did at Balnagown. An invitation to tender, the only one from this period shown in the *British Newspaper Archive*, appeared in March 1842 when estimates were wanted for 'Mason, Carpenter, Slater, Plaster, and Plumber Works of Alterations and Repairs to be made on BALNAGOWN CASTLE. Plans and Specifications may be seen with Mr Laidlaw, the Factor at Balnagown Castle.'[4] It is tempting to think that Andrew was employed to supplement the work of Lady Mary on the east wing, perhaps to ameliorate problems arising from the previous absence of a professional architect. The work would probably have gone beyond Lady Mary's lifetime, as she died in September 1842.

As we will see in the next chapter, the first three estates for which Andrew is clearly recorded as having received commissions were all close to Balnagown, so his work there must have gained him some local reputation.

A connection with Sir Walter Scott

Mackenzie and Durham relate that in later life Andrew retained 'fond memories' of William Laidlaw. As we saw earlier, when Andrew was working in Edinburgh he set type for Sir Walter Scott's works. It is possible that he met Laidlaw at that time. He clearly met him, however, whilst working at Balnagown, where Laidlaw was the factor between 1838 and 1843.

William Laidlaw, born in 1780, was one of Sir Walter Scott's closest friends, his amanuensis, and steward of Abbotsford. Scott had met Laidlaw in 1801 when he was searching for material for the third volume of the Border Minstrelsy. Laidlaw was a friend of James Hogg, the Ettrick Shepherd, who kept sheep on Laidlaw's father's farm. Laidlaw furnished Scott with the ballad of *Auld Maitland*, which he had recovered from a recitation, perhaps by Hogg's uncle. The Maitland in question was not our Andrew or his ancestors: he is thought to have been Sir Richard Maitland, who is said to have possessed the Thirlestane estate in 1250.

Laidlaw was appointed Sir Walter's steward, or factor, at Abbotsford in 1817 and Scott became more and more dependent on him as a companion and as a correspondent during his absences. Andrew Maitland used to recall in later life that he asked Laidlaw whether as amanuensis he made any suggestions to Sir Walter. Laidlaw had replied that he had done so on more than one occasion, but that usually Sir Walter put up his hand and said with a smile 'Go on, William, we will hear that when I am done'. Laidlaw was in constant attendance during Scott's final illness, and was presented by Scott's eldest son and his wife with a brooch which they had given Sir Walter at the time of their marriage and which had been worn by him up to his death. Andrew would have seen this brooch, since Laidlaw wore it for the rest of his own life.[5]

Laidlaw left Abbotsford after Scott's death in 1832. He became successively factor of the Seaforth estates in Ross-shire and in February 1838 of the Balnagown estate. As factor he would have been heavily involved in the building programme at Balnagown. Given his earlier involvement with Abbotsford and its reconstruction he would have enthusiastically approved the style of architecture favoured by Lady Mary.

By all accounts Laidlaw was an amiable and affectionate man. But his health was delicate and he had to retire from Balnagown with an annuity from the Ross family, a new factor succeeding him by August 1843. Laidlaw retired to his brother's house at Contin, where he died in May 1845.

Working in Tain

In the 1840s a number of ferry services ensured that the Black Isle and the Easter Ross peninsula were better connected than they are to-day. Three of these serviced Resolis - the Balblair or Inverbreckie Ferry, using Telford piers at Invergordon and Balblair, the Alness Ferry from Alness to Alness Ferry in Resolis, and the Foulis Ferry (probably to Toberchurn).[6] It was thus not unusual for someone living on one peninsula to find work on the other.

Even before he worked at Balnagown, Andrew may have become familiar with Tain. We know that William Robertson visited Tain in 1838 to advise on the location of a proposed new prison.[7] Elizabeth Beaton observes in her *Ross & Cromarty*, moreover, that two Tain houses, No.10, Knockbreck Street (opposite the then parish church, now the Duthac Centre) and Mayfield in Morangie Road, are both in the manner of William Robertson.[8] Andrew could well have assisted Robertson on some or all of these projects, perhaps supervising the work, and he might have been attracted by the opportunities in Tain and the surrounding countryside.

What appears to be the earliest definite record of Andrew doing work in Tain appears in the Tain Free Church minutes of 1843.[9] They show that at the same time as he was working on the new church at Resolis Andrew was performing a similar function in Tain, where the vast majority of the congregation had followed the Rev. Charles Calder Mackintosh out of the Church of Scotland and into the new Free Church.

The congregation secured a site in Back Street (now Queen Street), the site later occupied by the Maitland-designed church of 1891-92 which is now the Tain Parish Church. They quickly erected a wooden church, at the same time making plans for a permanent one. Though the latter was to stand for nearly fifty years, its construction neatly illustrates the aphorism that a committee is an animal with four back legs. On 23rd June, only five weeks after the Free Church was formally constituted, a committee of the newly formed Tain Free Church Association, presided over by Mackintosh, considered printed suggestions and plans, provided from Edinburgh, of new Churches. They appointed a sub-committee 'to consider the mode of proceeding and such other particulars as they shall consider useful'. In view of the demand for sittings they later recommended that the new church should contain room for 1,100 sittings at 18 inches each and walls 2 feet higher than contemplated in the Edinburgh plans. On 8th August the sub-committee's report was presented, along with 'Mr Maitland's plan of the Church' and estimates received for 'the execution of the mason work in terms of the plan and specification prepared by Mr Maitland'. The lowest tender was from Donald Munro, a Tain builder, in the amount of £160, and Munro had bound himself to have the work completed by 1st November, so as to be ready for roofing, under penalty of £50. Eight days later it was noted that 'Mr Maitland's specifications did not allow for the difference in the level of the ground and in consequence a considerable quantity of underfounding will be required'. (One wonders whether the committee had had the site surveyed.) The committee now also wanted the walls a further 3½ feet higher. In October a tender by Alexander Gair of £690 for carpenter, slater and plumber work was accepted. It was decided the following May that a gallery should be erected and other alterations and improvements made 'according to plans and specifications by Mr Maitland'. A reluctant Gair was only persuaded to do the additional work by being promised £136-2s-0d, £10 more than Andrew's estimate. The result was a long, low church typical of those built at the time of the Disruption, plain looking except for a bellcote.

2.2 The Rev. Charles Calder Mackintosh.

15

Settling in Tain

Whilst Andrew was producing plans for the new churches in Resolis and Tain Henrietta was again pregnant. Their second son, Alexander, was born on 19th November, 1843. The baptismal records of Resolis Free Church show that Alexander was baptised there on 4th December.[10] Andrew was described in the register as 'Architect, Braelangwell'. Less than three months before he had, as we saw earlier, been described in the Resolis Free Church minutes as 'Architect, Tain'.

This suggests that Andrew, newly self-employed, was taking work where he could get it - whether it was in Resolis where he may still have been doing supervisory work at Braelangwell (the remodelling of which was not completed until 1845), at Balnagown, or in and around Tain. What is less clear is the timing of the Maitland family's move to Tain. Henrietta, their one year old son and their new baby were presumably still living at Braelangwell at the time of Alexander's baptism in December 1843 and they are perhaps unlikely to have moved from Resolis to Tain during the winter. It thus seems reasonable to assume that the family settled in Tain in 1844.

His involvement with the building of the new church, on top of any earlier work he may have done in Tain for William Robertson, would have enabled Andrew to see the opportunities from having a home and office in Tain. These opportunities were ones for which the other offshoots of William Robertson's practice, the young Reids and Thomas Mackenzie, both then based in Elgin, were less likely to compete. The only potential competitor in Tain, moreover, seems to have been Donald Munro, who had done the mason work on the new church. Munro was an architect / builder, who had designed a Parish Church in Edderton. It was perhaps telling that the new Tain Free Church Association had consulted Andrew rather than Munro. As we will see in the next chapter, Munro was to give Andrew major problems by going 'vexatiously slow' on one of his first major commissions.

The new Tain Free Church was opened on 17th October, 1844. The church, it was reported 'is seated for more than 1,200, and as the seats are all taken it is thought that an additional gallery will be necessary'.[11] Andrew and Henrietta, who were surely present on that day, were to worship here for the rest of their lives; and half a century later the last project in which Andrew Maitland was to take an interest was to be that of a replacement church on the same site.

References and Notes

[1] *Balnagown - Ancestral Home of the Clan Ross*, Brompton Press, 1997, p.78 - a fascinating and lavishly illustrated account, by an un-named author, of Balnagown and its owners over the centuries.

[2] *Balnagown*, p.74.

[3] William T. Russell, *My Brothers Past*, vol. 1, 1761-1899, Librario Publishing Ltd, 2002, p.66.

[4] *Inverness Courier*, 21st March, 1842.

[5] *The Modern Scottish Minstrel*, vol. II, *The Songs of Scotland of the Past Half Century*, Charles Rogers (Editor), online at www.gutenberg.org/ebooks/22515.

[6] *Resolis, 'Slope of Light'*, written and published by Dr Jim Mackay, Cullicudden, 2009, pp. 59-64, 54-5 and 127 respectively.

[7] See chapter 5.

[8] Beaton, *Ross & Cromarty*, p.80.

[9] Tain Free Church Deacons' Court Minutes 1843-1899, Highland Archive Centre, CH3/748/2.

[10] Resolis Free Church Kirk Session, Baptisms 1843-68, Highland Archive Centre, CH3/1296/1.

[11] *Inverness Courier*, 23rd October, 1844.

3. IMPROVEMENT AND CLEARANCES

The heritors

For a quarter of a century between his arrival in Tain in 1844 and a vast explosion of demand for houses and civic, commercial, ecclesiastical and other urban buildings which began around 1870 Andrew Maitland's practice was, with one or two important exceptions, a rural one. His work was critically dependent on the heritors, the factors who managed many of their estates and a new class of tenants.

The heritors were the principal landowners in each parish, holding their land directly or indirectly from the Crown without limit of time. They had a propensity to up-grade their own principal residences from what they had inherited, but their most common requirement for an architect was for 'improved' farm buildings. The heritors of each parish also had a statutory responsibility for maintaining the established church, manse and schoolhouse and for appointing and paying the minister and schoolmaster. Schools and ecclesiastical buildings were thus a further source of potential work.

Significant changes were taking place in the pattern of land ownership. In the half century or so after Waterloo some two-thirds of the estates in the Highlands changed hands, and Easter Ross was no exception. Established families were often burdened by debt resulting from over-ambitious territorial expansion, from succumbing to the blandishments of southern society, or from annuities paid to widows and other dependants. At the same time others were making fortunes - some in the Lowlands or England from sources such as industry, banking and the law, some elsewhere in the Empire - and were keen to buy estates from impoverished Highland proprietors.

In the most fertile parts of Scotland, including the eastern coastal plain in which Andrew Maitland was particularly starting to seek business, landowners and their tenants had long practised the farming methods of Improvement. In the straths and glens further west and north of the coastal fringe townships had often been cleared for sheep farming, and sporadic episodes of the Highland Clearances still continued. Both Improvement and the Clearances, as we will see, affected the sort of buildings Andrew was called on to design.

An early client - the Cromartie estates

Work seems to have come slowly for Andrew in his early years in practice on his own account. Information on what is probably the earliest work he obtained after he settled in Tain in 1844 is to be found in the Cromartie Muniments, deposited with the National Records of Scotland by the present Earl of Cromartie. The Muniments are a rich seam of information, mined by Eric Richards and Monica Clough to produce one of the finest accounts of Highland social history.[1]

John Hay-Mackenzie of Cromartie lived at Tarbat House, an imposing classical Georgian mansion in Kilmuir Easter, some six miles south west of Tain. This part of his estates was contiguous with that of Balnagown, where Andrew had worked before settling in Tain. Hay-Mackenzie's factor, John Scott, had his office near to Tarbat House and would certainly have come into contact with William Laidlaw, the Balnagown factor for whom Andrew had worked. Joseph Mitchell recorded that Hay-Mackenzie 'was an agreeable, kindly man, took no interest in county affairs, but sang a good song. His lady was cold and taciturn in manner'.[2] His mother, The Hon. Mrs Maria Hay-Mackenzie, the head of the Cromartie dynasty, was still alive. Her grandfather, the third Earl of Cromartie, had suffered the forfeiture of his estates and the attainder of his title after his involvement in the Jacobite campaign of 1745-46. But the estates had been repurchased by Maria's uncle, John Mackenzie, Count Macleod,[3] son of the third Earl. Maria had conveyed the title of the estates to her son John Hay-Mackenzie in the 1820s. He thus owned land in most of the 20 or so enclaves spread across Ross-shire for which the first Earl of Cromartie had achieved recognition as Cromartyshire.

But the costs of the repurchase of the estate by Count Macleod and of his rebuilding of Tarbat House, the annuities enjoyed by Maria and other female relations, and John Hay-Mackenzie's own propensity to spend money had all combined to put the Cromartie estates into dire financial straits.

The earliest surviving reports bearing Andrew's signature appear to be two valuations on cottages and farm buildings on the Cromartie estates at Kinettas in Strathpeffer, both dated 26th May, 1844.[4] One is signed by Andrew alone, the other jointly with James Ross - probably the James Ross who completed the remodelling of Braelangwell after the death of William Robertson. In September of the following year Andrew reported to the Presbytery and heritors of Lochbroom, of whom Hay-Mackenzie was the principal one, on a recently built parish church designed by Andrew's former colleagues, William Robertson's young nephews Alexander and William Reid.[5]

The earliest surviving record of an architectural design by Andrew himself also appears to be for the Cromartie estates - a plan dated 1845 of a square of farm offices at Polnicol Farm, close to Tarbat House and on the main coastal road from Invergordon to Tain.[6]

But, as the Cromartie estates teetered on the edge of bankruptcy, most of the work given to Andrew continued to be for inspections, including a further report on steadings at Kinettas and Auchterneed in 1846 and a report on a tenant's liability for fencing at Fodderty in 1848.[7]

In 1849, however, the fortunes of the Cromartie estates took a dramatic new turn. John Hay-Mackenzie's daughter Anne married the Marquess of Stafford, son of the second Duke of Sutherland, and Hay-Mackenzie himself died a fortnight later. The Cromartie estates now fell into the control of the mighty Sutherland empire. James Loch, Commissioner of the Sutherland estates, was astonished to find an immense financial black hole and urged retrenchment.

Andrew Maitland's work for the Cromartie estates had been pretty small beer, but it led, as we shall see, to involvement with the Sutherland estates, an important step in his career. It is also likely to have been instrumental in gaining work for some of the other Ross-shire estates mentioned in this chapter.

Improvement in Easter Ross

The overwhelming bulk of Andrew's work related to the low-lying parts of Easter Ross, which form the bulk of the peninsula. This area is part of a coastal plain which covers great swathes of eastern Scotland. It has an exceptionally low level of precipitation and a relatively mild climate, and it boasts rich agricultural land. The emphasis in the 1840s was on arable farming, particularly grain. As a result of Improvement there had been huge changes in the rural economy of Easter Ross in recent decades, and these changes were still taking place as Andrew sought work.

Historically the majority of these proprietors had derived the bulk of their wealth from the land. In past centuries most of Scotland's arable land had been organised on the open-field system, with most of the fertile land being worked by small tenants. This land had been divided into strips or 'rigs', and each tenant held land intermixed with that of his neighbours. Tenants had usually lived in 'towns' or 'townships', clusters of perhaps 10 or 12 single-storey buildings which typically had two rooms, a byre at one end, and a peat fire on the floor. They had virtually no security of tenure and paid their rents in kind.

The Age of Enlightenment had brought in its train agricultural 'Improvement'. The principal aims were the improvement of the land already under cultivation and the bringing into cultivation of land not previously capable of being cultivated. A key element in this was the conversion of land formerly tenanted by small farmers into larger farms. In 1841 James Cameron, a surgeon in Tain, produced a report which was incorporated into the social reformer Edwin Chadwick's Report to the Poor Law Commissioners. Cameron estimated the average size of the new large farms in Easter Ross at about 400 acres, as compared with the average of 20 acres for the former small farms.[8] Fields were enclosed with thorn hedges or dry-stone dykes, and land was drained.

The Easter Ross landscape became one of planned farms. Some heritors with adequate resources financed improvements themselves. But most of the farms were tenanted by a new class of more substantial farmers with some capital, who were typically offered 19 year leases. The tenant farmers had, Cameron noted, generally 'received a respectable education, were able, when steady and circumspect, to live comfortably and to lay by something toward the education and settlement of their children'. Many of them came from the Lowlands, where they had learned the best modern farming practices. The enclosure of the new large farms meant of course that the old 'towns' disappeared. Some of the former inhabitants left Easter Ross for the fast expanding cities of the Central Belt or became part of the great Scottish diaspora. Some went to the planned villages of the area. Others remained - not as the social equals of their former joint tenants but as labourers or 'farm servants' employed by the new class of tenant farmers - and were housed in 'improved' farm cottages.

Farm buildings in the age of Improvement

The creation of the new improved farms was reflected in three principal types of buildings - farmhouses for the tenant farmers, cottages and bothies for farm servants, and steadings of farm 'offices'. Andrew Maitland would certainly have had pattern books to assist him and his patrons in designing farmhouses, cottages and steadings. The designs, in an ordered and symmetrical way, reflected both the efficiency of the new farming systems and the social divisions to which they had given rise.[9]

The tenants usually occupied two-storey three-bay farmhouses constructed of stone, with lime mortar, often harled and with slate roofs. Typically there were five or six main rooms, with the kitchen in a back wing.

Farm servants were less fortunate. James Cameron noted that there were on average four or five farm servants on an Easter Ross farm, half of whom were generally married. The married servants lived in single-storey cottages, typically with two rooms and a closet. The cottages were sometimes detached but commonly in rows of two, three or more. They were usually built close to the steading on an approach road to the farm house or in similar terraces in a position closer to outlying fields. 'Most of them have pigsties either before or behind', Cameron reported, 'but rarely immediately attached to them. [They] are usually constructed of stone or mud-work. The flooring is made of earth or clay, wood flooring being seldom used'. John Gifford notes that cottages of more substantial construction, with mortared stone and slated roofs, were uncommon before the mid nineteenth century even on large farms. He quotes from a letter written by Andrew Maitland in 1855: 'I have done all in my power in this quarter [Easter Ross] to induce Proprietors and their Factors to improve Labourers Cottages but without success, - my proposals having been met with the answers, "too good for them", "ridicolous" *(sic)*, &c &c.' [10] Unmarried labourers, hired at six-monthly feeing markets, were usually accommodated in bothies, which could be within the steading or in separate buildings which Cameron described as 'barrack-like'.

The creation of the large improved farms was accompanied by the building of steadings of farm offices. Nearly all arable farms kept some livestock, and nearly all livestock farms grew some root and or cereal crops. A typical requirement was thus stables for housing the draught horses that worked the land (with more stabling required if riding or gig horses were kept), along with accommodation for carts and implements. A second common requirement was provision for storing and processing harvested crops: harvested grain would be stored in stackyards, close to which there would be a thrashing (i.e. threshing) machine, sometimes worked by wind, sometimes by horses, sometimes by water, and sometimes by steam - each of which required different architectural solutions; it would then be stored in granaries, typically above the cart and implement sheds. A third typical requirement was housing for livestock and their produce - byres, cattle courts, dairies, poultry houses, pig houses, etc. To accommodate these various requirements steadings were designed symmetrically, typically round three or four sides of a square. Tenants were usually responsible for farmsteads, though the lease might provide for compensation for improvements. But many of Andrew's commissions were for the mains farms of the landlords themselves, and the landlord was also often involved when he needed to improve facilities to attract new tenants.

The nineteenth century saw a constant demand for new farmhouses, farm cottages and steadings, and also for repairing, adding to and up-grading existing ones. These buildings, along with the fields enclosed by dry-stone dykes and thorn hedges, gave us the rural landscape of Easter Ross we still see to-day. A high proportion of them were to be designed by the Maitland family, for whom this became the major part of their business.

The tenanted farm of Lochslin, belonging to the Macleods of Cadboll, provides a good example of Improvement. The farm, about six miles from Tain, was beside Loch Slin (now known as Loch Eye). On it were then the ruins of Lochslin Castle, standing on an eminence and 60 feet high, and described in the *New Statistical Account of Scotland* as 'one of the most conspicuous objects in this country'. In 1820 it had 147 arable acres and it was claimed that 'Much of the Lands previously waste or in pasture can be advantageously improved and made Arable'. Land was drained, crops were rotated and crofts occupied by sub-tenants were incorporated, and when a 19 year lease was advertised in 1846 there were 227 acres of 'excellent' arable land. That September Andrew Maitland sought tenders for building a dwelling-house on the farm.[11] From about 1852 the farm and the house were occupied by Kenneth Murray, brother of William H. Murray of Geanies, Provost of Tain, and himself Agent of the Commercial Bank in Tain and a future Provost. Kenneth Murray was already persuading his bank to lend large sums to agriculturalists of enterprise. As a manager and, after his brother's death, as proprietor of the estate of Geanies he increased the arable acreage from 2,016 acres in the 1840s to some 4,000 in 1876.

The man whose estates featured most frequently amongst Andrew Maitland's work in his early years as an architect was, however, the recently deceased Hugh Rose Ross of Glastullich and Cromarty,[12] a well-known Improver.

The legacy of Hugh Rose Ross

The death in 1846 of Hugh Rose Ross, the largest landowner around Tain and recently Provost of the Royal Burgh, was followed by one of the most impressive funerals in the history of the area, with a procession a mile long and 5,000 people present. His death, and the subsequent fragmentation of his estates, led directly and indirectly to many opportunities for Andrew Maitland and his sons in this and, as we will see in later chapters, the following decades.

Hugh Rose Ross is one of the most colourful characters in the history of the area. He is particularly remembered by Tain Royal Academy (where his portrait still hangs) as the most energetic and successful of its original promoters; and historians regard him as one of the leading Highland agriculturalists of the age of Improvement. But there was a darker side to him. These activities were largely funded by a fortune he had made in the West Indies from supplying stores to the British Fleet as deputy paymaster general - a fortune enhanced by some highly dubious transactions. He was also a partner in a sugar plantation, relying heavily on slave labour, in Berbice (later part of British Guiana). He had, moreover, a penchant for litigation and for duelling.[13]

Hugh, whose father the Rev. Hugh Rose had been minister of Creich and later of Tain, chose Easter Ross as the area in which to invest his fortune. To the south of Tain he purchased the estates of Calrossie and Glastullich, to the north west of Tain the estates of Tarlogie and Morangie, and along the Scotsburn Road and into the Burgh itself various farms, and in Nigg he purchased the Bayfield estate. The adjacent farms of Calrossie, Glastullich and Arabella were run by him personally. He enclosed the fields with 40 miles of hedges - and the copper beech hedges, burnished by low sunshine in winter, are still one of the glories of the area. He drained them in the new fashion of tile-drainage, and he erected his own tile manufactory. His residence, 'built in the style of a *cottage ornée* and with 22 Apartments' was at Calrossie House, but he preferred to designate himself Hugh Rose of Glastullich.

His first wife was Arabella Phipps, daughter of a rich planter who had become paymaster general for the West Indies and had appointed Hugh to his position in the commissariat. But the marriage only lasted seven years. A memorial

3.1 Hugh Rose Ross, by H.W. Pickersgill R.A.

tablet in the Collegiate Church in Tain records that Arabella 'in the act of preparing Medicine for the relief of a sick and indigent family suddenly expired on 9th November, 1806 aged 27 years'. Local legend has it, however, that she was murdered by her husband's quadroon mistress, whom he had brought back to Bayfield from the West Indies. Both her Christian name and her surname live on, however, as Hugh changed the name of a farm he reclaimed from The Bog to Arabella. He also gave the name Phippsfield to another farm, on which he built a tile manufactory. Arabella bore Hugh one son, Hugh Munro St Vincent Rose, St Vincent being the title taken by his godfather Earl St Vincent, ennobled after his triumph in the great sea battle of Cape St Vincent in 1797, in which he flew his flag in *H.M.S. Victory*. The name St Vincent was also used for a farm on the Scotsburn Road outside Tain (owned by members of the author's family from 1882 to 2014).

Under the common law of Scotland the moveable property of a married woman, including rents received, vested in her husband, who enjoyed a right of administration of her heritable (immovable) property. This gave men an incentive to wed heiresses. In 1815 Hugh married again. His bride was Catherine Munro, heiress of Duncan Munro of Culcairn. On Duncan Munro's death the estates of Culcairn and Dalmore, near Alness, fell into Hugh's empire. One of his tenants, Donald Sutherland, established a distillery in 1839 at Dalmore, with which, as we shall see, Andrew Maitland and his sons were to be involved on several occasions. Meanwhile Hugh had another target - the more substantial estate of Cromarty. Catherine was the great-niece of George Ross of Cromarty and had a claim to be the heiress of entail. Hugh pursued her claim right up to the House of Lords. He succeeded in getting the putative heir declared illegitimate and therefore unable to inherit, so that the estate passed to Catherine. When he entered into possession of the Cromarty estate in 1830 he styled himself Hugh Rose Ross of Glastullich and Cromarty.

In 1844 Hugh Rose Ross, then aged 76, sought tenants for the farms of Arabella, South Calrossie and Glastullich 'which have for a long number of years been in the natural possession of the Proprietor, who has spared neither trouble nor expense in making them in every way well worth the attention of farmers of capital and skill'. Efforts by Rose Ross to let the farms and after his death in September 1846 by the estate factor, James Strachan, who occupied the farm of Phippsfield, continued for three years. One of the obvious constraints on letting was clearly the absence of separate farm buildings, which had not been needed when Rose Ross had the farms in hand. Farmhouses were thus erected at Glastullich ('a very superior dwelling house, equal to any in the district') and at Calrossie and a steading of offices at Glastullich; Andrew Maitland clearly designed the latter two buildings[14] and probably also the first.

Most of Rose Ross's estates in Easter Ross were inherited by his son by Arabella, Major Hugh St. Vincent Rose as he now styled himself. The Cromarty estate in the Black Isle and the estates of Culcairn and Dalmore in Easter Ross remained the property of his widow Catherine and were inherited on her death in 1852 by their son Colonel G.W.H. Ross. Major St. Vincent Rose was soon to get a nasty shock. His two sisters now inherited their mother Arabella's fortune of £40,000. His father's lawsuits had involved 30 years of argument about title to the Cromarty estate and its debts, a 15 year dispute with Donald MacLeod of Geanies, a 6 year dispute with Mrs Hay-Mackenzie about salmon fishing rights (all three of which went to the House of Lords), and further fishing disputes with Mackenzie of Ardross and the Duke of Sutherland. The costs were reputed to be in excess of £100,000. Hugh Rose Ross's depleted personal estate amounted to £22,396-13s-11½d. The residual beneficiaries under a deathbed will and codicils were his second wife Catherine, who was sole executrix, and her children Colonel Rose and his sister, another Arabella. Major St Vincent Rose not only got nothing but was also required to pay over to the executrix the value of the stocking and moveables on the Easter Ross farms. To his dismay St. Vincent Rose's advisers insisted that he must sell Calrossie, cherished as his childhood home, Arabella and Glastullich as well as Bayfield. He also tried - but without success - to sell the neighbouring estates of Tarlogie, Morangie and Cambuscurries north west of Tain. He thus continued to own the Morangie estate, which included the Morangie Brewery, converted in 1849 by a tenant, William Matheson, into the Glenmorangie Distillery - a business with which Andrew's family were to be heavily involved. He also continued to own Tarlogie, which became his Ross-shire seat (though he lived mainly in Norwood in Surrey), and he styled himself Major St. Vincent Rose of Tarlogie.[15]

James Strachan continued to act as factor for both the estates in Easter Ross and the Cromarty estate, but moved his office from Easter Ross to the Black Isle. Andrew Maitland was engaged in 1847 to design for him 'a new house and small offices on the estate of Cromarty, adjoining the town'.[16] The house was initially known as known as Rosenberg Cottage. Its occupant made himself highly unpopular in the Cromarty area. David Alston quotes a contemporary account of Strachan's 'tyrannical oppression' written by one tenant whom he removed as part of his improvements: Strachan was 'full of vainglory and void of all principle', evicting tenants, refusing compensation for improvements, refusing to allow widows to retain tenancies, and defacing the beauty of the estate by tearing down hedges and cutting down wood.[17] It was perhaps appropriate for such a factor that Rosenberg Cottage was no ordinary cottage, being described in the 1871 Ordnance Survey Name Book as 'a very fine house surrounded by a small plantation on the terrace which skirts the town and for several miles extends along the bay'. The 1851 census shows that Strachan had two servants living in the house, and items in an advertisement for the sale of Strachan's furniture, etc. after his death later that year included 'a new Four-wheeled CARRIAGE, a light and comfortable PHAETON, and good GIG'. The house is today an up-market bed and breakfast establishment, known as The Factor's House.

Although the Rose Ross estates in Easter Ross were substantially reduced, Andrew Maitland continued to receive commissions. One, in 1851, was for the restoration of a farmhouse at Ardjachie, which had apparently been difficult to let. Another was for servants' houses at Tarlogie in 1854, and a third, also at Tarlogie, was for extensive additions and repairs to the farm steading, including the erection of an engine-house and stalk, together with a liquid manure tank.[18] As we will see in later chapters, moreover, the fragmentation of the vast estates once owned by Hugh Rose Ross was to be a major theme in the ownership of land in Easter Ross for the rest of the nineteenth century. It was also to lead to numerous commissions for Andrew Maitland and his sons, including one from another flamboyant landowner, the Count de Serra Largo of Tarlogie, for major alterations and additions to the mansion house of Tarlogie.

The Highland Clearances

In the straths and glens of the mountainous areas beyond the Eastern coastal plain recent decades had also seen change - but it took a different form, known to history as the Highland Clearances. The inhabitants of the small settlements, or *bailtean,* had for centuries produced black cattle, sheep and, if they were fortunate with the soil and the weather, some crops. Following the introduction of hardy Cheviot sheep landowners saw the financial advantages of clearing the *bailtean* to make way for massive sheep-walks. Sometimes, too, they could see the opportunity for shooting lodges, which could be rented out to further improve the estate's income. Whereas in the arable eastern fringes of the Highlands many of the small tenants dispossessed by Improvement had found employment as agricultural labourers on the new large scale farms, there were few such options for those cleared from the new sheep-walks. The destruction of communities and migration to the cities and to Canada and Australia were thus major consequences of the Highland Clearances. These trends were intensified by the tragedy of a potato famine from 1846 to 1850 which affected a population highly dependent on the potato for sustenance.

Many of the large-scale clearances had taken place during and in the years following the Napoleonic Wars. Several of Andrew's early landowning clients were thus beneficiaries of clearances by their predecessors. But there were further sporadic clearances, particularly in the 1840s and 1850s, and one of Andrew's earliest clients was a man known to history for organising two of the most notorious of these, at Strathconan and Glencalvie.

James Falconer Gillanders - a 'hard and ambitious' clearer

One name that recurs in the newspaper advertisements relating to Andrew's earliest commissions is that of 'James F. Gillanders, Esq., Highfield Cottage, by Beauly'. As the notorious Patrick Sellar, the organiser of many of the early Sutherland clearances, survived until 1851, James Falconer Gillanders may not have been the greatest living expert on clearances; but in the 1840s he was the expert most frequently employed by proprietors who wished to clear small tenants from their land, and he gained a reputation similar to that of Sellar. He himself had pretensions to gentility. His father owned the Highfield estate. His mother was the sister of George Falconer Mackenzie of Allangrange, who, following the verdict of a 'highly respectable

Jury' in Tain in October 1829, claimed the disputed title of Chief of the Clan Mackenzie. Gillanders, described as a 'hard and ambitious man', features as one of the leading villains in John Prebble's famed, but sometimes controversial, *The Highland Clearances*.[19]

In July 1845 Gillanders advertised for quotations for works of addition to the farmhouse of Newmore and a square of offices for the farm of Pollo, according to plans to be 'found with Mr Maitland, Inspector (*sic*), Tain and here at Highfield Cottage'.[20] James Gillanders was acting as factor for his uncle Francis Mackenzie Gillanders, who had bought the Newmore estate, some three miles from Invergordon, in 1843. By the spring of 1845 he had according to one account 'weeded out' 16, or to another account 20, families from the estate. By October, 1847 Andrew's plans for the farmhouse must have been executed, for Gillanders was able to seek a 19 year lease on the farm of Newmore, with 410 arable acres and a modern and complete dwelling-house, a 'superior and extensive arable farm', recently limed and drained - seemingly the very model of an 'improved' farm.[21]

The Newmore clearance, however, was nothing to what Gillanders was already achieving for the Balfour family on the estate of Strathconan. Strathconan, or as it is nowadays spelt Strathconon, is a beautiful glen some 25 miles long, and was then part of one of the main routes to Wester Ross from the east of the county. James Balfour of Whittinghame, known to the irreverent as 'the Nabob', had made an immense fortune supplying provisions to the British Navy in Indian waters, and after he retired he had bought numerous estates around Scotland, including the 77,000 acre Strathconan estate in 1839. He married Lady Eleanor Maitland - no relation to Andrew, but the daughter of the Earl of Lauderdale. When he died in 1845 he left the colossal sum of a million pounds. His estates were inherited by his son James Maitland Balfour, who made an even more prestigious marriage, his wife being Lady Blanche Gascoyne-Cecil, whose brother Robert was to become the 3rd Marquis of Salisbury and Prime Minister. Their own eldest son was the languid philosopher-politician Arthur James Balfour, who was appointed by his uncle as Chief Secretary for Ireland in 1887 - giving rise to the catch phrase 'Bob's your uncle' - and who followed his uncle as Prime Minister.

James Balfour and his son James Maitland Balfour cleared, according to Alexander Mackenzie's calculations, some 500 people from Strathconan between 1840 and 1850. Through most of the period Gillanders acted for the Strathconan estate. These clearances were aimed not just at 'improvement' and the creation of larger sheep farms, but also at adapting land for sporting purposes. The Scardroy part of the estate had for some time been used for grouse shooting, and a shooting lodge had been built there in 1835-36. The estate already included a so-called deer forest, and this was continuously extended, eventually reaching 27,500 acres by 1877. In February 1846 quotations were sought from contractors for work 'agreeably to Plans and Specifications prepared by Mr Maitland, Tain' for a farm-steading, school-house, dog-kennels and repairs on Scardroy Lodge.[22] Recent research has shown that Scardroy Lodge, the farmstead and other buildings were built on the site of the cleared township of Keanloch Beanchran.[23] A year later Andrew Maitland sought quotations for another shooting lodge '(and out-houses), of large accommodation, to be erected at Lochgowan, on the Estate of Strathconan, near to the Lochcarron Parliamentary Road, according to the Plans and Specifications prepared by Mr Maitland, Tain'.[24] The result, Ledgowan Lodge, was a two-storey, three-bay building with semi-dormer windows with decorative cast-iron finials. Somewhat clunky in design, and surprisingly urban looking, it lacks the grace of later Maitland shooting lodges. It has had a curious history. In 1904 its then owner, John M. Ross, a civil engineer, replaced it with a new and more elegant Ledgowan Lodge on higher ground a few hundred yards away. After the second World War, however, this was detached from the estate and became the Ledgowan Lodge Hotel. The original Maitland-designed lodge is still in use and carries the name Ledgowan Lodge. It was reported in 2017 that it was for sale with an 11,105 acre sporting estate for offers over £4.5 million, and later that it was being sold to a Danish billionaire who was the grandson of the inventor of the plastic toy Lego and had previously purchased the Strathconon and Scardroy estates.

3.2 Ledgowan Lodge - lacking the elegance of later Maitland shooting lodges.

But it was for his clearances in the parish of Kincardine on the estate of Strathcarron, owned by the Robertsons of Kindeace, that Gillanders achieved notoriety on a national scale. Strathcarron, a valley running westwards from the Kyle of Sutherland, was divided into two, Greenyards and Glencalvie. In 1842 Gillanders advertised these as sheep-walks, but he met resistance when he tried to clear the small tenants from Glencalvie. When he tried again in 1845 the people of Glencalvie, where 18 families lived, took the extraordinary step of placing in *The Scotsman* a petition against impending clearances. They were actively supported by the Free Church minister of Creich, the Rev. Gustavus Aird. In the latter part of the century Aird, a noted preacher and Moderator of the Free Church General Assembly in 1888, was to become familiar with Maitland-designed churches: one was to be built at Migdale for his own congregation, and he preached at the inaugural services of new Free Churches at Helmsdale, Portmahomack and Tain (now the Parish Church). The Glencalvie affair became a national *cause célèbre* when the *Times,* investigating conditions ahead of new Poor Law legislation, began a campaign about abuses of landlord power. A *Times* correspondent was taken to the glen by Gustavus Aird at the time of the clearance and reported that 80 dispossessed people had taken refuge in a tent in the churchyard at Croick; some of them had scratched messages on the east window of the church - 'Glencalvie people was in the churchyard here May 24 1845', and, thinking themselves to have upset the Almighty, 'Glencalvie, the wicked generation'. The inscriptions remain visible to-day in this most evocative of places.

In 1852 Gillanders married Margaret Amy, the daughter of Major Charles Robertson of Kindeace. Two years later Robertson ordered a further, and equally famous, clearance, this time from Greenyards. Differing reports were published - varying from melodramatic press accounts later published as a pamphlet entitled *The Massacre of the Rosses*, through a more sober report in the *Inverness Courier*, to an official account by Sheriff Taylor. It appears, however, that Taylor was accompanied by about 35 or 40 men, mainly police constables, when he arrived from Tain to deliver the removal summonses; that he was faced by a crowd of about 300, two-thirds of them women; and that a fracas ensued in which 15 to 20 women and some 4 men were injured.[25] The publicity engendered by the clearances of Glencalvie and Greenyards was so injurious to the interests of landlords that there were no more mass evictions in the Highlands.

It was almost certainly through the Gillanders connection that in the same year of 1854 Andrew Maitland received a commission from Major Robertson. A week after the affray at Greenyards the major sought tenders for work on farm offices at Kindeace in Kilmuir Easter 'according to a Plan and Specifications prepared by Mr Maitland, architect, at Tain'.[26]

Half a century later, when the economics of estate ownership had shifted towards sporting lets rather than sheep-walks, both Glencalvie and Greenyards were to be locations for Maitland-designed shooting lodges.

The Easter Ross Union Poorhouse

By the end of the 1840s Andrew Maitland was clearly making his mark locally, and this was sufficient to enable him to gain his first two prestigious commissions. The first was for a new Court House in Tain, an interesting project, misinterpreted by twentieth century writers, and worthy of a chapter of its own. The other, of no great architectural merit, but nevertheless important for Andrew's reputation for efficiency, was for a poorhouse near Tain.

Reform of the poor law had been very much on the political agenda since the early 1840s. Reports such as that of Edwin Chadwick, which incorporated the report by James Cameron on Tain and Easter Ross featured in the next chapter, were influential in securing change. Historically the main instrument of poor relief had been the Kirk Session of the Church of Scotland in each parish. The relief given was almost invariably 'outdoor relief', i.e. financial relief in the home. Although existing legislation permitted parochial assessments in order to raise funds, funding in the Easter Ross parishes, as in many other parts of Scotland, was somewhat haphazard and often dependant on the generosity or otherwise of the heritors. The needs of the poor were exacerbated by an increasing reliance on casual farm labour rather than employed farm servants, since the casual labourers found it difficult to earn enough to tide them over the rest of the year. Delivery of poor relief was blown apart in 1843 by the fragmentation of the Kirk Sessions of the established church in the wake of the Disruption.

In 1845 an 'Act for the Amendment and better Administration of the Laws relating to the Relief of the Poor in Scotland' transferred the control of poor relief to Parochial Boards. The property qualifications for these ensured that, even with an elected element, control was in the hands of the larger landowners. The Boards had to raise funds to relieve the poor, either voluntarily or by compulsory assessments on the annual value of property. The building of poorhouses to provide 'indoor relief' to the sick and indigent - but not the able-bodied - poor was encouraged, the poor-houses being intended to be at once a safety net and a deterrent to claiming relief.

In February 1848 representatives of all the nine parishes of Easter Ross approved a report by a committee chaired by Henry Dunning Macleod recommending that the system of giving money as relief should as far as possible be abolished and that the nine parishes should unite in building a common poorhouse. Macleod, a 27 year old Etonian reading for the English bar, soon became President of the Board of Management. His appointment perhaps owed not a little to the fact that he was the second son of Roderick Macleod of Cadboll, formerly M.P. for Cromartyshire, and the largest landowner in Easter Ross.

The fact that Andrew Maitland had, as we saw, recently designed a farmhouse at Lochslin on the Cadboll estate may have helped to bring him to the attention of Henry Macleod and his Board.

The Board took two acres at North Glastullich on the Scotsburn Road as a feu at £1-15-0 per acre and engaged Andrew Maitland both to to draw up plans and specifications and to act as inspector. In August the lowest of four tenders for the main part of the contract, £2,475 from the Tain architect/builder Donald Munro, was accepted for completion on 1st September, 1849.

Unfortunately Munro delayed the start by seven months, and in October 1849 Andrew Maitland reported that 'the works are going on vexatiously slow'. The Board did not get possession until May 1850, 35 weeks late. At a general meeting of all the Parochial Boards Henry Macleod was highly critical of Munro, but 'had the greatest pleasure in bringing to [the Board's] notice the invaluable services of Mr Maitland, our architect and inspector. He drew out the whole of the plans and specifications himself. He had never seen anything of the kind before, yet he prepared the whole of the details with such care and forethought that the extra work only amounts to £3-4s-11½d'. Macleod noted that 'the usual fee of a professional architect is 5% and if he acts as an inspector it is 2½ % additional.[27] He [Maitland] had been subjected to 8 months extra trouble and had to visit 3 or 4 times a week, sometimes every day'. The amount of Andrew's charges was £80, but Macleod recommended that 'the Board should present him with £20 additional accompanied by a letter conveying in the strongest terms our satisfaction at his conduct'.[28]

The plaudits were for Andrew's skills in designing to budget and in cost control rather than for the architectural merit of the building. For as Macleod reported in 1851, 'its cost per head of the inmates is unusually low … the cost [of other poorhouses] has exceeded it by 50 to 80 percent. This result has been attained by strictly limiting everything to its lowest amount compatible with efficiency'.[29] As a result the buildings were functional - a Master's house fronting the road, with two gaunt, austere and high buildings (both now long since pulled down to accommodate a housing development), for men and women respectively, forming a rectangular 'U' shape with the Master's house as its base, and ancillary buildings in between.

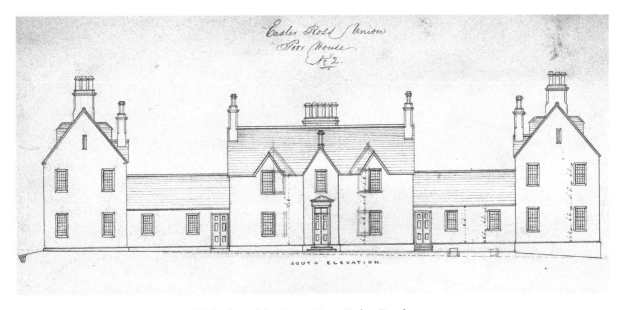

3.3 A plan of the Easter Ross Union Poorhouse.

The Board advertised for a married couple 'able to write well and [with] a thorough knowledge of Accounts' to act as Master and Matron at a combined salary of £50 p.a.[30] From 19 candidates they chose William Bell, a colour-sergeant to one of the companies in the 93rd regiment, and his wife. The regime they maintained was spartan and involved not providing meat to persons who never tasted it in their own homes. The authors of a contemporary guidebook noted that the paupers 'never were so elegantly or comfortably housed before, but ... rather shrewdly regard the place as a sort of state prison'.[31]

Henry Macleod remained President of the Board for some years, and the Easter Ross system, about which he wrote a book, was much imitated throughout Scotland. He achieved wider, if transient, fame from his 13 books on political economy. He tried to win the chairs of political economy at three universities; but 'as his idea of candidature was abuse of Ricardo and John Stuart Mill, followed up by self-praise for having created the "science of economics" single-handed ... his lack of success is not surprising'.[32] His failure was probably also due to his conviction in 1856, along with his fellow directors of a bank, for conspiracy to defraud. Though he is forgotten to-day, he did enrich the economic vocabulary by originating the still-used name 'Gresham's Law' for the principle that 'bad money drives out good'.

In 1930 the poorhouse became the Arthurville Poor Law Institution, and it later became a council-run home for the elderly. Much of it was subsequently demolished and the site, including some residual buildings, was given over to residential use.

References and Notes

[1] Eric Richards and Monica Clough, *Cromartie; Highland Life 1650-1914*, Aberdeen University Press, 1989.

[2] Joseph Mitchell, *Reminiscences of my Life in the Highlands* (1833), vol.I, reprinted for David & Charles (Publishers) Ltd, 1971, p.256.

[3] John Mackenzie was the eldest son of the third Earl of Cromartie, and bore the courtesy title Lord Macleod. At the age of 18 he took part in the Jacobite Rising of 1745-46 and was taken prisoner, later pleading guilty to high treason and receiving a pardon. He served in the Swedish army, becoming a Lieutenant-General and a Count of Sweden. He later became a Major-General in the British Army, repurchased the forfeited estates and built Tarbat House.

[4] NRS GD305/2/378.

[5] NRS GD305/2/520.

[6] NRS RHP34737.

[7] NRS GD305/2/378 and GD305/1/132/9.

[8] James Cameron, *Report on the Sanitary Condition and General Economy of Tain and the District of Easter Ross, made to the Poor Law Commissioners*, in *Sanitary Inquiry, Scotland*, H.M. Stationery Office, 1842.

[9] Invaluable secondary sources for this section have been John Shaw, chapters 20-22 in *Scottish Life and Society, Scotland's Buildings*, Tuckwell Press, 2003, and Miles Glendinning and Susanna Wade Martins, *Buildings of the Land, Scotland's Farms, 1750-2000*, Royal Commission on the Ancient and Historical Monuments of Scotland, 2008, chapter 2.

[10] Gifford, *Highlands and Islands* p.73.

[11] *Inverness Courier*, 9th September, 1846.

[12] The estates of Cromartie and Cromarty both feature in this chapter and thus need to be distinguished. Sir George Mackenzie (later Viscount Tarbat, later still first Earl of Cromartie, and a leading statesman through four reigns) acquired much of the burgh of Cromarty and adjacent lands in the late seventeenth century. He obtained an Act of Parliament which allowed him to annex his other properties across Ross-shire to the sheriffdom of Cromarty - the origin of the county of Cromartyshire, which lasted until it was subsumed into Ross & Cromarty in 1889. He transferred the property in and around the burgh of Cromarty to his second son, whose own son sold it in 1741, but the rest of the estates remained in his possession and were inherited by his elder son, the second Earl of Cromartie. A useful convention later grew up whereby the estate in and around the burgh of Cromarty, later acquired by Hugh Rose Ross, was spelt "Cromarty" and the remaining estates (owned from the early nineteenth century by the earl's Hay-Mackenzie descendants) were spelt "Cromartie".

[13] For a fuller account see Hamish Mackenzie, *Tain, Tarbat Ness and the Duke, 1833*, Tain & District Museum, 2012, Chapter 4.

[14] *Inverness Courier*, 4th May and 9th November, 1847.

[15]   Much of the information on Hugh St. Vincent Rose is taken from a privately printed Rose family history, of which the Tain & District Museum has a copy.

[16]   *Inverness Courier*, 7th April, 1847.

[17]   David Alston, *My Little Town of Cromarty*, Birlinn Ltd, 2006, p.252.

[18]   *Inverness Courier*, 19th June, 1851, 13th July, 1854 and 15th February, 1855.

[19]   John Prebble, *The Highland Clearances*, Martin Secker & Warburg, 1963, Chapter 5.

[20]   *Inverness Courier*, 9th July, 1845.

[21]   *Inverness Courier*, 12th October, 1847. In 1854 Andrew Maitland designed additions to the Newmore Farm steading.

[22]   *Inverness Courier*, 4th February, 1846.

[23]   *Report on Phase Two of a Project to Identify, Survey and Record Archaeological Remains in Strathconon, Ross-shire*
North of Scotland Archaeological Society, 2007; and Highland HER MHG54367. The society has also published (2011) Meryl Marshall's *Strathconon - The History and Archaeology of a Northeast Highland Glen*, which gives an excellent account of these clearances and their context.

[24]   *Inverness Courier*, 10th February, 1847.

[25]   See Eric Richards, *The Highland Clearances*, Birlinn Ltd, 2008, chapters 2 (re Glencalvie) and 16 (Greenyards).

[26]   *Inverness Courier*, 6th April, 1854.

[27]   An distinguished architect advises the author that little has changed in 150 years. Architects have widely varying fees, but he recognises these percentages in relation to much of his own work.

[28]   *Inverness Courier,* 30th May, 1850.

[29]   *John o' Groat Journal,* 19th December, 1851.

[30]   *Inverness Courier*, 24th April, 1850.

[31]   George and Peter Anderson, Route IV 11, *Guide to the Highlands and Islands of Scotland, including Orkney and Zetland,* Adam and Charles Black, 1850.

[32]   *Oxford Dictionary of National Biography,* Oxford University Press, 2004-13, entry for Macleod, Henry Dunning.

4. TAIN IN THE 1840s

4.1 '*The Town of Tain*, drawn on the spot by J. Clark and engraved by Robt Havell, 1828.'

Tain - the most important canvas of the Maitland dynasty

Although Andrew Maitland and his architect sons were to execute a vast amount of work across the Northern Highlands, Tain was the canvas to which they returned again and again over the years. But others had already worked on that canvas, and some were still working on it when Andrew came to Tain. It might perhaps be of interest to look at Tain in the early 1840s, particularly at buildings that pre-dated his arrival or were contemporaneous with it - thus differentiating them from those designed by the Maitlands.

The Royal Burgh of Tain, with a population of 2,287 in the 1841 census, was the largest mainland town north of Inverness. It was the administrative hub of Easter Ross and was the market town and commercial centre not only for that area but also for parts of Sutherland. When the Maitland family settled in Tain the burgh had been in a modest expansionary phase for nearly half a century, and the expansion was slowly but actively continuing. The majority of the pre-Maitland buildings that we see to-day had either been built in this period or were still in the process of construction.

The main driving forces behind this expansion were agricultural improvement in the rich farmland of Easter Ross described in the last chapter, and Tain's position in an improved road network.

The raised beach

The bulk of Tain was, to a proportionately greater extent than to-day, set along a narrow and relatively flat ledge, one of the 'raised beaches' characteristic of the Dornoch, Cromarty and Beauly Firths. In the 1840s exponents of the nascent science of geology were fascinated by phenomena such as raised beaches. One such exponent was a former stonemason, born a mere 15 days before Andrew on a raised beach at Cromarty - Hugh Miller, one of the greatest literary figures of Victorian Scotland. He recognised that 'in some era this continuous bank [the edge of the raised beach] formed the line of coast and that the plain at its base was covered by the waters of the sea'; but - like his contemporaries - Miller found the timing of that era 'impossible to fix'.[1]

Above the raised beach rose the Hill of Tain. A track led up the hill from Tain to quarries on the hill. 'Those at present wrought', we read in the *New Statistical Account of Scotland*, compiled in 1837, 'are the common property of the burghers. .... The procuring of the finest white sandstone is attended with no expense but that of quarrying it. … The material now employed in every construction above a hut is the fine white sandstone from the hill'.[2] The so-called 'white' sandstone was actually an attractive honey colour. Its frequent use down the ages has given Tain an essential harmony. It has also put Tain into the bright and cheerful rather than the dour category among Scottish towns. Though durable, the sandstone was easy to work. Hence the unusually high quality of stonework to be found in the urban architecture of Tain. Andrew and his two architect sons were to become the supreme exponents of its use. Andrew Junior and James were also to lease the quarry from the Common Good Fund in the 1870s and 1880s.

Below the raised beach was a sandy 'flat', or plain, which bordered the Dornoch Firth and stretched eastward across the Fendom to the fishing village of Inver and onwards towards Tarbat Ness at the end of the peninsula. Through the flat, just below the centre of Tain, the Tain River meandered towards the Firth. It was generally believed that the earliest Tain settlement had been close to this river. The only remaining vestiges of any settlement, set on an eminence round which the river looped, were the ruins of the ancient Chapel of St Duthus, the patron saint of Tain. The area around the chapel was used as a graveyard - one, sadly, soon to be well-known to Andrew and Henrietta. On the raised beach itself were both the historic central area of Tain and two significant and more recent extensions of the town.

The centre of Tain

Since medieval times the principal buildings in the centre of Tain had been grouped into a cluster in and around what were to become High Street, Tower Street and the roads going uphill and downhill from them. The original focus had been the Collegiate Church, started around 1370 and probably nearly completed in 1458, into which the relics of St Duthus had been moved.[3] So venerated was St Duthus that Tain had been one of the leading places of pilgrimage in medieval Scotland. Andrew would have learnt that the most illustrious pilgrim had been James IV, who visited it at least once in nearly all of the 25 years of his reign until his death at Flodden in 1513. He might not perhaps have been told that the King usually organised his journeys so as to combine the spiritual solace he derived from the saint's relics in Tain with the physical solace which his mistress 'Flaming Janet' Kennedy provided at Darnaway Castle, near Forres. James V was less zealous than his father, but in 1527 he travelled barefoot, using a footpath across a moor above Tain known as the King's Causeway, to the Collegiate Church. After the Reformation the Collegiate Church had continued as the parish church of Tain. But even with wooden lofts, two tiers high in places, its capacity of 720 had been insufficient for it to continue in this role. When a new parish church was completed in 1815 the old one had been abandoned. By the 1840s Andrew would have seen signs of significant decay. In due course he would be called upon to orchestrate repairs.

Tain's ecclesiastical origins and its role as a pilgrimage destination were reflected in an appearance and a layout distinct from that of the generality of Scottish towns. Many of the older burghs had developed within town walls, with gates where taxes were collected, and had been laid out in a traditional pattern of narrow burgage plots running off a main street. Tain's development was more piecemeal, perhaps starting with manses for the collegiate canons, mainly built to the west of their church in and around the area that was to become Tower Street, and with a high street to the east, 'probably dominated by shops, inns, souvenir vendors, mountebanks and service buildings - particularly stables (and probably shoemakers, unless [the pilgrims] all came barefoot'.[4]

Andrew would have observed that the dominant feature of the centre of the town, and the one most instantly recognisable on the Tain skyline, was the Tolbooth with its distinctive conical steeple crowned by a weathercock and surrounded by four bartizans. The Tolbooth, probably the third on or near the existing site, was built between 1706 and 1733 by Alexander Stronach, a master mason from Tarbat, who also built the smaller of the two girnals (storehouses for grain) and the original pier at Portmahomack, as well as a manse in Tain, now Manse House.[5] The present tower originally had a contemporary 'counsell house of two houses hight adjoyned thereto', also used for imprisoning debtors and criminals. This was replaced when estimates were sought in 1825 for 'a Court House and an Enlargement of the Jail' next to the Tolbooth, together with 'Repairs on the Four Cells in the Ancient Tower'.[6] Unfortunately, however, as the *New Statistical Account* recorded, the 'handsome town and county house … was not constructed fire-proof; and the upper rooms, being appropriated for the confinement of debtors, were, a few years ago [1833], by some accident inflamed. Several lives were lost and the building was almost burnt to the ground. It has not since been rebuilt, and what was once an ornament, is now the greatest deformity in the place'. As we will see, Andrew's first major achievement was to design a Court House, still in use as the Sheriff Court, to occupy the vacant space.

The Lodge St Duthus, completed in 1787, stood in a prominent position at the end of the High Street and occupied more or less the site on which three decades later the present Royal Hotel, designed by Andrew Maitland, would be built. The Lodge itself used a large upstairs room, and derived an income from letting out shops and cellars below.

After the Reformation and the end of pilgrimages Tain had become something of a backwater. It was not until the end of the eighteenth century and the first decades of the nineteenth century that several factors combined to put Tain into a more expansionary phase. One major factor was the construction in the 30 years from 1771 by the Commissioners of Supply, influenced by Donald Macleod of Geanies, of 600 miles of roads in Ross-shire and Cromartyshire, mainly in the east. Early in the nineteenth century Tain became a staging post on the road from Inverness to Wick and Thurso. At the same time, the burgh as the most significant town in the area was a natural beneficiary of the agricultural improvement of the period. These developments opened up commercial opportunities, not least in hotels and in banking.

Andrew would soon have discovered that Tain had two flourishing hotels. The leading one was occupied by Mrs Isabella Ellison, and was known variously as the George and Dragon and Mrs Ellison's Hotel (and later as the Royal Hotel). It stood in the High Street adjacent to the site of the 'handsome town and county house' destroyed by fire in 1833. A posting house, it had stables, coach houses, yards and offices going down the west side of what is now Castle Brae. Two Maitland buildings, the Court House and a lodge for the caretaker of the Collegiate Church (now housing the Tain & District Museum), would later be erected on its site. The other hotel was run by Houston Mackay and was known as the Crown & Anchor (but was later in the century to be called the St Duthus Hotel). It formed part of the complex of buildings owned by the Lodge St Duthus on the corner of the High Street and St Duthus Street, later replaced by the present Maitland-designed Royal Hotel.

Banks did not stint themselves when it came to constructing new branches, nearly always with ample living accommodation for their agents, who were important figures both in the local economy and socially. In 1828 the Commercial Bank of Scotland had built ornate premises on the corner of the High Street and Bank Street (now the Highland Council Service Point). Soon after Andrew settled in Tain work began in Tower Street on a handsome classical building, with a pilastered doorpiece, designed by George Angus for the British Linen Company's Bank (now the Bank of Scotland).

Pigot's 1837 Directory shows the High Street and Lamington Street as full of shops, with more round the corner in Market Street and no less than five fleshers (butchers) occupying a long narrow building, dating from 1820, situated in Market Street and forming part of the Market Place. In later years Market Street would be reconfigured according to designs by Andrew, and later still A. Maitland & Sons would design a bank (later the Clydesdale Bank) across the road from the Market Place. Many of the shops in the main streets would, moreover, be renovated or rebuilt to Maitland designs.

This period also saw two new ecclesiastical buildings. The first, in what is now known as King Street, was a Secession Chapel (now the Associated Presbyterian Church), with 300 sittings. This was built in 1838-39 for a group whose breakaway from the Church of Scotland preceded the Disruption. Andrew would no doubt have appreciated the fine masonry work on its frontage. The other, in what is now Queen Street, was the new Free Church, built, as we saw in chapter 2, from a mixture of printed plans produced in Edinburgh and plans and specifications produced by Andrew Maitland himself. On this site nearly half a century later a replacement, one of the best known Maitland buildings and now the Parish Church, would be built.

Soon after the Free Church was completed Andrew would have observed work on a new prison, backing on to, and to the west of, the church and with its entrance in the Scotsburn Road. It was reported in September 1846 that 'the new prison has now been built; but it is not yet ready for use'. A prisoner had lately made his escape owing to the insecurity of the old building.[7] The site of the new prison was as far as Tain went uphill to the south of the High Street. The prison was opposite fields on which half a century later Maitland-designed villas would be built.

Expansion - westward and eastward

Two extensions of the town had taken place prior to Andrew's arrival in Tain, both of them on the level of the raised beach.

The first of these was at the western end. During the seventeenth and eighteenth centuries development of the area known as Little Tain, including Hill Street and Well Street to the south and Dunrobin Street to the north of Academy Street, had started. Early in the nineteenth century this area was further developed and more closely linked to the rest of Tain, the catalyst being the foundation of Tain Royal Academy. The Academy building, completed in 1813, was designed by the Inverness architect James Smith. The *New Statistical Account* saw it as 'one of the chastest and most handsome erections in the north of Scotland'. The liberal education it offered was a magnet for upper and middle class pupils from all over the Highlands. It was in this part of Tain that Andrew and his family were to settle, and it was to the Academy that he was to send his sons and daughters.

The other extension, known as the New Town of Tain, was at the eastern end of the town. Donald Macleod of Geanies had started to feu lots in 1789 in Geanies, Ross and Lamington Streets. In 1813 he sold to the magistrates and heritors for £181-1s-0d a site for a new parish church, which was completed in 1815.[8] The new church (to-day the Duthac Centre) was also designed by James Smith. His Gothic building was described in the *New Statistical Account* as 'a substantial but rather heavy looking edifice; a tower is its great *desideratum'*. Even without a tower it did, however, give the New Town a focal point. A series of further feus starting in 1826 led to a more significant phase of development of the New Town in the grid pattern we see to-day.[9] By the late 1830s and early 1840s the new parish church's capacity of 1,200 worshippers was becoming insufficient. But the problem was alleviated when a schism led to the building of the Secession Chapel mentioned above. It was finally solved when the majority of the congregation defected to the Free Church in 1843.

Until not long before Andrew arrived in Tain the most common form of lighting had been by fish and whale oil lamps, with tallow candles being used in more prosperous circles. In 1839, however, the Tain Gas Light Company was formed. It built a gas works in Shore Road, expenditure on capital account reaching £1,754 by 1842. Gas was now being used in 'almost all respectable houses' and in prominent buildings such as the Mason's Lodge. The largest shareholder and main customer, for street lighting, was the Tain Burgh Council. Half a century later there was to be a monumental struggle between the gas company and the council. James Maitland was to play a major role in this and in rebuilding the gas works.

Water was obtained from wells, but in December, 1841 the Council resolved that it was 'necessary for the comfort and cleanliness of the inhabitants that a permanent supply of water should be introduced'.[10] From then on the subject was discussed again and again, and Andrew Maitland was to be involved in attempts to solve the problem.

A surgeon's perspective

The 1842 report of the Tain surgeon James Cameron to the Poor Law Commissioners provides an additional perspective.[11] 'During the last three years the town has increased in size', Cameron wrote, 'and on the main street and other parts a number of elegant dwellinghouses and places of business have been erected, which have imparted to the town an aspect superior to that of most burghs of its size and population. ... There are in Tain several families in good circumstances; and, indeed, a considerable proportion of the population consists of respectable individuals in the middle rank of life'. There were upwards of 72 shopkeepers, 'none of them to be reckoned among the lower orders', and several with 'large establishments'. But that was only part of the story.

'There are', Cameron noted, 'two or three covered sewers; but these are not sufficient for keeping the town free of impurities. .... There are three courses of water that run through the town. In summer they are scantily supplied; but in winter they are sometimes converted into torrents. They are in a great measure undefended, and in some places overflow their banks after heavy rain. The courses are not kept clear, and, in consequence, filth proceeding both from animal and vegetable matter is allowed to remain in them'. The three watercourses are shown on a map of the burgh produced by the Boundary Commission in 1832. Two of them were close to the centre of Tain and were both known as the *Aultmatach* (with many spelling variations), or 'foul stream'. They had been bridged - one to facilitate development of the New Town, the other across Tower Street - but still presented problems. Thus it was reported to the burgh council in April, 1842 that George Murray Senior, a member of the council who owned several properties in 'the street leading from the High Street to the Secession Chapel'[12] had 'recently covered over part of the Burn of *Altmatach* with the intention of including it as part of his garden'. In order to widen the street the council had to purchase this from him and to get him to move a proposed new house further back. Andrew would also have observed improvements in Tower Street following the agreement of the burgh council in October, 1846 that the other '*Altmatach*, or Foul Burn' should be 'arched and causewayed' at a cost of £48 (to which they agreed to contribute only 10 guineas, with the balance to come from neighbouring property owners - the Mason Lodge £22, and the British Linen Bank and Mr Mackenzie, Writer, each 7 guineas). Thirty years later a Maitland-designed Public Hall would be opened immediately to the east of the burn. The legacy of the raising of the street levels that resulted from these various initiatives was a subterranean world which continues to fascinate people - tunnels, drainage channels and a series of cellars from which access had originally been gained to the street.[13]

'In front of the houses of the poorer classes', Cameron wrote, 'the channels of the streets and roads are not kept open, water being allowed to remain in a stagnant state, and all sorts of refuse being thrown into these channels, and collected there in heaps, in order to form dunghills. There are numerous houses in a decayed and useless state, which are converted into reservoirs for all sorts of filth. There are various causes which render the collecting of manure profitable to the inhabitants: their food principally consisting of potatoes, of which vegetable they raise large quantities, it requires all their ingenuity throughout the year to collect a sufficient supply towards a succeeding crop; and the farmers in the neighbourhood are in the habit of purchasing cart-loads from them, for which they pay from 1s. 6d. to 2s. 6d. per load. Thus the greatest pains are taken by the inhabitants to procure and collect impurities of all descriptions; such as ashes, dirty water, decayed and decomposed matter, &c.: and this mass is husbanded with the greatest care and attention, and lies at their doors during most part of the year'. The practice of keeping pigs was very common, with pigsties 'of necessity near the houses'.

The local economy

The author of the *New Statistical Account* observed that Tain 'seems to owe its existence and prosperity' to its position as a market town for the whole surrounding countryside. It was primarily in this surrounding countryside, with agricultural improvers as clients, that Andrew Maitland began building his professional practice.

'The only manufactories properly so called in the parish', the *New Statistical Account* reported, were an iron-foundry and 'a brewery which supplies the most of the neighbourhood with excellent ale'. The brewery took its power from the Burn of Morangie, a mile west of the town, which also 'gave motion separately to a sawing, a carding, a grinding and a dyeing-mill'. The source of the Burn of Morangie was the Tarlogie Springs. Both the springs and the burn with its brewery were on the estates of the largest landowner in the parish, Hugh Rose Ross of Glastullich and Cromarty. Within a few years Andrew was to be briefly involved with the Tarlogie Springs when the burgh council sought to harness them to provide the much sought after water supply to the town.

The brewery was, however, to play a more significant role in the lives of the Maitland family. The tenant, Colin Mackenzie, died in 1841 and his heirs vacated the premises in 1844. A new lease was taken in 1848 by William Matheson, who the following year converted the brewery into a distillery. The distillery, Glenmorangie, was destined to achieve world-wide esteem - and Andrew's sons, as designers and investors when the distillery was re-built, and also as managers, were to be among those responsible for that success.

References and Notes

[1] Hugh Miller, *Scenes and Legends of the North of Scotland*, first published 1835 and revised 1850, reprinted B&W Publishing 1999, p.27.

[2] *New Statistical Account of Scotland,* vol. 14, pp. 281-91, Parish of Tain, drawn up by Mr William Taylor, August 1837.

[3] For a scholarly account see Harry Gordon Slade, *The Collegiate Kirk of St Duthac of Tain and The Abbey of Fearn*, Tain & District Museum Trust, 2000.

[4] *Reconsidering the Scottish Town*, a paper by Professor Charles McKean, 11th August, 2008.

[5] *Tain Tolbooth*, Estelle Quick, Tain & District Museum Trust, 1998 is a well-researched history.

[6] *Inverness Courier*, 10th March, 1825.

[7] *Eleventh Report of the Inspectors of Prisons*, summarised in *John O'Groat Journal*, 11th September, 1846. For the story of the building of the prison see chapter 6.

[8] Instrument of Sasine, 13th January, 1813 re Disposition 14th December, 1812 (copy in Tain & District Museum), and W. Macgill, *Old Ross-shire and Scotland from the Tain and Balnagown Documents,* vol. ii, The Northern Counties Newspaper and Printing and Publishing Company, 1911, no. 1265.

[9] The story of the development of the New Town, the financial woes of Donald Macleod of Geanies and the acquisition of the New Town by the first Duke of Sutherland is one of the main themes of a book by the present author: Hamish Mackenzie, *Tain, Tarbat Ness and the Duke, 1833*, Tain & District Museum Trust, 2012.

[10] Minutes of Tain Burgh Council, Highland Archive Centre B70/6/4.

[11] James Cameron, *Report on the Sanitary Condition and General Economy of the Town of Tain and the District of Easter Ross*, made to the Poor Law Commissioners, in *Sanitary Inquiry, Scotland*, H.M. Stationery Office, 1842.

[12] This street was variously known in the early and mid nineteenth century as Dog Street, King's Street and its present name of King Street - the latter names commemorating the fact that James IV and James V entered the centre of Tain by this route during their pilgrimages.

[13] See *Remembering Hidden Tain*, a report produced for the Tain & Easter Ross Civic Trust by Cait McCullagh of ARCH (Archaeology for Communities in the Highlands), 2012 following oral history sessions - online via www.archhighland.org.uk .

5. THE TRUE STORY OF THE TAIN COURT HOUSE

5.1 A print for sale in 1850 of the new Tain Court House and Council Chambers.

The Tain Tolbooth and Court House

The most widely recognised and cherished image of Tain, reproduced again and again over the years, is that of the eighteenth century Tolbooth, its tower and bartizans a prominent feature of the skyline, and the adjacent nineteenth century Scottish Baronial style Court House with its smaller bartizans echoing those of the Tolbooth. Andrew Maitland's first major success was to design the Court House and to make ornamental changes to the Tolbooth itself which brought the two into harmony - plans with which the civic leaders were 'much pleased'.

But modern writers on Tain's buildings have not acknowledged Andrew's contribution, and most have ascribed the design to a better known, but on this occasion unsuccessful, competitor. This chapter, utilising the minutes of the Tain Burgh Council,[1] contemporary newspaper reports, and some detective work, aims to tell the true, though somewhat convoluted, story and thereby to restore Andrew's laurels.

The civic leaders of Tain

In the countryside, the economy was based, as we saw in the last chapter, on land ownership. And land ownership gave power - and also responsibility - to the heritors. Indeed they retained a major role in local government until the formation of the Ross and Cromarty County Council in 1890. But in Royal Burghs like Tain the burgh councils enjoyed wide powers. Hence an architect like Andrew looking for work had to look not only to the heritors but also to councils.

Historically the councils had been dominated by the heritors, but reforms of the franchise in 1832-33 had been transformational. The 'close system' of self-perpetuating councils, which favoured the landed interest, had been abolished. Instead public elections were held every year for one-third of the council seats, at which £10 householders could vote. In Tain up to 70 electors voted annually to elect 5 councillors for a three year term. This wider franchise skewed the social base of the council towards wider middle-class representation.

The sitting councillors when Andrew settled in Tain included five professional men (three writers [solicitors], one bank agent, and one accountant), eight tradesmen (four merchants, two grocers, one druggist and one draper), an Inspector of Roads, and George Murray of Rosemount. The council was thus essentially middle class in complexion, albeit covering a wide spectrum of that class. The apparent exception was George Murray. But, despite the designation 'of Rosemount', he had no aristocratic lineage. His family had long been merchants and bankers in Tain. They had shown a remarkable propensity to become Provosts of Tain, and he himself was currently the Provost. Members of the family had invested in estates at Pitcalzean (which they re-named Westfield) in Nigg, at Rosemount near Tain, and at Geanies in Tarbat - a prime example of an upward social mobility so often observable in this period.

All the evidence is that the Tain councillors overwhelmingly shared the political and religious preferences of the Highland middle classes - Liberalism and the Free Church. Thus Tain and the other Northern Burghs were represented in Parliament by James Loch, sitting as a Whig and later as a Liberal, from 1832 to 1852. All the Tain councillors, with one exception, had joined the Free Church at the Disruption, when over 80% of the population had seceded. When a wooden temporary Free Church was erected 'the people of Tain followed [the Rev. Charles Calder Mackintosh] in an almost unbroken mass. ... There was witnessed a sight which was seen in only one other burgh in Scotland. The Magistrates of Tain (as if it were a little State by itself) walked in procession followed by their red-coated halbert-armed officers to take their place opposite the pulpit in the Free Church, as they had long been wont to do in the Church Established. And this they continued to do, Sabbath after Sabbath, until a hint was received from Edinburgh that such an official proceeding was of questionable legality'.[2] The council minutes of the period show, too, that the members were not afraid to confront the heritors. Battles included ones over poor relief in the aftermath of the Disruption, payments for the parish school and schoolmaster, and the Duke of Sutherland's alleged interference with the Tain Mussel Scalps.

Civic pride - and the myth of 'the oldest Royal Burgh in Scotland'

Another aspect that comes over strongly from the council minutes is the sense of civic pride felt by council members. This was particularly marked during a long-running battle between Tain and Dingwall as to which should be 'Head Burgh', or county town, of Ross-shire. The council had declared in 1832 that 'Tain had enjoyed this privilege from time immemorial' and that they had in their possession a document showing that King Malcolm Canmore had granted this privilege in 1057. An extrapolation of this claim, with the date later adjusted to 1066, seems to be the basis of the myth - widely quoted nowadays, not least by by estate agents and those who write tourist brochures - that Tain is the oldest Royal Burgh in Scotland. The myth is contradicted by the fact that there were no Royal Burghs until the reign of David I (1124-53) and by the absence of Tain from all early lists of Royal Burghs. It is further undermined by the absence in Tain of burgh walls with gates like those at which medieval burghs collected taxes.[3]

Despite 'memorials', petitions and objections from the Tain Council, an Act passed in August, 1843 appointed Dingwall as Head Burgh. The battle was lost, but the councillors continued to manifest a sense of civic pride, which led particularly to a concentration on enhancing the look of the town through such improvements as road straightening and levelling and the location and appearance of key buildings. This civic pride was to provide work for Andrew Maitland and his family right up to the time of the Great War.

Work for Andrew

From 1847 onwards Andrew Maitland's name appears frequently in the minutes of the Tain Burgh Council. During the late 1840s and through the 1850s he produced numerous reports on and valuations of property owned by the council or in dispute. In February, 1848 he and Andrew Ross were appointed Road Assessors 'for laying on the road assessment on property within the Royalty of the Burgh for the current year'. Successive Acts of Parliament had imposed a duty to pay for the road system, and, under the Ross and Cromartyshire District Roads Act, 1847, £50 had to be paid by the burgh (which had to be found through local assessments) and £50 by the heritors.

In August, 1849 the council decided that the pavements, which were presumably irregular as a result of the road levelling, were 'to be improved by doing away with the steps in such a way as shall be approved by Mr Russell or Mr Maitland'.

Andrew's appointment as a valuator for the road assessments was renewed annually until 1855, when a local merchant was appointed with a remuneration of £2 per year 'with the usual allowance for collection'. By this time Andrew was certainly able to find more remunerative work.

With one exception, the council did not require any architectural work during the 1840s. One reason might be that the council was chronically short of money. In 1849 it had to increase its credit from the British Linen Bank from £385 to £600, and it had no financial control until after the Treasurer, James Munro, was forced to step down in November, 1855 when he was unable to pay up the stated cash balance of £299-17s-4½d and had to appeal to his friends to 'come forward and make up any deficiency to the Burgh'. The one exception was, however, an important one for Tain and for Andrew Maitland. It was to give Tain its Court House, aligned with the Tolbooth, and it was to establish Andrew's reputation.

The Tolbooth and the adjacent ruin

The Tolbooth was a proud symbol of Tain's burghal status. Tolbooths, often with adjoining administrative buildings, were a key feature of Scottish burghs, usually occupying a prominent position near to the mercat cross. Medieval monarchs had given burghs a special status and trading rights which included holding annual fairs and weekly markets. The tolls levied on these were an important source of burgh income and were collected in the tolbooth. Tolbooths became the meeting place of burgh councils. From the sixteenth century they became places where courts were held, and from 1597 burgh councils were required to provide a secure prison.[4]

As we saw in the last chapter, the fire of 1833, which destroyed the 'long contemplated and much required new Gaol and Court House of the burgh', had left an ugly ruin beside the Tolbooth. For some years after the fire the council had met, and courts been held, across the road in the Lodge St Duthus, where the Royal Hotel now stands. At the same time the Tolbooth appears to have been pressed back into service as a prison. The surgeon James Cameron, almost certainly referring to the Tolbooth, commented in his report to the Poor Law Commissioners that 'the present gaol is narrow in its accommodation, and anything but a wholesome place'. Not surprisingly one of the burgh council's major concerns became the provision of a new prison and and court house. In so doing, however, they had to deal not just with the heritors but also with a new Ross and Cromarty Prisons Board. County Prisons Boards had been established by an Act of 1839 to take over from burghs the management of local prisons. They were given responsibility for maintaining existing prisons and erecting new ones, and were empowered to raise finance by an assessment of the burghs within their area of jurisdiction. From the council minutes of the period we can observe the Tain Burgh Council's concerns about the visual aspects of the proposed new facilities, and we can see how Andrew was able to satisfy the council's wishes.

Enter William Robertson and Thomas Brown

The Tain Burgh Council noted in June 1840 that 'in consequence of the New Prison Act for improving prisons and prison discipline a new prison was required for Easter Ross'. The present one was in their view 'incapable of being made sufficient'. The new Prisons Board of Ross and Cromarty met in Dingwall in February 1841. William Robertson, the Elgin architect who was then Andrew Maitland's employer, reported that he had visited Tain (perhaps with Andrew to assist him?) and found that there were 'four situations more or less eligible as a site for a Jail'. His preferred site was immediately opposite the north end of Geanies Street, on a one in ten slope, and he recommended that the building 'should not be conspicuous and should not be ornamental'. Later that month, however, the burgh council expressed a wish for 'a more ornamental building than that which the Board proposed'.

William Robertson died, as we have seen, in June 1841. The County Prisons Board then turned to Thomas Brown, who had worked in the office of the highly regarded William Burn and had been appointed architect to the Prisons Board of Scotland in 1837. In May 1842 the Ross and Cromarty Prisons Board sent to the burgh council plans for a new prison and court house prepared by Thomas Brown.[5] The council were not impressed. They noted that these had been prepared 'on the Supposition of the Court House and the Prison being combined on the site of the old one in the centre of the Town'. They preferred separate sites. They acknowledged that Brown had prepared plans for Dingwall, Tain and Stornoway - the first having the prison behind the Court House, and the latter two beside it - and that Brown was confident that joining the two would cost less and estimated a total of £1,900. But even this was not sufficient to persuade them.

In August 1842 the Town Clerk received a letter from Thomas Brown saying he 'would be prepared to prepare plans to meet the views of the council', and in the following month a committee was appointed to consider these plans and to confer with the heritors to make the most favourable arrangements they could for the council. By December it had been agreed that the County Prisons Board would give up the Tolbooth to the heritors ('who were empowered by [the Act] 5 and 6 Will 4 Cap 98 to provide a Court-House and other relative accommodation in the district') on the heritors becoming the owner of the site of the old Court House. The heritors agreed to provide, in the new building to be erected adjacent to the Tolbooth, offices for the Town Clerk and a room for meetings of the council.

In April 1843 the County Clerk sought tenders for 'a Prison and inclosing Wall, in the Burgh of Tain' [but not a Court House], a prison and Court House in Stornoway and repairs to the prison of Cromarty, all according to plans to be seen in Dingwall or of Thomas Brown, Esq. in Edinburgh.[6] In September 1843 the Tain Burgh Council regretted that the plans 'have been much altered for the worse' and offered the free use of their stone quarry if the Prisons Board would consult their wishes. The Prisons Board would not agree. By June 1844 the council were in dispute with Messrs Mitchell & Brand who stated that they had contracted for the new prison and requested permission to open quarries on the council's land. The council submitted a Memorial to the General Prisons Board of Scotland 'with a view to having a more suitable building and better accommodation than proposed by the County Board and giving local tradesmen a fair chance of obtaining the Contract'.

The council seems to have lost this battle, for the prison was built in 1846 and prisoners were transferred to it in November of that year. But the council's defeat was tempered by the fact that they had ensured that the new prison was neither adjacent to the Tolbooth nor in a prominent position. A photograph in the Tain & District Museum shows the prison, set back from the eastern side of the Scotsburn Road, near the foot of the road, and backing on to the site then occupied by the Free Church built with Andrew Maitland's help after the Disruption (the site of the present Parish Church) and the Free Church School (designed by Andrew Maitland, and now the Parish Church Hall) behind it. It appears as a T-shaped building, with bars on the windows, and is surrounded by high walls. The photograph is indistinct, but it almost certainly reflects plans by Thomas Brown - probably those referred to in the advertisement of April 1843 - which have been deposited in the National Records of Scotland.[7] The prison is also shown on the first Ordnance Survey map, surveyed in 1871. The Ordnance Survey Name Book prepared for this map show that it housed five criminals and two civil prisoners. The building is to-day used by the Care & Learning Service Easter Ross Family Team.

But the council was clearly determined not to lose the battle for a Court House in the centre of the town and worthy of the ancient Royal Burgh. Andrew Maitland was engaged to come up with designs. He came up with plans in the Scottish Baronial style, making use of bartizans to echo those of the the adjacent Tolbooth and of emphatic crenellations.

'The Council are much pleased with the plans prepared by Mr Maitland'

The council minutes of 17th April, 1847 record that 'the plans prepared by Mr Maitland of the proposed Court-House were laid before the Council and the Council having examined them are much pleased with them as likely to be ornamental to the Town'. But 'the Heritors are not likely to adopt these plans unless the Burgh contribute to the expence [sic] of the ornamental work in addition to the statutory proportion of the remaining expence'. Mr Maitland had 'estimated the expence of the ornamental work at £162 and the Council considering the desirableness to the Town of having the building made in a style which will be creditable to the Community give the Provost or Senior Bailie ... a discretionary power to offer on behalf of the Burgh ... a subscription not exceeding the said amount in addition to the Burgh's legal share'.

A year later Andrew's plans were still being discussed. Provost George Murray of Rosemount's 25 year old nephew William H. Murray of Geanies successfully moved a resolution at a meeting of a Committee of the Heritors of Easter Ross that the district should agree to proceed with Mr Maitland's original plan, excepting that the building to the back in which it was proposed to place the Sheriff's room be dispensed with and that the new entry should be through the Tower (presumably rather than through the doorway in the middle of the new building, which is now used as the entrance).

Provost George Murray of Rosemount died, however, on 13th March, 1848. His young nephew William H. Murray of Geanies was co-opted to the council in his place at a meeting on 3rd April and was immediately elected Provost. His first item of business was consideration of the Court House plans. The council agreed to grant to the heritors 'the site and materials of the old Court-House to be employed for the erection of the new Court-House', and also 'to pay the additional expence to be incurred in making the outside of the Court-House ornamental instead of plain and on the exterior of the Tower, as the same shall be ascertained by one or more persons to be agreed by the Heritors and the Council'. Invitations to builders and contractors to tender were published in May.[8] A building contract was then drawn up on terms agreed by the council, including those as to the additional costs of the ornamentation.

On 1st September, 1848 the foundation stone was laid in a ceremony of a type enamoured by nineteenth century Tain. 'Old and young, to the number of about three thousand, assembled on the High Street of Tain to witness the proceedings.' At two o'clock members of the St Duthus Lodge and other lodges in full masonic costume were joined by the Magistrates and Council, and marched 'through the principal streets, the fair sex filling every door and window'. They then took their places on a raised platform, where the Rev. Lewis Rose 'delivered a most eloquent and soul-stirring prayer'. Coins and documents were laid in the cavity of the foundation stone and a masonic formula proceeded with. William H. Murray of Geanies as Provost and Master of the St. Duthus Lodge then gave a lengthy address to the vast crowd. 'He could not', he said, 'express how much pride he felt that he was permitted to preside on so auspicious an occasion - and it was an additional satisfaction that the architect, who has displayed such elegance of taste, and the contractors are of our own people'. The ceremony ended after nearly three hours, and about 100 people dined afterwards at Mr Ellison's George and Dragon Hotel.[9] Three days later the council gave retrospective approval and agreed to defray the expenses of the procession and the ceremony - presumably including the dinner.

During the construction of the Court House Andrew Maitland acted as Inspector and was entrusted with various related tasks. Thus the council agreed to place 'a device in stone or iron over the Court-House door' and authorised 'procurement of such a one as Mr Maitland ... will approve of'; and the Town Clerk was 'authorised to order furniture for the Council Chamber and to take assistance of Mr Maitland, Architect, in designing the furniture'.

The new Court House

A newspaper account written as the work neared completion gives a clear account of both the exterior and the interior.[10] The reporter thought the new building was too close to the street: 'were it twenty yards farther back, it ... would look as well as any of the kind in any town like ours in Scotland'. Otherwise he was complimentary. 'The Court House is battlemented and ornamented at each corner, and at the middle top of the front elevation, with neat turrets. One of them above the doorway is very handsome and looks uncommonly well, giving a set-off to all the others. To be equal with the building at its side the old tower that has seen so many centuries has been stripped of its dark coat of age and long service'. (The Victorians liked to expose original stonework. Was the old Tolbooth perhaps harled?) 'The old iron barred windows in it', the report went on, 'have been replaced with modern ones and that which is to be the principal entrance to the Court House has been placed in it. A Lion, the town's arms, executed in vitrified stone, has been placed immediately above this door, and also looks very well. ... The whole range of buildings provides a very pleasing spectacle'.

'But', the report continued, 'the inside of the building is more pleasing still'. The old winding stairs in the tower had been replaced. 'Splendid specimens of the plastic art' adorned the walls of the handsome court room on the second floor. Below it was a commodious council room and offices for the Sheriff, Fiscal and Sheriff Clerk. At the back were 'unexplorable dungeons', one of which was to be converted to a lock-up or police office. The architect, Mr Maitland and the contractors, the Messrs Ross, 'certainly had reason to be satisfied with their handiwork'.

The new Court House was opened on 23rd January, 1850. Sheriff Taylor gave an address on the occasion of his occupying the bench for the first time in the new building. After thanking the heritors and the burgh magistrates he went on to say that the building was 'an edifice which is an ornament of the town - worthy of its progressing prosperity. The convenience of the interior arrangements, as well as the design of the elevation, they owed to the judgement, skill, and good taste of the architect, Mr Maitland; and when it was recollected that he was necessarily limited in point of space, and, it might be added, in point of funds too, it must be admitted that he had, in these unfavourable circumstances, accomplished the task of planning out the required accommodation with a success which reflected much credit on his professional talents ... So complete and accurate were his specifications that ... the whole of the extra work [required] had only amounted to eleven shillings! - rather a novelty in building experience'.[11]

The finished building was illustrated in a contemporary print.[12] This shows the new building in the Scottish Baronial style, in tooled ashlar, and joined to the Tolbooth (which is shown in polished ashlar rather than its actual coursed and dressed rubble). Several ornamental features of the new building, all observable to-day, can be clearly seen. The most prominent is the crenellated roof with bartizans at each end and a central gable with smaller bartizans - the bartizans echoing those of the Tolbooth. Another feature is the arched central door and four arched ground floor windows of the new building with a continuous hoodmould above, these being matched by a similar new arched door and arched west window in the old Tolbooth, also under the continuous hoodmould. A third feature is the lion rampant in relief above the door of the Tolbooth, which must be the device 'such as Mr Maitland will approve of'. The Historic Environment Scotland listing describes the Court House as 'a good composition of Scots Baronial and Tudor features, ... [which] demonstrates the confident adaptation of this mid-19th century country house style to public architecture'.[13]

This was not, however, the end of Andrew's involvement with the Tolbooth and Court House. As we will see, in 1873 he was to design an addition at the east side of the Court House, continuing down Castle Brae, and in 1878 A. Maitland & Sons were to supervise the installation of a clock on the Tolbooth.

Andrew's contemporaries recognised that he had made a significant contribution to the development of the ancient Royal Burgh. Soon after the completion of the Court House, in what appears to be an early sign of approval by the influential masonic fraternity, Andrew who had joined Lodge St Duthus (of which his two architect sons would both later become Master) was raised Master Mason on 12th February, 1850.[14]

But in the twentieth century Andrew Maitland's laurels are taken away

When Andrew Maitland died in 1894 various newspaper obituaries listed his major works. The first mentioned was the Court House.

At some stage during the twentieth century, however, Andrew Maitland was robbed of the credit for his design. Thus Historic Scotland's listing in 1971 did not give the name of the architect of the main part of the Court House and ascribed only the 1873 addition to Andrew Maitland. The Highland Council's Historic

Environment Record, with 1983 photographs,[15] followed suit. Since then every single one of the distinguished architectural historians who have written about Tain has ascribed the Court House of 1848-50 to Thomas Brown and only the 1873 addition to Andrew Maitland. By 2014 what is now Historic Environment Scotland had also decided that Thomas Brown was responsible.

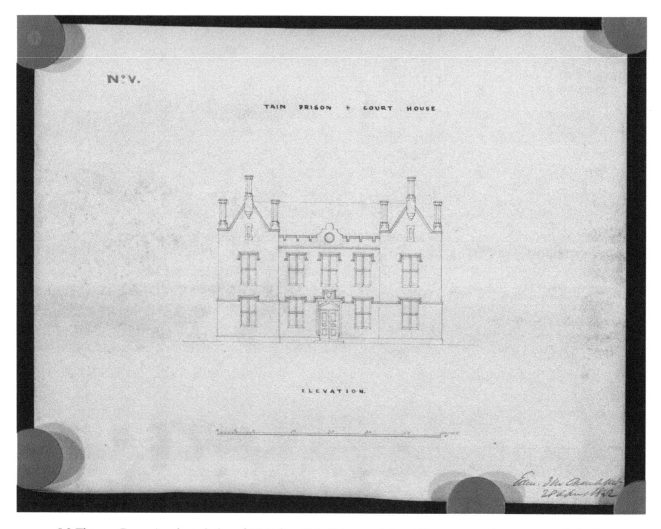

5.2 Thomas Brown's rejected plan of 1842 for a Tain Prison and Court House - not what was actually built.

The most likely reason for this is that Brown's rejected plans of 1842 for a combined prison and Court House were deposited with the National Records of Scotland and have been mistaken for the real thing. But Brown's plans show a Tudor style building dominated by tall octagonal chimneys not unlike those in the Court House designed by Brown at Stornoway. This is of course not what was actually built - and his design is so far removed from the building we see to-day that it is inconceivable that Andrew Maitland merely adapted Brown's designs.[16]

Fortunately at least parts of the original Maitland plans do appear to exist.

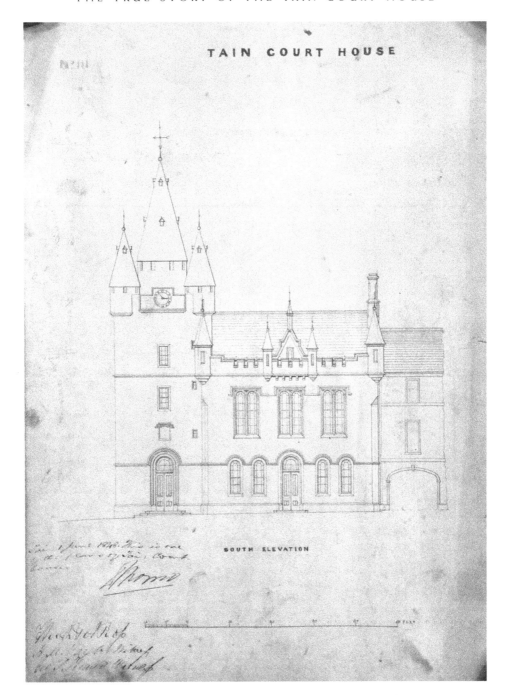

5.3 Plan in Andrew Maitland's style and dated 1st June, 1848 of the Tain Court House -
linked at right to the then Royal Hotel. Surely the original?

The Highland Archive Centre in Inverness holds the plans of the main elevations of the extension to the Court House carried out in 1873-75, whose Maitland provenance has never been disputed. Filed inside the bundle are six smaller scale plans showing the Court House without the later extension. They are each certified (by someone whose signature is illegible) 'Tain 1st June 1848. This is one of the plans of Tain Court House'. The plans themselves are not signed but they are in Andrew Maitland's characteristic style, and the draftsmanship matches that of the later extension.[17] They must surely be the original plans.

Every single piece of contemporary evidence indicates that the Court House was designed not by Thomas Brown but by Andrew Maitland. It would be good to see credit restored to him for the iconic building which established his reputation.

References and Notes

[1] Tain Burgh Council Minutes, Highland Archive Centre, B70/6/3 to 5.

[2] The Rev. William Taylor, *Researches into the History of Tain: Earlier and Later*, Northern Chronicle Office, Inverness, 1882, p.100.

[3] A charter of 1588, the first of two granted by James VI, is the earliest extant proof of Tain's status as a Royal Burgh. It declared that Tain was 'by our noble ancestors of good memory ... erected and constituted from ancient time with each and all of the liberties ... appertaining to our free royal burghs ...'. This royal testimony fails, however, to tell us how ancient that time was.

[4] For a helpful account see Caroline A. MacGregor, *Buildings of Administration*, chapter 13 in *Scotland's Buildings*, Tuckwell Press, 2003.

[5] Plans dated 28th April, 1842, National Records of Scotland RHP21791 to 21795.

[6] *Inverness Courier*, 19th April, 1843.

[7] National Records of Scotland, RHP21800 to 21823. The plans are marked '1843?'

[8] *Inverness Journal*, 5th May, 1848; *Inverness Courier* 23rd May, 1848.

[9] *Inverness Courier*, 5th September, 1848.

[10] *John O'Groat Journal*, 2nd November, 1849.

[11] *Inverness Courier*, 31st January, 1850.

[12] Tain & District Museum, TANDM 2103.1.

[13] Historic Environment Scotland LB41867.

[14] William T. Russell, *My Brothers Past*, vol. 1, 1761-1899, Librario Publishing Ltd, 2000, p.76.

[15] Highland HER MHG8667.

[16] National Records of Scotland, RHP 21791 to 21795, dated 28th April, 1842 .

[17] Highland Archive Centre, CRC/9/3/3/5/3.

6. THE MAITLANDS AT HOME

6.1 Andrew Maitland, photographed by William Smith.

A growing family … and a poignant memorial

Andrew and Henrietta brought with them to Tain two sons, both, as we have seen, born in Resolis - George (born in 1842) and Alexander (born in 1843). The years after they settled in Tain saw the birth of five more sons: James (born 3rd June, 1845) and Andrew Junior (born 13th March, 1847), who were the only two of their generation destined to become architects and who both became Provosts of Tain; followed by Henry (born 26th October, 1848), William (born 30th September, 1850), and Thomas (born 15th August, 1852). From at least 1851 Henrietta's younger sister Helen Andrews was living with them. She was described in the census for that year as a house servant, aged 23. In the 1861 census she had, somewhat strangely, only advanced to 29 and she had no occupation listed.

When Henrietta became pregnant once again in 1853 she and Andrew must have wondered whether their eighth child was to be yet another son. Sadly, however, before they found out Thomas died on 7th March, 1854, aged only 19 months. On the 28th of the same month their first daughter, Henrietta Margaret, was born. 1856 was an even more unhappy year. First Henrietta Margaret died of tubercular disease of the lungs on 28th April, aged only two years and one month. Then another son, Gordon, was born on 12th June but died on 29th June. The next year, 1857, also saw mixed fortunes. First, George, the eldest of the Maitland children, who had been ill for two years, died of phthisis pulmonalis (tuberculosis of the lungs, with progressive wasting of the body) on 10th May, shortly before his fifteenth birthday. Then another daughter, Christina Helen Jane, was born on 12th July. The eleventh and last child, a second Henrietta Margaret, was born on 6th October, 1859.[1]

Thus four of the eleven children of Andrew and Henrietta had died in infancy. One of the most poignant sights in Tain was a small marble tombstone at the base of the hillock on which the ruined chapel of St Duthus stands. The first inscription commemorated Thomas, who died in 1854, and this was followed by the names of the first Henrietta Margaret, Gordon and George, and then by Henrietta herself in 1887. The words 'Thy will be done' appeared beneath these inscriptions. There was insufficient space on the original tombstone to commemorate Andrew himself, and when he died more marble had to be added for this purpose. By this time he had outlived three more of his children. This tombstone has fragmented in the present century. Fortunately a much larger tombstone, at the top of the hillock and close to the chapel, survives and recapitulates the same information. Presumably his architect sons were responsible for this.

Esther Place

Where the Maitland family lived when they first came to Tain is not known. By the time of the 1851 census, however, they were living in what was variously described as Esther Row or Easther Row, but later came to be known as Esther Place. This is a short cul-de-sac at a right angle to Hill Street, a street going uphill from Academy Street to Manse Street. There were at this time three two-and-a-half-storey terraced houses, 'high slated and in firstrate condition' in Esther Place. The Maitlands' home was at the western end of the terrace, gable end on to Hill Street.

Andrew initially leased the house from the Trustees of the Westfield (or Pitcalzean) Estate - one of the many estates in Easter Ross that had been acquired by members of the Murray family as they climbed the social ladder. In July, 1856, however, the Westfield Estate offered for sale by public roup (auction) various properties, including 'the house now occupied by Mr Maitland'. The sale was advertised to take place at Macgarrow's hotel at 2 o'clock in the afternoon of the 18th of that month.[2] Andrew took the opportunity to buy the house. The Valuation Rolls show a significant increase in its valuation from £7-1s-6d in 1856 to £12-0s-0d in 1857. We can almost certainly infer from this that it was in the months between these two valuations that Andrew built the substantial, and still extant, rear extension on the Hill Street side of the house.

Andrew was to live here until his death in 1894. It was from Esther Place, too, that Andrew conducted his business for the rest of his life, his office being on the first floor of the 1856-57 extension. Slater's Directory for 1861 gives Andrew's business address as Esther Row. As we will see in chapter 13, the building on the corner of Tower Street and Rose Street frequently described as 'Andrew Maitland's Office', and frequently dated as 'around 1870', was in fact built by his sons within months of his death nearly a quarter of a century later. We can be certain that Andrew Maitland never worked in this building, his office always being at Esther Place.

Andrew appears to have had no interest in activities outside his work except for those connected with the Free Church. In 1867 he was elected a Deacon of the Tain Free Church, the Deacons' Court being responsible for discharging the material and financial business, as opposed to the spiritual business, of the congregation. The Deacons' Court then appointed Andrew as one of two members of 'a standing committee to look after, and take charge of, and order all necessary repairs that might from time to time be required for the proper maintenance of the Ecclesiastical buildings belonging to the Congregation'.[3]

Educating the young Maitlands

Esther Place was conveniently close to Tain Royal Academy, then a well-respected, fee-paying school, with the level of fees alleviated by endowments.

The Academy had opened in 1813. But, nearly three decades on it had become apparent that the founders had 'fixed the salaries of the teachers somewhat higher than their resources warranted', and the number of teachers had to be cut back, and so the 'usefulness of the school was limited very considerably'.[4] Costs of around £1,000 in pursuing to the House of Lords the dismissal of the master of the Classical Department had exacerbated the situation, and the school had been closed. But it was re-opened in 1843 when a donation of £200 was received from James Matheson M.P.(later Sir James Matheson of the Lews and Achany). Its financial position was bolstered in 1844 by collections made, mainly from members of their families, in Calcutta by David Jardine and in China by James's nephew Alexander (later Sir Alexander) Matheson. No-one expressed concern that these founding families of the Jardine Matheson empire had accumulated much of their prodigious wealth from selling opium to the Chinese, thus precipitating the Opium Wars; but then no-one had expressed concern in 1812-13 that a significant part of the funds raised to found the school was derived from operating plantations worked by slaves.

The records of the Academy have not survived for the period during which the Maitland children were educated. In their history of Tain, however, R.W. and Jean Munro quote a report on the Academy published in 1872. 'With about 100 scholars on the roll - three-quarters of them boys, one-quarter girls - it was reckoned that the total cost of a full 10 year course was about £37. The parents were mostly clergymen, farmers, merchants, and "the more comfortable class of master tradesmen", and they could choose which courses they wished their children to follow.'[5]

Newspaper accounts of the period suggest that the Academy provided a good education in the Mathematics, Classics, and English and Writing Departments. Rigorous examinations were conducted in public each July by external examiners, many of whom were Ministers. The annual prize lists were usually published in the *Inverness Courier*. In 1848 the name of the 7 year old George Maitland appeared. In the years thereafter his name and those of Alexander, James, Andrew Junior, Henry and William all appear. In 1864 both Christina and Henrietta Margaret received prizes for English - as did Barbara Lindsay, who was to marry James Maitland. By 1868, however, Christina and Henrietta Margaret were attending Miss Macleod's Classes in Castle Brae and winning prizes there.

Andrew and Henrietta must have taken pride in the success of all the children who survived to school age. James was clearly a star pupil at the Academy, sometimes in the same class as his elder brother Alexander, and sometimes being placed above him in the prize list. In 1861 James won the prestigious Provost's Medal for Mathematics, whilst Andrew Junior, another star pupil, was first in Junior Mathematics. In his last year James had the honour of becoming dux, or top student in the school.

Whilst still a boy James was already showing an interest in buildings. A charming drawing from 1862, signed by the 17 year old James, survives of a house in Shore Road designed by his father for the Manager of the Tain Gas Light Company. The house still exists, albeit overlaid by subsequent accretions.

6.2 A drawing of the Gas Manager's house by the 17 year old James Maitland.

Andrew's house, then and now

Houses that architects design for their own use are often of particular interest. James and Andrew Junior were to build fine houses for themselves, but their father never did so - perhaps surprisingly in view of the limited space available for a large family. The 1861 census shows that Andrew and Henrietta were living in Esther Place with Helen and seven of their children, who must have been crammed into top floor bedrooms under the pitched roof. Within a few years James and Andrew Junior were working with their father in the small office in the rear extension he had built.

6.3 Andrew Maitland's house, Esther Place, Tain.

In 2003 Justine Golesworthy, keen to acquire a traditional house, bought what is now known as Borreraig in Esther Place. She was particularly pleased by a number of Victorian features. Interested in its history, she found it on a map of 1783 and she also discovered that it had been the home of Andrew Maitland. She has since worked so hard to sustain a Victorian ethos that if Andrew and Henrietta were able to see it they would quickly feel at home. She uses Andrew's office as the office for her IT recruitment consultancy. All she lacks, and not for want of trying, is a blue plaque outside to commemorate the house's occupation by its distinguished previous owner.

References and Notes

[1] The dates of births from 1845 to 1854 are taken from the Tain Free Church Baptismal Register, Highland Archives, CH3/748/4, and those of deaths prior to 1856 from the family tombstone.

[2] *Inverness Courier*, 10th July, 1856.

[3] Minutes of Tain Free Church, Highland Archive Centre CH/3/784/2, 7th October and 18th December, 1867.

[4] The information on the history of Tain Royal Academy is taken from contemporary newspaper accounts - particularly *Inverness Courier*, 19th February, 1841, 20th December, 1843, and 16th October, 1844.

[5] R.W. and Jean Munro, *op. cit.* p.124.

7. THE HERITORS IN THE 1850s AND 1860s

Andrew Maitland's clients in the 1850s and 1860s

In the 1850s and 1860s the heritors remained the primary source of commissions for architects in the Highlands, mainly for houses and farm buildings on their estates. By 1850, with the Tain Court House and the Easter Ross Union Poorhouse both completed, Andrew Maitland had established a local reputation and was obtaining a regular flow of work.

His greatest single source in the 1850s and early 1860s was almost certainly the Cromartie estates and the vast Sutherland estates, into whose superintendence the former had fallen. In aggregate, however, by far his most numerous commissions in these decades were from Easter Ross. He worked for a high proportion of the heritors on the peninsula, particularly for new or improved farm buildings and farm houses. This was the age of 'high farming' and the landlords and tenants of Easter Ross were among its leading practitioners.

One notable feature of these decades was the demand from men who had made their fortunes elsewhere. Thus Andrew Maitland's client list included Alexander Matheson, M.P., nowadays best remembered for opium trading. Some of these commissions reflected the needs of high farming. Others, particularly in the northern and western Highlands, related to sporting activities, and the future Duke of Westminster and John Fowler of Forth Bridge fame were among Andrew's clients. At the same time indigenous landlords such as Osgood Mackenzie, the creator of Inverewe Gardens, were seeking to boost their income from letting out shooting and fishing facilities.

The Hay-Mackenzies and the Sutherlands

As we saw earlier, on the marriage in 1849 of Anne Hay-Mackenzie of Cromartie to the Marquess of Stafford, the heir to the second Duke of Sutherland, the Cromartie estates had come under the superintendence of the Commissioner of the Sutherland estates.

Andrew continued to produce reports for the factor of the Cromartie estates, Andrew Scott. These show a painstaking attention to detail and a strong commitment to the client's interest, often to the detriment of contractors - features which must have commended him to heritors and their factors. In 1851 Andrew was responsible for additions to Castle Leod at Strathpeffer (later to become the seat of the Cromartie family), adapting designs by David Bryce. The additions to the predominantly seventeenth century tower house were a single-storey addition to the east and a low wing to the north (later substantially rebuilt).[1] Also for the Cromartie estates he designed in 1859 a forester's house at Fodderty and in 1864-65 servants' houses at Kinettas.[2]

In addition to this he began to deal with the factors of the Sutherland estates, who reported until 1855 to the formidable James Loch and thereafter to his son George Loch. He also obtained commissions directly from the Duke's tenants, whose improvements were commonly financed by the Duke, the tenant paying interest or an equivalent increase in rent.

The vast wealth of the Sutherlands, and the propensity of the second Duke to utilise it in building, clearly offered opportunities to an architect working for the wider Sutherland estates. The favoured architect was not, however, Andrew Maitland but William Fowler, a former pupil of David Bryce. Fowler was appointed Estate Surveyor in 1857 and designed numerous farmhouses, cottages, schools and shooting lodges. Many of these reflected the influence of the London country house architect George Devey, who developed a characteristic Sutherland style.[3] The pickings for Andrew were thus mainly inspections and reports, but there were nevertheless some interesting commissions for buildings.

In October 1856 Andrew wrote to Evander Maciver, factor at Scourie for the western and central part of the Sutherland estates, saying that he was glad that a successor to Robert Brown, Inspector of Buildings on the estates, had been appointed. 'As for my self', he wrote, 'I could not, nor would not have undertaken the whole duties had the situation been offered me. ... The new appointment will put an end to my labours in the Duke's Interest for some time at least, and perhaps for ever'.[4] The appointment referred to might have been that of William Fowler, and Andrew's comment probably reflected the fact that he was now obtaining a good flow of commissions which included the design of buildings, particularly in Ross-shire. But it was not, however, the end of Andrew's work on the ducal domain.

Andrew placed five advertisements for tenders for buildings on the Sutherland estates between 1856 and 1861.[5] The first, in late 1856, was for a cottage and farm offices at Cambusmore, near Loch Fleet. In 1858 Andrew obtained a commission at Ribigill, near Tongue in the north of Sutherland. Ribigill had been part of the estates of Lord Reay, chief of the clan Mackay, who had carried out massive clearances in the first two decades of the nineteenth century, including the clearance of three townships to create the farm of Ribigill. Burdened by debt, Lord Reay sold his estates to the Marquess of Stafford (later first Duke of Sutherland) in 1829. At Ribigill Andrew Maitland designed alterations and additions to the farm house, a new manager's house and a shepherd's house. The tenant of the 28,875 acre sheep farm, where 3,000 sheep were managed by eight shepherds and three turnip herds, was William Mitchell. In 2009 Mitchell's great great grandson David, a well known comedian, participated in a television programme 'Who Do You Think You Are?' He visited his ancestor's farm, and was relieved to find that his family had not themselves been involved in the clearance that had facilitated the creation of the sheep farm. All he could see, however, was sad ruins.

The name Sellar, one with huge resonance in Highland history, appears in relation to two further commissions in 1858. Andrew's client was Patrick Plenderleith Sellar, whose father Patrick Sellar had cleared much of Strathnaver in one of the most notorious of all the Sutherland clearances, which had led in 1816 to his trial for homicide. Following his acquittal Sellar senior had been dismissed from his role in the administration of the Sutherland estates and had concentrated on his other role as a sheep farmer. Much of Strathnaver became a huge sheep farm. After another clearance in 1819-20 he had added to it the farm of Langdale. The previous population of over 2,000 people in Strathnaver was replaced by 19 shepherds from the Borders. When Patrick Sellar died in 1851 his son had taken on the tenancy of Langdale, and it was for him that Andrew designed a new farm house, a manager's house, two shepherd's houses and a steading. Patrick Sellar had been a strong advocate of 'away wintering', the practice of moving lambs during their first year from the vast sheep farms of the far north to areas where there was better grazing and better weather. These included the 400 acre farm of Culmaily, south of Golspie, on which he also had a lease. Patrick Plenderleith Sellar acquired the tenancy of Culmaily also, and in 1858 Andrew Maitland was commissioned to design a new steading, later described as 'exceptionally good' and 'commodious, convenient and substantial'.[6] By the 1860s the younger Sellar was also leasing two farms near Tain, those of Hartfield (where he lived) and North Glastullich.

In February 1861 the Marquess of Stafford succeeded his father, becoming third Duke of Sutherland. Later that year Andrew, instructed by Joseph Peacock, the duke's factor at Golspie, designed farm buildings at Evelix, near Dornoch. His 'labours in the Duke's Interest' seem to have petered out after this, though it was not the end of the Maitland family's work for the Cromartie estates of the new duke's wife.

There were, moreover, three significant commissions linked to the ducal family still to come in Sutherland. These catered for the opposite ends of the social spectrum - a poorhouse and two shooting lodges.

The Sutherland Combination Poorhouse

Andrew's success in designing and controlling the costs of the Easter Ross Union Poorhouse and his work for the Sutherland estates were no doubt significant factors in securing for him a commission for the Sutherland Combination Poorhouse. As in Easter Ross, parochial boards had been set up in the 13 parishes of Sutherland in the wake of the 1845 Act. The difference was that the duke was the principal ratepayer in each parish. Thus the major part of the costs of 'outdoor relief (financial relief in the home), given to the sick and indigent poor - but not the able-bodied poor - fell on him. George Loch, who had succeeded his father as Commissioner of the Sutherland estates, was concerned at the rising costs of this - £5,211 in 1862, when there were 1,001 people on the poor roll. He could see that the option of giving 'indoor relief' would save money, and accordingly orchestrated a scheme for a poorhouse serving all the parishes. The adoption of this scheme was facilitated by the fact that most of the parochial boards were chaired by Sutherland estate factors.[7]

7.1 The Sutherland Combination Poorhouse.

Andrew Maitland was engaged to design the new poorhouse at Bonar Bridge, though he found himself under pressure on the costs from the Board of Supervision, who regarded his initial plans as too ornamental. Tenders were sought in 1863.[8] The poorhouse was completed in 1865 at a cost of about £6,000. Despite the cost pressures it has a certain elegance, with a dignified H-shaped two-storey building with a distinctive cupola and steep gables and a matching single-storey entrance block at the west side of the site. But contemporary accounts indicate that paupers were reluctant to leave their own homes and its capacity of 110 was substantially under-utilised. By May 1866 the only inmates were the governor and his wife (who was the matron), a porter and a servant girl. Six paupers who had entered at the opening had all left.[9] In 1927 the name was changed to the Swordale Institution. It became an NHS hospital in 1948, was renamed the Migdale Hospital in 1958, and survived as a hospital until 2011. The NHS sold it to a private buyer in 2013, but at the time of writing its future remains uncertain.

Shooting lodges in Sutherland

Around 1867 Andrew was engaged by two Englishmen for buildings for the use of a very different class of occupant.

One of these clients was Samuel Whitbread M.P. Notable features of Victorian society were the acceptance of wealthy brewers into the ranks of the gentry and the propensity of members of brewing families to marry into the aristocracy. Whitbread was the son-in-law of a peer and he married an earl's daughter. He leased deer forests from the Duke of Sutherland and commissioned Andrew Maitland to design Loch Assynt Lodge, a shooting lodge on the north shore of the loch, about six miles north east of Lochinver.[10] The lodge has survived into the twenty first century and is available to rent for stalking and trout fishing.

Between 1867 and 1872 Andrew substantially remodelled and added to a shooting lodge for an even grander client. Hugh Lupus Grosvenor, Earl Grosvenor, who succeeded as Marquess of Westminster in 1869 and became first Duke of Westminster in 1874, was the son of a daughter of the first Duke of Sutherland and he married a daughter of the second Duke of Sutherland. He inherited enormous revenues from the ground rents of Belgravia and Mayfair, and when he died was reputedly the wealthiest man in Britain. He built and extended a prodigious amount of buildings, including shooting lodges on deer forests he leased in north west Sutherland from his first cousin the Duke of Sutherland. One of these was Lochmore Lodge, originally built in 1851-52. When Grosvenor became the tenant he wanted it substantially remodelled and enlarged to receive large parties of distinguished guests.

Lochmore Lodge, Reay Forest.

7.2 Lochmore Lodge, remodelled for the first Duke of Westminster - a love nest for the second Duke and his mistress, Coco Chanel.

The result of Andrew's work was a seven-bay, multi-gabled building in pink granite, which the Historic Environment Scotland listing, citing the quality of the sanitary ware, the game larders and the kennels, describes as an important example of the nineteenth century shooting lodge.[11] The Grosvenors must have entertained on a grand scale, for Evander Maciver, who was their factor (as well as being one of the Duke of Sutherland's factors), recounted a meeting with the Prince of Wales at Lochmore and also two other royal visits.[12] In the 20th century Queen Elizabeth II, Prince Charles, Winston Churchill, and Neville Chamberlain are all reputed to have stayed at Lochmore Lodge. So too did the legendary fashion designer Coco Chanel, mistress for ten years of 'Bendor', the second Duke of Westminster, who was said to hide diamonds under the pillows of his mistresses.[13] During a stay in 1927 Churchill wrote to his wife about Chanel's skill at fishing: 'she fishes from morning till night, and in two months has killed 50 salmon'.

Even though in its prime the lodge was fit for royalty, in 2011 the sixth Duke of Westminster sought planning permission to demolish it, which prompted a listing to be initiated. It was put on the market in 2014 at a knock-down price of £450,000. It failed to attract any buyers, and in 2019 planning permission was obtained for consolidating it into its original frontage elements, removing rear extensions and developing an estate archive in a detached building.

'High farming' and a growing prosperity

Landlords and tenants in Easter Ross had watched in dismay during the 1840s as the repeal of the protectionist Corn Laws and the import of cheaper foreign wheat, oats and barley appeared more and more likely. The Easter Ross Farmers Society even petitioned Parliament against what they saw as impending disaster. In the event, however, even though free trade began in 1849, its effects were neither immediate nor total. Transportation was not yet available to facilitate imports of the cheaper North American grain, and world prices increased to nearer British levels. Agriculture, not least in Easter Ross, grew to a new prosperity during the third quarter of the nineteenth century.

The period from 1850 to 1914 is commonly described as the era of 'high farming' - a system of agriculture supported by substantial capital investment and dependent on scientific and technical advances.[14] Cereal crop yields were enhanced by the use of imported chemicals and manures, notably guano (the excreta of South American seagulls). Animal husbandry was bolstered by the use of animal feeds, particularly ones extracted as a by-product from vegetable oil crops such as linseed and rape. 'Improvement', as described in chapter 3, continued to be pursued - through land reclamation, systematic drainage, and concentration into larger farms - and was assisted by technical advances. Thus by 1850 cylindrical drainage tiles were taking over from the earlier horseshoe shaped tiles and their use was encouraged by government backed improvement loans. At the same time improvements in the efficiency of steam power increasingly led to threshing mills being powered by steam rather than water or horses. From Cadboll Mount in Easter Ross - built by an eighteenth century Macleod of Cadboll to look down on his neighbour, kinsman and rival Macleod of Geanies - 18 steam stalks could be observed in 1876, most of them erected in the last 25 years.[15] Steam power was also harnessed by John Fowler (not to be confused with the great railway engineer of the same name, who plays a part in the Maitland story) to power steam ploughs and traction engines. During the 1850s and 1860s many local farms diversified into dairying and fat-cattle production or into growing seed potatoes, which was to prove a useful buffer when grain and mutton prices slumped in the 1870s.

For the Maitland dynasty high farming had two important consequences. First, there was a substantial demand for farm buildings through the 1850s and 1860s and beyond. New farming practices necessitated new steadings and the improvement and extension of existing ones. At the same time tenants were moving up the social ladder and wanted new houses, usually further away from the steadings and the labourers' cottages, or at least improvements to their existing dwellings. Secondly, the general increase in the prosperity of the region had a significant effect on Tain as the commercial centre of Easter Ross. A consequence was a significant increase in the wealth of the local middle classes. As we will see in later chapters, they were gaining the clout and the spending power, collectively and sometimes individually, to become an additional source of work for Andrew and his family in the last three decades of the century.

As high farming prospered so did Andrew's order book, particularly on the Easter Ross peninsula.

High farming commissions in and around Easter Ross

The 1855 Valuation Rolls show that the entire area, excluding burgh properties, glebes and mortified land, of the 11 parishes on the peninsula east of Dingwall was made up of 41 estates, of which a dozen or so were small ones round Tain (which particularly reflected the break-up of the once proud possessions of Hugh Rose Ross). Of the 18 highest valued estates in the area Andrew Maitland obtained commissions during the 1850s and 1860s from at least 15.

Some of these were from clients for whom he had previously worked. But these decades also saw many changes of ownership - particularly where old established families, burdened by debt, sold out to new owners who had made their fortunes in cities further south, or overseas, and who sought the prestige of land ownership and sporting facilities in the Highlands. The propensity of these new owners to upgrade their estates frequently benefited Andrew.

The estate of Sir Charles Ross of Balnagown was one of those for which Andrew had done work in earlier years and provided at least four commissions during these decades. One of these was a major restoration in 1862 of the stables at Balnagown after they had been destroyed in a fire[16] - no run-of-the-mill stables but an impressive two-storey eleven-bay building with carriage houses in the outer bays and now a listed building[17]. The Tarlogie estate, belonging to Major St. Vincent Rose and later his son Hugh Law Rose, provided at least two more commissions, and the estate of Gillanders of Highfield at least one more, in addition to those described earlier.

The largest proprietor in Easter Ross was Macleod of Cadboll, whose seat was at Invergordon Castle. As early as 1846 Andrew had designed a farm house for the Cadboll estate at Lochslin Farm. In the years after Robert Bruce Æneas Macleod, fifth of Cadboll, succeeded his father in 1853, Andrew received at least half a dozen commissions. R.B.Æ.Macleod was the elder brother of Henry Dunning Macleod, who, as we saw in chapter 3, had lavished praise on Andrew for his contribution to the Easter Ross Union Poor House. He was a leading exponent of high farming and spent some £40,000 on improvements, particularly to steadings, over the next quarter of a century. His tenants also expended 'a very large amount which it would be difficult to calculate'. The 'able and energetic' factor with whom Andrew dealt was James Young, who himself was the tenant of two of the farms (Cadboll and Cadboll Mount) on which new buildings were constructed.[18]

Other commissions for new clients in the 1850s and 1860s included three for the Geanies estate and two for the Pitcalzean or Westfield estate, both estates having been purchased by members of the upwardly mobile Murray family of Tain, and ones for the Munro of Allan, Shandwick, and Pitcalnie estates in Easter Ross, the Invercharron estate in Kincardine and the Allangrange estate in the Black Isle.

Alexander Matheson, opium and whisky

Andrew also gained work as a result of the prodigious expenditure of Alexander (later Sir Alexander) Matheson M.P., the largest proprietor in Ross-shire. Matheson had acquired an immense fortune in the Far East, succeeding his uncle James (later Sir James) Matheson as *taipan* of the great trading house of Jardine Matheson & Co. The firm's most profitable commodity was opium, sold illegally to the Chinese. Alexander Matheson had himself been in the midst of the incidents which precipitated the First Opium War between Britain, which supported the opium trade, and the Chinese empire. He used the fortune gained from these activities to acquire 220,433 acres in Ross-shire by 1870, spending the prodigious sum of £1,460,000 on land purchases and improvements.[19] According to Joseph Mitchell, Matheson had 'an unhappy shyness and coldness of manner', but he was regarded as very public spirited.

7.3 Sir Alexander Matheson, painted by W.N. Owlife in 1879.

In 1854 Andrew Maitland was responsible for the rebuilding of farm offices at Lower Gledfield, a farm near Ardgay owned by Matheson. Matheson's most dramatic scheme, however, was at Ardross, 10 miles inland from Alness. George Rhind designed an enlargement of the existing house.[20] The surrounding Ardross estate was developed under the supervision of the factor, William Mackenzie, an engineer, and, in the words of Joseph Mitchell, 'a gentleman whose tact and intuitive perception for works of this nature amounted to genius'. 4,000 acres were reclaimed by draining and trenching, 50 miles of road made and 27 crofts and farms laid out. Matheson thus both created employment and increased his rent roll. Whether or not Andrew Maitland was involved in designing farm houses and buildings is unclear, but we do know that the resultant increase in population necessitated a school, that William Mackenzie was responsible for procuring one, and that in 1857-58 Andrew Maitland was commissioned to design it.[21] On one account it was attended by 140 pupils in 1877, and on another it had an average attendance in 1879 of 65 pupils. It survives to-day, a long single-storey and attic building with distinctive crow-stepped gables, as a private house.

Matheson also acquired a distillery. In 1854 Colonel G.W.H. Ross of Cromarty, the son of Hugh Rose Ross and his second wife Catherine Munro of Culcairn, put up for sale the adjacent estates of Dalmore and Culcairn, near Alness; he also offered separately a 19 year lease on the farm of Dalmore, with 330 acres of arable land and a distillery in 'complete order and repair'.[22] Colonel Ross's wish to sell assets would almost certainly have reflected the financial pressures which, as we saw earlier, had followed his father's death. But he appears to have regarded the farm with its distillery as an investment worth retaining. The distillery had been founded in 1839 by a tenant of the farm, Donald Sutherland, who had recently died. According to the advertisement for letting, during the last 14 years the tenant had 'successfully and profitably' operated a distillery constructed to produce about 40,000 gallons of spirits a year and capable of being 'largely extended'. In 1855 Alexander Matheson bought the the Culcairn and Dalmore estates and also, believing in ownership rather than taking 19 year leases, Dalmore farm with its distillery.[23]

Almost all accounts of the history of the Dalmore distillery credit Alexander Matheson with having founded it in 1839, and much praise is lavished on his vision and enterprise in doing so. Records of the period show, however, that he could not have founded the distillery: when Donald Sutherland began distilling at Dalmore in 1839 he was a tenant not of Matheson but of Hugh Rose Ross, and Matheson did not appear on the scene until 1855.

Matheson's purchase created an opportunity for Andrew Maitland. In 1860 Andrew was commissioned to alter and repair the distillery and dwelling house.[24] Whilst the work was in hand he would have heard gossip and read newspaper reports about a local *cause célèbre*, the 'Dalmore Bankruptcy'. Donald Sutherland's widow, claiming her *jus relictae*, had taken over the distillery operation, and her brother had become manager. Her father, Provost James Sutherland of Inverness (who had founded a distillery, Glen Albyn, in Inverness in 1846), and her brother had used cashflow from the Dalmore distillery to stock the farm of Parks of Inshes and had thus 'dragged the widow into bankruptcy'. Alexander Matheson had lent her £800 on the security of the utensils and machinery of the distillery, but 'the management of the distillery was a canker-worm which would eat up everything within its circle and could not be appeased with this poor flea-bite of £800'.[25] The Sutherlands gave up the tenancy of farm and distillery in 1860, handing over the crops and utensils at valuation to Matheson, and it was after this that Andrew Maitland's services had been engaged. By 1865 the distillery had been leased by Robert Pattison (not to be confused with the Robert Pattison, a whisky blender, whose fraud precipitated a major crisis in the whisky industry at the end of the nineteenth century). In 1867 Andrew Mackenzie, son of Matheson's factor William Mackenzie, became the tenant of Dalmore. Under the Mackenzie family's management the distillery was to thrive and to provide more work for the Maitlands in 1873 and, more significantly, in the major reconstruction of the 1890s.

Matheson's propensity to up-grade newly acquired farms may have been responsible for a commission in 1861 at Pollo, where Andrew Maitland appears to have added to farm buildings he designed in 1845, and for additions to three farm houses and offices in 1870.[26] Thereafter work for Matheson seems to have tailed off.

The Munros of Foulis and the Munros of Novar

In the early 1860s Andrew was commissioned by two Munro estates, both at the western end of the Easter Ross peninsula, that were to produce a flow of work in years to come.

The first was that of Munro of Foulis, an estate in the parish of Kiltearn We know of commissions at Ardullie (a new farmhouse and additions to the steading) in 1863, on four separate farms in 1864 and at Mains of Foulis (altering and repairing the steading and for the 'machinery of a water-power thrashing mill and forming a mill-dam and lead') in 1865. In September, 1869 Andrew (but apparently not Henrietta), along with many of the leading proprietors of Ross-shire and tenants of the Foulis estate, was a guest at 'one of the most sumptuous and elegant of dinners' held in a large granary at Mains of Foulis to celebrate the coming of age of the grandson of Sir Charles Munro, Chief of the Clan Munro. This invitation suggests that Andrew might have been known to the estate for more than just these two commissions earlier in the decade.[27]

The estate of the Munros of Novar, distant kinsmen of the Munros of Foulis, provided at least half a dozen commissions during this period. Novar, mainly in the parish of Alness, at this time was owned by Hugh Munro, whose uncle, General Sir Hector Munro, had acquired a large fortune in India. In 1820 Hugh, who is castigated as the 'young and rakish young laird' in John Prebble's *The Highland Clearances,* had cleared Culrain in the Kyle of Sutherland in order to put it under sheep. Hugh lived, according to Joseph Mitchell, a 'sensuous life'. Himself an artist, and friend, travelling companion and executor of the great artist J.M.W. Turner, he collected some 2,500 contemporary and old masters, and on some days he opened his private gallery in London to the public. What appears to be the first of many Maitland commissions for the Novar estate, in 1853, was the conversion into dwelling houses of the Secession Chapel in Evanton, a prominent building with a tower in the centre of the front, which closes the end of the main street. This had been built in about 1824 for a group which had broken away from the Church of Scotland, but the congregation had melted away, perhaps in the wake of the more dramatic Disruption of 1843.[28]

In 1855 Andrew received the first of at least three Novar estate commissions for which Peter Brown of Linkwood acted for the estate - a house for the tenant at Culcairn. Brown was factor not only for the Novar estate, which included land at Findhorn, but also for the estate of the Earl of Seafield. He was an eminent agriculturalist, with an estate of his own at Linkwood, near Elgin, where in 1821 he established the Linkwood Distillery - happily still going strong. He was, according to Joseph Mitchell, 'so upright and honest that in any dispute throughout the north of Scotland both parties generally referred to him and were contented with his decisions'.[29] His brother, who lived with him in the last years of his life, was General Sir George Brown, a hero of the Peninsular War and commander of the Light Division in the Crimean War. Peter Brown was also involved with two commissions in 1863, one for a farm house at Aultdearg and the other for 'additions and alterations to the lodge in the deer forest of Gildermorie'. (As we will see, Gildermorie - now known as Kildermorie - Lodge was to undergo further Maitland additions in 1891, following its sale to the furniture manufacturer and retailer Walter Shoolbred.) By 1865, when Andrew was engaged to design a dwelling house and steading on the combined farms of Upper Park and Drummore, James Forbes had replaced Peter Brown as the Novar factor.[30]

In the 1860s Andrew Maitland was engaged by two men who left footprints on the sands of time to work on new buildings on their recently acquired estates in Wester Ross - Sir John Fowler, remembered for the creation of the iconic Forth Rail Bridge, and Osgood Mackenzie, celebrated for establishing the world-famous gardens at Inverewe.

Sir John Fowler, the railway engineer, and his lost mansion

The great engineers of the nineteenth century enjoyed an extraordinary degree of celebrity. John (later Sir John) Fowler, who bought the Braemore estate near Ullapool in 1865 and the adjoining Inverbroom estate in 1867 was one of the most famous. He had built his reputation - and earned remuneration which others envied - particularly on railway engineering. His most notable achievement had been the creation of the first underground railway, the Metropolitan Railway, for which he also designed engines. He was soon to build other railways which to-day form the bulk of the London Underground Circle Line. His greatest work was two decades later - the Forth Rail Bridge, for which he was engineer-in-chief, the largest civil engineering structure of the nineteenth century. The bridge was sometimes called the eighth wonder of the world, and even to-day travelling over it is awe-inspiring.

In buying his estates Fowler, as he later explained to the Napier Commission, was motivated both by health considerations, wanting to spend two months a year in the Highlands, and by 'a great weakness for improving properties'.[31] He was a keen shot, and no doubt regarded shooting as good for his health. He acquired his estates for £130,000 from Duncan Davidson of Tulloch, who had earned the nickname 'The Stag' by sireing 18 children and at least 30 illegitimate children, and had blown an ancestral fortune acquired in the eighteenth century West Indies. The sale proceeds enabled Davidson to emerge from a chateau in the Forest of Ardennes, in which he had taken refuge from his creditors, and to return to Tulloch Castle, in Dingwall.[32] Fowler actively set about improving his newly acquired 43,000 acres. He planted nine million trees, bridged the Corrieshalloch Gorge, improved the arable land and farm buildings and earned a reputation as a good landlord.

Fowler also built a grand house at which he was to entertain the good and the great of Victorian Britain and to give them opportunities for shooting and fishing. In March 1866 an advertisement appeared in the *Aberdeen Journal*: 'TENDERS are Wanted for the various Works to be done in the Erection and Completion of a NEW MANSION at BRAEMORE, Lochbroom, in the County of Ross. Plans and Specifications may be seen at the Office of the Architect, JOHN JOHNSON, Esq. of 9, John Street, Adelphi, London; or of Mr MAITLAND, Architect, Tain, who will give any explanation required by parties tendering'.[33]

In July, 1867 Fowler wrote to his father, reporting that 'The house is a serious undertaking, both as regards

7.4 Sir John Fowler, by Millais.

the carrying out of such a work in such a wild and uninhabited part of the country and as regards its cost. ... It is so far advanced that no doubt we shall be able to cover it in by the end of October and have it ready for occupation next season. … The people in the country have been much astonished by my building the house 700 feet above the sea, instead of following the old Scotch practice of burying it in the lowest place I could find'. The bulk of the stone, he explained was gneiss, blue in colour and wonderfully durable, obtained from a quarry about a quarter of a mile from the house, but 'it cannot be worked into anything requiring an acies or edge and therefore we have window-heads, sills, plinths, etc. brought from Glasgow ... to the head of Loch Broom and then carted six miles to the house.'[34] The house, suffering from dry-rot, was demolished in the early 1960s, but surviving photographs show an imposing building with a *porte-cochère* which sat beneath crow-steps flanked by two pinnacles and led to a grand entrance hall. Its visitors' book contained the names of many of the most eminent Victorians, drawings by Sir Edwin Landseer and a series of sketches by Sir John Millais.

What was Andrew's role in the building of the house? The advertisement makes it clear that 'Mr Maitland' was regarded, both socially and professionally, as ranking behind 'John Johnston, Esq'. Johnson was part of an élite group of civil engineers, architects and decorative artists in Victorian London, and is best remembered for his work on Alexandra Palace. The support of an architect from Tain, who had knowledge of Scottish sporting estates and of local stone, and was more easily able to travel to the site, might therefore have been considered useful. Andrew may therefore have had some input into the design and a role in the supervision of the building.

As well as working on the 'new mansion' Andrew is thought to have obtained other commissions on the Braemore estate. One, in 1868, was for a new steading and repairs to farm buildings at Achindrean. Later that year, following a change in tenancy, he designed additions to farmhouses on the adjoining estate of Inverlael.[35]

Braemore House, near Ullapool

7.5 Braemore House

Osgood Mackenzie, his garden at Inverewe and another lost mansion

Osgood Hanbury Mackenzie of Inverewe achieved fame during his lifetime - and wider fame posthumously - for the creation of the world-renowned garden at Inverewe in Wester Ross. His mother, the Dowager Lady Mackenzie, the widowed second wife of Sir Francis Mackenzie of Gairloch, bought the estates of Kernsary and Inverewe for him just as he was coming of age in two transactions in 1862 and 1863. 'After taking about two years to settle where we should build our home', he wrote in his autobiographical *A Hundred Years in the Highlands*, 'we finally settled on the neck of a barren peninsula as the site of the house. The peninsula was a high, rocky bluff, jutting out into the sea'. His own obsession, second only to what a more censorious age might regard as the wholesale massacre of wildlife on an industrial scale, was gardening: 'I started the work in the early spring of 1864 … perfectly ignorant of everything connected with forestry and gardening … but I had all my life longed to begin gardening and planting'. Fortunately for the young Osgood 'my mother undertook the whole trouble of house-building'.[36]

The result was a building fairly typical of the Highland shooting lodges of the period, but, as contemporary images show, distinguished by a three-storey conical tower. The architect and heritage consultant Andrew Wright makes a compelling case for Andrew Maitland having designed it. He notes similarities in the details of the designs to those of Loch Assynt Lodge (referred to earlier in this chapter), which Andrew Maitland is known to have designed. He also quotes from a letter written in February 1869 by William Fraser of the Caledonian Bank in Inverness to the factor

7.6 Osgood Mackenzie as a young man.

of the Cromartie estates: 'Maitland would like the Freestone for this job taken from the same quarry in Glasgow as those in Mr Fowler's house Loch Broom'. He surmises that this indicates Andrew Maitland's involvement in both projects.[37] Further pointers to this involvement are perhaps to be found in the fact that, as we shall see, Andrew was engaged in the 1870s by Osgood's half-brother Sir Kenneth Mackenzie to design the Gairloch and Loch Maree Hotels and to alter the Kinlochewe Inn on the Gairloch estate, and also that in later decades Osgood himself was to engage the Maitland firm on a number of occasions.

Osgood Mackenzie was, however, to spend little time in Inverewe House. Pauline Butler has written a fascinating account of his multi-faceted life, an account which fills in many gaps in Osgood's autobiography[38] - including Osgood's failure to mention that he had been married and had been involved in well-publicised matrimonial disputes. Osgood was perpetually short of money. He found it more economical to rent out Inverewe House to shooting tenants and to stay elsewhere - particularly with his mother in a house, designed by Matthews & Lawrie, he built on his estate at Tournaig. Thus in most years from 1872-73 up to the Great War Inverewe House was let. Tenants included prominent businessmen such as members of the Coats and Thomas Cook dynasties, and guests appear to have included H.H. Asquith, Winston Churchill, Thomas Lipton and David Lloyd George.

In 1877 Osgood, later to be accused of marrying for money, married Minna, daughter of a wealthy Liverpool businessman, Sir Thomas Edwards Moss. The relationship of Osgood and Minna was acrimonious from the start. Arguments intensified after the birth of a daughter, Mairi, in 1879 and they were soon living separate lives. From 1881 to about 1891 Minna, when in Gairloch, lived at Pool House, across the bay from and within sight of Inverewe House. When Osgood and Minna passed they cut each other dead. Sir Thomas leased Pool House and shootings at Inveran, Isle Ewe and Mellon Charles from Sir Kenneth Mackenzie. It is very likely that it was Sir Thomas who paid for 'additions and alterations' to Pool House in 1882 and also for 'large additions and alterations' in 1889. The architects in both cases were A. Maitland & Sons.[39] Meanwhile Osgood, aided and abetted by his mother, took charge of their daughter Mairi, and lived mainly at Tournaig. Minna fought a long battle, with limited success, for access rights. She also put up a successful defence in three widely reported divorce actions which Osgood brought, the last in the House of Lords.

As we shall see, Inverewe House was seriously damaged by fire in 1914 - but not before the Maitlands had been further involved with Osgood Mackenzie and his family.

References and Note

[1]   Highland HER MHG6283.

[2]   National Records of Scotland GD/305/2/320 and GD/305/2/378.

[3]   See Elizabeth Beaton, *Sutherland,* particularly pp.6-7.

[4]   Sutherland Estate papers, NLS Dep. 313/1423. Evander Maciver of Scourie was the author of "*Memoirs of a Highland Gentleman, Being the Reminiscences of Evander Maciver of Scourie*", T. and A. Constable, 1905 - reminiscences which suffer from over-emphasis on his own genteel origins and on his hobnobbing with dukes.

[5]   *Inverness Courier*, 4th December, 1856, 5th August, 1858, 14th October, 1858, 11th November, 1858, and 31st October, 1861.

[6]   *Transactions of the Highland and Agricultural Society of Scotland*, 4th Series Vol. XII, 1880, On the Agriculture of the County of Sutherland.

[7]   The above account relies particularly on Annie Tindley, *The Sutherland Estate 1850-1920: Aristocratic Decline, Estate Management and Land Reform*, Edinburgh University Press, 2010, pp.23-26, and www.workhouses.org.uk/Sutherland.

[8]   *Inverness Courier*, 2nd July, 1863.

[9]   *Inverness Courier*, 17th May, 1866.

[10] See SCRAN 000-000-523-585-C.

[11] Historic Environment Scotland listing LB51897.

[12] Maciver, *op. cit.*, pp.174 and 224.

[13] Lochmore Lodge was clearly not sufficient for the couple. Bendor bought the Rosehall estate in East Sutherland in 1926, with a classical mansion house which Elizabeth Beaton notes as being in the style of William Robertson, Andrew Maitland's one time employer. Coco redecorated and furnished Rosehall House.

[14] For an excellent account of high farming and its consequences for building see Miles Glendinning and Susanna Wade Martins, *Buildings of the Land, Scotland's Farms, 1750-2000*, Royal Commission on the Ancient and Historical Monuments of Scotland, 2008, chapter 3.

[15] *Transactions of the Highland and Agricultural Society of Scotland*, 4th series vol. IX, 1877 - J. Macdonald, On the Agriculture of the Counties of Ross and Cromarty.

[16] *Inverness Advertiser*, 17th January, 1862.

[17] Historic Environment Scotland LB7867, Highland HER MHG16521.

[18] *Transactions of the Highland and Agricultural Society of Scotland*, 4th series vol. IX, 1877 - J. Macdonald, On the Agriculture of the Counties of Ross and Cromarty.

[19] *Dictionary of National Biography*, entry for Matheson, Sir Alexander, first baronet.

[20] Later incorporated into a spectacular Scottish Baronial castle designed by Alexander Ross.

[21] *Inverness Courier,* 18th February, 1858.

[22] *Inverness Courier*, 23rd March and 13th April, 1854 respectively.

[23] *Inverness Courier,* 10th January, 1856. The same paper of 4th June, 1857 reported a dinner given for Alexander Matheson to celebrate his recent acquisition - a dinner at which Matheson was not present.

[24] *Inverness Courier*, 20th September, 1860.

[25] *Inverness Courier,* various articles, particularly 10th January, 1861; and *John O'Groat Journal*, 31st January, 1861.

[26] *Inverness Courier*, 3rd October, 1861 and 7th April, 1870 .

[27] *Inverness Courier,* 2nd April, 1863, 23rd March, 1865 and 16th September, 1869.

[28] *Inverness Courier,* 12th May, 1853.

[29] Joseph Mitchell *Reminiscences of My Life in the Highlands*, vol. one (1883), re-printed David & Charles, 1971, p.142.

[30] *Inverness Courier*, 29th March, 1855, 23rd July, 1863, 17th December, 1863, and 9th March 1865.

[31] Examination of John Fowler, C.E., Proprietor of Braemore, by the Napier Commission, Ullapool, 30th July, 1883. The commission had been appointed by W.E. Gladstone's government to enquire into the condition of crofters in the Highlands and Islands.

[32] Joseph Mitchell, *op. cit.*, p.262. (Despite this sale the finances of the Davidsons of Tulloch remained in a parlous state in the years leading up to the restoration of the castle by the Maitlands in 1890-91 - see chapter 18.)

[33] *Aberdeen Journal*, 21st March, 1866 and *Inverness Courier,* 8th March, 1866.

[34] Thomas Mackay, *The Life of Sir John Fowler, Engineer*, John Murray, 1900, p.322.

[35] *Inverness Courier*, 9th April and 16th July, 1868 respectively.

[36] Osgood Hanbury Mackenzie of Inverewe, *A Hundred Years in the Highlands*, Edward Arnold and Co., 1921 (reprinted Birlinn Ltd, 1995), pp.195-96.

[37] Andrew P. K. Wright, *Inverewe House Conservation Plan*, produced for the National Trust for Scotland, March, 2008. The author is grateful to Pauline Butler for bringing this to his attention, and to Andrew Wright for allowing him to quote from it. The detailed similarities he cites include the relationship of the window dormers to the wallheads, the manner in which the ground floor windows are larger than those at the first floor, the narrow apertures at the head of each gable, and the projecting ground floor bay windows.

[38] Pauline Butler, *Eighty Years in the Highlands - The Life and Times of Osgood H. Mackenzie of Inverewe, 1842-1922*, Librario Publishing Ltd, 2010.

[39] *Inverness Courier*, 26th January, 1882 and 22nd January, 1889.

8. CHURCH RIVALS AND CIVIC NEEDS,
1850s AND 1860s

A broadening client base

During the 1850s and 1860s Andrew Maitland found work that made him less critically dependant on the estates of landed proprietors.

By the early 1850s the Free Church had substantially completed its task of creating a new religious infrastructure for Scotland. But there was still some unfinished business, not least in Tain. The heritors, moreover, retained responsibility for the provision and upkeep of the churches of the established Church of Scotland, and for manses and schools. There was an ongoing need for repair and sometimes for new buildings. Also during these decades the civic authorities in Tain began their long reliance on the Maitland family, a reliance which was to lead in the final three decades of the century to some of the finest buildings in Tain. And at the same time policing became high on the political agenda and police stations were needed over a wide area.

Work for the Free Church …

At the start of the decade after that in which the Disruption took place the Free Church congregation of Tain had a recently built church, with whose building Andrew Maitland had, as we saw, been involved - but it had neither a manse nor a school.

8.1 Tain Free Church manse, built for the Rev. C.C. Mackintosh in 1852 and now a guest house.

In the year to March 1852, however, the Tain Free Church congregation paid £20 to Andrew Maitland for plans and specifications for a new manse for the Rev. Dr Charles Calder Mackintosh - of which Andrew appears to have paid back £4 as a 'subscription'. They then paid £331-10s-2d for the site for the new manse and glebe (between the road south past Knockbreck and the road, fringed by the 'Woody Braes', to Portmahomack), £847-2s-10d to Donald Munro for building the manse in full and £90-16s-9d for dykes, paling, trees, etc. Andrew received another £20 for inspection.[1]

The total cost of over £1,300 seems surprisingly high, but ministers of the Free Church were not usually expected to stint themselves, and Mackintosh was provided with a spacious and elegant building. His failing health soon, however, 'necessitated removal to the lighter charge of Dunoon'. He was succeeded in 1858, after a four year gap, by the Rev. Thomas Grant, who was minister for the next 43 years and whom Andrew knew well for the rest of his life. House hunting early in the present century, the present author and his late wife considered the possibility of buying the former manse and living in the style of a mid nineteenth century Free Church minister - albeit without servants. But, as so often happens with substantial Victorian houses, the vendors planned to build another house in the garden. Today it is a well-regarded guest house.

The Free Church scholars in Tain, and their teacher, had to wait much longer than their minister. The Deacons' Court found difficulties with financing a new school, even though what the congregation raised could be matched from central funds. In June 1859 the popular young teacher, Peter Bain, read in the *John O'Groat Journal* that a new Free Church school in Tain had been opened, with Mr Peter Bain as teacher. 'As I believe myself to be the only teacher in Tain represented by that name', he wrote to the editor, 'I could not help feeling a little surprised to find myself still labouring in the old building. ... I would like to know where [the new school] is, as it would be desirable to get into it as quickly as possible, now that the warm weather renders us rather uncomfortable where we are.' The editor replied that the reference was meant to be to another Tain, in the parish of Olrig in Caithness.

In 1860, however, plans for a new school, drawn up by Andrew Maitland, were approved. In May 1861, 18 years after the Disruption, it was reported that a 'very handsome and commodious school-house has been erected in the open field to the south of the Free Church. ... The school, now so efficiently taught by Mr Peter Bain, assisted by two Government pupil-teachers, is generally attended by 130 to 140 boys and girls. ... [It had] occupied a dilapidated building for the last 18 years'. The outlay, financed by private subscriptions, was about £320. The new building was used as the Free Church School until, in the wake of the educational reforms of the 1870s, it became a church hall in 1878. Relations with the established church school seem to have been good, as an Easter Ross Schoolmasters' Association was formed in June 1861, with agreement on a uniform scale of school fees and on the 'Saturday School Question'. In 1895 substantial alterations were made to the building, including a large addition at right angles to the west end to create the L-shaped building that is used today as the Parish Church Hall.[2]

But not all his work for the Free Church during the 1850s and 1860s was in Tain. In 1852 the Free Church congregation of Kincardine advertised for the mason and carpentry work of a new schoolroom and teacher's residence to be erected in Lower Gledfield, near Ardgay. A sign of the times was that the plans and specifications lay not with a heritor or his factor but with Mr Ross, post-master at Bonar Bridge - though it was reported that Sir Charles Ross of Balnagown, the main heritor in the parish, had given the site and that 'the factor on the estate, Mr Williamson, has generously encouraged the object by a donation of £10. .... The plans and specifications are by Mr Maitland, architect, Tain and are executed with his usual taste and accuracy'.[3]

Another Free Church commission in 1865-66 took Andrew back to Resolis, the parish in which he and Henrietta had lived before they moved to Tain. The Rev. Donald Sage, the Minister at the time of their marriage, was still in post. Though infirm and seeking an assistant, he was conducting services in a church at Jemimaville, hurriedly built at the Disruption and considered inconvenient for much of the parish. Mr Shaw-Mackenzie of Newhall donated 12 acres for a new church, manse and glebe. A replacement church was built to plans drawn up by two architects - Andrew Maitland and an Inverness based architect, William Munro, about whom little is known.[4] The church, simple in design, was rectangular, with lattice-glazed windows, a minister's porch at the south and a ball-finialled birdcaged bellcote at the west. The church is still in use and stands, in open country, close to a manse designed by A. Maitland & Sons and built in 1880. As we will see in chapter 17, this replacement of a Disruption church was the forerunner for the building of numerous others, nearly always on a grander scale, in the following decades.

... and work for the established rivals

The Disruption had had a significant effect on the provision of education in the traditional established church pattern. In Tain the heritors owned jointly with the provost, magistrates and council what was variously called the grammar school, the parish school or, more formally, the Burgh and Parochial School.[5] The burgh made an annual payment towards it. After the Disruption the Free Church had become the main provider of education for those whose parents could not afford the fees of Tain Royal Academy. The grammar schoolhouse was thus sold in 1847 in the expectation that the remaining children would be educated at the Academy and the funds united. However the Commissioners of Supply (a body of the principal heritors) appointed a new schoolmaster, despite the protests of the council, whose members were overwhelmingly adherents of the Free Church. On his application a new grammar school and schoolmaster's house, for which Andrew Maitland sought tenders in April 1851,[6] was erected at the joint expense of the council and the landward heritors. The building (which appears to be the school shown at the top of Gower Street in the 25 inch to the mile Ordnance Survey map surveyed in 1871) was sold when the new Maitland-designed Tain Public School was opened in 1878 in the wake of the Education Act of 1872.

Other work by Andrew Maitland included the Ardross School mentioned in chapter 7, a new manse at Creich in 1855, and a new school at Logie Easter and rebuilding a school at Alness, both in 1863.[7] The list of additions, alterations and repairs for which Andrew was responsible was extensive, including (usually more than once) buildings in the parishes of Rosskeen, Logie Easter, Lochbroom, Tarbat, Fearn, Kilmuir Easter, Kincardine and Nigg. Elizabeth Beaton describes Andrew's 1864 alterations to the long, low, venerable and predominantly eighteenth century Nigg Parish Church as 'sympathetic to the building'.[8] Reports by Andrew in 1855 and 1856 to the heritors on the ecclesiastical buildings of Lochbroom survive and reveal an impressive attention to detail.[9]

As we saw earlier, the Collegiate Church in Tain had been abandoned as the parish church in 1815 in favour of the castellated Gothic building now used as the Duthac Centre. It was in a ruinous state. The heritors remained responsible and met in 1859 to agree work to be done and to draw up a subscription list. A committee headed by Provost John McLeod was formed 'to repair, as far possible, the injuries inflicted on this ancient edifice by time and neglect'. They sought to raise the £320 estimated by a competent architect to be required, including work on the windows and buttresses. The 'competent architect' was Andrew Maitland, who was paid £2-17s-0d for his services. The money seems to have run out in the 1860s, and it was not until the 1870s that more substantial work was done.[10]

Tain - civic needs

If there was one subject to which members of the Tain Burgh Council returned more often than any other in the mid nineteenth century it was that of the provision of a supply of water.[11] Most householders had wells, but the water was brackish. There were four springs in the old town, a fountain in the Newtown of Tain and a large well at the foot of Castle Brae.[12] But people remembered a cholera outbreak in 1832 and the report of James Cameron quoted in chapter 4 drew attention to the need for a new and fresh source.

A shortage of funds precluded action in the early 1840s, but in March 1844 the council demanded somewhat peremptorily that the great Aberdeen architect Archibald Simpson should 'come here by the *Duke of Richmond* Steamer on as early a day as he possibly can' to draw up a specification and an estimate for a water supply. Simpson was at this time extremely busy, not least with his Triple Churches in Aberdeen, 'frequently referred to as the "Cathedral of the Disruption" and one of his greatest and most ingenious efforts'.[13] He must have declined the work in Tain, since the council then consulted another architect with Aberdeen connections, William Leslie. Leslie had been involved with the reconstruction of Dornoch Cathedral and was currently assisting with the reconstruction of Dunrobin Castle. It appears to have been an opinion given by Leslie that led to Andrew Maitland being asked in October 1850 to draw up plans to convey water from the *Fuaranbuie*, or yellow stream, near Hartfield on the Aldie estate 'for the amount of money at the disposal of the Council'.

In 1851, however, Dr James Vass and other councillors became enthusiastic about using water from the Tarlogie Springs, which was, they thought, 'not appropriated to any useful purpose' - a view from which modern connoisseurs of malt whisky would dissent, for the springs provided water for the Glenmorangie Distillery, which had been opened in 1849. Andrew Maitland was instructed to cost and plan catchment tanks and a pipeline for a new water system for the burgh. Fortunately for future generations of whisky drinkers, May, June and July 1851 were exceptionally dry months, and Andrew reported that the springs were 'much diminished and not to be calculated on for a permanent supply'. Andrew could thus be said to have saved a distillery which was to play a major part in the lives of his sons Andrew and James, and also to have ensured that it continued to use the hard and mineral-rich water of the Tarlogie Springs, which is believed to contribute, along with the unusual stills, to the unique taste of Glenmorangie.[14] The plans for the Tarlogie Springs were then abandoned, and a contract for supply from the *Fuaranbuie* 'in terms of Mr Maitland's specifications for the sum of £113' was signed. The work was completed in December 1851.

But by 1855 'the footing on which permission had been given by Mr Ross of Aldie was precarious and the expence [*sic*] of carrying water into the Town not warrantable'. Hence in 1861 Andrew Maitland was consulted 'on the mode in which the supply of water can best be arranged'. It was, however not Andrew but James Leslie (an Edinburgh engineer) and Charles Gordon (a surveyor in Tain), who produced plans in 1865 for a much more ambitious scheme on the lands of Scotsburn Glen, Lamington and Culpleasant, with a reservoir beside St David's Well and a pipeline of 3 miles, 6 furlongs and 88 yards to Tain.[15] Another alternative, diverting water from the Lairgs of Tain, was considered, but plans by William Paterson C.E. of Inverness for the St David's Well scheme were finally agreed. Paterson assisted Kenneth Murray of Geanies at a formal opening at St David's Well, attended by 1,400 people, in September 1871. Tain thus got 'a most copious supply of excellent spring water'.

Another matter with which the Council concerned itself was the improvement of Market Street, where the Common Good Fund derived an income from stalls leased out annually by the council and used mainly for selling meat and fish. Andrew Maitland drew up plans in 1860 for lowering and widening the street and a new railed market place wall. 'Large as the sum may be' [£94-15s-0d in the event], a committee reported, 'the Council will see the propriety of carrying out the proposed improvements which will benefit the inhabitants and is widely more called for than any other, being more frequented and consequently having more traffic than any other street in the Town'.

Police stations

The maintenance of law and order came on to the agenda of central government in the middle of the century, reflecting particularly the growth of urbanisation. This provided work for Andrew over a wide area. Policing in burghs was sparse - Tain only spent £14-14s-0d on 'police expenses' in 1846-47. In the countryside it was rudimentary. In 1852 the heritors of Easter Ross commissioned Andrew to design a police lock-up house in Invergordon with rooms for a police officer.[16] A major advance was the Police (Scotland) Act of 1857, which required the Commissioners of Supply in each county to form a committee to administer a police force, permitted burgh magistrates and councils to consolidate the burgh police with the county force, and provided for an Inspector of Constabulary to report on the efficiency of local forces. The Inspector reported in 1862 that there were only 20 constables in the whole of Ross-shire, which then included the 'Island of Lews' (Lewis). Lock-ups and stations for the constables to reside in were, he noted, 'very much called for' in several burghs, including Tain, Dingwall, Fortrose and Stornoway. Sutherland was similarly deficient.

Andrew gained several commissions as a result. In Dornoch he was responsible for a police station built in the Square in 1861 and now a private residence.[17] Its style, with prominent crowsteps, appears to echo, so far as the budget of some £400 would allow, those of the neighbouring Jail and Sheriff Court, both designed by Thomas Brown in the 1840s. An advertisement for sale (at £325,000) in 2018 noted that it retains many original features, including a pitch pine staircase, window shutters, deep skirtings, ornate cornicing and wood panelling. In Dingwall in 1864 Andrew designed a police station and lock-up house joined to the Sheriff Court (another Thomas Brown building)[18], and later used as an assessor's office. This was followed in 1865 by another police station in Fortrose.[19]

8.2 The former Dornoch Police Station.

In Tain a police station was erected to Andrew's designs, close to the prison in the Scotsburn Road, in 1864-65. His plans show a building, one room deep to the right of the front door, the room being a kitchen which must have been the family's main living room. They show it two rooms deep to the left - an office and behind it two cells, each with a window so small that the occupants would have been unable to escape. Upstairs were three bedrooms, one above the cells.[20] The Inspector of Police was thus very much living on the job. His family's sleep would have been disturbed if anyone in the cells below was too unruly - and a policeman's lot would not have been a happy one. This building was acquired in 1898 by Provost Fowler and used to accommodate his farm grieve, and is to-day a private residence, Mansfield Cottage.

In Stornoway a further police station and lock-up house was built in 1867 to designs by Andrew Maitland.[21] The police office was soon to be occupied by Donald Cameron, Superintendent of Police, his wife and nine children, and a general servant, with separate quarters being occupied by three police constables. Cameron, widely respected, exercised a moderating influence in the so-called 'Bernera Riots' of 1874, when crofters of Bernera, who had been evicted from traditional grazing lands wanted by Sir James Matheson for sporting purposes, marched on Stornoway, in protest at one of their number being apprehended and conveyed to the Maitland-designed lock-up.

References and Notes

[1] Minutes of Tain Free Church Deacons' Court, Highland Archive Centre CH 3/784/2.

[2] The Tain & District Museum has copies of Andrew Maitland's plans of 1860 and of those (unsigned but surely by the Maitland partnership) of 1895.

[3] *Inverness Courier,* 22nd July and 5th August, 1852. Historic Environment Scotland LB7178. The Maitland partnership was responsible for alterations and additions to the schoolteacher's house in 1893, *Inverness Courier,* 25th April, 1893.

[4] *Elgin Courier*, 26th January, 1866; Highland Council HER MHG16423; Historic Environment Scotland LB14946.

[5] The information in this paragraph has been provided by Margaret Urquhart and is based on an Opinion of Counsel in 1891 relating to a dispute between the Tain Burgh Council and the Board of Governors relating to an annual payment of £25.

[6] *Inverness Courier*, 17th April, 1851.

[7] *John o' Groat Journal*, 21st December, 1855, *Inverness Courier* 12th February and 23rd July, 1863.

[8] Beaton, *Ross & Cromarty*, pp. 68-69.

[9] National Records of Scotland GD305/2/520.

[10] Harry Gordon Slade, *The Collegiate Church of St Duthac of Tain and The Abbey of Fearn*, Tain & District Museum Trust, 2000; *Inverness Courier*, 1st March, 1860.

[11] The main source of information on Andrew's involvement in the Tain affairs covered in this section is the Burgh Council Minutes, Highland Archive Centre B70/6/4-5 (to 1862) and BTN 1/1/1 (from 1862).

[12] R.W. and Jean Munro, *Tain through the Centuries*, Tain Town Council, 1966, p.115.

[13] David Miller, *Archibald Simpson - His life and times*, Librario Publishing Ltd, 2006, p.266.

[14] It was not until 1989, however, that Glenmorangie actually bought the springs and 650 acres of surrounding land.

[15] NRS RHP282274.

[16] *Inverness Courier*, 8th October, 1852.

[17] *Inverness Courier*, 1st August, 1861, LB24639.

[18] *Inverness Courier*, 7th April, 1864 and Highland HER MHG16510.

[19] *Inverness Courier*, 5th October, 1865.

[20] *Inverness Courier*, 1st September, 1864. Plans Highland Archive Centre, CRC 9/3/3/5/5. Surprisingly a Chartulary recording Burgh Feus shows that it was not until 1875 that David Ross Vass, brother of (the soon to be Provost) James Vass conveyed the land for this use.

[21] *Inverness Courier*, 21st March, 1867.

PART II

THE GOLDEN YEARS -
THE MAITLANDS FROM 1870 TO 1898

9. THE TRIUMVIRATE

The second generation

The 1861 census shows Andrew and Henrietta living in Esther Place with the seven surviving of their eleven children. Three of these children left Tain permanently - Alexander (who emigrated to Sydney, where he married, became a storekeeper and was said to be 'never weary of doing a good turn for a fellow Scot', and died without issue in 1896), Henry and William. By the 1870s there were thus only four in Tain - James and Andrew Junior, and the younger daughters, Christina and Henrietta Margaret, both of whom continued to live with their parents.

Only James and Andrew Junior were to follow their father as architects. In doing so they provided not simply additional pairs of hands but a dynamism which was to take the Maitland business through its golden years of the 1870s, 1880s and 1890s. Through most of this period the Maitlands were a triumvirate.

James Maitland

After leaving Tain Royal Academy, where he had been dux, James Maitland was clearly interested in a career in architecture, and he became apprenticed to his father in the 1860s.

Architecture was by this stage a more structured profession than it had been in Andrew's early days. As a result of economic and social change the client base was expanding beyond its traditional limited, and mainly aristocratic, range. Architects now sought a higher social status and wanted recognition as professionals in the same way as advocates, solicitors, surgeons and physicians. They were now tending to organise themselves into professional partnerships rather than family operations. Efforts were made to set up a unified Scottish professional body of architects, but, particularly owing to personal rivalries, the profession remained somewhat fragmented. The normal way of learning architecture had become apprenticeship with an architect, supplemented by training in classes.

It was against this background that James pursued his architectural studies in Edinburgh. One newspaper obituary states that he 'gained further experience during his course of service in the office of Mr David Bryce, R.S.A., Edinburgh, who was then recognised as the leading architect of the day'. Another obituary, the text of which for the most part so closely follows the first that it must have been written by the same author, says that 'he entered the office of Sir Rowand Anderson, the famous Edinburgh architect'. Both David Bryce and Rowand Anderson were operating in Edinburgh at this time and for a brief period in 1873 they were partners. Bryce also ran an architectural training academy in addition to his practice. It is thus entirely possible that James was trained by or assisted both these eminent architects, but that neither of the newspaper editors had room in the obituaries they published for both their names.

Bryce, as we saw in earlier chapters, was one of the leading proponents of the Scottish Baronial style and also the designer of the additions to Castle Leod which Andrew senior adapted in 1845. In Edinburgh he enjoyed a significant reputation. During the period that James was in Edinburgh Bryce was at work on several of his iconic buildings. One was Blair Castle at Blair Atholl, which he transformed from an English country house look-alike to a full-blooded Scottish Baronial castle. In Edinburgh they included Fettes

College and the reconstruction of the Head Office of the Bank of Scotland on the Mound. Around 1870 Bryce slipped on an icy station platform and thereafter suffered ill-health, which may be why he took Rowand Anderson into partnership. Anderson, whose wife was the daughter of a tenant farmer in Contin, Ross-shire, was at this time little known, his main work being on churches, particularly for the Episcopal Church. He appears to have been a difficult and arrogant man. In later years he was to gain fame for works including two of Scotland's architectural masterpieces, both in a secular Gothic style, the National Portrait Gallery in Edinburgh and the flamboyant Mount Stuart on the Isle of Bute. In 1902 he was knighted for work at Balmoral.

At the time of the 1871 census James was at his parents' home at Esther Place and was described as an architect's assistant. By 1873 he was in Petley Street in the 'New Town' of Tain. The Valuation Rolls for 1876 to 1880 show him as the tenant of his father's house at Esther Row.

On 11th August, 1880 when he was 35, James married Barbara Lindsay, the daughter of Hugh Lindsay and his wife Catherine Cruickshank. Barbara, who was 22, had been born and brought up in Tain at Glenmorangie Cottage, a small one-storey cottage on the Tarlogie estate, which her father occupied as Excise Officer at the Glenmorangie Distillery. At the time of the marriage her father had retired and she was living with her parents at 62, Cromwell Street, Glasgow. The wedding took place at their home according to the forms of the Church of Scotland. After the marriage James became the tenant of a house in Hartfield Street, Tain, where they had one general domestic servant living in. Their next door neighbours were the present author's grandfather, John Mackenzie (then a Managing Law Clerk and later to have frequent dealings with both James and Andrew Junior), and his widowed mother. From about 1883 until 1892 James was tenant of a house in Lamington Street.

Andrew Maitland Junior

Like his elder brother James, Andrew Junior followed his father into the architectural profession. His training almost certainly followed the pattern of that of his brother in Tain and Edinburgh.

It would no doubt have been in Edinburgh that he met his future wife, Eliza Chapman. Eliza had been born in St Vincent, in the West Indies, where her father had been a planter. They married at her widowed mother's house, 23 London Street, Edinburgh on 23rd September, 1873. The ceremony was a Free Church one. Andrew Junior, however, unlike his father and James, at some stage switched his allegiance to the established Church of Scotland, becoming a leading member of the Tain congregation.

From about 1878 to 1884 Andrew Junior took a lease of a house in Lamington Street, Tain. He was thus for a few years a near neighbour of his brother James. During these years three sons and then two daughters were born to Andrew Junior and Eliza. Their eldest son, Andrew Gordon, died in infancy. Their third son, born in 1880, and also christened Andrew Gordon (but known as Gordon), was destined to become the fourth and last in the line of family members who were partners in A. Maitland & Sons.

9.1 Andrew Maitland Junior and his wife Eliza Chapman.

Andrew Junior soon showed that he was very much an entrepreneur. The quarry in Tain (referred to in the council minutes as 'the Freestone Rock' or 'the Rock') which formed part of the Common Good assets of the burgh, had been let by the burgh council to an Inverness builder in 1864 at an annual rent of £23. This lease came to an end in 1875. The Rock was then exposed to set by public roup (auctioned) for the purpose of opening and working the quarries for 5 years at an upset yearly rent of £15. The new tenant would have the right to work the quarries already opened and to open and work new quarries. He would also be 'bound to supply preferably - but on equal terms with others - the inhabitants and feuars of the Burgh with whatsoever stones shall be required by them from the Rock hereby let'. The roup was held on 31st December - then a normal business day. No offers were, however received, and the Rock was re-exposed to set the following February at an upset price of £12 p.a. This time Andrew Maitland Junior appeared and offered the upset price on behalf of himself and his brother James - the first of several business ventures.[1]

Andrew Junior's next initiative was to stand for election in November 1877 to the Tain Burgh Council. Five councillors were elected every year to serve a three year term. There were eight candidates, five of them retiring councillors. Andrew, at the unusually young age of 30, was elected in fifth place with 84 votes, well ahead of the next candidate who received 59.

Almost immediately he showed that he was not afraid to challenge the powers that be. The burgh was entitled to send an Elder to the General Assembly of the Church of Scotland. For some years a Mr Reid of Edinburgh had performed this function, but he was now in ill health. The redoubtable Bailie Alexander Wallace, a keen adherent of the Free Church, moved at a council meeting in March 1878 that no election should be made to replace him. Andrew Junior proposed an amendment that a local baker should be elected to represent Tain. Voting on the amendment was tied at six votes to six, and Andrew's amendment was lost on the casting vote of Provost Vass. Young Andrew then secured a special meeting of the council to call for a further meeting on the disputed election. This time the Provost moved, and Bailie Wallace seconded, a motion that the council should not meet for this purpose. Again the voting was six to six, and again the Provost exercised his casting vote against a replacement Elder. The minority apparently had the right to meet to elect an Elder to represent the Burgh if they were so disposed. The minority of six accordingly held a meeting and nominated an Edinburgh solicitor to represent Tain. In April 1879 Andrew Junior returned to the fray, this time winning the election of an Elder to represent the burgh, in the teeth of opposition by the Provost and Bailie Wallace, by seven votes to five. In April of the following year the election of an Elder to represent the burgh was agreed with no-one recording dissent. Andrew Junior had won an unequivocal victory on an issue about which he obviously felt passionately. (But this was not the end of the story. The dispute became an annual ritual, lasting into the 1890s. As late as 1888 Vass and Maitland were at it hammer and tongs. The council minutes, prepared by the author's grandfather, are circumspect, but a newspaper account gives a more direct flavour. Maitland said that by not sending an elder the council acted illegally in abusing a sacred trust which belonged to the inhabitants of Tain. Provost Vass retorted that it was a bit of tomfoolery for the council to patronise a church the door of which the majority of them never darkened. On this occasion Maitland won by seven votes to four, with three abstentions.)[2]

In 1882 Andrew Junior was re-elected to the council, this time in third place behind Provost Vass and Bailie Duff. Out of a constituency of 235 male and 44 female electors (who had the right to vote in municipal elections for the first time) 81 males and 14 females voted. Again in 1888 when the electorate had increased to 318 and 264 votes were cast he was re-elected in third place.

Unlike his father, Andrew Junior had a wide variety of interests outside architecture. He branched out in a number of different directions, taking on civic responsibilities, leadership of the the freemason's lodge, and the managing directorship of the Glenmorangie Distillery. He was knowledgeable about the history of Tain, and he often spoke proudly about it in the council, at masonic functions and at the innumerable formal dinners at which the Victorians loved to listen to numerous speakers proposing toast after toast.

Andrew Senior

In order to distinguish himself from his father the younger Andrew used until his father's death the style of 'Andrew Maitland Junior', even signing documents this way. His father was usually designated simply 'Andrew Maitland', but sometimes (as in his Will) signed himself 'Andrew Maitland Senior'. In order to avoid confusion this latter style has been generally used in the rest of this book.

Andrew Senior remained very active for two more decades after he was joined by his two architect sons in the early 1870s. Rosemary Mackenzie and Jane Durham paint a vivid portrait of him. 'His tastes took a strong artistic turn and he used brush, palate and canvas freely. Assignments began to flow in and multiply. He was an indefatigable worker. At his desk at 9 o'clock every morning, he seldom finished before 8 o'clock at night. He wrote all his specifications himself, and in those days specifications were very detailed documents indeed. He would write until his fingers were numb, and his cure for this was to put his hand under the cold tap to restore circulation and then start again. He kept this pace up until the age of ninety when he consented to retire.'

As we saw in chapter 6, he had been elected a Deacon of the Tain Free Church in 1867 and had been given responsibility for the maintenance of its buildings. He remained an officer of the Church whilst his health and *anno domini* permitted. This seems to have been his only activity outside the professional work to which he was so dedicated. He was, however, a strong supporter of Gladstone and was listed among the distinguished persons present at a meeting in Tain of 150 people whom George Loch, newly elected as the Liberal M.P. for the Northern Burghs, thanked for the exertions made on his behalf in the General Election of 1868.

The collapse of the City of Glasgow Bank - and financial disaster

From the early 1870s, apart from absences whilst one or other of the brothers trained elsewhere, until 1892 when Andrew Senior retired, the three Maitlands worked together. For a further six years thereafter the two brothers continued to collaborate. These were years in which the Maitlands well and truly left their mark on Tain and the Northern Highlands. But in the early days of the partnership there occurred an event that had a profound effect on two of them and their families.

Disaster struck, suddenly and out of the blue, in 1878. Andrew Senior, holding two £100 shares and James, holding one share, had invested in the City of Glasgow Bank, regarded because of its rising dividends as 'a favourite investment among small capitalists and more especially with widows and persons retiring from business on a small competency'. The bank had 1,264 shareholders and they would have been reassured in June of that year to learn that the bank had 133 branches, had deposits of £8,000,000 and was paying a dividend of 12%. On what was to be its last business day each £100 share was priced at £236. It was therefore a huge shock to learn in October that the directors had decided to close the bank after other banks had refused assistance. The pages of *The Scotsman* record day by day a deepening crisis. It soon emerged that there was a deficiency of £6,200,000. The bank had over-extended itself with large advances to a small number of customers, notably the Racine & Mississippi Railroad (later the Western Union) in America. Worse still, in order to hide the deficiency the accounts had been falsified over a number of years. The directors were arrested. One became a witness for the prosecution, but the rest were convicted at the High Court in Edinburgh in January 1879. (Scottish justice was commendably swift in those days.) The Manager, Robert Stronach, and another director of 20 years standing were both sentenced to 18 months imprisonment for fraud, and the others to 8 months.

The collapse of what was one of Scotland's leading financial institutions led to a major financial crisis, not just in Glasgow, where hundreds of businesses collapsed, but throughout Scotland. The worst effects were felt by the shareholders and their families. The liability of shareholders and those who had held shares in the past year - together 1,819 potential contributors - was unlimited. Nineteenth century governments did not bail out failed banks (though interestingly the Commissioners of Stamps and Taxes waived £10,000,000 of fines for falsification of the bank's bullion returns). The burden of funding the deficiency of £6,200,000 thus fell on the 1,819 current and recent shareholders. Calls aggregating £2,750 were made on each £100 share they held. Only 254 of them were able to pay in full. A substantial number were ruined. The lawyers had a field day arguing the liability of trustees.[3] Andrew Senior and James, whose shares had apparently been together worth £708 now had to find £8,250 - the equivalent of more than three times the cost of building the Tain Public Hall.

In Ross-shire, it was reported, 'a generous spirit prevailed'. A fund had already been set up under the auspices of the county authorities to 'consider the claims of necessitous shareholders of the Caledonian Bank', who were in a similar, though far less severe, predicament. The Tain Burgh Council held a special meeting on 14th November 'to consider raising a fund for the relief of the sufferers by the failure of the City of Glasgow Bank'. After an exchange of telegrams between Provost Vass and the County Convenor, Sir Kenneth Mackenzie, it was agreed on 25th November to merge the fund being collected in Tain with the general county fund in order to relieve both the City of Glasgow and the Caledonian shareholders. On 12th December the council rejected the proposed merger of the two funds and appointed a sub-committee to collect subscriptions in the burgh and parish; clergymen were asked to have collections in their churches - God coming to the relief of Mammon?[4]

Notwithstanding these local efforts Andrew Senior and James were severely affected by the failure of the bank. Andrew Senior appears to have been among the 254 able to meet the calls on their shares. The generosity of his fellow citizens may have given a small measure of relief. But when he died in 1894 the value of his estate was very small compared to that of Andrew Junior four years later - almost certainly a reflection of the events of 1878. James, with less years in which to accumulate funds, suffered more distress. He had to make a complete surrender of his estate to the liquidators of the bank in order to obtain a discharge of his obligations for the bank's debts. This compromise was submitted for approval by the Court of Session in June 1879 - a heavy penalty for having bought a single share.

The aftermath

Houses designed by architects and builders for their own use are often among the most interesting. Remarkably, however, Andrew Senior never built a house for himself but continued to live in Esther Place until his dying day. But both his architect sons designed their own houses in areas of Tain characterised by up-market late Victorian development.

As we will see, Andrew Junior, unaffected by the bank collapse, was the first to do so. In 1884 he had the very distinctive Lauderdale built in Morangie Road, where two further children were born. Even though married, his brother did not follow suit until the next decade - perhaps for financial reasons. By 1893 James, now the father of a seven year old son, Henry, had acquired the feu of land near the foot of the Scotsburn Road on which he built an elegant villa for his own family.

References and Notes

[1]   Tain Burgh Council Minutes, Highland Archive Centre BTN1/1/2 - also the main source of the two following paragraphs.

[2]   *Aberdeen Evening Express*, 28th March, 1888.

[3]   This account relies on a paper by Professor Kenneth G.C. Reid, *Embalmed in Rettie: The City of Glasgow Bank and the Liability of Trustees*, Edinburgh University School of Law Research Paper Series No. 2013/21, 2013.

[4]   Tain Burgh Council Minutes, Highland Archive Centre BTN 1/1/2.

10. AN EXPLOSION OF DEMAND

The golden years

From about 1870 Andrew was assisted by either or both of James and Andrew Junior. He took them both into partnership in 1873, the business becoming A. Maitland & Sons. The years from 1870 until the death of Andrew Junior in 1898 were golden years for the Maitlands in terms both of the volume and the quality of their work.

They were also golden years for the fabric of Tain, years in which the Maitlands designed many of the public and private buildings which were key elements in giving Tain the charm, the dignity and the individuality which it retains to this day. But, as we will see in the following chapters, it was not only on Tain that the Maitlands left their mark, but also right across the Northern Highlands.

A burgeoning demand for architects' services

Clearly the Maitland practice had gained immeasurably from having two additional Maitlands, both young and energetic, at work. But this is by no means a sufficient explanation for the growth in the number and the significance of the commissions the Maitlands received in and after 1870. The other side of the coin was that demand for architectural work was increasing in the wake of huge social and economic changes.

One of the key aims of this book is to explore who commissioned the buildings that the Maitlands designed and why they did so. By looking separately in the next few chapters at the Maitland civic buildings, commercial premises, hotels, schools, distilleries, churches, agricultural and sporting buildings, and private houses of these decades we may perhaps get some sense of the various reasons for this burgeoning demand. The approach taken in chapters 12 to 20 of this book, which take the story up to the death of Andrew Junior in 1898, is therefore thematic, though broadly chronological within each of the themes.

Before we explore these themes, however, it is perhaps worth looking at some over-arching factors, factors that were significant in the history of Tain and the Highlands.

The railways

One major factor can be dated with some precision - the coming of the railways.[1] This took place in Highlands some decades later than it did further south. By 1858 Inverness was connected to Aberdeen, and thus indirectly to the south, and in September, 1863 directly to Perth and the south. Meanwhile a line between Inverness and Invergordon was constructed, opening for traffic to Dingwall in June 1862 and to Invergordon in May, 1863. An extension through Tain to Ardgay was opened in October 1864. All of these lines were planned and supervised by the able and dynamic civil engineer Joseph Mitchell. Mitchell, born the year after Andrew Maitland Senior, had been trained by the great Thomas Telford and had enormous experience of roads, bridges and harbours all over the Highlands, experience which he brought to bear on the creation of railways. Mitchell was also involved - albeit with disputes with another railway engineer,

John Fowler of Braemore, a client of Andrew Maitland whom we met earlier - with the Dingwall & Skye line. This had a stop at Achnasheen which facilitated travel to the Gairloch area, in which the Maitlands were to be active. It initially terminated at Strome Ferry when it was opened in August 1870, and it was later extended to Kyle of Lochalsh. Sections of a line from Ardgay to Wick and Thurso, initially surveyed by Mitchell, were completed in July 1874, connecting Caithness and the east of Sutherland. On the Black Isle a branch line from Muir of Ord to Fortrose was opened in 1894; but it never reached Cromarty, which became something of a backwater.

10.1 The Highland economy was transformed by the coming of the railway,
which reached Tain station (shown above) in 1864.

We saw in chapter 7 the positive effect that the advent of the railway system had on farming and thus the demand for new and better farm buildings. But the railways had a much wider effect on life in the Highlands - relatively more so perhaps than in more populated regions. Goods of all sorts could be more easily moved. This allowed Highland architects to offer their clients a wider range of features in the villas they commissioned. It also facilitated supplies to distilleries and the distribution of their whisky, and it is noteworthy that all the distilleries designed by the Maitlands had railway sidings. People of all classes could more easily travel, both within the area and to and from more southerly parts of Britain. Tourism boomed, creating a demand for more and better hotel accommodation, a demand which the Maitlands helped to satisfy, particularly in Tain and Gairloch. Better off members of the middle class were more easily able to travel to towns like Tain, where they could build summer homes or settle in permanent homes that were now better connected to the south - homes which architects like the Maitlands were often commissioned to design. They and the traditional aristocracy could, moreover, travel with greater convenience to the northern and western Highlands for shooting and fishing, thus boosting the demand for shooting lodges, with which the Maitlands were particularly associated.

The middle classes and their values

But the majority of the increasing volume of commissions received by Highland architects in the late nineteenth century were not from incomers but from the indigenous population. One of the key features of the period was the increasing prosperity of the middle classes, particularly in burghs and towns. Individuals, particularly professional men and successful merchants, were able to build new houses, offices and shops, or to extend existing ones - often with the assistance of an architect.

More significant commissions came, however, from the collective efforts of the middle classes. Their involvement - particularly as members of local councils, of school boards after the Education (Scotland) Act of 1872, and of Free Church congregations - was hugely beneficial to architects.

In the latter part of the nineteenth century the middle classes assumed political power in towns throughout Scotland - power which, in the days before the welfare state and the centralisation of government, was significantly devolved to burghs and parishes. Their values were thus the predominant ones.

Their political values were for several decades overwhelmingly Liberal. In the words of a leading article in the *Ross-shire Journal* in 1900, 'before 1886 to be anything but a member of the Liberal party was to invite the ostracism of the mob'. The Liberal Party itself was a confederation of various interests - Whigs, voters enfranchised by the Reform Acts of 1832 and the so-called Second and Third Reform Acts of 1868 and 1885, radicals, and Peelite free traders like W.E. Gladstone himself. Its most spectacular period of office was Gladstone's first administration of 1868-74, which delivered reforms including the beginnings of the modern educational system - a reform which was to lead to commissions for the Maitlands to design new schools across the Highlands.

One of the the most vivid manifestations of support for the Liberals in Easter Ross occurred in Tain in October 1884. A holiday was observed in the town and a great part of the population of the area joined in a demonstration in support of the Franchise Bill, which was to become the Third Reform Act, then being resisted by the House of Lords. The speakers, followed by 120 mounted men, 18 different trades amounting to about 700 people, about 1,400 representatives of the agricultural interest and 500 fishermen from the fishing villages marched from Burgage Farm round the town to the Links, where some 10,000 to 12,000 people surrounded a platform. Provost Vass, chaired the meeting, and several people who were or were to become clients of the Maitlands, including Sir Kenneth Mackenzie of Gairloch, Ronald Munro Ferguson of Novar M.P., and Andrew Mackenzie of the Dalmore distillery, also spoke. After passing resolutions the meeting ended with cheers for the Queen and Mr Gladstone.

In 1886, however, the Liberal party suffered its own disruption when those opposed to Gladstone's Irish Home Rule Bill and concerned about possible Scottish Home Rule seceded and became Unionists. Unionist candidates for the Northern Burghs constituency were thereafter widely perceived as heirs to the historic Liberal tradition, and results in the elections in the two decades that followed were highly volatile. Andrew Maitland Senior himself had been a follower of Gladstone, but fell out with his party over the issue of Home Rule. The Tain Council election of 1887 was fought on party political lines, and the results, in which Andrew Junior headed the poll, were perceived as a decisive victory for the Unionist cause. In the early twentieth century James Maitland, a keen Unionist and an organiser of their parliamentary election campaigns, was to became involved with local government at three levels, parish, burgh and county.

Throughout these decades there was a strong sense of civic pride. In burghs like Tain this was based on a long and proud history and was nurtured by successive moves towards more democratic governance, particularly by local people themselves rather than by a centralised state. It was this that led many men from a wide spectrum of the middle classes to seek election to councils such as that of Tain and to serve as bailies and provosts. In Tain, as elsewhere in Scotland, this also found its expression in a number of public buildings and in projects designed to improve the burgh's facilities. The Maitlands were involved in the majority of these.

The political involvement of the middle classes was paralleled by their religious involvement. The predominant religious institution continued to be the Free Church, which was undoubtedly the major social institution of the Highlands, not least in Tain. The middle classes, particularly their upper ranks, came to dominate the Free Church, often becoming elders. As very few of the gentry became members of the Free Church the middle class dominance was unchallenged. Among the strong characteristics of the Free Church were strict Sabbath observance and a strong emphasis on morality. This particularly meant sexual morality, with fornication being condemned by admonishment by the Minister in front of the congregation. For many adherents morality extended to the evils of drink - though, given their heavy involvement in distillery architecture and in running Glenmorangie, it is not surprising that the younger Maitlands were not among the supporters of the Temperance movement.

But the middle class Free Churchmen also liked their own comfort. They frequently looked for new and better - and usually more imposing - churches than those that had been hurriedly built in the wake of the Disruption of 1843. Space, heating and ventilation were important. With a wider distribution of wealth, raising funds for building such churches was now easier. Free Church congregations were to be among the most important clients of the Maitlands in this period, with commissions for churches over a wide area of the Highlands - one of the biggest and best of them in Tain itself.

Another area that saw increasing middle class involvement was freemasonry. There is nowadays an element of suspicion about freemasons and the influence they are perceived to have, but little knowledge about their identities and what they get up to. In sharp contrast to this, the activities of freemasons in Victorian times were remarkably public, and the leading men (for there were no women freemasons) played a prominent and well-publicised role. Contemporary newspaper reports of the openings of buildings such as those the Maitlands designed, of funerals and of great public events like the Jubilees of Queen Victoria, routinely described masonic processions through the streets. The middle classes who now dominated freemasonry could now emulate, and enjoy the chance to socialise with, the gentry who had previously held sway. And masonic ritual may have served as an antidote to the rigours of Free Church Presbyterianism.

Lodge St Duthus in Tain and its *dramatis personae* are well chronicled in two books by William Russell.[2] Andrew Maitland Senior had, as we saw earlier, become a Master Mason in 1850. His sons James and Andrew Junior were initiated in 1876, and both were to become Right Worshipful Masters of Lodge St Duthus - James for four separate terms. The Lodge was to be heavily involved with three Maitland buildings - the Royal Hotel, the Town Hall and the Lodge's own building.

Competition for the Maitlands

The Maitlands were of course far from being the only architects to satisfy the increasing demand in the Highlands in the later decades of the nineteenth century. There was a marked increase in the number and workload of architects working in the region, and professional partnerships were increasingly common. The new railway lines, moreover, facilitated travel by architects over a wider area. Although the Maitland's reputation stood them in good stead in their heartland of Easter Ross they were competing there, and even more so further afield, with other architects, particularly those based in Inverness.[3]

As we saw earlier, the death in 1841 of Andrew Senior's employer William Robertson had been the catalyst for the development not only of Andrew's own practice but also those of Robertson's nephews, A. & W. Reid, and of his principal assistant, Thomas Mackenzie.

From the 1840s to the 1890s the Reids produced a range of buildings comparable to that of the Maitlands. For a time they had an Inverness office, and they gained several commissions in the Black Isle between the early 1850s and the mid 1870s; but thereafter they concentrated their efforts on Moray, Banffshire and Aberdeenshire from their base in Elgin and served a different market from the Maitlands.

Although Thomas Mackenzie had died in 1854 his surviving partner James Matthews, first in his own name and later in partnership with William Lawrie, built up a substantial practice in the years up to 1887, both in their base of Inverness (where they designed the impressive Town House) and further afield. Matthews & Lawrie thus obtained several commissions in the 1870s and 1880s in the Black Isle and Wester Ross, areas in which the Maitlands were operating.

Another Inverness based practice, also undertaking several commissions in Ross-shire, was that of John Rhind. Like the Maitland brothers he was of the second generation, having taken over a business set up by his father George in 1842; and like them he was involved in burgh politics, becoming an Inverness councillor and Dean of Guild. Rhind's preference was for expensive mansions and shooting lodges.

But the leading Highland architect of the latter half of the nineteenth century had no such constraints. The *Dictionary of Scottish Architects* lists nearly 1,000 works by Alexander Ross or his firm between 1853 and 1923, covering, as did the Maitlands, buildings of every type. At the age of only 19 Alexander Ross had taken over from his late father, James Ross (whom Andrew Maitland would have recalled both from his time at Braelangwell and from a joint commission on the Cromartie estate in 1844). Alexander Ross only retired when he was 88. During this time he was responsible for numerous well known buildings, including Inverness Cathedral, Ardross Castle, Duncraig Castle and the lay-out of Ness Walk, Ardross Terrace and Ardross Street in Inverness for Sir Alexander Matheson. At the same time he undertook a prodigious amount of small and medium-sized commissions. John Gifford sees Ross as 'the colossus among Highland architects … in Ross are drawn together the threads of 19th-century Highland architecture, eclectic, practical and at times touching on genius, at others of the drabbest but always stamped with a force of personality which is less often to be found in the recent productions of architects or designers in the Highlands.'[4]

In the course of Ross's career he entered into four partnerships. One of his partners was William Cumming Joass, whom he installed in an office in Dingwall in 1859. This enabled Ross & Joass to gain a significant number of commissions in Ross-shire. In 1865 Joass, still in Dingwall, set up on his own account and practiced until the Great War. Joass, like the Maitlands, operated in a variety of styles. He left his mark on Dingwall to a significant degree. Away from Dingwall the commissions he obtained were in areas which substantially overlapped with those of the Maitlands - indeed many of the estates for which they worked were the same. Another of Ross's partnerships, lasting from 1887 to 1907, was with his former assistant R.J. Macbeth. Ross & Macbeth did comparatively little work as far north as Easter Ross, though one significant commission they won was for St Andrew's Episcopal Church in Tain in 1887. This, in an Early English style with a distinctive steep roof, is one of the few major buildings in Tain not designed by the Maitlands during their eight decades of activity.

Analysis of advertisements for tenders in the newspapers of the period makes it clear that the Maitlands were predominant in and around Easter Ross, where they had home advantage. Further afield, however, they had to compete with other architects, particularly W.C. Joass in the area around Dingwall, and elsewhere in the Northern Highlands with Matthews & Lawrie, John Rhind, and Alexander Ross and his various partners. But across the Northern Highlands as a whole the Maitlands do seem to have been the most prolific architects of their time - indeed of any period.

The next chapter features an example of competition between architects - together with a début for one of the next generation of Maitlands.

References and Notes

[1] Joseph Mitchell in his *Reminiscences of my Life in the Highlands*, Vol. 2 pp.204-26 provides an entertaining account of his work on the Highland railways and justifications of his stance in the disputes it entailed. This volume was so outspoken that it was suppressed to avoid lawsuits. David Ross in his well-researched *The Highland Railway*, Tempus Publishing, 2005,

argues cogently that mainstream historians have given insufficient weight to the effect of the railways on the economic and social history of the Highlands.

[2]   William T. Russell, *My Brothers Past*, Vol. One 1761-1899 and Vol. Two 1900-2002, Librario Publishing Ltd, 2002.

[3]   The most informative study of Highland architects in the period so far published is by John Gifford, *Architects of the Highlands in the Nineteenth Century - a Sketch*, in *The Scottish Georgian Society Bulletin no*, 7, 1980.

[4]   Gifford *op.cit*. p.43.

11. A DÉBUT IN INVERGORDON

11.1 Invergordon Town Hall, James Maitland's first work of note, nowadays wrongly ascribed to another architect.

Invergordon Town Hall - and a strange co-incidence

Readers of the *Inverness Courier* or the *John O'Groat Journal* in 1870 would have learned that the Burgh Commissioners of Invergordon had 'selected a design by Mr Maitland, architect, Tain, for a public hall'.[1] This was correct - but the Mr Maitland involved was not the one most of them would have expected. It was not Andrew Senior but his son James.

As we saw earlier, Andrew Senior had received plaudits in 1850 for his first work of note, the Court House adjacent to the Tolbooth in Tain, but architectural historians in our own day have wrongly credited the design to Thomas Brown, architect to the Prisons Board of Scotland. By a strange co-incidence, twenty years later James was praised for his own first work of note, the design of the Invergordon Town Hall, but similarly lost credit for it when the design was later attributed to another architect.

Invergordon and civic pride

Invergordon, some ten miles south west of Tain, and on the main road that linked Inverness and Wick, had grown during the nineteenth century as a planned village organised by the principal landowners, the Macleods of Cadboll, who had their seat at Invergordon Castle. The use of its sheltered harbour by steamships had made it the main link between Easter Ross and the south, and the coming of the railway in 1863 had given it a further boost.

The mid nineteenth century saw significant reforms of local government in Scottish towns. Between 1833 and 1862 a series of statutes allowed local ratepayers in 'populous areas' to vote for their area to be recognised as a police burgh. Elected police commissioners were given powers which included not just the preservation of law and order but also much of the social legislation of the period - the provision of water, sewage, waste disposal, paving, lighting and sanitary standards. Central government thus recognised both the wish and the ability of the emerging middle classes to exercise local government - a far cry from the centralisation that has been such a feature of recent decades. In 1864 Invergordon took advantage of the General Police and Improvement (Scotland) Act of 1862, which extended police powers by allowing towns of more than 700 inhabitants to become police burghs. The Senior Magistrate of Invergordon, Robert Bruce Æneas Macleod of Cadboll, was *ex officio* a police commissioner. Though a police burgh was less grand than an historic Royal Burgh like Tain, Invergordon nevertheless had a sense of civic pride. In this the Senior Magistrate and the commissioners sang from the same hymn sheet - although they were not always perhaps on the same line.

The Town Hall

The story of the Invergordon Town Hall, and James Maitland's involvement, emerges from the pages of the *Inverness Courier*.[2] The major proponent of the idea of building a town hall was Macleod of Cadboll, who had been the source of several commissions for Andrew Maitland in the two previous decades. Cadboll as Senior Magistrate of the burgh had played a major role in arranging a water supply in 1853, and in his view 'the next thing the town required was a public hall where the inhabitants could meet for instruction and amusement with comfort and respectability'. But such projects needed local funding and the town hall project had been overtaken by the building of a Free Church (now the Parish Church). When the loans raised for these two projects were nearly paid off the town hall project was revived. Cadboll donated the site in the High Street and the Police Commissioners took up the project as representatives of the community.

On 20th August, 1870 Cadboll and distinguished guests drove from Invergordon Castle to the site in the main street of Invergordon. The walls were already going up. Mrs Macleod of Cadboll laid, somewhat belatedly, the foundation stone, and a bottle was deposited in the cavity below. This contained copies of current newspapers, coin of the realm and a document recording the occasion and including the names of those involved, including that of the architect, James Maitland.

Cadboll himself made a congratulatory, and sometimes self-congratulatory, speech. He recalled that he himself had requested an architect, well known in the country, to produce a plan, but that the Commissioners thought it 'unworthy of the place. ... The Commissioners said with one voice that if they had a hall they would have a good one. ... Another architect was employed, who produced a plan which is now being carried out almost without alteration. It shows great merit on the part of the young man who drew it up, and is well suited to the requirements of the community'. That architect was James Maitland.

A town hall was not a municipal building as in England, but, as Cadboll explained, it was 'for our intellectual instruction and amusement'. He instanced particularly scientific lectures and music, and there was a room to be opened as a school of art.

The building was completed in 1871. It had a handsome facade, Italianate in style, with a grand pediment and three decorative urns on the skyline. Behind the facade the building was 100 feet deep, with space at the front for two offices, to be let at a fair rent, and a hall which, with a gallery, would seat 450 people. The Historic Environment Scotland listing comments that 'it is a good example of its type, making effective use of the Italianate detailing. Its compact and well-proportioned principal elevation adds greatly to the interest of the street scene'. This was enhanced by a relief carving, set in the pediment, of Neptune with cornucopia, sculpted by Davidson of Inverness.[3] The new Town Hall was opened on the evening of 20th March, 1871, the Highland Railway Company running special trains to Invergordon from Tain (on which the Maitland family doubtless travelled) and Dingwall.

The Town Hall was converted into a cinema in 1934 and an Arts Centre in 1988. By 2019 the Highland Council, finding it increasingly expensive to maintain and run, were consulting on proposals for its disposal. A local councillor noted that the roof needed attention and the sandstone was falling off in chunks. At the time of writing the local community appears determined to secure the future of the building.

Somewhere along the way the design was credited not to James Maitland, but to W. C. Joass, a fine architect who was responsible for many buildings in Dingwall, and who may have been the 'well known' architect referred to by Cadboll as producing a design 'unworthy of the place'. The listing, the Highland HER[4] and architectural guides all give credit to Joass but fail to mention James Maitland. The truth lies in the cavity beneath the foundation stone.

References and Notes

[1] *Inverness Courier*, 28th April, 1870, *John O'Groat Journal*, 5th May, 1870.

[2] *Inverness Courier*, 25th August, 1870.

[3] Historic Environment Scotland LB35077.

[4] Highland HER MHG8770.

12. CIVIC PRIDE

12.1 Tain High Street before 1872, the Freemasons' Lodge athwart the end of the
street and the then Royal Hotel at the head of Castle Brae.

Tain transformed

In the last three decades of the nineteenth century more of Tain's distinctive buildings were constructed than at any time before or since. The Maitlands were responsible for the majority of the listed buildings of this period, buildings which form a major part of their enduring legacy.

The Tain Burgh Council, imbued with a sense of civic pride, was heavily involved with several key ones, and successive Provosts gave a strong lead. Most of the Maitlands' public commissions are thus well documented in the council minutes, which have been one of the key sources of information for this chapter.[1]

The trigger for the construction of several of the public buildings of the period was the coming of the railway to Tain in 1864. Access to the station, downhill from the centre of the town, presented problems and opportunities which led to commissions for the Maitlands.

Dr James Vass and his inheritance

Dr James Vass, born in 1821, was one of the major figures in Tain during the second half of the nineteenth century. On the death of their mother in 1856 he and his brother had inherited several properties in Tain. Their mother was the sister and residuary legatee of Donald Ross of Mineralbank (a small estate outside

Tain), a successful and prosperous merchant in Tain who had 'lived in family' with her and her husband until his death in 1842. Donald Ross had commissioned a considerable quantity of Tain silver, produced by several fine craftsmen who worked in Tain in the eighteenth century and the first half of the nineteenth. Much of his collection descended to Dr James Vass, whose grandson made a generous bequest which forms an important part of the Tain & District Museum's collection of silver.[2]

One of several properties which James Vass inherited was a hotel in Tain known as the Royal Hotel. The sale of this hotel was to result in three commissions for the Maitlands on land previously occupied by the hotel, and also in two more as a consequence of its replacement.

The Royal Hotel was the principal hotel in Tain. It was also a posting house, where tired carriage horses could be replaced if necessary and sent back to the posting house that had supplied them. It was situated on the north side of the High Street and was adjacent to the Court House (now the Sheriff Court), which had been designed by Andrew Maitland Senior

12.2 Dr James Vass.

and completed in 1850. It occupied the ground on which the eastern extension to the Court House would be constructed and, with its 'substantial and commodious' stables and other buildings, it extended somewhat erratically down the western side of the tracks known as Church Yard Brae or Castle Brae. When the railway came in 1864 the main route from the centre of the town to the station was thus composed of two inconveniently narrow and merging tracks, both accessed through archways on the High Street.

Although he enjoyed a rental income from the hotel (£70 in 1865), James Vass does not seem to have regarded it as investment he wished to retain. As early as 1857 he was advertising it 'to be let or sold' and if let to be available for sale to the incoming tenant during the currency of his lease. In 1863, noting that Tain 'will have Railway Communication extended to it in the Spring of 1864' and that the tenant's lease expired at Whitsunday 1864, Vass again advertised the hotel for sale. In 1864 Vass tried to sell the hotel by public roup, with set up price of £850.[3]

But these repeated failures to sell the hotel did not discourage Vass. The good doctor had been elected a councillor in 1849 and a bailie in 1852. He had considerable local influence and connections (including marriage in 1868 to a daughter of George Murray Senior, a member of the family of merchants and bankers who played a conspicuous role in the civic life of late eighteenth century and nineteenth century Tain). One suspects that his connections may have helped him, for he was able to get two official bodies interested in buying his property.

Court House extensions

The first body to show interest was the Burgh of Tain. The question of access to the station was first raised in 1862, two years before the railway reached Tain. In 1865 Provost John McLeod, a Tain draper, put to a meeting of electors a proposal to buy the hotel, knock it down and improve the access to the new railway station; but the meeting thought that the railway company should be responsible.[4] Undeterred, the Provost repeatedly raised the issue with the burgh council. 'I believe [the plan] to be calculated to promote the well being and prosperity of the inhabitants, encourage strangers to reside among us, maintaining the reputation of our ancient Burgh, and remove the reproach cast upon us by the press of having the worst access connected with the railway system in the north', he later told them. The council voted by a majority in 1867 to purchase the Royal Hotel, Dr Vass, abstaining.

There was, however, only some £600 in the council's kitty, and it therefore welcomed a complementary proposal from the Commissioners of Supply for the (still legally separate) counties of Ross-shire and Cromartyshire. The Commissioners were a committee of the principal heritors of each county, first appointed in 1667 to collect the national cess (or land tax). Through the eighteenth and nineteenth centuries they had acquired further responsibilities, including the maintenance of roads and bridges and the administration of the police force in the county. By the 1860s they were responsible for the provision of court houses, and they had access to central funding. They were particularly interested in improving the facilities in Stornoway, Dingwall and Tain. Their architect of choice was Andrew Maitland Senior, who, as we saw earlier, had designed several police stations for them. Andrew was sometimes described as 'the county architect'.

The Commissioners' biggest concern was about plans for the Court House in Stornoway that had been prepared by Robert Matheson, who was born in Tain in 1808 and was now Clerk of Works for Scotland in H.M Office of Works. Matheson proposed to pull down the Tudor style Court House of 1843, with its battery of tall octagonal chimneys (which had been designed by Thomas Brown in the style rejected for Tain) and to build a new one on a much larger and grander scale. The Chairman, Sir Kenneth Mackenzie, asked Andrew Maitland to cost this plan and to come up with a reduced alternative. Maitland estimated the cost of the Matheson plan at £3,585. His own plan involved extending the existing building in the same Tudor style and with similar tall chimney stacks corbelled out from the wallhead, and he estimated the cost at about £1,400 exclusive of furniture. The Commissioners preferred this. The addition of further rooms and the use of freestone from Glasgow and of rubble from Isle Martin were presumably responsible for an increase to 'upwards of £2,000' by the time the Maitland designed extension was completed in 1870.[5] Robert Matheson appears to have been somewhat unhappy that his plan was not chosen (though he was later to get his own back). The Stornoway Sheriff Court was the scene of the famous trial in 1874 of the 'Bernera Rioters', crofters who had challenged the clearance of their ancient grazings by Sir James Matheson's vindictive Tain-born factor or 'Chamberlain of the Lews', Donald Munro. The rioters were acquitted after Munro had been taken apart with devastating skill by their defence counsel, and Munro's reputation was so badly damaged that Matheson soon dismissed him. This victory for croftrers has been described as the first shot in a battle which led to the Napier Commission and to land reform which gave crofters security of tenure.

Andrew Maitland had already designed a police station in Dingwall joined to the Court House built in 1842-45 (also to designs by Thomas Brown). He was now engaged to produce designs for additions and alterations to the Court House itself, advertising for tenders in June 1872.[6] The work on the Court House appears to have been minor.

Meanwhile a deal was being cobbled together for Tain between the Commissioners and the burgh council, who insisted that the Court House extension 'should be in unison with the present Court House'. Dr Vass agreed to sell the Royal Hotel for £900 - smart business considering that he had failed to find a buyer at £850. The burgh council would pay £200 towards this and would obtain 'a road of not less than 22 feet in lieu of the existing two public roads through the archways'. The Commissioners, assisted by a government contribution of £450, would pay the balance. James Vass, who had (temporarily at least) retired from the council, got his money - though not without delay.

Andrew Maitland Senior, as both the preferred architect of the Commissioners of Supply and the architect of the original Court House, was the natural choice as architect. He drew up interesting plans which can be seen in in the Highland Archive Centre.[7] These show on the left the existing building and on the right, using a flap which could be pulled back, two alternative versions of the proposed extension. The larger version, the one actually built, was stamped on behalf of the Home Secretary on 20th June, 1872. (The plan of the main elevations is now filed in the Highland Archive Centre along with six smaller plans which all bear the certification 'Tain 1st June 1848. This is one of the plans of Tain Court House', accompanied by an illegible signature. As suggested in Chapter 5, there is every reason to believe that these are the original plans, widely attributed to Thomas Brown but actually by Andrew Maitland.)

Tenders were sought in March 1873.[8] But matters did not go smoothly. The council insisted that John Ross, the contractor for the mason work, should replace stone removed by him. Alexander Ross, builder, Tain, had a dispute with the Town Clerk about access, and A. Maitland & Sons had to give a written undertaking to the council about access and completion. There were problems with dampness in the safe in which the Burgh's records were kept. Robert Matheson, the unsuccessful contender for the work at Stornoway, produced a report in November 1875 implying criticism of A. Maitland & Sons, which recommended to the council that they should deduct 'abatements' of £30 from the £290 due to the Commissioners of Supply as their share of the building costs.

The appearance of the extension is such that anyone who did not know that it was completed a quarter of a century after the main part of the building could be forgiven for thinking that it was part of the original. It allowed the Commissioners to meet new Government requirements, and it also provided a room for the Tain Burgh Council to meet - a room now adorned with paintings of former Provosts of Tain, including both Andrew Maitland Junior and James Maitland. It is used to-day, in an era when all the powers once enjoyed locally have been centralised in a behemoth based in Inverness, by the Tain Community Council.

Progress on the other principal raison d'être of the purchase and demolition of the old Royal Hotel was, however, to be much slower. Arguments as to whether Castle Brae was the most appropriate route to the station, and as to how any new route was to be financed, impeded any decision. The Highland Railway offered a donation of £500, but when this was not accepted they formed a carriage route from the station, parallel to their track, which joined the shore road near the gas works. (Oddly enough in these times of one-way streets this has become the exit route from the station.)

The Royal Hotel

Meanwhile the demolition of the old Royal Hotel had created an opportunity. The Lodge St Duthus of freemasons owned another hotel, of three storeys and with stabling attached, then known as the St Duthus Hotel. It formed the southern part of their complex of buildings closing off the western end of the High Street and continuing up St Duthus Street to include much of the site of the present car park. They had tried unsuccessfully to sell it, and eventually let it at £27 per year. The Lodge themselves occupied a large room forming the upper floor of an adjacent three-storey building to the north, effectively on the site of the present Royal Hotel. At a meeting in March 1871 it was suggested that they should sell the Lodge buildings and garden for £700. An auction of the Lodge property took place in August 1872, with the purchaser being bound to build a new hotel and the Lodge retaining a piece of ground at the rear, bounded by Tower Street and the *Aultmatach* burn, where it was intended to build a Public Hall.[9]

James Vass was hardly likely to invest in a replacement hotel, but fortunately his tenant was. Roderick Finlayson had been a waiter in Dingwall and Invergordon. He seems to have quickly become a remarkably popular figure in Tain. Within a year of his taking a lease of the old Royal Hotel in 1857 'upwards of fifty gentlemen of Tain and district entertained him to a public dinner, in token of their respect for his personal character and in appreciation of his management of the hotel'.[10] As well as being a hotelier he was a farmer, a pillar of the Free Church and was to become a councillor in 1875. Finlayson must have realised the potential additional business from visitors to Tain, and he purchased for £800 the property the Lodge did not wish to retain.

Andrew Maitland produced the design for Finlayson's new hotel and in October 1872 sought tenders.[11] There were, however, problems during the construction phase, both with the carpenter work and the mason work.

12.3 The Royal Hotel, Tain - an early twentieth century view.

The carpenter, Alexander MacKenzie, died the following May at the age of only 34. His death was reported by his next door neighbour in Petley Street, James Maitland.[12] Curiously the Dingwall Sheriff Court records show that only 17 months earlier MacKenzie had signed, apparently at the insistence of his prospective father-in-law, Robert Ross, farmer at Wester Seafield, Portmahomack, an antenuptial Contract of Marriage under which he was obliged to marry Isabella Ross, to put £200 plus a life assurance policy for £200 into a trust for her benefit and to renounce any claims on all property she had or may later succeed to. One of the two trustees was James Maitland. After MacKenzie's death his brother took over some of the work on the hotel.

In August 1873 it was reported that a party took a 'pleasant drive' to Tain. They found that 'there was nobody in'. It was the annual holiday. The Reading Room, known long and familiarly as 'St Duthi's', had gone and on its site an 'elegant new hotel' was being raised. But they found only two men at work, 'who could not possibly complete the building in 100 years'. They were told that the rest of the workforce had left *en masse*. Their employer, the mason contractor, had taken the job far too cheaply, drawn larger sums of money than the work justified, and then 'skedaddled', as did the men, some of them having 'about £4 to get'.[13] The contract for mason work was then awarded to William Fraser, who completed it successfully.[14]

The hotel, French Gothic in style, has several distinctive features still apparent to-day.[15] These include projecting gabled bays at left and right, the latter with a tower in close proximity to the adjacent Maitland-designed Public Hall, and in between the bays a stone verandah looking, over cast-iron railings, straight down the High Street.

'As a mark of the regard entertained for Mr Finlayson, the proprietor of the NEW ROYAL HOTEL' the Town Clerk and the Secretary of the Easter Ross Farmers' Club organised an 'Opening Dinner, tickets One Guinea' in October 1874. Finlayson ran the hotel for a quarter of a century. It catered for the upper range of travellers, and provided 'a fleet of wagonettes and brakes which were widely used by sports clubs in their season and by parties going off for a day's outing'.[16] The burgh accounts show that Finlayson's wagonettes were frequently used by the council. They, together with newspaper reports of the period, demonstrate too that his hotel played a prominent role in the life of the town, with frequent formal dinners, auctions, meetings of the Easter Ross Farmers' Club and, all too frequently, examinations of bankrupts - and in 1894 a banquet for Earl of Rosebery, then Prime Minister, and the Duke of Sutherland after the presentation to them of the Freedom of the Burgh.

The Tain Public Hall

We saw in the last chapter how James Maitland had designed a town hall for Invergordon, built in 1870-71. John Gifford notes that town or public halls, built primarily for public events and sometimes also to provide a room for burgh council meetings, were an expression of nineteenth century civic pride.[17] Among the examples he cites is the fine Flemish Baronial Town House in Inverness of 1876, designed by Matthews & Lawrie. Tain got its public hall in the same year, but the need for such a building had been long felt.

Thus at a concert for the benefit of the poor held in the Court House in Tain on 11th February, 1870 the Chairman, Kenneth Murray of Geanies, in thanking the performers remarked that the only drawback had been the crowded state of the room and passages. 'As I see my worthy friend Mr Maitland, who built this hall, present,' he went on, 'I propose that we now, at once, give him an order to build a larger one - worthy of the good old town. (Great cheering) The want of such a hall is a great drawback to our prosperity and enjoyment, and I for one am prepared to give a helping hand to remove it'.[18]

Kenneth Murray did indeed give the project a helping hand. He was well placed to do so. A scion of a family of merchants who had played a prominent role in the affairs of Tain for generations and had deployed their wealth into buying estates in Easter Ross, he had been agent for the

12.4 Kenneth Murray of Geanies.

Commercial Bank in Tain and factor for a number of estates. He was also a noted agriculturalist and writer on agricultural subjects. On the sudden death in 1867 of his elder brother, ex-Provost William H. Murray, he had succeeded to the estate of Geanies, and he had followed him as Master of the St Duthus Lodge of freemasons. He had been one of the three Bailies of Tain since 1851 and was regarded as the 'ruling spirit' of the burgh council.

It was not, however, to the burgh council that Kenneth Murray looked to advance plans for a public hall. The council's financial constraints noted above would have made that route impossible. The key to the project lay partly in the decision of the Lodge St Duthus (no doubt influenced by Kenneth Murray as Master) to retain land at the rear when they sold the main part of their property to Roderick Finlayson for the new Royal Hotel, and partly in the contacts which enabled Murray to raise funds. Kenneth Murray promoted a Joint Stock Company, the Tain Public Hall Company Limited. The land was then feued to the company by the Lodge, which also provided a bond of £500 to go towards the costs of the proposed building. It was agreed that the freemasons should have the right to use the hall on St John's Day and for their quarterly meetings.[19] Andrew Maitland was commissioned to design the new hall and sought tenders in March 1874.[20]

The cost of the new building was 'upwards of £2,500'. The Duke and Duchess of Sutherland contributed £200, about half of the funds required by the new company were found by the heritors of Easter Ross, and Bailie Wallace 'set the ball rolling a-rolling in the streets [of Tain] with a hundred grand reasons why we should keep it moving'. Andrew Maitland Senior, like many of his fellow townsmen, subscribed for shares, in his case four of £5 each, and Andrew Junior took three. Four days before the official opening of the new hall the freemasons held a meeting in it at which James and Andrew Maitland Junior were initiated. Both were later to become Masters of the Lodge St Duthus.

12.5 Tower Street, Tain, with the Public Hall (later Picture House) at right, flanked by the north elevation of the Royal Hotel.

The hall was opened on 18th January, 1876. 'Of course', said a very full report,[21] 'the opening was not to pass without a public demonstration worthy of the occasion'. There was a one and a half hour torchlight procession, marshalled by Kenneth Murray, who two months before had been elected Provost of Tain following the retirement of John McLeod. About 60 freemasons and 60 members of the Tain or 1st Ross-shire Volunteers paraded through the principal streets of the town, followed by an immense crowd. There was then a concert in the new hall, at which Kenneth Murray, amidst great acclaim, declared the hall open.

The building[22] was in a French Renaissance style. Facing Tower Street were two projecting towers surmounted by pointed gables and between them an entrance at the head of a flight of 10 steps, flanked by a parapet and railing, stone pillars and two globular gas lamps. Inside was a hall 72 feet long, 32 feet wide and 32 feet 6 inches high, with a gallery at the street end, and total seating for 500 to 600.

The hall became the venue for concerts, bazaars and great events, such as the conferring of the Freedom of the Burgh on Lord Rosebery and the Duke of Sutherland in September 1894, referred to above. A few weeks later a 'very large audience' attended an entertainment by a 'troupe of darkies' in aid of the Golf Club's funds. But the hall company was not a financial success. Thus when Andrew Senior died in 1894 his four fully paid shares of £5 each were valued at only one shilling each, and when Andrew Junior died four years later his 3 shares were valued at a mere two pence each. As we will see, the interior of the hall was to undergo a makeover by James Maitland after a benefaction by Andrew Carnegie in 1903.

Provost Kenneth Murray did not live long after the opening of the hall. His forebears had been shopkeepers in Tain, but he had climbed to new heights on the social ladder. He had become a personal friend of the third Duke of Sutherland, for whom he supervised the construction of 17 miles of railway from Golspie to Helmsdale and major land reclamation works at Lairg. He died in July 1876, aged only 52, whilst staying with the duke at Dunrobin Castle. In his memory a monument, a 'small scale Dec[orated] Gothic version of the Scott Monument in Edinburgh',[23] was erected, overlooking the High Street, in what had been his garden as agent of the Commercial Bank and is now the Rose Garden.

The Collegiate Church and a Caretaker's Lodge

By 1876 the sale of Dr Vass's Royal Hotel had thus played a role directly in the construction of an extension to the Court House, of Roderick Finlayson's new Royal Hotel and indirectly in that of the public hall. But nothing had been done about the burgh council's original plan to use the land purchased from Dr Vass to improve access to the railway station. Following Kenneth Murray's death James Vass, who had stood down from the council in 1868, was hastily parachuted in as a councillor and as Provost, and he became the leading proponent of the proposed improved access.

Early in his Provostship a bequest from Frederick Campbell Taylor, a former Treasurer of the burgh, was used for the purpose of erecting a clock for the Tolbooth with three faces connected to the central mechanism. A report from 'Mr Maitland' (probably Andrew Senior) in September 1878 indicated that it was now complete, the costs of tradesmen and architects being £125-13s-8d and of the clock £164.

Meanwhile, however, a major project was coming to fruition. This was the restoration of the old Collegiate Church - not as a place of worship, but for monumental purposes as the 'Valhalla of Ross-shire'. Following an appeal for funds, the work was in the hands of Robert Matheson, whose path had crossed that of Andrew Senior in relation to the Court Houses at Stornoway and Tain. Matheson added four new buttresses, and was able to call upon the services of Edinburgh colleagues - John Rhind to restore the five large traceried windows, and James Ballantine & Sons to produce the magnificent stained glass in those windows, together one of the glories of this building.[24] Matheson died, however, in March 1877 and so did not see the finished windows. Another major feature, installed after Matheson's death but based on his recollections from his boyhood in Tain, was the restoration of the pulpit. In the words of a contemporary historian, at the Reformation 'the people of Tain became such decided Protestants, that their zeal procured the notice and approbation of the "good regent" Murray [illegitimate half brother of Mary, Queen of Scots], who, in acknowledgement of it, bestowed on them the gift of a finely carved oaken pulpit for their church . .... A lamentable negligence ... had suffered [it] to be broken and its ornamentation carried away by wanton hands'.[25] The framework had escaped destruction and portions of the ornamentation ('all the pieces of the original which could be found') were recovered from private hands, and thus the pulpit was restored to its original beauty.

There exists a 'plan of the Collegiate Church and elevations of the insides of the walls' dated 27th October, 1881 and signed on behalf of his firm by Andrew Maitland Junior. The plan is accompanied by two drawings of proposed arrangements for mural monuments.[26] It would appear that the Maitlands had been asked to design further improvements to the Collegiate Church, but that these were not proceeded with. At least one later student of the plans, the leading historian of the Collegiate Church, was not impressed. 'Monument is piled on monument, the walls are loaded with pinnacles, carbuncles, columns, busts, tablets, mini-Scott monuments in all known, and a good many unknown, styles, both gothic and baronial, in stone, metal, marble and granite. Fortunately it did not happen.'[27]

Whilst the project to restore the Collegiate Church proceeded minds turned once again towards the proposed improvements to the access to the station and how they could be made more decorative. A Memorial presented to the Burgh Council in November 1876 (to which ex-Provost McLeod and Robert Matheson were signatories) sought removal of the old stables of the former hotel in Castle Brae, a new parapet wall with handsome iron railings, and an entrance gate to the churchyard. The council requested A. Maitland & Sons to report on the matter 'with a view to utilising the subjects for revenue' - probably selling the stones from the old stables. But their report was not acted upon. In November 1879 Provost Vass proposed that Messrs Maitland should prepare a plan for a more comprehensive scheme, but a decision on the resulting plan was deferred, mainly on cost grounds, at meeting after meeting. In August 1880 a Petition signed by 198 inhabitants sought to have the works carried out. The Maitland firm estimated the costs at £2,160. But a decision foundered on financial considerations: could the Council, still paying off the debt for a water supply, afford the scheme and also the necessary land purchases? or could the Common Good Fund be used to defray the costs?

Whilst these debates continued the Council received a letter in September 1882 from John Mackintosh of Calcutta, 'a native of Tain, offering to build a lodge for a caretaker of the St Duthus Old Church [the Collegiate Church] on the ground belonging to the Burgh immediately behind the Court House, and also to create an ornamental gate giving access to the Church Yard on its South Side in memory of his father Mr Lachlan Mackintosh, an esteemed Burgess of Tain'. The Council 'heartily accepted' and agreed to remove the coach house and stables of the former Royal Hotel. Before the work he was sponsoring had even started John Mackintosh was one of several benefactors to receive a gift that well illustrates the sense of civic pride felt in that era. The Rev. William Taylor, son and brother of former Town Clerks of Tain, had just published his history of Tain, which focussed particularly on the stories of St Duthac and of Tain's glory days during the reign of James IV. The Council presented him with a copy of his own book, with a suitable inscription, bound in boards of oak from a portion of the Regent Murray's pulpit which had not been used in its restoration. Similar presentations were made to John Mackintosh, and also to A.B. Macqueen Mackintosh (who had presented the widely admired Ballantine east window in memory of his father and brother, ministers in Tain from 1797 to 1858) and to George McLeod (son of Provost McLeod and a liberal contributor to the restoration of the Collegiate Church). Four years later Provost Vass was also presented with a copy.

The Maitland firm prepared plans for the Caretaker's Lodge in 1884 and advertised for tenders in January 1885. The building, in the early Gothic style, single storey with a steeply pitched roof, is described in the Historic Environment Scotland listing as 'picturesque, asymmetrical cruciform'.[28] The caretaker, Sergeant

William A. Ross, was allowed to use a garden on Castle Brae for 2/6d per year on condition that the council, still hoping to build the new road to the station, could resume possession at any time. The *Inverness Courier* commented that 'the disparity between the neat appearance of the new lodge and the ruinous tumble-down old stables of the former hotel must make every well-wisher of Tain devoutly desire the immediate clearance of the unsightly pile'. It urged the Corporation no longer to sustain the anomalous reputation of being one of the wealthiest in the North and having one of the worst approaches to the station.[29]

To-day the former Caretaker's Lodge houses the Tain & District Museum.

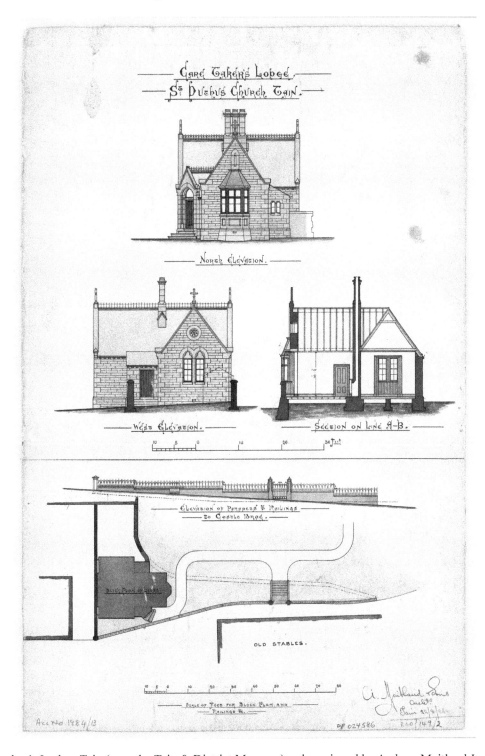

12.6 Caretaker's Lodge, Tain (now the Tain & District Museum) - plans signed by Andrew Maitland Junior, 1884.

Dr Vass and the Mercat Cross

Dr James Vass, in ill-health, retired as Provost in 1890, with the long-running saga of the access to the station still continuing. He retired to Morningside in Edinburgh, but he did not sever his connections with Tain and he was responsible for one of the more unusual of the Maitlands' commissions.

In August 1894 Vass wrote to the Council: 'It has for many years been my desire and purpose to give some visible expression to the Town Council and the Community of Tain of my warm interest in, and kindly feeling towards, that ancient Royal Burgh'. He recalled that some years ago he had succeeded in recovering some fragments of the 'Lion' which had surmounted the Tain Mercat Cross. He now sought 'the privilege of erecting a new Mercat Cross in imitation and on the site of the former Mercat Cross'. He had recovered the original socket in which the shaft of the Cross was erected, and he proposed 'using it for the new Cross and placing at the base of the structure the fragments of the old Lion with a view of preserving all that is ancient and historic of it'.

Mercat crosses had been an important feature of Royal Burghs in medieval times, serving as a focal point for markets and fairs and for important public events. In the Victorian era several burghs erected replicas, sometimes incorporating original elements. It is not surprising that in the wake of the restoration of the Collegiate Church and the publication of Taylor's history, with its emphasis on the antiquity of the town, Dr Vass's offer should have been received with enthusiasm.

A committee was appointed to see the new Mercat Cross constructed and erected. The project was entrusted to the Maitland partnership. The result of their work was an octagonal shaft surmounted by a lion holding an armorial shield and standing on a weathered base which Gifford describes as 'probably C16'.[30] The *Ross-shire Journal* reported that the replacement lion was sculpted from Dumfries sandstone by Birnie Rhind, A.R.S.A., Edinburgh, and the shaft hewn from yellow Balintore sandstone by William Fraser, mason, Tain.[31] The paper regretted that the committee had disregarded ex-Provost Vass's wish to have the new Cross erected on its former site. When functional it had stood on the opposite side of the High Street, but it had been moved in 1778 because it obstructed traffic.[32] According to the above report it had then been erected west of the Tolbooth door, but 'over 50 years ago it was easily demolished in a drunken lark'. Vass and his contemporaries would have regarded this as the 'former', and perhaps original, site. The committee preferred, however, to put the new Cross to the east of the door, in the inner angle of the Tolbooth and the Maitland-designed Court House, 'where it is … most effectively hidden until one is within three or four feet of it'.

12.7 The restored Tain Mercat Cross.

Castle Brae and access to Tain station

James Vass was succeeded as Provost in 1890 by Edward Matheson. The council immediately noted that resolutions in 1880 had committed them to improving the access to the station according to the Maitland plans. Despite the Provost's support a decision was again put off. Many inhabitants of Tain also felt strongly about the issue, and a petition signed by 170 ratepayers seeking 'immediate construction' of the road was presented in 1892. The Maitland plans of 1880 were again dusted down. Some councillors thought them too expensive, and the Chief Engineer of the Highland Railway, Murdo Paterson C.E. (who had taken over the construction of the railway through Tain when Joseph Mitchell suffered a stroke in 1862) was instructed to come up with alternative plans. The council deemed both plans impracticable because of the costs of purchasing land. James Maitland was instructed to come up with a third scheme. This involved a new branch road behind Orchard Place and a total cost of £960. In 1896 James Maitland was again consulted on the proposed steps and railings for Castle Brae. He insisted that steps must be built otherwise there could be no improvement, as the decline was too steep.

12.8 Castle Brae, photographed by William Smith - the steps were the culmination of years of dispute about access to the station.

The first real progress was made in 1897, when a steading belonging to Donald Rattray was purchased for road widening. In November that year Provost Matheson retired and was succeeded by Andrew Maitland Junior. The improvement of Castle Brae and the access to the station became the main issue of his all too brief tenure of that office. People were crying out for the improved access, but the council was £1,300 in debt. Counsel had advised on what the Common Good Fund could and could not be used for. James Maitland was thus advising on two alternative schemes, via Castle Brae or via Chapel Street. It fell to the Town Clerk, John Mackenzie (grandfather of the present author) to organise a plebiscite of ratepayers. They had to choose between:-

No.   *Scheme*
1.   *Recently adopted Improvement Scheme, including Chapel Street and Station Road   Improvement, costing about £600 to be paid out of the Common Good Fund.*
2.   *Direct Traffic Road from Railway Station to High Street, estimated to cost about £2,500 to be repaid principal and interest by an Assessment on Proprietors and Tenants.*

Out of 335 cards issued 277 votes were cast, 146 for Scheme 1 and 127 for Scheme 2, with 4 for neither. And so, a quarter of a century after Dr Vass's hotel had been purchased in order to facilitate access to the station, Rattray's steading was pulled down, Chapel Street was widened, the angle of the British Linen Company's Bank's (now the Bank of Scotland and Abbian House) dyke was taken away and rounded 'next Shandwick Place', attractive cast-iron railings, with a gate, were erected to enclose the Collegiate Church and its Caretaker's Lodge, Castle Brae was widened and the footpath was constructed with the flights of steps that James Maitland had insisted on - giving very much the pattern we see to-day. Final accounts were submitted by James Maitland in January 1900, along with his own account from 1893 to 1900 for £35-10s, which the council deemed 'extremely moderate'.

The Common Good Fund and its assets

The Tain Common Good Fund had therefore been used to solve a problem that had bedevilled Tain for more than three decades. The Maitlands were also involved professionally and personally over several decades with various assets of the fund. What, the modern reader might ask, was the Common Good Fund? A judicial definition was given in the Court of Session by Lord Wark, who said that there was no dispute that 'all property of a royal burgh or a burgh of barony not acquired under statutory powers or held under special trusts forms part of the common good'.[33] The origins of the common good can be traced back to the Crown Charters which established Royal Burghs from the reign of David I (1124 - 1153) onwards. As previously noted, the earliest extant charters granted to Tain as a Royal Burgh, confirming claims that had been made for a century, are those of James VI in 1588 and 1612. Tain's best known common good asset, the Mussel Scalps, was granted in the 1612 charter. It was still providing revenue in the late nineteenth century, albeit reduced by poor management.

Another well known common good asset was the quarries on the Hill of Tain. We saw earlier that Andrew Junior and James Maitland had taken a lease in 1876. Their lease expired in 1881. They do not seem to have been keen to renew it, but a council 'Committee on the Tain Quarries' could not decide what to do and left the quarries in the Maitlands' hands until 1884. When the quarries were then exposed to set, with very prescriptive terms as to the prices the tenant could charge for stone, no offers were received. The Maitlands were then asked to remove their plant, and a report which recommended that people requiring stone should be authorised by the council to quarry it themselves - a report which appears to have been critical of the Maitlands' management of the quarries - was presented and approved by the full council. The report was said to be based on consultations with 'practical men'. Andrew Junior dissented from the report and demanded to know the names of the 'practical men', but it was thought 'unnecessary' to divulge them. In 1887, after permissions to quarry had been granted to individuals on an *ad hoc* basis for 3 years, the council thought that that arrangement was unsatisfactory. Andrew Junior accused the quarries committee, whose Convenor was Duncan Cameron, of favouritism as to who got permission. The position was not resolved until 1888, when the quarries were again exposed to set. This time two offers were received, the successful offeror paying £7 per year plus dues of 2d per ton on all stones exported beyond the Royalty of the Burgh. But the falling-out of Andrew Junior and Duncan Cameron was to be the precursor of a much more serious dispute over the Glenmorangie distillery, a dispute which ended up in the Court of Session.

A large part of the lands belonging to the burgh mentioned in the charter of 1612 had been lost, particularly in the late eighteenth and early nineteenth centuries, through encroachments by neighbouring landowners and by the magistrates of Tain feuing out the town's moors (originally amounting to some 3,000 acres) often to the advantage of themselves and their close associates. In the last three decades of the century some of the remaining properties required attention from the Maitlands, ranging from very minor alterations to the construction of new buildings. There were two farms, the farm of Lairg, or the Lairgs of Tain, and the Hill Farm, for which valuations were done. The tenant of the latter, Donald Mackay, who also owned the farm of St Vincent, had financial problems and by 1881 was unable to pay his rent. John Cormack (great grandfather of the present author) retired from day to day management of the family fish-curing business in Wick and bought St Vincent at a roup. He then offered to take an assignation of Mackay's lease of the Hill Farm, but pointed out the dilapidated state of the farm offices. A. Maitland & Sons reported to the Council that the farm offices needed entire renewal and should be shifted northwards. This did not happen, and John Cormack was able to claim rent rebates for several years.

Another burgh property was the High Mills, a pair of mills, one a corn mill and one a saw mill, sited one above the other, both using the same lade to provide water power. In 1893 James Maitland was responsible for major repairs to them, and in 1897 for a reconstruction to convert the corn mill to a 'new and commodious woollen mill' for a new tenant, John Skene & Co. More recently the mills, a listed building, have been converted to residential use.

The burgh's property also included the Links, between the Highland Railway and the Dornoch Firth, on which rough pasture and arable land was let, areas were used for tennis, cricket, skating and curling, and quarterly fairs were held just east of Gallow Hill for the sale of cattle. On the other side of the railway track, on the site of what is now a light industrial park, the Council owned the Meadowfield (sometimes known as 'The Meadow').

The Tain Public Shambles

The Meadowfield was conveniently close to the railway station, and in the last two decades of the century parts were given over to new uses - a Public Shambles or Slaughterhouse and an auction mart.

A shambles originally meant a place for slaughtering animals - a usage that was still extant when the slaughterhouse was built in Tain - though the meaning has come to encompass scenes of carnage, destruction or disorder.

The Tain Public Shambles or Slaughterhouse,[34] built in 1885, remains one of the curiosities of the town - a purely functional building, but sitting behind an ornate castellated frontage described as being in the Lombardic style. The project originated with a committee of the Commissioners of Police of the Burgh of Tain, chaired by Bailie Wallace. Royal burghs were allowed by the Burgh Police Acts to have a 'parallel police system', run by elected police commissioners and co-existing with the burgh council. As we saw in the case of Invergordon in chapter 11, 'police' powers included the oversight of paving, drainage and cleansing and regulation of infrastructure in order to improve sanitary standards; constabulary was an option. In 1854 Tain adopted a policing system without the constabulary provisions. During the mid to late nineteenth century health and social concerns led to the elimination of private slaughter and to slaughterhouses, regulated by law, being set up away from the centre of towns and often, as in Tain, located conveniently close to to railways. The Police Committee got tired during 1884 and early 1885 of seemingly endless communications with three fleshers (butchers) who continued to operate unlicensed slaughterhouses and with an 'officious' sanitary inspector. They were able to provide building materials worth some £400 and they recommended that a public slaughterhouse should be erected at a further cost estimated at £650, to be paid from the Common Good Fund rather than by assessment. The burgh council agreed on condition that any income derived from the slaughterhouse should be paid into the fund.

A. Maitland & Sons provided the plans. Sheep and pig pens were on the left, the slaughterhouse in the centre and two cow sheds and three meat stores on the right. The Maitlands sought tenders in January 1885[35] and the building was opened in February 1886. The early years of operation were not without problems: the Police Commissioners operated it themselves for a couple of years as they did not know what rent to ask for, and the first tenant had to be ejected.

In 1888, when professionally organised auction marts were taking the place of cattle sales at locally run fairs, a portion of the Meadowfield to the west of the slaughterhouse was laid out according to a sketch by A. Maitland & Sons and was later let out as an auction mart. In the following year the Invergordon Burgh Commissioners decided to instruct A. Maitland & Sons to prepare plans and receive estimates for a slaughterhouse for their burgh.[36] This soon competed strongly with the one at Tain, as a railway line was run into it and carriage rates were 5 shillings per ton lower.

Both the Tain Shambles and the auction mart have long since closed. By 1970 the Tain Burgh Council was advertising the Shambles for lease either as a slaughterhouse or for alternative use. To-day, forlorn and disfigured by utilitarian additions, it remains a relic of a bygone age. The auction mart building has become a workshop and store.

A hard fought battle over gas

The Shambles was not, however, the end of of the Maitlands' involvement in public buildings on the lower land north of the raised beach or narrow terrace on which the main part of Tain stood.

In July 1890 a major dispute, in which the Maitland brothers played a prominent role, erupted in Tain. It led to consequences which were extensively reported in the *Ross-shire Journal* and in the national press. The town was lit by lamps whose gas was produced from coal by the Tain Gas Light Company at its works in Shore Road. Andrew Maitland Junior was the burgh's representative on their board, though he dissented from several of their decisions. The gas works and plant were half a century old. The council regarded them as 'worn out and dangerous' and noted that the lamps were found to be unlit on 108 occasions in the last lighting season. James Maitland was requested to report on the cost of buying the gas works and putting it into 'a thoroughly efficient condition'. In early September he reported that it would cost £2,585 to do so and that a new gas works could be erected for £2,630. On the basis of this the council offered to buy the company for £1-10s-0d per share (£740 in total), the figure used in James's calculation. The shareholders refused this offer, wanting £2 per share. A parallel dispute arose as to the price the council should pay for gas used for street lighting.

An impasse was reached. The company refused to supply gas. Bailie Edward Matheson and Andrew Maitland Junior were adamant that the council's offer could not be increased. After a period when the town was in darkness (and 'some of the evil youths took advantage of it') the council hired a lamplighter and lit the streets with paraffin. Householders too had to use paraffin for lighting and heating - as was still the practice outwith the predominantly urban areas served by gas companies. The council adopted the Burghs Gas Supply Act (Scotland), 1876 which enabled municipal control of town gas supplies. Then, encouraged by Matheson and Andrew Junior, they adopted a policy of waiting for the other side to cave in. This worked. In November 1891 the gas company finally accepted the offer of £1-10s-0d per share. In March 1892 the council, meeting as Gas Commissioners, heard a report by James Maitland, and it was remitted to him, along with the works manager and the Gas Committee of the council, to 'execute the works forthwith'. The cost was estimated at £1,750. A. Maitland & Sons sought tenders for reconstructing the gas works in June 1892,[37] and the following month an advertisement appeared for builders at '8d. per hour and sheds in wet weather'. Modern readers might find it strange that at no stage had it been suggested that Andrew Junior had a financial interest which should disbar him from participation in the council's deliberations.

Public buildings beyond Tain

As well as those in Tain and Invergordon, the Maitlands designed four more public halls in the last three decades of the nineteenth century. The first two were both initially promoted as drill halls for the Volunteer Force.

With government encouragement volunteer rifle corps and artillery corps had begun to be formed throughout Britain from 1859. The military requirements of the Crimean War had exposed the inadequacy of home defences, and there were fears about the intentions of the French Emperor Napoleon III. Volunteers provided their own uniforms and paid an annual fee. Professional men and tradesmen, who could attain ranks that in the regular army were the prerogative of the gentry, were particularly attracted. Volunteers often felt a social obligation to provide a hall to be used both for drill and by the wider community.

Thus in 1879 A. Maitland & Sons sought tenders for building a drill hall for the Bonar Bridge Battalion of the Sutherland Rifle Volunteers.[38] The hall soon became a venue for meetings connected with the so-called Crofters' War of the 1880s, including a hearing by the Napier Commission in 1883, the launch of the Crofters' Party's 1885 general election campaign, and meetings of the Highland Land Law Reform Association and the Crofters' Commission established by Gladstone.

12.9 The Victoria Hall, Cromarty.

In Cromarty, on the Black Isle, where, as David Alston notes, the 1st Cromarty Artillery Volunteers were 'an important focus of activity and a source of pride for the community, Walter Ross of Cromarty co-ordinated local efforts to have a drill hall erected'.[39] In 1887 A. Maitland & Sons designed the Victoria Hall, advertising for tenders in May and receiving plaudits for the design at an opening ceremony in December.[40] The hall became the first of a number of new buildings in the town and is still at the centre of community life. The hall[41] has a distinctive facade, including an eye-catching round window above the entrance, with spokes radiating from a central clock. Further local fund-raising, including events in the Victoria Hall, led to the building of the Cromarty Cottage Hospital on land donated by Walter Ross. A. Maitland & Sons advertised for tenders for the hospital in 1893, their designs said to have been an adaptation of plans by Mr Butler of Dublin, and they supervised the building of a 'neat and comfortable cottage hospital' which was opened in June 1894.[42]

In Evanton, another landlord, Major Randle Jackson of Swordale, 'a bluff, English north countryman with military bearing', was the prime mover in the construction of a public hall to commemorate the Diamond Jubilee of Queen Victoria in 1897. Jackson, as we will see later, had himself already engaged the Maitlands to design a mansion house, Swordale House. So it was perhaps no surprise that A. Maitland & Sons were commissioned to design the Diamond Jubilee Hall. But the planning of the hall sparked another controversy. Jackson, like the Maitland brothers, was a Unionist. He had contested the 1895 General Election as the Unionist party's candidate for the Ross & Cromarty constituency. He had fought a vigorous, though unsuccessful, campaign, during which he met considerable personal criticism. Among his opponents was another local landlord, also a client of the Maitlands - Ronald Munro Ferguson of Novar (later Viscount Novar), a Liberal who had been M.P. for the county in 1884-85 and had succeeded W.E. Gladstone as M.P. for the Leith Burghs in 1886. Novar and his factor were accused by the pro-Unionist *Ross-shire Journal* of standing outside the polling booth trying to influence voters, many of whom would have been tenants, against Jackson. The animosity continued during meetings on the hall, leading to Jackson suing Novar's factor, John Meiklejohn, for slander. Jackson averred that Meiklejohn had accused him and another trustee of a dishonest scheme to gain control of the hall in order to enable them to use it for sectarian and other purposes in defraud of the purposes for which money had been subscribed. The Court of Session did not accept Jackson's interpretation of Meiklejohn's remarks and awarded costs against him.[43]

The foundation stone of the Diamond Jubilee Hall was laid on the penultimate day of the Jubilee year by Jackson's daughter, Annie Constance. The hall was completed in November, 1898. It cost about £800 to build and was designed to seat 500 people. The *Ross-shire Journal* reported that the opening ceremony included a concert to which Major Jackson brought his gramophone, which was new to the audience who 'marvelled much at the speaking and singing machine'. A prominent feature inside the hall is a life-scale painting of the magnificently be-whiskered Major Randle Jackson, clutching (appropriately for a former captain of the St Andrews and St Duthus [Tain] Golf Clubs) the blade of a iron club.

Four miles away in Alness another public hall was also the subject of controversy. The Rosskeen Parish Council deemed an existing hall gifted by Sir Kenneth Matheson to be too small and in need of renovation, and wished to convert it into cottages and build a bigger hall. Strong objections were raised, and in 1896 Mr Maitland (which one was not specified) was called in to report. He recommended building a new hall and was asked to produce plans. These were accepted and a new hall 'of no mean pretensions', costing £1,100, was opened in 1898. The opening ceremony was conducted by Major Randle Jackson under the 'genial presidency' of Andrew Mackenzie of Dalmore, for whom the Maitlands had rebuilt a distillery and designed a new mansion house. The hall, 'seated for the accommodation about 500 persons', had what Gifford describes as 'an agreeably old-fashioned Georgian castellated detail on the gable front'.[44] The debt incurred by the parish council was soon paid off by fund raising, towards which the Maitland firm contributed by knocking £14 off their business account. The hall is now used by youth groups.

References and Notes

[1] Highland Archive Centre, BTN 1/1/1 to 4.

[2] See Estelle Quick, *The Tain Silver Collection in Tain & District Museum*, Tain & District Museum Trust, 2012, particularly pp.89-90.

3 *Inverness Courier*, 1st January, 1857, 20th August, 1863, and 11th February, 1864.

4 *Inverness Courier*, 16th February, 1865.

5 *Inverness Courier*, 17th October, 1867, 23rd January, 1868 and 4th August, 1870. Historic Environment Scotland LB41710.

6 *Inverness Courier*, 13th June, 1872.

7 Highland Archive Centre CRC 9/3/3/5/3.

8 *Inverness Advertiser*, 4th March, 1873.

9 William T. Russell, *My Brothers Past*, vol. 1, 1761-1899, Librario Publishing Ltd, 2002, pp.85-86.

10 *Inverness Courier*, 3rd December, 1857.

11 *Inverness Courier*, 17th October, 1872.

12 Information provided on the Dictionary of Scottish Architects website, scottisharchitectcts.org.uk by Alexander MacKenzie's great granddaughter, Morag Cruden.

13 *Aberdeen Journal*, 27th August, 1873.

14 Information from the Rev. John MacLeod, great grandson of William Fraser.

15 Historic Environment Scotland LB41858.

16 The Rev. R.W.A. Begg, *Parish of Tain* in *Third Statistical Account of Scotland, Ross & Cromarty*, Edinburgh 1987.

17 Gifford, *Highlands and Islands*, p.66.

18 *Inverness Courier*, 17th February, 1870.

19 William T. Russell, *op. cit.*, p.86.

20 *Inverness Advertiser,* 31st March, 1874.

21 *Inverness Courier*, 20th January, 1876.

22 Highland HER MHG16708, Historic Environment Scotland LB41918.

23 Gifford, *Highlands and Islands*, p.461.

24 Harry Gordon Slade, *The Collegiate Church of St Duthac of Tain and The Abbey of Fearn*, Tain & District Museum Trust, 2000, pp.19-20.

25 The Rev. William Taylor, *Researches into the History of Tain: Earlier and Later*, John Menzies & Co., 1882, p.51.

26 Documents on indefinite loan from the Tain & District Museum in Historic Environment Scotland archives, RCD 122/5, 122/3 and 122/4.

27 Harry Gordon Slade*, op. cit*., p.20.

28 Plans, lent by the Tain & District Museum, held by Historic Environment Scotland; tenders sought *Inverness Courier* 1st January 1885; Historic Environment Scotland LB41844; Highland HER MHG42329.

29 *Inverness Courier*, 22nd January, 1886.

30 Gifford, *Highlands and Islands*, p.460. Historic Environment Scotland LB41868.

31 *Ross-shire Journal*, 13th September, 1895.

32 W. Macgill, *Old Ross-shire and Scotland as seen in the Tain and Balnagown Documents*, The Northern Counties Newspaper and Publishing Company, Limited, 1909, No. 955 identifies the original site as 'in the present High Street near its south side, or even further, and close to ex-Bailie W. Ross's present property'; the property, now no. 5, has a commemorative plaque on the wall.

33 Magistrates of Banff v Ruthin Castle Ltd, 1944, quoted in Andy Wightman, *The Poor had no Lawyers*, Birlinn Ltd 2010, pp.220-21.

34 Highland HER MHG8676; Historic Environment Scotland LB44944; *Inverness Courier,* 1st January, 1885.

35 *Inverness Courier*, 1st January, 1885.

36 *Ross-shire Journal*, 17th May 1889.

37 *Inverness Courier*, 3rd June, 1892.

38 *Inverness Courier*, 29th May, 1879. The drill hall has sometimes been identified with the Gair Memorial Hall in Bonar Bridge. This latter was built in 1915 as a Free Church hall and is still in use; it commemorated a local merchant, Robert Gair,

whose widow donated the feu and 'a substantial sum of money': *Aberdeen Weekly Journal*, 25th June 1915. Gifford, *Highlands and Islands*, p.558 ascribes the Gair Memorial Hall of 1915 to A. Maitland & Sons: this may well be correct, but the 1879 hall was certainly a Maitland building.

[39] David Alston, *My Little Town of Cromarty*, Birlinn Ltd, 2006, pp.270-73.

[40] *Northern Chronicle and General Advertiser for the North of Scotland*, 25th May and 21st December, 1887.

[41] Highland Council HER MHG21875.

[42] *Inverness Courier*, 23rd February, 1893, *Ross-shire Journal*, 29th June, 1894. The reference to Mr Butler comes from the *Dictionary of Scottish Architects* entry for Cromarty Cottage Hospital.

[43] The above account is based on a section on Kiltearn Gentry in the *Evanton Oral History Project, 1991-93*, edited for web in 2010, online at spanglefish.com/evantonoralhistoryproject. See also *Glasgow Herald*, 6th December, 1899.

[44] *Ross-shire Journal*, 7th August, 1896 and 1st April, 1898; Gifford, *op. cit.*, p.381.

13. COMMERCIAL NEEDS

Growing prosperity

In the last three decades of the nineteenth century the towns in which the Maitlands operated saw an acceleration in the rate of construction not just of new public buildings but also - reflecting a wider level of prosperity - of commercial buildings.

The most prominent of these were banks. John Gifford remarks that 'rapid expansion of the banking system during the nineteenth century quickly established the rule that a bank in any prominent town should have the character of a public building'.[1] The Maitlands designed three banks that conformed to this pattern - one of them, unwittingly, for the use of a bank agent who was defrauding his customers.

Among other commercial buildings designed by the Maitlands during these decades were an unusually grand warehouse in Tain and an office for the Maitlands themselves. What is often described as 'Andrew Maitland's office' is a picturesque and often remarked feature of the Tain townscape, but its origins have been widely misunderstood.

The most numerous commercial buildings of these decades were, however, shops. Up-grades to shops were frequent when businesses prospered or ownership changed, though these are seldom well documented. Even when architects are known to have been employed it is often not possible to discern which premises were involved. Thus invitations to tender for work on shops in Bonar Bridge, Alness and Hill of Fearn were published in newspapers of the period, but we know relatively little about them. We know more, however, about several commissions in Tain undertaken by the Maitlands in this period. These show that in the late nineteenth century successful merchants in the burgh, often from humble backgrounds, were among those who could afford to employ architects. Many of these merchants played a prominent role in local affairs - particularly as burgh councillors, elders of the Free Church, and members of school boards - and in the freemasons.

The banks extend their branch networks ...

Commissions from banks received by the Maitlands in the 1870s included three lots of alterations and improvements to the well-established Commercial Bank in Tain (dating from 1828 and now the Highland Council Service Point), and also improvements to the Bank of Scotland in Beauly and to the British Linen Company's bank in Golspie. But now, with the growth of commerce, banks were extending their branch networks, sometimes adapting existing premises, sometimes erecting new buildings. One bank expanding its network was the Aberdeen based North of Scotland Bank, later merged into the Clydesdale Bank. In 1872 the Maitlands designed a new branch for the North of Scotland Bank in the Invergordon High Street.[2] It was immediately opposite the Town Hall which James Maitland had designed two years previously. The bank was a gabled building with three storeys, presumably to allow accommodation for the bank agent. A century later its ground floor has been wrecked by a hideous extension.

In Tain Andrew Maitland Junior signed plans on 1st October, 1878 for a new branch of the North of Scotland Bank opposite the arcaded market in Market Street.[3] Ironically, on that same evening the City of

Glasgow Bank, in which Andrew Maitland Senior and James were shareholders with unlimited liability, closed its doors for the last time. Over the next few weeks the story of the vast scale of the bank's deficiency, the fraudulent conduct of the directors, and the liabilities of shareholders all over Scotland unravelled with terrifying consequences. As we saw earlier, the collapse of the City of Glasgow Bank wiped out much of the savings Andrew Senior had accumulated over the past three decades and led to James becoming bankrupt.

Whatever feelings the Maitland family may have had about the mis-management of banks or the liability of their shareholders did not, however, disrupt the completion of the new North of Scotland Bank branch. On 21st November A. Maitland & Sons advertised for tenders.[4] The two earlier nineteenth century banks in Tain, the Commercial Bank and the British Linen Company's Bank, had been sizeable, classical buildings designed not just to accommodate a banking function but also to provide office and residential space for bank agents appropriate to their role as factors and advisers to the major estates in the area. The new bank, one of six banks in Tain by 1882, was a more modestly sized single-storey building reflecting the banking requirements of a growing volume of commercial and private customers.[5] The part of the building visible from the street contained the telling-room at the left and an office for George MacLeay, a member of the Tain Burgh Council and one of the two solicitors who acted as part-time joint-agents, at the right. Behind this were safes, a lobby and offices for the other joint-agent, Murdoch Mackenzie, and for law-clerks. But the exterior elevations show that the bank was determined not to be outdone stylistically by its older rivals, paying for what Gifford calls 'a fine Renaissance presence disproportionate to its size'.[6] A distinctive feature in this, one of the more charming buildings in Tain, is the use of ornate cast-iron cresting on the ridge and cast-iron railings at the front elevation.

Sadly the Clydesdale Bank has now closed its Tain branch and the future of the building is uncertain.

... and the Dornoch banker who had his fingers in the till

On the other side of the Meikle Ferry Dornoch was emerging from the doldrums. Until 1868 the Dukes of Sutherland had been Provosts, but in that year the first (moderately) democratic elections were held. The middle classes slowly began to flex their muscles. The later years of the nineteenth century saw a rising prosperity, fuelled particularly by the attractions of the golf course. This was to lead to several commissions, particularly for houses, for the Maitlands. It also led to another expanding bank, also Aberdeen based, the Town & County Bank, opening a branch in Dornoch. In 1889 the bank appointed as joint agent John Mackintosh, a farmer at Proncy, three miles from Dornoch. Mackintosh seemed to be highly respectable: he was a total abstainer and lived an unostentatious life, and he became commander of a company of Volunteers, Clerk of the School Board, and a county councillor. But, unbeknown to the bank's directors, Mackintosh was soon embezzling their customers' money.

Mackintosh's fellow joint agent was a Dornoch solicitor, John Leslie. Leslie served for ten years as captain of the Royal Dornoch Golf Club, and was said to have been responsible for an important step in 1886 when the services of the legendary golfer Old Tom Morris were secured and the course was extended to 18 holes. In 1893, whilst Mackintosh's fraud remained undetected, Leslie decided to build new premises in Castle Street, the main entrance to the town. A. Maitland & Sons produced plans and sought tenders for a new classical style building.[7] Inside were bank offices, which Leslie let to the Town & County Bank, law offices and living accommodation for himself and his family. Beaton describes it as a 'plain, somewhat conventional bank building, the symmetrical two-storey front enhanced by simple pilastered doorpiece and tri-partite (three-light) ground floor windows'.[8] John Leslie, who had become Sheriff Clerk of Sutherland, died in 1900 and John Mackintosh then became sole agent.

There was great excitement in Dornoch in March 1908 when Mackintosh was arrested and committed to Inverness Prison. In May he pleaded guilty in the High Court of Justiciary to having embezzled a total of £1,753-2s-6d between 1889 and 1907. In mitigation his counsel asserted that in regard to at least half of the deficiency Mackintosh had not personally fingered a penny of the money. A number of customers had overdrawn accounts. The bank had strict rules and had instructed him that certain customers should not be accommodated. In order to oblige them, however, Mackintosh had honoured cheques and bills drawn on their accounts and had met these by paying into their accounts money taken from other customers. Mackintosh might have expected a sentence of penal servitude (imprisonment with hard labour), but the Lord Justice Clerk, apparently impressed by this Robin Hood argument and perhaps also by Mackintosh's colonelcy in the Volunteers, sentenced him to only 15 months imprisonment.

Like the North of Scotland Bank, the Town & County Bank later became part of the Clydesdale Bank, but the Dornoch branch no longer operates. The building, now listed,[9] and the first in a series of dignified premises flanking the approach to the centre of Dornoch, is now a bed and breakfast establishment.

A warehouse for William Russell Ross

The first identifiable commission received by the Maitland partnership from a merchant was for a warehouse in Tain for William Russell Ross, a fellow councillor of Andrew Maitland Junior and a former Treasurer of the burgh. Ross dealt in a surprisingly wide range of goods. Directories of the period show that these included groceries, wines and spirits, leather goods, seeds, and coal, and that he was an agent for Pullars of Perth, dyers. He traded from and lived in elegant premises at 16-18, Tower Street (a listed building which is now a solicitors' office). These initially belonged to the widow of a former grocer and leather merchant, whose maiden name was Russel (sic) and could have been related, but William Russell Ross later appears to have acquired ownership.

This was the age of 'High Farming', a system of agriculture - explored in other chapters of this book - which depended on technical and scientific advances. Crop yields were enhanced by chemicals and manures, including guano, and animal husbandry was improved by feeds, particularly ones extracted from vegetable oil crops. Suppliers to farmers could prosper, and William Russell Ross, himself a farmer's son, appears to have seen the opportunities in a prime agricultural area like Easter Ross. His Tower Street premises with cellars below were clearly inadequate for storing bulkier agricultural products, and in 1884 he engaged A. Maitland & Sons to design a warehouse.[10]

13.1 William Russell Ross's warehouse (centre right) and the Tain Public Shambles (centre left), both Maitland-designed.

This was in Shore Road, and it was convenient for the station. Part had three storeys and part two storeys, and it included stores for guano and manure, and above them an oil cake or seed store, a hay loft and a grain or seed store. It had stables in one of the side wings and was surrounded by a yard with a cart shed and coal stores. As with the nearby Maitland-designed Public Shambles or Slaughterhouse, the exterior was remarkably ornate for such a functional building. As the description in Historic Environment Scotland's *Scran* service points out, the use of inset arches on the main elevations reduces the apparent bulk of the building and enhances its status.[11]

Ross's business appears to have prospered. When he died intestate aged 68 in 1896 he left the substantial sum of £17,665-18s-5d, and he was buried beneath the grandest monument in the old cemetery in Tain. In the years following his death his building was used for a variety of commercial purposes, and early in the twenty-first century it was tastefully converted into flats and re-named The Granary.

'Andrew Maitland's office'

There is an eye-catching Arts and Crafts style building in Tain at the corner of Tower Street and Rose Street which is widely regarded as having been Andrew Maitland Senior's office. Thus the Historic Environment Scotland listing describes it as 'Built as architect's office of Andrew Maitland of Tain (d.1894), perhaps in 1870s. Cottage style building in Andrew Maitland's distinctive picturesque style with decorative barge-boards and timber-framed, painted walls, slated roofs with deep eaves and red ridge tiles'.[12] Both the assumption that Andrew Senior designed this office for his own use and the dating to around 1870 are almost universal, though John Gifford, who remarks that the building 'seems to have escaped from the seaside', puts it at c.1900.[13]

Documents of the period indicate that Gifford's dating is rather more accurate.

Andrew Senior's Will, which he signed in December, 1891, shows the location of the practice's office at that date. He left to his only surviving daughter Christina possession and occupancy of his house in Esther Place so long as she remained unmarried. But 'the furniture of the business office in the said dwelling house with all the drawing instruments, drawings, plans, specifications, business papers and Architectural books and works, so far as belonging to me' were left to James and Andrew Junior. His Will further provided that 'So long as during the occupancy of said dwelling house by my said daughter my sons the said James Maitland and Andrew Maitland Junior shall continue to occupy the business office therein they or he shall be bound to pay my said daughter a rent of Ten pounds *per annum* for the use thereof and the supply of fire and gas thereto'. It is clear from this that as late as the end of 1891 the office in Andrew Senior's house in Esther Place on the first floor of the 1856-57 extension was not only that of Andrew Senior but also that of his sons.

Further evidence comes from the *Ross-shire Journal.* It reported in July 1893 that 'the masons have now commenced work on Messrs Maitlands' new offices in Academy Street, and these, when finished will no doubt add greatly to the amenity of the town, and especially to the part in which it is situated'.[14] When the new office was finished Andrew Junior installed the first telephone in the district, linking it with his other main place of work, the Glenmorangie Distillery.[15]

The last project in which Andrew Senior took an interest was the construction of a new Tain Free Church, now the parish church, in 1891-92. We can be absolutely certain, therefore, that, notwithstanding the weight of expert opinion to the contrary, Andrew Senior did not design this building or use it as his office, that James and Andrew Junior built it in 1893-94 following their father's retirement and that it was completed shortly before his death.

The Valuation Rolls show that the office continued to be used by A. Maitland & Sons into the 1920s, even after the the last Maitlands had retired. The building was later used as the Procurator Fiscal's Office, until it was damaged by a fire which - so legend has it - was started by a ne'er-do -well who thought he might escape punishment if the records were destroyed.[16] The Highland Buildings Preservation Trust later acquired it for £1 and found funding of £153,000 early in the present century to restore it. The external panels were painted in their original terracotta colouring. The building was then sold, very appropriately, to another architect. Notwithstanding this, at the time of writing the future use of the building - variously described as Andrew Maitland's Office, the Procurator Fiscal's Office and the Red House - is uncertain.

13.2 The office, in Arts & Crafts style, built in Tain in 1893-94 by the Maitland brothers when their father retired.

Shops in Tain

In the early nineteenth century most shops in Tain, as in towns throughout Scotland, had been converted from residential accommodation, occupying the ground floor of houses of two or more storeys or single-storey cottages. This often meant low ceilings, narrow windows and a poor display of goods. As the century developed architects began to design purpose-built shops with residential accommodation above. With improvements in glass technology it became possible to abandon astragal frames and to use large sheets of glass to lighten shops and facilitate window displays. By the 1890s the Maitlands were designing such premises.

One such commission was in Tower Street, Tain, where 'handsome and commodious premises prepared for the Post Office ... adjoining the County and Municipal Buildings' were opened in May 1894.[17] The interior design was said to reflect great credit on the architects, Messrs A. Maitland & Sons. The premises were gutted by fire only six years later, so that our knowledge of the building is somewhat sketchy and derives mainly from reports of the fire.[18] The block was built for John Mitchell, who was a grocer and also postmaster. It contained a post office, Mitchell's shop and a printing works on the ground floor, and a dwelling house on the upper floors. The building was restored after the fire, to give us the present Tower

Buildings, 24-28 Tower Street.[19] The post office remained there until it was replaced by a Maitland-designed post office in the High Street in 1910.

Another fire, in January 1895, on the north side of the High Street, at premises numbered 18 and 20 which were owned by Bailie Donald G. Munro, also led to work for the Maitland partnership. The tenant was Andrew MacDuff Ross, who had married Andrew Maitland Senior's daughter Henrietta Margaret in December 1890 - a short-lived marriage as Henrietta Margaret had died in November 1891. MacDuff Ross carried on a drapery business in the premises, which were known as London House. The fire was massive and destroyed the building. Munro's loss was apparently covered by insurance, but that of MacDuff Ross was understood to be only partially covered by two policies of the gross value of £1,600. The adjoining premises occupied by William Ross, a jeweller, were also damaged. The watching crowd burst open his door and carried out the stock to the street, and many articles were broken and damaged.[20]

During this year Andrew MacDuff Ross re-located to temporary premises, remarried, and secured election to the burgh council. In 1896 he purchased premises on the south side of the High Street, where he lived above the shop. Numbers 13, 15 and 17 became the new London House. It retains the name to-day, and there are still metal plates below the plate glass windows engraved with the name 'A. MacDUFF ROSS & SONS'. The elegance of the premises suggests that MacDuff Ross involved his Maitland former brothers-in-law in the refurbishment of the building.

Meanwhile William Ross took the opportunity to build his own premises, and the Maitlands were definitely involved. The son of a master carpenter, William Ross had set up business in 1888. As well as being a jeweller he was also a silversmith, a watch maker and an optician. Within a few years he had prospered sufficiently to own a family house (and also a guano store) in Moss Road and another house round the corner in Hill Street, occupied by his father. He was also a keen supporter of the then fashionable sport of cycling, being a prime mover of the Easter Ross Cycling Club, of which he was secretary and treasurer, Andrew Maitland Junior a vice-president and James Maitland a member. Some cyclists rode 'pneumatics', others 'cushions'. An advance guard of local cyclists, no doubt including Ross, escorted the Prime Minister (the Earl of Rosebery) and the Duke of Sutherland from the Meikle Ferry to the Royal Hotel when they received the freedom of the burgh of Tain in September 1894. In August 1896, A. Maitland & Sons advertised for tenders for new buildings for William Ross, jeweller, at 18 and 20 High Street.

The result, named Victoria Buildings, was a three-storey building with a door in the centre giving access to the upper floors and shop fronts on each side of it.[21] The style of the facade was French Renaissance and its detailing remarkable for a building of this type. William Ross himself occupied the shop on the left and his name remains on a mosaic floor at the entrance. The shop on the right was let (a later tenant being the Bank of Scotland, whose name also appears on a mosaic floor), as was the upstairs accommodation. The *Ross-shire Journal* gave a glowing report of the opening in October 1897: it attracted a constant stream of purchasers and well-wishers for three hours, the like of which had never been seen in the ancient burgh, all determined to see a collection of the freshest and most rare jewellery ever shown in the north. William Ross later extended his business to Invergordon and the ultra-fashionable spa resort of Strathpeffer. Like the Maitland brothers, he became Master of the St Duthus Lodge, a councillor and (in 1924-30) Provost of Tain. He was always seen with a hat, being known as 'Willie Hattie'. Given to Spoonerisms, he once managed, on a visit to Dingwall, to leave his dings at Bagwall.

Another Tain merchant who prospered sufficiently to build new premises was James Robertson. The son of a farm servant, he advertised in June 1877 that he had opened a 'Baking Business in all its Plain and Fancy Branches' in King Street. He hoped 'by diligent attention to business, good workmanship and by only using the finest flour, to merit a large share of the public patronage'. Twenty years later this hope had clearly came to fruition. In 1897 he was able to commission the Maitlands to design Gladstone Buildings, on a prominent site beside his bakehouse at the top of King Street and facing down Queen Street - in a style which Gifford calls 'endearingly dumpy Renaissance'.[22] The new building,[23] with cellarage below and residential accommodation above, was large enough for two shops, one being let to a draper and the other used by Robertson himself for his bakery and confectionery business. At a celebratory dinner James Maitland proposed the health of Bailie James Robertson (who was to succeed him as Provost in 1921). John Mackenzie proposed the health of the architect, James Maitland, 'a worthy successor to his widely known and greatly esteemed father, the late Andrew Maitland Senior'.

13.3 Gladstone Buildings, Tain, designed in 1897 by James Maitland for a baker.

Hotels around the Highlands

The latter part of the nineteenth century saw the building of new hotels and the re-building of existing ones across the Highlands on a hitherto unparalleled scale. The chief factor was clearly the growth of tourism, which was significantly boosted by the extension of the railway network.

One of the most important commission for a hotel received by the Maitlands was for a new Royal Hotel in Tain, an integral part of the transformation of the town centre which we explored earlier. Other commissions included ones in 1885 for 'alterations and large additions' and in 1894 for further additions to the Bridge Hotel at Bonar Bridge,[24] and in 1895 for 'extensive additions' to the Sutherland Arms Hotel, which, until it was destroyed by fire, closed off the main square in Dornoch.[25]

In 1896 the Maitland brothers prepared plans for a new venture in a scenic location, Marine Terrace in Cromarty. In the 1820s the buildings on the site had included an inn tenanted by their maternal grandfather, George Andrews. They drew up 'very elaborate plans for the adaptation of the premises into a first-class family and tourist hotel, a want which is very much felt in Cromarty'. The improvements, for Mrs Davidson, the new owner of what became the Royal Hotel, were 'on a very extensive scale. … When it is completed it will be one of the most attractive and comfortable hotels in the north'.[26]

The Maitland legacy lives on, moreover, in several Highland hotels which were originally designed as private houses. As we will see in later chapters, the Morangie House and Mansfield House (later styled

'Castle') Hotels in Tain, the Kincraig House (also later styled 'Castle') Hotel near Invergordon and the Tulloch Castle (a genuine historic castle) Hotel in Dingwall were all private residences designed or substantially added to and/or altered by the Maitlands.

But the best known Maitland hotels were in Gairloch. Their story is an interesting one, worthy of a separate chapter.

References and Notes

[1] Gifford, *Highlands and Islands*, p.68.

[2] *Inverness Advertiser*, 11th March, 1872, Highland HER MHG21245.

[3] The plans are held by Historic Environment Scotland, RCD/36/1-4.

[4] *Inverness Courier*, 21st November, 1878.

[5] Historic Environment Scotland LB41890.

[6] Gifford, *op. cit.*, p. 461.

[7] *Inverness Courier*, 6th June, 1893.

[8] Beaton, *Sutherland*, p.33.

[9] Historic Environment Scotland LB24635, Highland HER MHG16970.

[10] *Inverness Courier*, 21st August, 1884. Listed Building (B) 41903, Highland HER MHG8687.

[11] *Scran* ID 000-000-187-419-C.

[12] Historic Environment Scotland LB41912, Highland HER MHG 22764.

[13] Gifford, *Highlands and Islands*, p.461.

[14] *Ross-shire Journal*, 28th July, 1893 and 4th May, 1894. Further evidence as to the date of the building comes from the Valuation Rolls. There is no sign of any Maitland office separate from Andrew Senior's house before 1894/95. The Valuation Rolls for that year show for the first time an office belonging to A. Maitland & Sons in Tower Street. These Rolls would have been surveyed between the autumn of 1893 and the summer of 1894. Map evidence also supports this interpretation, the Maitland office first appearing in the 25 inch to the mile Ordnance Survey Map, surveyed in 1904.

[15] *Inverness Courier*, 1st May, 1894.

[16] Information from Margaret Urquhart.

[17] *Ross-shire Journal*, 25th May, 1894.

[18] *The Scotsman*, 21st February, 1900, *Ross-shire Journal*, 23rd February, 1900.

[19] The Historic Environment Scotland description for LB41919 gives a somewhat different account of the building, describing it as a mid nineteenth century terrace, raised to three storeys circa 1870-80, but the sources for this are not given.

[20] *Glasgow Herald*, 23rd January, 1895.

[21] *Inverness Courier* 4th August, 1896; Historic Environment Scotland LB41869, Highland HER MHG22847.

[22] Gifford, *Highlands and Islands*, p.462.

[23] Highland HER MHG22830.

[24] *Inverness Courier*, 2nd April, 1885, 24th May, 1885 and 5th June, 1894.

[25] *Ross-shire Journal*, 24th May, 1895.

[26] *Ross-shire Journal*, 15th May, 1896.

14. GAIRLOCH - AND A HOTEL FIT FOR A QUEEN

The parish of Gairloch

In 1872 Andrew Maitland sought tenders for two hotels in the parish of Gairloch in Wester Ross. Two years later A. Maitland & Sons were commissioned to design a third, and eight years later a major extension to one of them. Woven into the history of the construction and operation of the Gairloch hotels are the stories of a powerful and enterprising landlord and of an entrepreneurial hotelier who entertained no less a person than Queen Victoria - but who fell spectacularly from grace.

John Dixon of Inveran published in 1886 a guide to the parish of Gairloch - a minor classic which presents a vivid picture of the area, including the three Maitland hotels and the pursuits and tourist attractions which lured their guests to Gairloch.[1] The parish was 30 miles long and 15 miles wide, with 'no town in the ordinary acceptation of the term' but about 34 villages or townships, 29 of which were on the coast and mainly dependent on fishing. The great changes of recent decades - the wider electoral franchise, the dominance of the Free Church, the poor law reforms, and the educational reforms - had brought a wider participation in local governance, but Dixon had little to say about the new participants. This clearly reflected the fact that virtually the whole of the parish was owned by a mere three heritors, whose influence was still paramount. Although the Maitlands were to win commissions from the school board and Free Church congregations in Gairloch, the middle classes still lacked the numbers and the individual and collective clout - and the propensity to commission new buildings - so evident on the east coast, not least in and around Tain.

Sir Kenneth Mackenzie - an enterprising landlord

The principal heritor, owning more than three-quarters of the parish, was Sir Kenneth Smith Mackenzie of Gairloch, 6th Baronet. Sir Kenneth was the 13th Laird of Gairloch and in direct line of descent from the redoubtable warrior Hector Roy Mackenzie, who had received a grant of lands in Gairloch from James IV in 1494. When Sir Kenneth was 11 his father had died. On coming of age in 1853 he had succeeded to the vast Gairloch estate in Wester Ross and the Conan estate near Beauly. A survey by the Land Ownership Commission in 1872-73 shows him owning 164,680 acres in Ross-shire. At the ripe old age of 24 he was appointed Chairman of the Commissioners of Supply and Convenor of Ross & Cromarty. In these capacities, and through his later appointments as Convenor of the Ross & Cromarty County Council and Lord Lieutenant, he became one of the prime movers of the county in the second half of the nineteenth century.

Sir Kenneth was the half-brother of Osgood Mackenzie of Inverewe, whom we met in an earlier chapter. He was to take the side of Osgood's wife Minna in the acrimonious divorce battle between them. Osgood nevertheless wrote that Sir Kenneth was 'far and away the most esteemed man in the county of Ross' and that he 'was at the head of everything that was good'.[2]

But Sir Kenneth had an uphill task. His father had been overwhelmed by financial problems and had died in an asylum. The Gairloch estate was critically dependent on rental income from crofters and suffered from an increasing population, poverty, and rents not being paid - a situation that had been exacerbated by the agricultural depression of the 1840s. The estate was entailed and could not be sold to raise cash.[3]

Sir Kenneth transformed the financial situation, but still managed to gain a reputation as a 'kindly landlord' with a 'generous and enlightened system of estate management'. His system of estate management included maximising his rental income from sporting activities and from the growth of tourism. Alexander Mackenzie, the leading Mackenzie historian of the nineteenth century, computed that in the 26 years from 1853 Sir Kenneth's rental income more than doubled from £4,671 to £9,387, with the contribution from angling and shooting on the Gairloch estate rising by £2,000.[4] The opportunities afforded at the three new hotels for angling and shooting must have contributed significantly to this, and in addition calculations based on the Valuation Rolls suggest that the contribution to rental income increased by some £950 as a direct result of Sir Kenneth's investment in the three hotels with which the Maitlands were involved.

Gairloch had in previous decades been popular with tourists, whose primary mode of access had been by steamers operating on the west coast. In 1870, however, the first stage of what became the Dingwall & Skye branch of the Highland Railway was completed, with a stop at Achnasheen, thus opening up the parish of Gairloch to visitors from Inverness and the south. Sir Kenneth saw the potential for travellers to be conveyed by mail-car the 10 miles from Achnasheen to Kinlochewe and the 29½ miles to the village of Gairloch, in each of which he owned small inns capable of extension or replacement, and also for building a new hotel beside the scenic Loch Maree. The mail-car was worked by Murdo M'Iver, described by Dixon as the 'much respected and courteous landlord of the Achnasheen Hotel' and as also offering open or close conveyances for hire by 'more luxurious tourists'.[5]

The hotels in Gairloch

Andrew Maitland Senior's work was well known to Sir Kenneth Mackenzie from his work for the Commissioners of Supply on police stations and court houses. He had, moreover, worked in Wester Ross for Sir John Fowler during the building of Braemore - and had almost certainly also been engaged by Sir Kenneth's step-mother to build the first Inverewe House for his half-brother Osgood Mackenzie. These connections no doubt explain why Andrew was commissioned to design the first two of Sir Kenneth's hotels, a replacement for the Gairloch Hotel and the new Loch Maree Hotel. Invitations to tender for work on both hotels appeared in February 1872.[6]

The Gairloch Hotel, tall and imposing and in a Jacobean style, was built on a fine site across the road from the beach at Loch Gairloch, a sea loch, and it enjoyed magnificent views of Skye. The hotel, 'now nearly complete', was advertised to let with entry at 26th May, 1873. The principal rooms were 1st and 2nd class coffee rooms downstairs, 18 bedrooms and one bathroom on the first floor, 10 bedrooms on the second floor and one bathroom, and above that seven attic bedrooms but no bathrooms. Something must have gone wrong very quickly, for in October James Munro, an Inverness draper 'and presently lessee and occupant of the Gairloch Hotel' was listed among Scotch bankrupts. By January 1874, however, the hotel had been let to James Hornsby, 'late of the King's Arms, Oban'.[7] Hornsby was soon advertising not only the beauties of the area but also the 'bathing machines and excellent sea-bathing on one of the finest beaches in Scotland'.

The Loch Maree Hotel, a gabled building in distinctive red sandstone, was smaller, with about twenty bedrooms, and was aimed at a more exclusive clientele. It was splendidly situated on the side of one of the most attractive lochs in Scotland and had fine views of the 3,218 feet Slioch and the islands of Loch Maree. One of the main attractions was fishing on the loch, which abounded in sea-trout and salmon. James Hornsby took a lease of this second hotel and was assisted for some years by his brother Robert.

14.1 The Loch Maree Hotel, with the Royal coat of arms on the chimney.

A writer in *The Scotsman* in 1875 noted that 'the landlord was a genial stout man with a keen eye, a handsome face, a well-shaped head, light brown hair and an unobtrusive manner'. The guests included 'a Dorsetshire baronet who had done the State some service - a man of the world in the best sense of that much-abused phrase … an ironmaster from Yorkshire, with a well-balanced judgement … and a man who had spent many years of his life in New Zealand, and who with his wife and handsome little daughter was out for a run through the Highlands'. The coffee room was 'a pleasant place at meal times', and Sir Kenneth had shown 'good judgement in placing the hotel where it is - opening up Loch Maree to the holiday maker and the angler'.[8]

The third hotel investment by Sir Kenneth was at Kinlochewe, a small village at the head of Loch Maree. There had long been an inn at Kinlochewe; but, as a press report of 1872 indicated, 'the dining-room of this hotel is not very spacious - in fact a newspaper spread out would nearly touch the four corners of it … [although] the pensive traveller may regale himself with a luncheon of excellent mutton, adding a trifle of Highland whisky, if he be so inclined'.[9] A. Maitland & Sons were awarded a contract for 'large alterations and additions' in 1875.[10] The hotel remained, however, the least significant of the three Maitland hotels in the parish of Gairloch, though Dixon regarded it as 'exceedingly comfortable' and noted that visitors had the privilege of fishing in the upper parts of Loch Maree.

The Maitland family would have followed with great interest the extensive newspaper coverage in 1877 of a stay at one of the three hotels with which they had been involved.

Queen Victoria's visit

Queen Victoria stayed in the Loch Maree Hotel from 12th to 18th September, 1877, she and her party taking over the entire hotel. This was to be the last in a series of royal excursions from Balmoral to other parts of the Highlands. The Queen's private secretary, Major-General Sir Henry Ponsonby, had sought advice from Sir Kenneth Mackenzie as to the relative merits of the Achnasheen Hotel, and two hotels owned by Sir Kenneth, the Kinlochewe Inn and the Loch Maree Hotel. Not surprisingly Sir Kenneth recommended the most suitable of his own properties.[11]

In her diary, extracts from which she published in 1884 and dedicated 'to my loyal Highlanders and especially to the memory of my devoted personal attendant and faithful friend John Brown', the Queen described the visit.[12] The hotel, she wrote, 'is a very nice little house, neatly furnished. To the left, as you enter, are two good rooms - a large one called the coffee-room, in which we take our meals, and another, smaller, next to it, in which the gentlemen dine. Up the winding staircase to the right come small, though comfortable, rooms. To the left [Princess] Beatrice's, and Brown's just opposite to the right. Then up three steps is a small passage; at the end to the left is my sitting-room, looking on to the loch, and to *Ben Sleach* [Slioch] and the road; it is very full of my things. At the other end is my bedroom, with two small rooms between for Wilmore and Annie'.

14.2 '*Loch Maree from the Hotel*', painted in September 1877 by H.M. Queen Victoria.

During the visit the Queen went for drives and walks, sketched, painted, read and wrote. Her activities on the Sunday caused some controversy. In anticipation of a royal visit the Gairloch parish church saw the biggest attendance since the Disruption, but the Queen did not attend, preferring to pray privately. 'At half past four', the Queen wrote, 'Beatrice, the Duchess of Roxburghe and I started in a four-oared gig, steered by Hornsby, the landlord, a very nice, quiet, youngish man, and rowed to the Isle of Maree'. Using a hammer they inserted into the bark of an old tree known as the wishing-tree a copper coin 'as a sort of offering to the saint who lived there in the eighth century, called Saint Maolruabh or Mulroy'. Such an outing on a Sunday caused some upset in an area dominated by the Free Church.

Two days later, 'at a quarter to nine we left with regret our nice cozy little hotel at Loch Maree, which I hope I may some day see again'. She never saw it again. But to commemorate her visit Sir Kenneth Mackenzie had a boulder of Torridon red sandstone carved with an inscription in Gaelic, literally translated by Dixon as follows:-

On the twelfth day of the middle month of autumn 1877 Queen Victoria came to visit Loch Maree and the country round it. She remained six nights in the opposite hotel, and, in her kindness, agreed that this stone should be a memorial of the pleasure she experienced in coming to this corner of Ross.

The hotel's frontage was later also decorated with a gilded Royal coat of arms - no doubt the only Maitland building so distinguished.

Hornsby's hotels prosper

The Maitlands received a further commission in 1878 to design a smoking-room and laundry for the Loch Maree Hotel.[13] Hornsby had a big problem, however, at the Gairloch Hotel, where the accommodation was insufficient for the masses of tourists who piled into Gairloch. A visitor reported in October 1876 that 'a week or two before 15 ladies had to sleep together in a drawing-room, and any number of gentlemen were billeted in the dining and smoking rooms'.[14] By September 1880 'A Weary Traveller' was complaining vociferously in *The Times* that 'at the only Gairloch hotel five beds were put into one small room (a sort of garret lit from the top). Each guest was charged the full value of the room. One of my party, affrighted at the prospect, asked if he might sleep in a bathroom, but was told they were all fully engaged. The guests in the sitting-room were turned out early to put beds in them. Sixty passengers have been landed late at night when there were only three rooms at liberty.'[15]

14.3 The Gairloch Hotel after the 1880 additions.

This was clearly the *raison d'être* of a further commission, in 1880, for the Maitland partnership to design substantial additions to the Gairloch Hotel.[16] After these were completed the hotel had sleeping accommodation for 150 visitors.

John Dixon devoted 50 pages of his guide to Gairloch to describing the approaches to and the excursions from Gairloch, with particular focus on the three hotels.[17] He also gave extensive coverage to the fishing, deer forests and grouse shooting available to visitors, and he waxed lyrical about excursions by steamer on Loch Maree, which afforded 'a means of viewing this queen of Highland lochs in a thorough and luxurious way'. The steamer was the *Mabel*, a 45 ft. steam launch built in 1882 and brought to Loch Maree by James Hornsby.

Hornsby's downfall - from Gairloch to Valparaiso

1886 saw the start of another widely reported story which the Maitlands would have followed with interest - and which might have been brought to the notice of the Queen. Two years after Her Majesty published her book, and in the same year as Dixon published his, both mentioning the hotelier with approval, James Hornsby's conduct began to be revealed in a different light.

Hornsby's estate was sequestrated on 15th September. In October he was subjected to a long and searching examination of his affairs, and he was summoned to appear in Dingwall for further examination. He failed to appear, sending a telegram from Euston saying that a letter would follow. It was alleged that he had put away large quantities of furniture and other goods, and a warrant was issued for his arrest. In Hornsby's absence dividends were paid to his creditors between 1887 and 1889.[18]

A clue as to where Hornsby had gone appears in an advertisement for an auction in the Glasgow City Sale-Rooms in July 1887. The items for sale included a costly ebonised Steinway grand pianoforte, solid silver communion plate, a powerful microscope, a theodolite and three rifles - all belonging to the sequestrated estate of James Hornsby, Gairloch, and recovered by order of David Rattray C.A. (trustee in the bankruptcy), from Valparaiso.[19] One can only admire the trustee's pertinacity - but was the recovery from Valparaiso cost-effective?

Two years later Hornsby's father, also James Hornsby, a builder at Gatehouse of Fleet, was sued for premiums on two life assurance policies which the younger James had assigned as security for advances in connection with his tenancy of one of the Gairloch hotels. It emerged that the elder James Hornsby had signed a blank sheet of paper sent to him by his son, which his son had then filled in as a guarantee of premiums on the policies. The Court of Session held that when the elder Hornsby signed he did not authorise a guarantee of payments and it absolved him of liability.[20]

Meanwhile a company had been formed to acquire a 10 years' lease of the Gairloch Hotel at the same rental (£657-17s-0d) as Hornsby had paid. Perhaps surprisingly, Hornsby's trustee in bankruptcy, David Rattray, was Managing Director of the new company. Its prospectus showed that Hornsby had drawn an average of £5,370-11s-0d per year in the last 4 years.[21] One is left wondering what on earth he had done with such large sums.

James Hornsby would recognise his hotels to-day. The Loch Maree Hotel, recently re-opened after years of uncertainty, still caters for the angler and those exploring the spectacular scenery. The Gairloch Hotel still has its fine views, and has recently returned to its original purpose after years of being used as a base for coach tours. And, as we will see in a later chapter, they have been joined as hotels by Shieldaig Lodge, a sporting lodge near Gairloch designed by the Maitlands for Sir Kenneth Mackenzie.

References and Notes

1   John H. Dixon, *Gairloch in North-West Ross-shire - Its Records, Traditions, Inhabitants, and Natural History, with a guide to Gairloch and Loch Maree*, Co-operative Printing Company, Edinburgh, 1886, reprinted Gairloch and District Heritage Society, 2004.

2   Osgood Hanbury Mackenzie of Inverewe, *A Hundred Years in the Highlands*, (first published 1921), republished Birlinn Ltd, 1995, pp.57-58.

3   For a good account See Pauline Butler, *Eighty Years in the Highlands, The Life and Times of Osgood H. Mackenzie of Inverewe, 1842-1922*, Librario Publishing Ltd, 2010, chapters I to V.

4   Alexander Mackenzie, article in *Celtic Magazine, 6* (1880), pp. 26-34 on Sir Kenneth S. Mackenzie of Gairloch, Bart.

5   John H. Dixon, *op. cit.*, p.301.

6   *Inverness Advertiser*, 27th February, 1872.

7   *The Scotsman*, 7th May, 1873; *Edinburgh Gazette*,7th October, 1873; *Inverness Advertiser*, 9th January, 1874.

8   *The Scotsman*, 31st August, 1875.

9   *London Daily News*, 21st August, 1872.

10   *Inverness Courier*, 9th December, 1875.

11   Pauline Butler, *op. cit.*, pp.311-12.

12   H. M. Queen Victoria, *More Leaves from the Journal of a Life in the Highlands*, Smith, Elder & Co., 1884, pp.334-58.

13   *Inverness Courier*, 28th February, 1878.

14   *Sheffield Daily Telegraph*, 19th October, 1876.

15   *The Times*, 8th September, 1880.

16   *Inverness Courier*, 14th December, 1880.

17   Dixon, *op. cit*, pp.299-349.

18   *Edinburgh Gazette*, 17th September, 1886, 31st May, 1887, 29th May, 1888, and 5th March, 1889; *Dundee Evening Telegraph*, 20th October, 1886; *Aberdeen Evening Express*, 26th October, 1886; *Scottish Highlander*, 25th November, and 2nd December, 1886.

19   *Glasgow Herald*, 27th June, 1887.

20   *The Scotsman*, 4th July, 1889.

21   *The Scotsman* , 5th February, 1887.

15. MAITLAND SCHOOLS

School buildings and educational reform

In earlier times most schools looked like the buildings around them and there was little need for architects. The main exceptions were those, such as Tain Royal Academy, whose endowments were sufficient to fund something more impressive. Various factors had combined during the early part of Andrew Maitland Senior's career to boost the building of schools that were differentiated from their surroundings - notably the introduction of state grants for voluntary schools, the wish of heritors to have more distinctive buildings on their estates and the entry of the Free Church into the provision of education. This entailed a modest amount of work for architects. Hence, as we saw in earlier chapters, Andrew Senior had designed a school built at Ardross in 1858, and in Tain a grammar school in 1851 and a Free Church school (now the Parish Church Hall) in 1861.[1]

In the 1870s, however, the pace of school building increased dramatically, and with it the role of architects. Numerous schools of a type we regard as typically Victorian were built, both in towns and in rural parishes. Many Maitland-designed schools are still a familiar feature of the Highland landscape, particularly in Easter Ross.

The catalyst was reform of the educational system by the Gladstone administration of 1868-74. Prior to this reform there was no shortage of educational facilities in Scotland, and school attendance was surprisingly high, particularly in Easter Ross and the Black Isle. But there was no compulsion, and there was a bewildering diversity of provision and of funding. The heritors in each parish were still responsible for the provision of a school, and, with the minister of the established church, for the appointment of a schoolmaster. The parish school legislation did not apply to Royal Burghs, where educational provision was left to private enterprise, the churches and charitable bodies. In many areas, particularly in the Highlands, parish schools were playing second fiddle to the Free Church schools set up in the wake of the Disruption of 1843. There remained some schools provided by the Society in Scotland for Propagating Christian Knowledge, set up in the eighteenth century to teach 'religion and virtue' in the Highlands and other 'uncivilised' parts of the country. There were 'ragged schools' for the poor, charitable schools, Gaelic schools, fee-paying private schools for the middle classes, and, increasingly, girls' schools.

The Education (Scotland) Act of 1872 made education compulsory between the ages of five and thirteen. Burgh and parish schools were transferred to school boards, elected every three years by rate-payers in every parish. The boards were given powers to levy rates and to borrow in order to build new schools. Other schools were allowed to continue, but without rate aid, and most joined the new state system. Fees continued (but were later abandoned), and those too poor to pay were given assistance.

A new role for architects

A key feature of the reform was the introduction of central standards for building materials, space and hygiene. The school boards set up by the new legislation took over the majority of existing schools. In towns such as Tain most of these were closed down as obsolete and unhygienic. To replace them, and to cater for the influx of new pupils, new 'public schools' were built. In rural parts of the Highlands the policy was to close down many smaller schools and concentrate on the parish school. But outlying areas still needed schools. Sometimes existing premises could be adapted, as at Edderton where the Maitlands altered and added to a mid nineteenth century house.[2] Where existing buildings could not be adapted to meet the requirements for stone walls, slated roofs and boarded floors new buildings were required.

To build the new schools, and to meet the new standards, school boards employed local architects, some of whom developed significant educational practices. The most prolific in the Highlands was Alexander Ross of Inverness, who designed some 40 schools in 1875 alone. But the Maitlands were dominant on their own patch.

As the franchise was property based (one-third of Scottish males were enfranchised after 1867 and two-thirds after 1884), as meetings were held on week-days, and as expenses were not reimbursed, the school boards were inevitably dominated by landed proprietors (particularly in rural areas) and the more successful members of the middle class.

Reflecting budgetary constraints, and also perhaps the speed with which the new schools had to be built, designs were usually plain, and there was a considerable measure of uniformity. Gifford remarks that 'most [of the schools] are cheap, with little more than a Gothic bellcote for emphasis, but Andrew Maitland & Sons produced boldly composed Gothic designs for schools at Cromarty, Kilmuir Easter and Tain'.[3] Internally there was typically one main room in which the head master taught and one or more smaller ones in which adult mistresses or teen-age pupil-teachers taught the younger children. The 1872 Act marked a significant turning point in the gender balance of Scottish teachers, with female teachers increasing between 1871 and 1901 from 49% of the total to 68% - albeit at average salaries of half the male rate.

Rural schools in Easter Ross

In the 1870s the rural parishes of Easter Ross were more heavily populated, and therefore had significantly greater educational demands, than to-day. Thus the parish of Tarbat had a population of 2,182 in 1871, whereas the 2011 census showed a total for the (similar) community council area of only 737. The 1871 figures reflected a booming agriculture, still only partially mechanised, and a fishing industry not long past its peak years.[4] Educational needs were served by a parochial school at Wester Seafield, a mile west of Portmahomack, which its promoter earlier in the century, Donald Macleod of Geanies, had regarded as 'centrical' to the parish, and by a Free Church school at Balnabruach.

The election of the first school board for the parish of Tarbat took place in 1873. As the historians of the parish wrote, 'the choice of the lairds of Cadboll, Geanies and Rockfield and the Ministers of the Established and Free Churches showed clearly where lay the seats of power'.[5] The first two lairds were heavily involved with two schools built by the board. Macleod of Cadboll gave the site for Tarbat Old Public School in what is now Tarbatness Road in Portmahomack. A. Maitland & Sons drew up plans and sought tenders for the school and an adjoining teacher's residence. The school was opened in early 1876. Simple in design, it was planned to accommodate 289 pupils. Attendance varied, but averaged 147 in 1884.[6]

But one school was not sufficient for all the prospective pupils in the parish. In 1875 the school board acquired from Kenneth Murray of Geanies a site for Tarbat West Public School at Toulvaddie. The Maitlands advertised for tenders in June of the same year.[7] The school, with accommodation for the head teacher and space for 68 pupils, opened in September 1876. Between these two dates Kenneth Murray became Provost of Tain and, eight months into his tenure of office, died. The Tarbat School Board restored the previous parochial school to his trustees.

15.1 An early photograph of Tarbat Old Public School, Portmahomack, now the local primary school.

To-day Tarbat Old Public School serves as the local primary school with a roll of around 36, but Tarbat West is a house in a settlement known as New Geanies.

In the neighbouring parish of Fearn the Maitlands designed three public schools for the school board - Hilton of Cadboll, Hill of Fearn and Balmuchy, for all of which tenders were sought in 1875.[8] The largest, Hilton, on the brae above the village of Hilton, served the fishing villages of Hilton and Balintore and nearby areas, and also from 1886 the fishing village of Shandwick in the parish of Nigg.[9] The building was designed to accommodate 178 pupils, but the children's assistance was so vital to the fishing, harvesting and potato planting and gathering that the school inspectors found 'a formidable amount of absenteeism, probably without parallel in that inspection district'. The building was replaced by the present Hilton of Cadboll Primary School on the same site in 1960 and only the schoolmaster's house remains. The school at Hill of Fearn, designed for 120 pupils, remains as a primary school, though now with a substantial and very basic 1940s extension. The small school (for 80 pupils) at Balmuchy closed in the 1950s and is to-day a house.

Meanwhile in another Easter Ross parish the Nigg School Board were attracting criticism from the School Inspector for continuing to cram pupils into the old parochial school, and the Scotch Education Board threatened to withdraw funding. Plans drawn up by A. Maitland & Sons were sent to London in August 1875, and tenders were sought in September 1876 for a new Nigg Public School designed to accommodate 100 pupils. At the same time they sought tenders for a smaller school at Pitcalnie to serve the eastern end of the parish.[10] The schools were built of red sandstone and given attractive finials.

In the nearby parish of Kilmuir Easter relations between the former parochial teacher, Thomas G. Meldrum, and the new school board were, in the words of the local historian (who was Meldrum's daughter), 'far from being of the most pleasant character'. The members of the school board were the proprietor of the Kindeace estate, the factors for the Cromartie and Balnagown estates, and the parish and Free Church ministers. There were disputes over how Meldrum's salary should be paid, and 'where any expenditure of money was concerned the members showed a grudging spirit'.[11] It is therefore perhaps remarkable that A. Maitland & Sons were able to design a new public school, designed for 160 pupils, that stands out from the majority of its more simply styled contemporaries.[12] Gothic in style, the school and schoolhouse (now a private house) has a tall bellcote and distinctive gables and gablets.

In the adjacent parish of Rosskeen the Maitlands designed two schools for the school board. The first, with accommodation for 205 pupils, was at Bridgend of Alness.[13] The other, with a similar capacity, was in Invergordon, 'low and rambling, with a Gothic bellcote'.[14] In our own day the pupils of what is now Park Primary School, did some research that vividly contrasts the past with the present. 'When the school opened, the building was already rather small for the numbers. All the children in the first three classes were taught together in one large room, which is now broken up to form the Infant Library, the Primary three classrooms and toilets and the rooms in the gallery in the roof space. All these classes were taught at the same time by the Infant Mistress and two pupil assistants with a great babble of noise. An early example of open plan education, perhaps! The floor was stepped, so that everybody could be clearly seen, and seven or eight pupils sat to a desk. The most cramped classroom was in the room which is now the Infant Library. The older children were taught in the area now occupied by the Primary 1 class. The headmaster's house was in the building now used for offices and Staff Room. At the opening service in the Town Hall, Mr King (the headmaster) made a speech expressing his hopes for the future but he did not remain in Invergordon to see them fulfilled; he resigned the following year.'[15] In 1881 the next head master, William Smith, was dismissed as he would not sign a memorandum by which his salary was to be lowered. The Lord Advocate refused to intervene when the issue was raised in the House of Commons, asserting that 'such agreements rest with school boards'.

Cromarty

The Maitlands also designed two new public schools in the Black Isle for the Cromarty School Board - one of them with a very distinctive and detailed design.

Hugh Miller - stonemason, geologist, writer, and Cromarty's most celebrated son - had been educated in the parish school by the sea-shore - a low, long, straw-thatched cottage, with a mud floor and an unlathed roof with naked rafters. At 'occasional intervals' the pupils heard 'the roar of death', the school being 'not thirty yards from a killing-place where from eighty to one hundred pigs used sometimes to die for the general good in a single day'.[16] In 1849 Andrew Maitland Senior had charged 12s for estimates and in 1850 £5-5s-0d for plans for a small replacement for the parish school.[17] But this was never built. By then, in the wake of the Disruption, the Free Church, which operated a substantial school on the Braehead, had become the main provider of education.

Following the 1872 Act, however, the Cromarty School Board commissioned the Maitlands to design a new public school on the Braehead, and also a smaller one at Peddieston four and a quarter miles to the south west.[18] These had accommodation for 300 and 120 children respectively - though the average attendances in 1880 were only 164 and 40.

The two schools were built in 1875-6 at a total cost of around £6,000. This appears to be well above the sums spent by the other school boards for whom the Maitlands worked. Thus Cromarty gained the most eye-catching of the Maitland school buildings. Constructed in a Gothic style, in red and yellow sandstone, the school was long and single-storey with decorative gables and buttresses. At the right was a prominent round bell tower and a two-storey teacher's residence. So remarkable was it that a fisher-wife was heard to say 'The like o' the Cromarty school was never seen north o' Aberdeen afore'.[19] To-day the school functions as Cromarty Primary School.

15.2 Cromarty Public (now Primary) School.

Tain - and 'sectarian animosities'

The Scotch Education Board tried to ensure that burghs with a population of less than 3,000 should share a school board with the parish in which they were situated. Hence the Tain School Board took responsibility for an area including the fishing village of Inver, six miles to the east of Tain. The Maitlands advertised in December 1876 for tenders for a school with accommodation for 70 pupils and a schoolhouse at Inver.[20]

The events leading to the construction of a public school in the burgh were far less straightforward. In June 1873 the Free Church agreed to transfer the school site behind their church in Queen Street (now the Parish Church Hall) to the school board. The board then considered alternatives, but found it difficult to decide on a suitable site. In April 1876 they intimated that 'in view of their intention to erect a public school at the east end of Tain they do not require the Free Church School', and they re-conveyed it to the Free Church.[21] A. Maitland & Sons then produced plans which were approved, and in February 1877 advertised for tenders.[22] There were delays in beginning building operations and then in occupying the new premises.

The new school, designed to accommodate 323 pupils, cost over £3,000. This allowed more architectural embellishments than did the tighter budgets for the other Maitland schools in Easter Ross. The long, low north elevation is flanked by Gothic gabled bays. The western gable is distinguished by a tall gableted bellcote with a wrought iron finial, and roundheaded windows linked by hoodmoulding and smaller outer gabled bays with stone finials.

At a ceremony in January 1879, attended by most of the members of the school board and of the town council, clergymen of the town and a 'large assemblage of townspeople', Captain Hugh Law Rose of Tarlogie, chairman of the school board since 1876, finally opened Tain Public School. He announced that the parish school teacher was retiring on his former salary, Mr Bain of the Free Church School had been appointed master, and Miss Bain one of his assistants - news received with great enthusiasm.

15.3 Tain Public School, later Knockbreck Primary School.

The Tain School Board was clearly dysfunctional. Captain Rose's grandfather, Hugh Rose Ross of Glastullich and Cromarty, had, as we saw earlier, built up vast estates in Easter Ross. Hugh Rose Ross's son had had to sell off many of these, but the captain was still the largest landowner in the parish. This did not, however, give him the power that the heritors retained in rural school boards. The majority of the seven members of the board were professional men and some of the more prominent merchants, though there was sufficient competition for Provost Vass and William Russell Ross (who was soon to commission the Maitlands to design a warehouse in Shore Road) to be rejected by the electors in 1882. The ministers of the Free Church and the established church also played a prominent role, and their ecclesiastical rivalry led to arguments so ferocious that they caught the attention of the press, and were characterised as 'sectarian animosities'.

Thus in the summer of 1884 a majority of the board voted to dismiss John Macdonald, the clerk and treasurer, who then refused to hand over the books. At the next meeting the Rev. Colin Macnaughton, the minister of the established church, proposed a new treasurer, but Bailie Matheson announced that at the next meeting the Rev. Thomas Grant of the Free Church, who was unable to be present, would seek the reinstatement of Macdonald, and the meeting broke up in disorder. The following meeting, after two and a half hours of wrangling, adjourned until the following week, having transacted no business. At the adjourned meeting it was reported that Professor Christie of Aberdeen, an inspector from the Society for

Promoting the Inspection of Religion in Schools, complained that when he had visited Inver Public School only 2 of the 74 pupils on the roll had presented themselves to be examined, and that at Tain Public School only 48 out of 270 had turned up. Mr Grant asserted that government inspectors were not allowed to examine in religious knowledge and that the Free Presbytery had examined the Free Church children. He considered himself a competent examiner, and asserted that Mr Macnaughton 'could not do what he likes in Tain'. The Rev. Mr Macnaughton said that he would not have believed that such a thing was possible in any part of Scotland, complained of boycotting, intolerance and and un-Christian spirit, and wished to move a motion of censure on the Rev. Mr Grant. Mr Grant said that Professor Christie had had matters misrepresented to him and that he felt sorry for him 'going down the long road to Inver on a very warm day and coming up again with a coldness at his heart'. The meeting then degenerated into a squabble, during which Mr Grant left the meeting, two other members threatened to resign, and none of the business for which the meeting had been called was discussed.

In 1912 Tain Royal Academy was, controversially, brought under the control of the school board and ceased to be a fee-paying school. The public school later became a primary school, acting as a feeder for the Academy, and became known as Knockbreck Primary School when a second primary school was opened in Tain.

Later commissions - alterations and extensions

The public school in Tain appears to have been the last of the commissions for new schools obtained by the Maitlands in the wake of the 1872 Act. But there was no prohibition on school boards providing education beyond the elementary stage, and from about 1878 a secondary system began to evolve. The leaving age was raised in 1883 to 14, fees were abolished for the elementary stages in 1891, and improvements to the facilities were frequently sought. As a result the Maitlands obtained numerous commissions for alterations and extensions, both to the 1870s schools and to earlier ones still in use. Many of these were outwith Easter Ross. They included in the 1880s a reconstruction of the school at Dornoch (now the Social Club) which gave it its present L-shape, and alterations to the school and schoolhouse at Embo (now a community hub); and in the 1890s additions to that at Bonar Bridge, a reconstruction of that at Melness in Caithness, alterations and additions to the schools at Achtercairn, Bualnaluib, and Inverasdale in Gairloch parish, and alterations and additions to the schoolteachers's house at Gledfield. The Maitlands were also responsible for further work on the public schools at Cromarty in 1890 and 1904, Invergordon (amidst great controversy) in 1891-92, Kilmuir Easter in 1895, Edderton in 1903, and Tain in 1908.

References and Notes

[1] For a helpful account of the history of school buildings see Robert D. Anderson, chapter 15 in *Scottish Life and Society, Scotland's Buildings*, Tuckwell Press, 2003, pp.294-305.

[2] Gifford, *Highlands and Islands*, p.410.

[3] Gifford, *Highlands and Islands*, p.67.

[4] In 1874 there were 95 resident fishermen in Portmahomack and 40 in Rockfield. Taking ancillary jobs, some part-time, into account fishing provided employment for 607 people in the parish.

[5] Finlay Munro (himself laird of Rockfield) and Alexander Fraser, *Tarbat: Easter Ross,* Ross & Cromarty Heritage Society, 1988, pp.101-07.

[6] School accommodation and attendance figures quoted in this chapter have been taken from Francis H. Groome, Ordnance Gazetteer for Scotland, Thomas C. Jack, Edinburgh, 1882-85.

[7] *Inverness Courier*, 10th June, 1875.

[8] *Inverness Courier*, 2nd September, 8th August and 30th September, 1875.

[9] See Jessie Macdonald and Anne Gordon, *Down to the Sea - An Account of Life in the Fishing Villages of Hilton, Balintore & Shandwick*, Ross & Cromarty Heritage Society, pp.137-43 for a fuller account.

[10] *Inverness Courier*, 14th September, 1876; see also *Nigg - A Changing Parish*, Anne Gordon, 1977, part 4, pp.21 and 30.

[11] *Kilmuir Easter - The History of a Highland Parish,* Helen Myers Meldrum, Robert Carruthers & Sons, Courier Office, Inverness, 1935, pp.49-58.

[12] *Inverness Courier*, 9th December, 1875.

[13] *Inverness Courier*, 30th March, 1876.

[14] Gifford, *Highlands and Islands*, p.427.

[15] *Victorian and Edwardian Invergordon*, compiled by the pupils of Park Primary School, 1991-7, pp.35-36.

[16] Hugh Miller, *My Schools and Schoolmasters*, 1889 edition, W.P. Nimmo, Hay, & Mitchell, Edinburgh, pp.42-44.

[17] *Catalogue of papers belonging to Cromarty Church of Scotland*, online at www.eastchurchcromarty.co.uk, 9.72.

[18] *Inverness Courier*, 28th January and 11th March, 1875 respectively.

[19] *Ross-shire Journal*, 19th May, 1876, quoted in Marinell Ash, *This Noble Harbour - a History of the Cromarty Firth*, Cromarty Firth Port Authority, 1991, p.63.

[20] *Inverness Courier*, 28th December, 1876. Early in the present century new school buildings were constructed for Inver Primary School beside the old and the schoolhouse was demolished.

[21] Minutes of the Tain Free Church Deacons' Court, 1843-99, Highland Archive Centre, CH3/748/2.

[22] *Inverness Courier*, 1st February, 1877.

16. MAITLAND DISTILLERIES

Maitland distilleries - and putting Tain on the world stage

The Maitlands designed at least five distilleries, all of them new or substantially rebuilt. The first two, Ben Wyvis in Dingwall and Gerston in Caithness, were as modern and innovative as any in Scotland, but have both since closed. Three others, Glenmorangie, Dalmore, and Teaninich, all in Easter Ross, are still going strong: the buildings of the first two retain to this day a strong Maitland influence, though the Maitland buildings at Teaninich have long since disappeared.

16.1 An early photograph of the Glenmorangie distillery by William Smith of Tain.

The Maitlands' most enduring achievement in the whisky industry, and one which helped to put Tain on the world stage, was at Glenmorangie. A mile to the north-west of Tain, close to the shore of the Dornoch Firth, and with stunning views of the Sutherland mountains, are the predominantly Victorian, and mainly Maitland-designed, buildings of Glenmorangie. But in this case the Maitlands' contribution went much further than its design. Andrew Junior and, to a lesser extent, James as investors and managers were key figures in propelling an existing small distillery into becoming a major player in the industry.

Whisky as a farmhouse industry

Whisky enjoyed such popularity in Scotland in the earlier decades of the nineteenth century that whisky distilling became a logical diversification for farmers able to grow grain, for the raw ingredient of malt whisky is barley. The process begins with malting the barley. Nowadays nearly all distilleries buy in malted barley from the big maltsters, but in earlier times distilleries used their own, or other locally grown, barley and had their own maltings. Whisky production was water intensive and farmers often had good water sources nearby. Peat was generally used not just, as today, for its smoke in the kiln but for drying the grain - and the Highlands were full of peat bogs. Many farmers had buildings that could be used for whisky production. Most distilleries had potential customers in inns, pubs and licensed victuallers in their local area.

Illicit distillation had been the norm until legislation culminating in the Excise Act of 1823 introduced a cost and taxation basis that made legal distilling a more viable proposition. In the decades that followed both landlords themselves and tenants set up new distilleries and refurbished old ones in many parts of Scotland. Easter Ross, a prime area for growing barley, with plenty of peat and with water from springs and rivers, was a natural beneficiary of the new regime.

But distilling remained a small-scale business. We saw in earlier chapters three instances where Andrew Maitland Senior had come into contact with distilleries. Each of these were small distilleries set up as the offshoot of a farm, often to utilise surplus barley. The first was the small distillery operated by his father-in-law, George Andrews, on the farm he leased at Braelangwell. The second was Glenmorangie, whose water source was the Tarlogie Springs. Andrew's finding that the springs were 'not to be calculated on for a permanent supply' of water for Tain had saved the distillery. The third instance was Dalmore. When Andrew had been commissioned in 1860 to alter and repair the distillery purchased five years before by Alexander Matheson M.P. its capacity was only about 40,000 gallons per year.

Andrew Junior recalled in a speech at a New Years Eve supper and dance in 1897 that the 'foundation stone' of his firm's significant involvement in distillery architecture was when William Mackenzie and his son Andrew had called at the Maitland office in 1873 and asked his father and himself 'to undertake the doubling of the Dalmore distillery … a fortunate day … as [we] shortly afterwards got the Balblair and Ben Wyvis distilleries'.

Boom times for whisky: blending, whisky barons, and an aphid

The last three decades of the nineteenth century saw the building of a remarkable number of new and much larger malt whisky distilleries and the reconstruction of old ones. Many of these were on Speyside, but several, including the Maitland-designed distilleries, were in the northern Highlands. This building programme reflected a vast growth in demand for whisky.[1]

A key factor in this had been the invention of the patent or Coffey still. Distillation in the traditional pot still is a batch process in which the right temperature, water and peat are critical. The new still made possible a continuous process with consequential advantages in volume and cost, and it allowed distilleries to be located anywhere. The product, which could be made not just from malted barley but also from unmalted barley and from other cereals was, however, different. It came to be known as grain whisky. Grain whisky distilleries were set up nearer the main centres of population in the Lowlands. The initial impact on the malt whisky distilleries, still reliant on pot stills, had been catastrophic.

But the malt whisky industry had been rescued by the introduction and spectacular growth of blended whisky, a mixture of malt whisky and grain whisky. The objective was to produce an acceptably flavoured whisky at a lower cost by blending in a mixture of malts to add flavour to the bland grain whiskies. By the mid 1860s blending was well-established. Among the blenders were the 'whisky barons', entrepreneurs with skills in branding, selling and advertising and also the ability to market their product in England and the colonies. Prominent names included Peter Mackie, the father of White Horse, Alexander Walker of Johnnie Walker fame, Tommy Dewar, James Buchanan, Arthur Bell, and the Haig dynasty.

A further stimulus to whisky sales came from an unexpected source - the *Phylloxera Vastatrix* aphid, which devastated French vineyards, reaching the Cognac region around 1875 and destroying 85% of the area under vine by 1895. The consequential reduction in volume and increase in the price of brandy gave a huge boost to sales of malt whisky.

The architect of choice for many of the distilleries of this period was Charles C. Doig of Elgin, famous for the invention of the attractive pagoda-shaped ventilators that are still a distinctive feature of so many distilleries. Doig designed his first distillery in 1889, but by then the Maitlands were well established and still able to secure commissions in the northern Highlands.

Ben Wyvis - a lost Maitland distillery

BEN WYVIS DISTILLERY.

16.2 Ben Wyvis Distillery, Dingwall - an engraving from Alfred Barnard's *The Whisky Distilleries of The United Kingdom* (1887).

During 1878 and 1879 A. Maitland & Sons advertised for tenders for a new distillery in Dingwall.[2] *The Scotsman* reported in the latter year that 'for the past two years Bailie D.G. Ross has been engaged in the construction of the "Ben Wyvis Distillery", one of the most extensive works of the kind in the Highlands. …. The site is on the side of a hill a few yards south of the town and is convenient to the railway station. The water supply is conveyed three and a half miles from Loch Ussie. … The site has been selected for its suitableness for conducting operations on the principle of gravitation, by which the material by successive stages from the granaries at the top of the hill, till it comes out as whisky at the bottom, on the level of the public road descends by successive stages … The whole works, which were designed by Messrs Maitland & Sons, architects, Tain, were entrusted to Ross-shire tradesmen … The output is expected to be 200,000 gallons of spirits annually.' On the other side of the road, and beside a railway siding, were warehouses, containing a granary and bonded stores.[3] The total cost was 'upwards of £21,000'.

The Maitlands' client, D.G. Ross, was a Dingwall merchant. He became Provost, despite an attempt in the House of Commons to remove him on account of a conviction and fine of £1 for travelling on the railway without a ticket - an attempt rebuffed by the Lord Advocate who noted that Ross had held a season ticket which had shortly before expired.[4]

Between 1885 and 1887 Alfred Barnard visited all 162 working distilleries in Great Britain and Ireland and wrote the first study of the industry, *The Whisky Distilleries of The United Kingdom*, an important work written at a turning point in the history of malt whisky. His descriptions of some of the unimproved distilleries are relatively brief, but he was more informative about modernised ones and particularly complimentary about the equipment and methods of working at Ben Wyvis.[5] Despite this D.G. Ross sold the distillery in 1887 to a company that went bankrupt two years later. The subsequent history of Ben Wyvis was chequered and it closed in 1926.[6] To-day the only remains are the warehouses, converted to residential occupation, and some offices and stores.

Gerston - another lost Maitland distillery

The Maitlands' next distillery commission was for a completely new one at Gerston, near Halkirk in Caithness. An earlier distillery at Gerston, though on a farmhouse scale, had achieved considerable fame, and Sir Robert Peel had been among the admirers of its product. After a change in ownership it had been closed in 1875. A few years later a London based company, the Gerston Distillery Company, attempted to repeat the earlier success. In 1885-87 the Maitlands designed and supervised for them the building of a new distillery (including the plant and machinery), houses for the manager and excise officer, workmens' cottages and stabling.[7] The second distillery was a mile or so from the old one and a similar distance from the new railway station at Halkirk.

The new distillery received a visit from Alfred Barnard, who wrote that 'the buildings and plant, are constructed on the most approved principles', and that 'the proposed output is ... about 80,000 gallons per year, but the Works have been so constructed that the output can, at little expense, be doubled if required. The whole buildings and internal fittings and plant have been carried out from the drawings and under the superintendence of Messrs A. Maitland & Sons, architects, Tain.'[8]

The second Gerston distillery was undoubtedly one of the most technically advanced in Scotland, but it failed to achieve the hoped for success. The flavour of the product appears to have been inferior to that of the predecessor distillery. A modern account queries whether the second distillery used the same water source and notes that, rather than using local barley, it shipped in barley from the Lowlands and the Baltic.[9] Local people, it says, 'bristled at a London based business that was not seen to be supporting the local community. Merchants who previously bought Gerston One spirit now shifted their trade to neighbouring distilleries such as Old Pulteney'. The distillery was sold in 1897, the new owners re-naming it Ben Morven, and it seems to have closed around 1911-14.[10]

Glenmorangie before the Maitlands - the 'mountain dew' of Easter Ross

The next Maitland distillery has enjoyed a much happier history, though it did involve a bitter dispute between the Maitlands and a representative of the founding family.

During his tour of distilleries in 1885-87 Alfred Barnard visited Glenmorangie. He was 'received courteously and entertained hospitably' by the proprietor, Mr Matheson. But he found that the distillery 'is certainly the most ancient and primitive we have seen, and now almost in ruins. At the time of our visit the proprietor was arranging to build a new Distillery on the same site'.[11]

Both Morangie Farm and a brewery, let separately from the farm and reputed to date from 1738, had formed part of the estates around Tain built up by Hugh Rose Ross. William Matheson, the father of Barnard's host, had taken a lease of the farm (but not the brewery, which was separately let) in 1843. After Hugh Rose Ross's death in 1846 his son, Major Hugh St Vincent Rose, under the financial pressures we saw earlier, had tried to sell the adjoining estates of Morangie, Tarlogie and Cambuscurries. In 1848, whilst these efforts continued, his factor James Strachan had advertised 'A BREWERY TO LET, NEAR TAIN: THE MORANGIE BREWERY, consisting of commodious Premises, will be let to an eligible tenant. ... There is an ample supply of water, with an excellent fall, and the Premises could, at very small expense, be converted into a DISTILLERY, there being a ready market in the District for such an Establishment. To a Tenant of enterprise, with capital, the Premises at Morangie will be found a first-rate opening, either for a Brewery or a Distillery'.[12] A tenant of enterprise, interested in a first-rate opening, had quickly emerged to take the lease. William Matheson was not only already tenant of Morangie Farm, but had also been a partner for 17 years in the Balblair distillery, as well as one of several people designated as managers of the Easter Ross Savings Bank, a campaigner for improved steam navigation, and a leading light of the Easter Ross Farmers' Society. At meetings of the Farmers' Society following the repeal of the protectionist Corn Laws, which took effect in 1849, landlords and tenants were expressing serious concerns about the effect of imported grain on sales and prices of British grain. The *Inverness Courier* reported in November 1849 the recent erection by Matheson of Glen-Morangie (*sic)*, a 'very neat and compact distillery', and commented that the diversification into distilling would be hailed by local farmers as providing an additional outlet for their barley.[13] The repeal of the Corn Laws could perhaps be said to have provided an impetus for the foundation of Glenmorangie.

In that same month William Matheson, promising prompt attention to 'Orders from Innkeepers and Private Families', respectfully requested 'a continuance of the liberal and encouraging support hitherto bestowed on him as a Distiller' at Balblair,[14] and also produced his first whisky. The date traditionally given for the foundation of Glenmorangie is 1843, the year in which William Matheson became tenant of Morangie Farm and applied for a distilling licence. The brewery was, however, let separately from the farm and it was not vacated by the heirs of the previous tenant until 1844[15] or occupied by Matheson until 1848. Thus if Matheson intended to distil whisky in 1843 he would have had either to use different premises from those first used in 1849 or to come to some arrangement that allowed use of the brewery.

Matheson survived a conviction for excise offences in 1852 (he was acquitted by a jury in the Court of Exchequer after pleading that his manager had disobeyed his instructions in his absence, but the Solicitor-General successfully argued in a second trial that the judge had misdirected the jury),[16] and he died in 1862. But he had sown the seeds of success. During the next quarter of a century his widow, their sons John (until his death in 1879) and William, their daughter Barbara and her husband Duncan Cameron (accountant and later agent for the Commercial Bank of Scotland in Tain, who was to be a thorn in the flesh of Andrew Maitland Junior) were involved in the ownership and management of the business. John and, after his death, the younger William described themselves as 'Distiller and Farmer'. The quality of their product seems to have been appreciated throughout Britain, 'The Glen Morangie Company' having an office and warehouse in London Wall and agencies in various English towns and cities. And not only Britain, for it was reported in 1880 that: 'We observed the other day, *en route* for Rome, a cask of whisky from Glen-Morangie Distillery, likewise several casks destined for San Francisco. Has his Holiness renounced the old *poteen* of the well-known story in favour of the mountain dew of Easter Ross?'.[17]

Andrew Maitland Junior appears on the scene

The next phase in the history of Glenmorangie was one in which the Maitlands, particularly Andrew Junior, were to be the main players.[18] Fortunately for anyone interested in these matters it involved a court case, *Duncan Cameron v The Glenmorangie Company, Limited and Others*, the reports of which, extending to 130 pages, provide a treasure trove of information both on the history of the distillery and on the life of Andrew Maitland Junior.[19]

In 1884 the younger William Matheson and his family wished to build a new distillery and therefore sought to buy the feu from the landlord, Major Hugh Law Rose of Tarlogie, grandson of Hugh Rose Ross. (Many accounts state that 'old William Matheson', the founder of the distillery, was responsible for initiating the plans, but he had been dead for 22 years.) A. Maitland & Sons were called in to value the existing distillery buildings as between the Mathesons and Major Rose, and also to prepare plans for the new distillery and plant. The Mathesons found, however, that they could not afford the costs. Nothing happened for a year or so until Andrew Maitland Junior, seeing an investment opportunity, approached William's brother-in-law Duncan Cameron suggesting the formation of a limited company. Cameron had recently joined Andrew Junior on the Tain Burgh Council, and their falling-out over the management of the Tain quarries (discussed in chapter 12) was yet to occur. They agreed to seek prospective investors through an advertisement in the London *Times*. A response to their advertisement came from Edward J. Taylor. Taylor was the proprietor of the Chelsea Distillery, in London, where he was a distiller and rectifier of spirits, and he had good connections in the wines and spirits trade. Taylor came to Tain to meet Maitland and Cameron, and it was agreed that Taylor and friends of his would initially put up £6,000 for 600 shares of £10 each, giving the 'London shareholders' a 50% interest in a company to be formed to own and operate the distillery. The other 600 shares were initially held as to 200 each by the younger William Matheson and his wife, Cameron, and Maitland.

The new business began on 1st November, 1886 and was registered as a limited company, The Glenmorangie Distillery Company, in October 1887. The company purchased the feu of ten acres with water rights, the old buildings and plant from Cameron, who had earlier purchased them from the widow of the first William Matheson.

The original architectural drawings, signed by the Maitland brothers, can still be seen in the distillery offices. One of these shows a new piggery: pigs were fed on the draff left after the mashing process.

By February 1888 A. Maitland and Sons were advertising for tenders for work on the new distillery.[20] The distillery was of advanced design and was the first malt distillery to have stills fitted with internal steam coils to prevent scorching. The design of the new stills, which has been followed ever since when stills have been replaced or added, is interesting. The necks of the stills at 16 feet 10¼ inches in height are the tallest in the industry, and

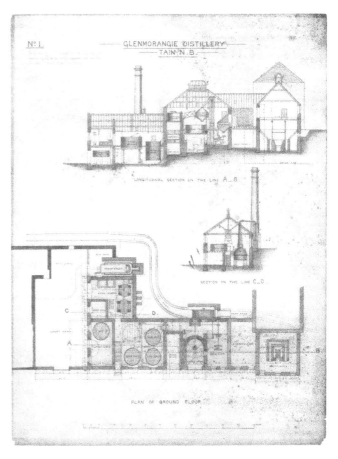

16.3 Glenmorangie plan No. 1.

the *cognoscenti* assert that this is one of the major factors contributing to the very special taste of Glenmorangie. Legend has it that the design originated with the first William Matheson who, in order to save money when fitting out the distillery in 1849, had bought stills that had previously been used in a gin distillery. This seems unlikely as there do not seem to have been any gin distilleries in the region. What we do know, from the cross-examination of Edward Taylor in the litigation referred to above, is that in 1888 the distillery was 'rebuilt to the designs of Mr Maitland' and that Taylor himself 'made practical suggestions as to the buildings and the stills, and so on to Mr Maitland', which involved 'constant correspondence' and 'a great expense of time and labour' to both of them. Taylor went on to praise Maitland as 'being very able in carrying out the suggestions that I could make'. It is likely therefore that the unusual design was the result of the correspondence between Andrew Maitland Junior and Edward Taylor in 1888.

Cameron, Taylor, Maitland and the younger William Matheson became directors of the new company. Initially Matheson was the 'indoor manager', responsible for the working of the distillery. Cameron was secretary and responsible for purchasing barley and selling the whisky, particularly to Taylor's contacts. Round about the time of the formation of the company, however, Matheson was incapacitated by a serious accident, and on 19th May, 1888, whilst building work on the new distillery was proceeding, he died of pleurisy at the age of only 37. Andrew Maitland Junior took his place as indoor manager and soon won the enthusiastic support of the London shareholders. They were, however, dissatisfied with the quality of the barley purchased by Cameron and very concerned about the low level of sales. In September 1888 Cameron was sidelined and Maitland was given the whole responsibility of management. As well as visiting the distillery almost every day whilst at home and also purchasing barley, coke, etc., Maitland travelled extensively in England and Southern Scotland, spending some two months a year visiting wholesalers. The results were in the words of Edward Cathie, one of the London shareholders and proprietor of Simpsons in the Strand, 'phenomenal'. Sales rose from 4,807 gallons in 1887 to 79,550 gallons in 1895, and the London shareholders ascribed this particularly to Maitland's exertions.

Duncan Cameron versus the rest

Edward Taylor and Andrew Maitland Junior worked well together. Maitland said at the 1890 Annual General Meeting that 'due to Mr Taylor's experience our new whisky is more mellow, and palatable and matures more quickly than any other on the market'. Taylor responded that he had been 'most ably seconded by Mr Maitland, who has spared neither time, trouble nor labour to grasp principles and details and apply them to actual workings in the distillery, even at the expense of his rest at night'.

But Cameron did not share such views. From 1888 onwards he seems to have been continuously at odds both with the London shareholders and with the Maitland brothers. He was replaced as secretary by James Stephen in 1890. In the following year he suffered the indignity of failing to gain re-election to the Tain Burgh Council, coming bottom of the poll by a large margin.

A major rift took place in 1893. Cameron objected to proposed payments to Maitland (whose only remuneration was a salary of £100 p.a.) of a commission of ½d per gallon on sales between 20,000 and 40,000 gallons - but he then failed to turn up at a shareholders' meeting which approved the arrangement. At the Annual General Meeting in December 1894 the Directors' Report noted that expenditure on further bonded warehouses and grain stores was required, and also that Maitland, in order to increase his influence in trade circles, desired an additional 200 £10 shares in the company and was willing to pay a premium of £1 per share - i.e. £11 each. Cameron objected. He ceased going to board meetings the following year, claiming that he was always outvoted, and he was replaced as a director by James Maitland. James's wife Barbara, whose father had been excise officer at the distillery, would no doubt have been pleased.

An Extraordinary General Meeting was held in August, 1895, when there were 1,200 £10 shares in issue, to discuss the allocation of 200 new £10 shares at £11 to Andrew Maitland Junior. Cameron cast his own 200 votes and the 100 of Mrs Ann Matheson against the issue. Maitland abstained from voting his existing 150 shares. But all 600 votes of the London shareholders plus the 50 of a local farmer and 100 belonging to James Maitland were cast in favour of the issue. The issue was thus approved by 750 votes to 300. Cameron then presented a Note of Suspension and Interdict against the company, Taylor, Andrew Maitland Junior and James Stephen to prevent the allocation.

Cameron's action was heard in the Outer House of the Court of Session before Lord Kyllachy in 1896. His case was that the shares were allotted at a price below their true value and the issue was *ultra vires* and illegal. The respondents' case was that Andrew Maitland Junior's services were specially valuable to the company, whose business he had pushed and developed at great expenditure of time and trouble, and that it was desired to give him a greater weight with customers, and to encourage further exertions in the company's interest. Shareholders, accountants and stockbrokers all gave evidence. Lord Kyllachy found that the issue was within the company's power and that the complainer therefore needed to make out a case of abuse of power, which he had failed to do. Costs of £300-10s-4d were awarded against Cameron.

The Maitland brothers thus together held 32% of the shares and had nullified the influence of Duncan Cameron and his use of the founding family's shareholding.

Two years later Duncan Cameron, who farmed at Edderton, was to suffer the further indignity of being asked to resign from the office of secretary and treasurer of the Easter Ross Farmers' Club in the face of alleged discrepancies in the accounts. James Maitland was among those present at an adjourned Annual General Meeting of the club in April, 1898 at which Captain Macleod of Cadboll successfully argued that the committee's investigations into the discrepancies did not go far enough: there were, for example, 151 members, but only 79 subscriptions had been accounted for; they had, he said, been living in a fool's paradise long enough and explanations on this and other points should be forthcoming.

The heyday of Andrew Junior: Sir Walter Scott, telephones and ærated waters

Whilst the dispute with Duncan Cameron had been rumbling on, Andrew Maitland Junior was putting his stamp on the distillery.

Around 1893 the company registered as a trade mark a label design for a pure malt whisky with the legend 'The Immortal Sir Walter Scott' and an image of Sir Walter which echoes that of the marble statue by John (later Sir John) Steell which forms the centrepiece of the Scott Monument in Edinburgh. Steell had associations with Tain and presented a plaster scale model of the famous statue to the Tain Public Hall Company, whose hall Andrew Maitland Senior had designed. (The model is now in the Tain & District Museum.) There were, however, other links with Sir Walter. Andrew Junior, and everyone associated with the distillery, would have been familiar with the large granite stone on the other side the road northward from the distillery which bears the inscription, albeit of uncertain origin, 'The Immortal Walter Scott, OB. 1832'. The connections between Andrew Senior and Sir Walter, which we saw in earlier chapters - helping to set the type for Scott's later works, and his friendship with Scott's amanuensis, William Laidlaw - may also have played a part in deciding on the branding.

Although Andrew Junior played an active managerial role at Glenmorangie he still had major responsibilities as an architect and in local affairs. Much of the day to day management at the distillery was delegated to James Stephen, the company secretary. Shortly after a new office was built for the Maitlands' architectural practice in Tain in 1894 the *Ross-shire Journal* noted that a telephone line, the first in the district, had been established from the office to the distillery.[21] No doubt Stephen would have been Maitland's main contact.

Andrew Junior and Stephen seem to have worked well together. They revived a defunct fizzy drinks business in Tain as the Highland Ærated Water Company. Premises were erected in Academy Street. The *Ross-shire Journal* reported that the building was 'lofty and commodious' and floored with concrete, and the machinery for washing and cleaning the bottles was a 'marvel of ingenuity' - though this does not seem to have stopped complaints about smoke issuing from the works. Although it was quite separate from Glenmorangie, the new business provided employment when work was slack at the distillery. The company is long since gone, but there is to-day an active trade online in its ginger beer bottles.

The rebuilding of the Dalmore distillery

The deep involvement of the Maitland brothers with Glenmorangie did not, however, stop the firm from designing the major reconstruction of another Easter Ross distillery. Dalmore, near Alness, was already familiar to the Maitland family, who had twice previously been involved with the distillery.

As we saw earlier, distilling had been started at Dalmore in 1839 by Donald Sutherland, then a tenant of Hugh Rose Ross, and later of his son Colonel G.W.H. Ross. When Sutherland died the Colonel had tried without success to find a new tenant for the distillery. Alexander Matheson M.P. (often incorrectly described as the founder of the Dalmore distillery) had purchased the distillery in 1855, and following the change in ownership Andrew Maitland Senior had been commissioned in 1860 to alter and repair the distillery and dwelling house.

In 1867 Andrew Mackenzie, the son of Matheson's well-regarded factor William Mackenzie, had become the tenant of Dalmore. Under his management, and for a time that of his brothers Charles and William, the distillery had prospered - so much so that in 1873-74 the Maitlands were engaged to undertake a doubling of the distillery.[22]

Alfred Barnard paid two visits to Dalmore. The first was during his tour of 1885-87, before the Maitlands' third involvement. He noted the favourable location, with a branch line from the railway, sea communication almost at its doors, a surrounding barley-growing district, an abundance of peats, and sole command of the river Alness. He was shown over the distillery by Andrew Mackenzie and noted that the distillery had been 'frequently enlarged' since 1839 and now had an annual output of 80,000 gallons.[23]

In 1886 Matheson, by then Sir Alexander Matheson of Lochalsh and Ardross, Bart., died. Five years later his heir, Sir Kenneth Matheson, sold to Andrew Mackenzie, now sole partner in Mackenzie Brothers, the property of Dalmore estate, which 'comprises the farm, distillery, mills, Belleport [a pier on the Cromarty Firth] and the salmon fishings'.[24] This was the prelude to a massive expansion. Output in 1892-93 for the first time exceeded 100,000 gallons and climbed to 271,694 gallons in 1895.[25]

This reflected a rebuilding of the distillery to designs by A. Maitland and Sons between 1893 and 1898. The original drawings can be examined in the collection of Historic Environment Scotland in Edinburgh. They demonstrate that, whilst nineteenth century distillery architecture may have been functional rather than visually inspiring, it demanded skill and attention to the detailed requirements of each part of the distillery.[26]

After the rebuilding Alfred Barnard paid a second visit to the distillery.[27] 'The buildings throughout', he recorded, 'are fully equipped with every detail of modern inventions and improvements which a long and practical experience could suggest, comprising methods comprehensive as they are ingenious, indicating that mechanical and chemical science has been brought to bear on the production of pure Highland malt pot still Scotch whisky, and showing that the art of distilling has been raised to that position to which its close affinity with the important science of chemistry entitles it'.

As we will see later, Andrew Mackenzie in his new role as a landed proprietor also commissioned A. Maitland and Sons to build a mansion house. at Dalmore.

Teaninich

The next substantial commissions for the renovation of a distillery were on the estate of Teaninich, in the parish of Alness and only a short distance upstream from Dalmore. Teaninich had a long history. Captain Hugh Munro of Teaninich, lost the sight of both eyes when hit by a musket ball at the battle of Tymeguen, returned home in 1794 to improve his estates, and founded the distillery in 1817. By the middle of the century, it was one of the largest distilleries in the north with an output of 70-80,000 gallons per year. It was put into good order by a new tenant John McGilchrist Ross, in 1864. But when Alfred Barnard visited Teaninich during his tour of 1885-87 he had little to say about it. He was in a hurry to catch a train to Dingwall, but one senses that he was there was insufficient evidence of up-to-date technology to excite him.[28]

When Ross gave up his lease in 1894 a lease was taken by the firm of Munro and Cameron of Elgin, who wanted a further up-grade. A. Maitland & Sons designed this and sought tenders for renovation and additions in 1895, for an excise officer's house in 1896, a bonded warehouse in 1897 and offices in 1898.[29]

The Maitlands' work at Teaninich was clearly substantial, but no evidence of it remains to-day. Successive expansions in the twentieth and early twenty-first centuries have involved the demolition of the nineteenth century buildings - and their substitution with functional modern replacements singularly lacking in charm. Alness itself has grown, moreover, so that the modern distillery is, fittingly, surrounded by an industrial estate.

From boom to bust

As late as 1907 Slater's Directory was describing A. Maitland & Sons as 'architects and distillery engineers', and it is likely that the Maitlands were involved with other distilleries besides those mentioned above. Thus in 1882 the *Ross-shire Journal* noted that the Balblair Distillery at Edderton, some five miles west of Tain, 'is about to be considerably enlarged under the superintendence of the Messrs Maitlands'.[30] Balblair was, however, rebuilt closer to the railway for a new tenant, Alexander Cowan, in 1894-95 to designs by Charles C. Doig, which included the iconic Doig ventilator. Newspaper reports also show the building of a new distillery, Glenskiach, near Evanton, in 1896-7, and one wonders whether the Maitlands may have been involved.

But to-day, with the Ben Wyvis and Gerston distilleries long since closed and the Teaninich buildings replaced, the only distilleries to retain substantial evidence of the work of the Maitlands are Glenmorangie and Dalmore.

Whilst the Maitlands were helping to add to the stock of malt whisky distilleries others were doing the same on an astonishing scale, particularly in Banffshire and Moray. At the beginning of this period of expansion there were 8 distilleries in Banffshire, but by 1897 there were 21, with several more being built and the original ones being expanded, sometimes eightfold. The 1890s alone saw 33 new distilleries built in the Highlands. Nearly 2 million gallons of malt whisky were warehoused in 1891-92, and this had increased to 13½ million by 1898-9 This expansion was paralleled by increases in grain whisky capacity further south and in the production of blended whisky. Much of this expansion was financed by imprudent bank lending. Speculators moved in: some built distilleries and then cashed in by floating their companies, whilst others invested in maturing whisky stocks.

But the iron laws of economics invariably prevail. Booms that get out of control always turn to bust. The proximate cause in this case was the dramatic failure of Pattisons Ltd, a whisky blending company that had invested in malt distilleries. The brothers Walter and Robert Pattison were flamboyant characters, given to extravagance both in their personal lives and in corporate advertising. They gave away 500 parrots trained to repeat phrases such as 'Buy Pattisons Whisky'. They deliberately missed trains and then ostentatiously hired private trains to make the journey. The Pattison brothers raised £150,000 in a public flotation in March 1896, but the company collapsed in December 1898. The liquidator subsequently found that the profits shown in the prospectus were only achieved by hiding invoices, that the assets shown were overstated by artificially inflating goodwill and by valuing stocks of Irish whisky bought at 11½d. per gallon as 'fine old Glenlivet whisky' worth 8s. 6d. per gallon, and that profits of £111,000 which the Pattisons claimed to have earned were non-existent. The Crown authorities followed the liquidation with interest. In April 1901 Robert Pattison, was arrested at his mansion house near Dunoon, donning an Inverness cloak and a Yankee hat before being taken away. Walter, catching a train at North Berwick, unexpectedly found himself accompanied on his journey by police officers.The brothers were tried in the High Court of Justiciary in July. After a nine day trial Robert was convicted on four counts of fraud and embezzlement and Walter on two counts.[31]

The effects on the whisky industry were traumatic. Pattisons Ltd owed at least £500,000 and the immediate impact was felt by its creditors, with ten other businesses also collapsing. But the whole market was affected: whisky prices collapsed and production was cut by a third in order to bring it more in line with demand. Thirty distilleries were closed, either temporarily or permanently, and those that remained limped on into the twentieth century and a prolonged depression. The first half of that century - characterised by the imposition by Lloyd George of heavy duties on spirits, the Great War, a major depression, and another world war - was not kind to the whisky industry, and closures included two Maitland distilleries, Ben Wyvis and Gerston. Glenmorangie, still under Maitland influence, was, as we will see, to be seriously affected by these pressures.

References and Notes

[1] Informative accounts are provided by Charles MacLean, *Scotch Whisky, a Liquid History*, Cassell Illustrated, 2005, chapters V and VI, and *The Scotch Whisky Book*, Tom Bruce-Gardyne, Lomond Books, 2005, pp.15-29.

[2] *Ross-shire Journal*, 15th March, 1878: *Inverness Courier*, 16th October and 28th December, 1878 and 16th October, 1879.

[3] *The Scotsman*, 16th October, 1879. A more detailed account was given in the following day's *Ross-shire Journal.*

[4] *Hansard*, 7th August, 1882.

[5] Alfred Barnard, *The Whisky Distilleries of The United Kingdom*, Proprietors of Harper's Weekly Gazette, 1887, reprinted by Birlinn Ltd, 2012, pp.167-69. Barnard gives the output as 160,000 gallons.

[6] Brian Townsend, *Scotch Missed - The Lost Distilleries of Scotland*, Neil Wilson Publishing 2000 and 2004, pp.40-42.

[7] *Ross-shire Journal,* 17th July, 1885 and *John o'Groat Journal*, 27th April, 1887.

[8] Barnard, *op. cit.*, p.159.

[9] www.lost-distillery.com/pages/gerston.

[10] Townsend, *op. cit.*, pp.42-43.

[11] Barnard, *op. cit.*, p.163.

[12] *Inverness Courier*, 18th July, 1848.

[13] *Inverness Courier*, 8th November, 1849.

[14] *Inverness Advertiser*, 13th November, 1849.

[15] *Inverness Courier*, 21st August, 1844.

[16] *Edinburgh Evening Courant*, 2nd December, 1852.

[17] *Inverness Advertiser*, 1st October, 1880. *Poteen* was a raw spirit or 'moonshine' first produced in Irish monasteries in the sixth century.

[18] The author is extremely grateful to Iain Russell, Brands Heritage Manager of The Glenmorangie Co. Ltd for sharing with him the results of his researches into the involvement in Glenmorangie of the Maitland family, for suggesting further lines of enquiry and for helpful comments on the draft of this chapter.

[19] National Records of Scotland, CS351/3405.

[20] *Inverness Courier*, 14th February, 1888. They also sought tenders for an excise officer's house and a bonded warehouse on 13th May, 1889.

[21] *Ross-shire Journal*, 4th May, 1894.

[22] *Inverness Courier*, 12th March, 1874 - advertisement for tenders for works on a new distillery, and tun-room, malt barn, granaries and water reservoir.

[23] Barnard, *op. cit.*, pp.164-65.

[24] *The Scotsman*, 25th January, 1892.

[25] University of Glasgow Archives Hub: *Summary of Records of Mackenzie Brothers, whisky distillers*, online at cheshire.cent. gla.ac.uk.

[26] Tenders: *Inverness Courier* 2nd May, 1893 for rebuilding, 12th February, 1895 and 19th May, 1896 for bonded warehouses. Architectural drawings: Historic Environment Scotland RCD 43/1 to 12.

[27] Alfred Barnard wrote, at an unknown date, a second report, *Dalmore - a Celebrated Highland Distillery*, perhaps as a plug for Dalmore. This report has been added to the Birlinn edition of Barnard, *op. cit*, and appears as pp.567-82.

[28] Barnard, *op. cit*, p.166.

[29] *Inverness Courier*, 5th July, 1895, 24th July, 1896 and 29th June, 1897, *Ross-shire Journal* 14th January, 1898. Tenders were also sought for another bonded warehouse in 1900.

[30] *Ross-shire Journal*, 9th June, 1882. Requests for further information from the distillery have not been successful.

[31] *The Scotsman*, 9th April and various dates in July 1901.

17. A SECOND WAVE OF CHURCH BUILDING

An age of religion - and of schisms

The Victorian and Edwardian periods saw church building in the Highlands on a remarkable scale. This reflected not just the the deep hold that religion had on society but also the perennial tendency of Scottish Presbyterianism to fragment and hence to require new premises. Most of this church building came in three great waves.

The first of these waves came in the immediate aftermath of the Disruption of 1843, when the Free Church built a new religious infrastructure modelled on that of the established church from which it had seceded. As we saw earlier, the new church had exhibited an extraordinary burst of energy in appealing for money, sites and materials and in constructing churches, manses and schools. But plans were supplied from Edinburgh, which reduced the scope for original designs by Highland architects such as Andrew Maitland Senior in his work in Resolis and Tain.

A second wave was taking shape in the mid 1860s, gained momentum in the 1870s and lasted to the end of the nineteenth century. The main thrust of this wave was the replacement by Free Church congregations of churches and manses built in the wake of the Disruption. This second wave, which led to the building of a dozen Maitland-designed new or replacement churches, including some of their finest works, is the main subject of this chapter. Contemporary accounts show that ceremonies for the laying of foundation stones were events of huge local interest, and that the new churches were packed for the opening services - usually one in English and one in Gaelic.

In 1900 the Free Church itself was to break into two. The major part formed a union with the United Presbyterian Church and styled itself the United Free Church. As we will see later, this was to lead to a third wave, particularly marked in the Highlands, of building churches and manses. The Maitlands were to design many of these.

Why a second wave of Free Churches?

The obvious question is why so many commissions for a second wave of Free Churches were appearing up to half century after the Disruption of 1843. The answer comes across very clearly if we look at the records of the Free Church for the two periods - and nowhere more clearly than in those of Tain.[1]

The Committee of the newly formed Tain Free Church Association met on 23rd June, 1843. The minutes record that 'The Committee had before them the printed suggestions and plans of new Churches, and being of opinion that the building of a Church should immediately be proceeded with, so as to be completed if possible before winter ... they remitted to a sub-committee to meet with tradesmen. ... The Church should be made to accommodate about 950 sittings'. Clearly they were in a considerable hurry, though in the event the church was not completed until October 1844. They had available, as early as five weeks after the Disruption, what were regarded as plans adequate for their requirements. When Andrew Maitland Senior had been called in to assist his role was not to provide a new design but working plans, specifications and estimates.[2] As John Gifford explains, 'Designs for cheap churches, built of wood and brick and roofed with felt, had been produced before the Disruption, but in the event most early Free Churches were plain versions of the 'Parliamentary' churches, rectangular or T-plan, with a birdcage bellcote, stone-built with slated roofs'.[3]

Nearly half a century later, on 22nd July, 1890, the Deacons' Court of the Tain Free Church considered a Report by A. Maitland & Sons on the ventilation of the 1843-44 church. This noted that 'the Church was built at the time of the Disruption - when necessity compelled the speedy erection and completion of a large number of Churches, and in consequence little attention was paid to comfort and sanitary requirements and it forms no exception in this respect to others built about the same period. The walls should have been at least 6 feet higher and the ventilation was unsatisfactory'.

In the late nineteenth century Free Church congregations, like that of Tain, would again and again find that it was desirable, or even necessary, to replace their original church, either on the original site or on a new one. By this period standards of living had improved, and the professional and merchant classes had assumed a more prominent role in the eldership. They wanted more comfort - more space to sit, heating systems, and sanitary facilities. They fancied loftier and more impressive places of worship, often superior to those of their established church rivals, and they liked pitch-pine furnishings. Their involvement made it easier to find donations for bigger and better churches, enhanced the ability to raise loans, and facilitated the success of bazaars and other fund-raising events. This second wave of Free Church building offered far more scope for architects than had the first. Externally there were more architectural features. Internally it became increasingly common towards the end of the century to rearrange churches and to build new churches in a different pattern. The pulpit, with the precentor's seat and communion table in front of it, had normally been in the middle of the long side of the building with the pews running from end to end and facing it, but it was now placed at an end with the pews running across the narrower axis and facing that end.

Building for the Free Church around the Highlands

Kilmuir Easter saw the first of the new wave of Free Church commissions received by the Maitland partnership. By 1875 the church, near the medieval Chapel of Delny, built immediately after the Disruption was thought to be dangerous. A Maitland-designed replacement was completed in 1876, 'an Early French Gothic edifice, erected at a cost of £1,500 and containing 500 sittings'.[4] 1876 also saw a commission for a new manse in Cromarty.

The early 1880s saw two very different Free Church congregations commission the Maitlands - those of the prosperous burgh of Nairn on the south shore of the Moray Firth and the rural parish of Creich in Sutherland.

Nairn, 13 miles east of Inverness, had been a place to which medical practitioners of the late eighteenth century sent their upper class patients for the restorative benefits of sea-bathing and sea air. Where the sick went the healthy followed, and where the upper classes went humbler folk followed. After Nairn was connected to

17.1 Nairn Free Church, now St Ninian's Church of Scotland.

Inverness by railway in 1855 a tourist boom ensued, and by the 1880s half the visitors to Nairn came from London and the south of England. Nairn became a popular place for retirement and was promoted as the 'Brighton of the North'.[5] As the population expanded membership of the Free Church congregation increased. The size of the Disruption church was considered too limited, and fund raising for a new church began in 1879. A commanding site at the top of the High Street was secured. The Building Committee invited architects to submit anonymous designs and unanimously chose that of A. Maitland & Sons, who advertised for tenders in March 1880.[6] The result won plaudits from the press. It was 'one of the handsomest erections in the North of Scotland', built of the local hard sandstone, the colour of dry sea sand. The design was an 'elegant Gothic. ... There can be no doubt that the *tout ensemble* seen under a bright summer sky or in brilliant moonlight is immensely superior to buildings in the "too Gothic" style with their bewildering gables in incomprehensible corners'. The frontage consisted of a fine tower and spire 156 feet in height at the west side, a central gable, and an octagonal tower at the east giving access to the gallery. The handsome woodwork was of pitch pine. At the rear was a building with a meeting hall, ladies room, session room and vestry. The cost was around £7,000. There were sittings for 1,200 persons, fully taken up for an opening ceremony in December 1881. This was performed by the Rev. Dr John Kennedy of Dingwall, the 'prince of preachers' and the author of *The Days of the Fathers in Ross-shire*.[7] The church, later used by the United Free Church, is now St Ninian's, Church of Scotland.

Creich was an extensive rural parish in the south of Sutherland, extending westward from within 3 miles of Dornoch for 35 miles along the north shore of the Dornoch Firth, the Kyle of Sutherland and the river Oykell. The Rev. Gustavus Aird had been Minister since shortly after the Disruption in in 1843 and was to remain there until 1896. Gustavus Aird was to preach at the opening of three more Maitland-designed Free Churches, typically at some length, and usually at Gaelic services. His unusual Christian name derived from the participation of one of his ancestors in the Thirty Years' War, fighting under Gustavus Adolphus, King of Sweden, at the battle of Lutzen in 1633. He was widely admired for his prominent role in opposing the clearances at Glencalvie in 1842-45 and for the quality of his preaching. He was to become, albeit with a show of reluctance, Moderator of the Free Church General Assembly in 1888. He had strong views and expressed them forcibly. Thus at a commemoration of the Covenanters in 1880 he is reported as lamenting the unsettling tendencies of the age, roundly abusing the Government and newspapers for their support of Atheistic and Popish tendencies and characterising the newspapers as 'nasty things that would do anything for money'. (The Prime Minister at the time was none other than William Gladstone, perhaps more famed for his religiosity than any other Prime Minister before or since. But Aird would have seen his High Church Anglicanism as a Popish tendency.)

The old church, erected at the Disruption 'with all the dispatch which the exigencies of the case required' had 'latterly assumed a dilapidated appearance'. In 1880 tenders were sought by A. Maitland & Sons for a replacement church on the site of the old one near Migdale Mill, east of Bonar Bridge, and also a replacement Free Church school. The replacement church, completed in 1881, contained 530 sittings and cost about £1,500.[8] Still in use as Migdale Free Church, it is in a simple Gothic style and is aptly described by Gifford as 'a big lanceted box, (with) angle buttresses at the gable front'. The interior has a gallery on three sides.[9]

In the early 1880s the Maitlands also received several smaller commissions for Free Church buildings. These included improvements to the church at Nigg, a replacement manse for Resolis, additions and alterations to the manses at Rosskeen and Kinlochbervie, and, also at Kinlochbervie an addition to the church built in the wake of the Disruption (now the parish church). In Stornoway, a busy fishing port where it had been found necessary to build an 'English Free Church' to cater for visitors who could not speak Gaelic, the Maitlands designed a manse for the new church.

In 1884 the Maitlands produced plans for and advertised for estimates for a Free Church congregation in the Black Isle, this time at Munlochy in the parish of Knockbain.[10] A new church and meeting hall were completed in August 1886. But there had been two decades of controversy in the parish. The new church was a bone of contention, with those in the south and west of the parish claiming that it had been built without proper authority. The General Assembly of the Free Church wrestled with the problem on three occasions and decided to divide the congregation into two. One section, along with the minister, moved to the new Maitland church, which became Knockbain Munlochy Free Church. A larger section of the congregation was named Knockbain West Free Church and built a new church close to the old one at Bogallan.[11] The Maitland church is another described by Gifford as a 'big lanceted box'.[12] Its congregation joined the United Free Church in 1900, and in 1929 it became the Munlochy Church of Scotland.

Two more churches, both in a simple Romanesque style, were designed by the Maitlands for the Free Church in the Wester Ross parish of Gairloch. One of these, built in 1888, was at Aultbea, where the church built at the Disruption was in a poor state and had to be replaced. The new church, still in use, occupies a prominent position on the main road fronting the bay. The other, built in 1889 at Poolewe, took the place of a meeting-house. Osgood Mackenzie of Inverewe, creator of the world-famous gardens, and, as we have seen, a client of Andrew Maitland Senior, was - unusually for a heritor - a member of the Free Church and he worshipped at both Aultbea and Poolewe. This did not prevent a major falling-out when the Free Church congregation took umbrage at Osgood signing a petition for the settlement of an assistant to a vacant living in the established church. Osgood wrote to three newspapers complaining of their intolerant attitude, and they in turn complained that he had contributed nothing to the fund for the erection of the two churches. The matter, like that of Knockbain, reached the General Assembly of the Free Church, which issued a mild rebuke to Osgood.[13]

Helmsdale on the East coast of Sutherland had been developed by the Sutherland estate in the wake of the Clearances as a fishing village. The objective had been to accommodate and provide work for tenants displaced, in favour of sheep, from the Strath of Kildonan and other inland straths. By the Victorian era it had become one of the most significant ports of the Scottish herring fishing industry. Here too the majority of the congregation had 'come out' in 1843. Hugh Miller had observed six to eight hundred people in the open in the fish curing yards, 'their Gaelic singing [was] more melancholy than usual. ... I hear that when the Duke passed through the place some of the women put out their tongues and began to "Baa" like sheep'. A jerry-built church and school had been very quickly erected, but by 1889 the church was found to be 'so worn out that it would be unwise to attempt to repair it'. A. Maitland & Sons were appointed as architects, and in 1890-91 the church and former schoolroom were demolished and were replaced close to the old church by a new Gothic church to hold 1,200 and a mission hall to hold 300. The cost was £3,212.[14] At the opening the ubiquitous Dr Gustavus Aird of Creich preached a sermon in Gaelic and a minister from Glasgow one in English.

Tain: 'If there be a willing mind the success of our object is sure'

The Maitlands' next ecclesiastical commission was in 1890-92, for the Free Church, now the Parish Church, in their home town of Tain - one of the firm's best known works. This is said to be the last commission in which Andrew Senior, nearing 90 when the church was opened, took an interest. Although he was a member of the Deacons' Court, which was responsible for property matters and fund-raising, he is not, however, recorded as appearing at their meetings or indeed at any other meetings connected with the new church. His son James was, however, heavily involved throughout.

What comes over strongly from the minutes of the various meetings connected with the project[15] is the sharp contrast between those responsible for commissioning ecclesiastical buildings in earlier decades and those now responsible. Andrew Senior had dealt with heritors and their factors on matters relating to the established church. James was now dealing with a broad spectrum of the middle classes on Free Church commissions. The Elders and Deacons included a bank agent, a solicitor, an accountant, a hotelier, several merchants and various tradesmen - and a colporteur (a distributor of religious publications). But the system of charging pew rents still prevailed. A Seating Committee, meeting before the new church was opened, fixed rentals at rates ranging from six shillings to one shilling per year depending on positioning. This had the obvious effect of differentiating between different social strata. Some historians believe that the system also reduced the appeal of the church to workers and the poor - though in Tain some free seats were reserved 'for Poorhouse and others requiring free seating'.

As mentioned above, in July 1890 the Deacons' Court had considered a report by A. Maitland & Sons on the church hurriedly built at the Disruption. They preferred 'an extensive renovation' to a simple re-seating and improved ventilation. This led, on 5th September, to 'a largely attended meeting of the Office Bearers, members and adherents of the Free Church Congregation of Tain, called by Public Notice'. The Rev. Thomas Grant, who had been Minister since 1858, presided. John Mackenzie (the present author's grandfather), a solicitor and Town Clerk of Tain, who was also Session Clerk and Treasurer of the congregation, narrated the various steps that had taken place since the Maitland Report had been prepared. The view had emerged that the old church had served its day and should be replaced. This view had gained impetus when he had been approached by Ronald Ross, of Ankerville Cottage, Tain, who had offered to contribute £1,000. Ross had told Mackenzie that for a new church he would give a thousand pounds, but for an old church not one penny.

Ross's ancestors had first acquired property in Tain in 1638, and he was the seventh or eighth eldest son to succeed to that property. He was the son of a mason and had made his money as a merchant in Liverpool. He was now 80 and not able to be present. In a letter he wrote 'If there be a willing mind, as there was when King David was collecting the Gold and the Silver for the building of the Temple, the success of our object is sure'. William Miller, a 79 year old retired draper and wine merchant, had offered a share of the residue of his estate, estimated at £500 to £800. His bequest had been made in a will of 1887; he had, however, yet to die.

Provost Edward Matheson proposed and William White, coal merchant, seconded a resolution approving the steps taken. This was carried unanimously. A Building Committee was appointed to 'carry out the Buildings to their completion'. No less than 51 members were appointed to this committee. These included many of the good and the great of Tain. James Maitland was appointed a member. Tradesmen were appointed to the committee 'on the express understanding that any one of them who is an offeror for any part of the work shall not be a member of the Committee who will consider the offers'.

The new Tain Free Church

Everything then happened remarkably quickly. The Building Committee met on 10th September, with James Maitland present, and approved plans submitted by his firm. It was noted on 21st October that the new church was to be on the same site as the old, but little was to be retained. 'The style of architecture adopted is Italian. While the external appearance has received due consideration, the main object kept in view by the architects has been to provide a thoroughly comfortable Church, where every sitter can both see and hear'.

By April, 1891 working plans were in place and contractors had been selected.[16] The contracts accepted amounted to £4,380, 'but', *The Scotsman* noted, 'if the upper stages of the tower be completed the cost will be £5,090. The style of architecture adopted is Italian Renaissance. The main front will have an elegant and imposing appearance, its principal feature being a tower at the north-east corner, with open upper stages, and having arched openings flanked by pilasters and columns of the Corinthian order, the whole being finished with a stone dome at the top, and rising to the height of 107 feet'.[17]

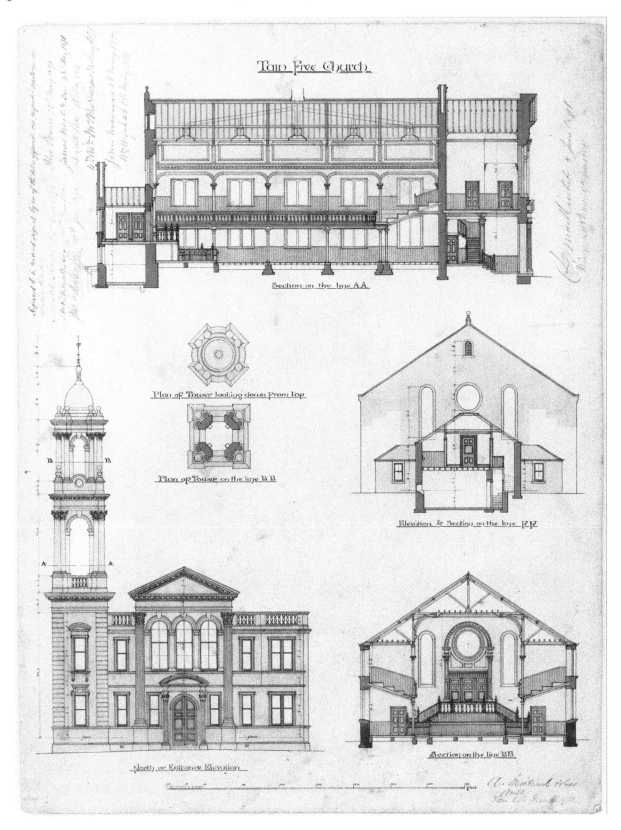

17.2 Plans, signed by James Maitland in 1892, for a replacement Free Church in Tain.

The building works were under the superintendence of A. Maitland & Sons. Most of the contractors chosen were local. They included Alexander Munro, (mason contractor), James Nicol and Son (carpenter work), Murdo Urquhart (cabinet maker, responsible for the turning work and carving), and plastering, painting, plumbing and slating contractors. Most were members of the church and are reputed to have done their work at cost.[18] (This perhaps contributed to Urquhart going bankrupt in March 1894.)

In May the old church was demolished within 10 days. On 13th July, 1891 the foundation stone of the new church was laid - with the customary deposits of documents, coinage and books - by Ronald Ross in the presence of 2,000 people. The Provost, magistrates (including Andrew Junior) and town council, attended by their halberdiers, were present in their corporate capacity. James Maitland sat on a platform with the ministers and Ronald Ross. Prayers were said by Thomas Grant and the much in demand Gustavus Aird. 50 workmen were entertained in the Maitland-designed Free Church Hall to a 'tea with meat', provided by Mr Finlayson of the Royal Hotel at 1/9d. per head.

John Mackenzie as Treasurer was again kept busy during the construction period. Earlier in the year, engaged to be married, he had acquired a house in Queen Street. This was immediately opposite the church, and was later appropriately named Tower Place. He married in Inverness on 1st July, had a honeymoon at the Foyers Hotel, and returned in time to attend to arrangements for the opening ceremony. He also found himself dealing with problems affecting the viability of the proposed tower. That same month ex-Provost Dr James Vass declared that he was 'not disposed to let the work proceed' because the tower encroached by 25 yards on a roadway that he used to access Alpin House. (Oddly enough the good doctor had

17.3 The Tain Free Church of 1892-93, now the Parish Church.

contributed £50 to the building fund.) Sir Charles Ross of Balnagown, who owned the Balnagown Inn, was then persuaded to agree to feu 25 yards of the inn garden adjacent to the road to facilitate Vass's access. But Vass would have nothing to do with this as he 'objected to becoming Balnagown's Vassal'. Dr Vass later agreed to sell to the congregation land referred to as 'the park' for £400 with conditions including a right of carriage from his garden to Queen Street. At the same time as he was negotiating with Dr Vass, John Mackenzie was involved with funding, and it was not until 1st October that funds (including the prospective bequest of William Miller, who still had seven months to live) were deemed adequate to proceed with the construction of the upper stages of the tower.

The imposing galleried interior was first occupied for the opening of the new church on 19th August, 1892, before the tower had been completed. Events and speeches were reported in considerable detail in a short-lived local newspaper.[19] The Rev. Dr Gustavus Aird popped up yet again to preach 'a very able, intelligent and appropriate sermon' during a Gaelic service in the morning. Then, the Town Council having recommended that merchants close their premises during the hours of an afternoon service in English, the church was 'well filled in every part'. At 7.00 P.M. an evening meeting was addressed by ten main speakers, each limited to ten minutes - though some must have over-run their allotted time. The main themes were praise and thanks - particularly to the Almighty, but also to those involved with the project. Whilst it is gratifying to a descendant to read the tributes paid to John Mackenzie ('I never in my life', said Roderick Finlayson of the Royal Hotel, 'and I am sixty years, saw one who carried on the work like Mr Mackenzie'), it is surprising to note that neither James Maitland nor his firm were reported as having been mentioned.

When the tower, reminiscent of an Italian campanile, was completed it not only complemented the facade but also gave the Tain skyline a distinctive feature still visible from afar and complementary to the steeple of the Tolbooth. Today the church is one of the most iconic features of the Tain townscape, and more photographed than anything except the Tolbooth.[20] But James Maitland's tower is a magnet for the seagulls with which Tain is plagued.

A red letter day at Portmahomack

The next Free Church project after that for Tain was for the congregation of Tarbat. 27th October, 1892 was an exceedingly cold day, punctuated by showers. Andrew Maitland Junior was involved in two ceremonies that day at Portmahomack, nine miles east of Tain and then a very active fishing village. They were the opening of a fountain and the laying of a 'foundation-stone - or rather a memorial-stone' for a replacement Free Church for the parish of Tarbat. Both ceremonies generated an extraordinary degree of local interest and were comprehensively reported.

Five years earlier gravitation water had been introduced to Portmahomack, hitherto dependant on spring water. To commemorate this event Peter Macdonald, a native of Portmahomack who had prospered as a rectifier[21] and wine merchant in Glasgow, presented a water fountain to the community. As a keen freemason he asked the brethren of St Duthus Lodge in Tain, whose Right Worshipful Master was Andrew Maitland Junior, to open the fountain with Masonic honours. Over twenty of the brethren drove from Tain with masonic flags flying, arriving at noon in Portmahomack, which was decorated with flags, bannerettes and streamers. With the masons, headed by a piper who played the 'Merry Masons', arranged around the fountain, Macdonald delivered a lengthy and nostalgic speech to a large crowd. After making a plea for the union of the Free Church and the Church of Scotland and pledging to take £1,000 worth of shares in a branch railway line then mooted from Fearn to Portmahomack, he invited Brother Bailie Maitland to declare the fountain open in due and ancient masonic form. The Brother Bailie then paid fulsome tribute to the donor and declared the 'fountain open by taking the first draught of its limpid contents, which he would drink to Mr Macdonald's health'.

Although the accompanying horse trough has long gone, the fountain, 'an exceedingly handsome and attractive acquisition to the amenity of the place', its centre-piece 'a bronze nymph sitting on a water jar underneath a prettily executed dome', still stands. With its scenic backdrop of the Dornoch Firth and the Sutherland mountains, it is a magnet for tourists' photographs.

The second ceremony, the laying of a memorial-stone of the new church, was witnessed by over a thousand people. 'One was almost inclined during the devotional part of the proceedings', wrote the reporter, 'to retain one's headgear for protection against the keenness of the uncharitable air'. The building which the new church replaced had been hurriedly built, with seating for 900 people, the year after the Disruption at a modest cost of about £500. The woodwork was immature and soon gave way, and during the last few years the church had been 'in quite an unsafe state for worship'. It had therefore been razed, and a new church, to be built on the same site, had been designed by Andrew Maitland Junior. This was also designed to seat 900 people, but in more space and comfort. The cost was estimated at £2,300, towards which £1,350 had already been raised locally and £250 promised by the central Building Committee of the Free Church.

After partaking of 'masonic refreshments' - the type of which was not reported - Andrew Junior took his place in the platform party for the second ceremony of the day, which began at 1.30 P.M. The Hundredth Psalm was sung, a 'commendably short … but much to the point' prayer of dedication said, and a document giving the facts leading up to the ceremony read out and then deposited, along with current coins and copies of *The Scotsman* and local papers, in a cavity beneath the memorial-stone by an Aberdeenshire worthy, William Ferguson of Kinmundy. Before inviting Ferguson to lay the stone, the minister, the Rev. Dugald Matheson recalled the ecclesiastical history of the parish. Ferguson, chairman of the Great North of Scotland Railway Company, was regarded as a very enthusiastic Free Churchman, but in a long speech after laying the memorial-stone he too took the opportunity to deliver a heartfelt plea for a reconstruction of the Presbyterian Church in Scotland by a re-union of the Free Church with the established church. This was to happen in large measure - but not for another 37 years, and not before a further schism that was to lead to another wave of church building in which James Maitland was to be heavily involved. After the second ceremony a 'large company', whose stomachs must by then have been rumbling, sat down to luncheon in the Public School - a building no doubt familiar to Andrew Junior, since his firm had designed it.

The new church, Gothic in style, with its gabled east front flanked by distinctive rounded gallery stair wings, was completed at a final cost of £2,400. It was formally opened in December 1893 by the seemingly omnipresent Rev. Dr Gustavus Aird of Creich. The debt incurred by the congregation was paid off by 1900.[22]

17.4 An early photograph of Tarbat Free Church, Portmahomack.

Rosskeen - the last of the wave of replacement Free Churches

The last years of the nineteenth century saw the end of the demand for replacement churches for the Free Church - though there were still congregations seeking renovation work (as at Stornaway where the Maitlands were commissioned by the Free Gaelic Church in late 1892).[23] The voices calling for change in the position of the Free Church were getting louder.

The last church designed by the Maitlands for the Free Church in the nineteenth century was for the congregation of Rosskeen, at Achnagarron. The original church had been opened there in 1845, and a separate charge with its own church (now the Parish Church) in Invergordon had been formed in 1861. The impetus for the building of a new church at Achnagarron came from the death of an elder, Mr Denoon, whose family had a grain merchant's business in Invergordon. At a meeting of the congregation in February 1898 the Rev. John Ross announced that Denoon had left 'something like £2,800' to the Deacons' Court for the purpose of building a new church or otherwise spending the money as they thought best in the interest of the congregation. It was agreed to build a new church on the existing site at Achnagarron. A. Maitland & Sons produced a design. On 6th July James Maitland, who (following the death of his brother Andrew Junior in May), was the sole surviving member of the triumvirate, presented tenders. These aggregated £3,218-5s-0d (all of which bar £127-0-0 came from Tain contractors) for a building to seat 1,000. The new church was opened on 14th June, 1900 with a Gaelic and two English services.[24]

Four months later the majority of the Free Church entered into a Union with the United Presbyterian Church, thus creating the United Free Church. The Rev. John Ross and most of the congregation joined the United Free Church. As we will see in chapter 24, extraordinarily bitter disputes ensued in Rosskeen and many other Ross-shire parishes between the United Free Church and the residual Free Church - disputes which led to another wave of church building in which James Maitland and his nephew were to play a prominent role.

The Rosskeen Free Church at Achnagarron is to-day a well known landmark, occupying a prominent position beside the A9 between Tain and Inverness. The view is, however, that of the back of the church as the main road no longer goes to the front of it. Thanks to Mr Denoon's benefaction the Maitland design, with its octagonal spire, is more distinctive than some of the other large box-shaped churches, and internally the church retains pitch pine woodwork of a high quality.

The established church

From the Disruption in 1843 until early in the twentieth century the Free Church remained the predominant religious and social institution in the Highlands. The bulk of the Maitlands' ecclesiastical work in the period, including some of their most cherished buildings, was thus for the Free Church.

They continued, however, to receive commissions for the Church of Scotland. With few exceptions the heritors remained in the established church after the Disruption (though later in the century some of the more anglicised ones joined the Episcopal Church). They lost the residue of their direct responsibility for education and school buildings when school boards were established in the wake of the Education (Scotland) Act 1872, but they remained responsible for the provision of ecclesiastical buildings of the Church of Scotland in each parish. Most of the numerous established church commissions received by the Maitlands in this period were for alterations, additions and repairs to older churches and manses. The only new church[25] appears to be that at Rosehall in Sutherland. Rosehall was in the parish of Creich, but was 14 miles from the parish church at Bonar Bridge. A 'missionary station' had been established there in the eighteenth century. A century later the parish minister pushed long and hard for a replacement for the mission chapel, which dated from 1808. Though he did not live to see it, the Maitland firm was commissioned in 1891 to design a new church. This was opened the following year in a ceremony at which the Rev. Dr James Joass of Golspie, a well regarded geologist and antiquarian, officiated. Dr Joass, who was the brother of the Maitlands' competitor William C. Joass of Dingwall, said that 'the design and appearance add another to the many evidences already existing of the skill and ability of the architects, Messrs Maitland'. Gifford, however, remarks on the 'cheap Romanesque detail'. The church is no longer in use.[26]

References and Notes

[1] Tain Free Church Deacons' Court Minutes 1843-1899, Highland Archive Centre CH 3/748/1 and 2.

[2] See chapter 2.

[3] Gifford, *Highland and Islands* p.38. (In an earlier wave of church building 32 new 'Parliamentary churches' had been built for the established Church under the Act for Building Additional Places of Worship in the Highlands and Islands of Scotland, 1823. This provided funds for building churches and manses to standard designs and budgets for the then growing population. The great engineer Thomas Telford supervised the project, though the designs were mainly by one of his surveyors, William Thomson.)

[4] *Inverness Courier,* 29th July, 1875 and F.H. Groome, *Ordnance Gazetteer of Scotland,* 1882-84. Much of the congregation joined the new United Free Church in the early years of the twentieth century, and this building does not appear to feature in any modern records.

[5] This account is derived from *Moray, Banff and Nairn,* Eric Simpson, John Donald Publishers Ltd, 1992, chapter 10.

[6] *Ross-shire Journal,* 26th March, 1880.

[7] *Aberdeen Journal,* 9th and 13th November, 1880 and 30th December, 1881; Historic Environment Scotland LB38442, Highland HER MHG16010.

[8] *Ross-shire Journal,* 11th February, 1881.

[9] *Inverness Advertiser,* 15th April, 1880; Historic Environment Scotland LB268; Highland HER MHG16954; Gifford *op. cit.,* p.589.

[10] Plans at NRS RHP97755, 6, and 7; *Inverness Courier,* 14th April, 1884.

[11] The controversy was reported in various issues of *The Scotsman,* particularly 1st June, 1886.

[12] Gifford, *op. cit.,* p. 439. Gifford attributes this church to John Rhind, but it is clear that A. Maitland & Sons produced the plans held in the National Records of Scotland and that they advertised for tenders. Rhind is generally credited with the other Knockbain church at Bogallan.

[13] Aultbea Highland HER MHG49557, Poolewe MHG33193. For a full account of the shenanigans see Pauline Butler, *Eighty Years in the Highlands, the Life and Times of Osgood H. Mackenzie of Inverewe,* Librario Publishing Ltd, 2010, pp.253-58; also *The Scotsman,* 7th March, 1889.

[14] This account is based on J.R.D. Campbell, *Some Helmsdale Memories,* Timespan Heritage Centre, 1998, pp. 34-35. See also Highland HER MHG29776, which has some fine photographs.

[15] Minutes of the Tain Free Church Deacons' Court, 1843-99, Highland Archive Centre, CH3/748/2.

[16] Invitations to tender *Ross-shire Journal* 10th April, 1891; plans held by Historic Environment Scotland, Canmore C47125 to 32.

[17] *The Scotsman,* 27th April, 1891.

[18] *The Passing Century, Tain Parish Church, 1892-1992,* the Rev. Alexander G. Macalpine, 1992.

[19] The *Tain Free Lance,* 23rd August, 1892, reproduced in *Tain, the Passing Century, op. cit.*

[20] Historic Environment Scotland LB41895.

[21] Rectifiers bought in whisky or other spirits, mixed or blended them, and sometimes added other ingredients.

[22] Highland HER MHG16528. See also Alexander Fraser and Finlay Munro, *Tarbat, Easter Ross - A Historical Sketch,* Ross & Cromarty Heritage Society, 1988, p.67.

[23] *Ross-shire Journal,* 7th October, 1892.

[24] Highland HER MHG8031; *Aberdeen Journal* 23rd February, 1898; and Janice Maclellan, *Ordinary People, Extraordinary God - Celebrating 100 years of God at Work in Rosskeen Free Church of Scotland,* Christian Focus Publications, 2000, pp.11-15.

[25] *The Dictionary of Scottish Architects* and Gifford, *op.cit.* both ascribe the present Kiltearn Parish Church in Evanton (built in 1893 as the Hogg Memorial Church) and also Kiltearn Manse (also 1893) to A. Maitland & Sons. It is clear, however, from the *Ross-shire Journal* of 5th May, 1893 that the architect of the church was William C. Joass of Dingwall.

[26] *Ross-shire Journal,* 17th April, 1891, *Inverness Courier,* 3rd June 1892; Gifford, *op.cit.,* p.590.

18. LAIRDS IN THE AGE OF HIGH FARMING

High farming - and an agricultural depression

The last three decades of the nineteenth century saw a continuation of what became known as 'high farming' - a system of agriculture based on capital investment, on the use of scientific techniques linked to the use of fertilisers and imported manures such as guano, on intensified animal husbandry, and on increasing mechanisation. The great bulk of the Maitlands' work in this period was for rural buildings in the rich agricultural areas of Easter Ross, the Black Isle and Mid Ross. The vast majority of these were for the farm buildings which are still such a prominent feature of the rural landscape, but increasingly, as we will see, they were for what were called 'mansion houses', and on occasion castles, for landowners.

The prosperity of estate ownership reached its high water mark in or around the early 1870s. Thus out of a total population of 80,955 in Ross-shire and Cromartyshire in 1871 a mere 49 people owned land representing 67% of the gross annual value for the twin counties, and, reflecting the lower rental values in Wester Ross, 90% of the land area.[1] In the countryside, unlike in burghs like Tain where power now resided with the middle classes, the heritors still played a prominent role in local affairs and enjoyed considerable social prestige. Even though their responsibilities for poor relief, and education had been lost, or were lost during these years, they continued to occupy important positions, particularly on school boards, voluntary organisations and, from 1890, the new county councils. As we shall see, their status was, fortunately for architects like the Maitlands, frequently reflected in a desire to improve and often to 'baronialise' (convert to the Scottish Baronial style) their ancestral homes, and, especially in the case of newly wealthy clients wishing to upgrade their social standing, to build prestigious new homes. At the same time their prosperity was critically dependant on rental income. To attract tenants with sufficient capital to invest in high farming it was necessary to build farm houses of a quality which reflected the status of prosperous tenant farmers, to provide steadings which reflected evolving patterns in farming, and to house the farm servants employed by their tenants.

But the territory on which the Maitlands operated was, like the rest of rural Britain, soon affected by a long and severe agricultural depression, which lasted from about 1873-74 until 1896. The depression could be said to have been a delayed response to the repeal in 1846 of the Corn Laws, which had protected British arable farmers from foreign competition. Key drivers were technical developments beyond these shores - particularly a huge expansion of the American railroad system after the Civil War ended in 1865 and reductions in the cost of bulk ocean transport. Together these facilitated large scale importation to Britain of cheap grain from the American prairies. The most dramatic consequence was a fall in the average price of wheat of some 51% between 1867-71 and 1894-98.

The fall in agricultural prices had a serious impact on farm rents. New tenants sought reduced rents. Andrew Hall of Calrossie, near Tain (where in 1876 the Maitlands had added to the farmhouse built by Andrew Senior in 1847 and designed a block of servants' houses) won plaudits in 1879 for remitting the half-yearly rents of tenants due to the depression - but he was certainly not alone. One response to the crisis was to borrow, which landlords did on an increasing, and often debilitating, scale. Another was the fragmentation of estates. Individual farms were sold off, sometimes to sitting tenants, who as owner-occupiers became potential clients of architects in their own right. Newspapers published, with increasing frequency, advertisements for the sale of 'desirable small properties' with farmland attached and an 'excellent site for a dwelling-house' (whose design would require an architect). Thus Highland architects, the Maitlands included, were able to ride out the depression.

Bigger and better mansion houses for the lairds of Easter Ross

In the 1870s and early 1880s the Maitlands were engaged by four heritors on their own home patch of Easter Ross to design new mansion houses. All four already lived in houses on their estates, but none of them deemed them grand enough.

18.1 Rockfield House.

In 1867 the 21 year old Alexander Munro had inherited the 382 acre estate of Rockfield, near Portmahomack and nine miles east of Tain. Rockfield had come into the possession of his family in an unusual manner. Alexander (later Sir Alexander) Matheson had, whilst building up his vast property empire, bought the Ardross estate and also several smaller estates nearby. One such estate he sought was Lealty. Through a mutual disposition in 1847 with Alexander Munro's grandfather, Finlay Munro of Lealty, Matheson had acquired Lealty and Munro had got Rockfield, which had come into the possession of Matheson's family. 'One reason for this exchange was a proprietor's dislike of having his property looked down upon from the property of another. … Had Munro remained at Lealty he would have overlooked the site on which Matheson was building Ardross Castle.'[2]

Alexander Munro's inheritance included good agricultural land, which he farmed himself, a 'very fine and large steam mill', the small fishing village of Rockfield and a 'small but neat mansion with ornamental ground'. Although he was still single, the latter was clearly not good enough for him, for in 1870 he engaged Andrew Maitland to design a replacement.[3] He married the daughter of the local minister in 1876, but died of softening of the brain and partial paralysis in 1878. His three-bay house is still occupied by the family. With four reception rooms, bay windows, and a servants' wing at the rear, it is little changed and retains many attractive period features.

One of the most distinctive examples of the Maitlands' work is Kincraig House, near Invergordon - Scottish baronial in style, white-harled and highly visible from the present A9.[4] Its present eye-catching appearance reflects the dramatic transformation that baronialisation could achieve.

18.2 Kincraig Castle Hotel, formerly Kincraig House, near Invergordon, baronialised by Andrew Maitland in 1872.

In recent times Kincraig House has become a hotel and it is now a popular and well-respected venue. One earlier hotelier tried to raise its profile by calling it the Kincraig Castle Hotel and describing it as the former seat of the chiefs of the Clan Mackenzie. Though the name has stuck it was never a castle, and it had no direct connection with any chief of the clan. The Mackenzies of Kincraig were a 'cadet' branch which descended from a sixteenth century Mackenzie clan chief, and at the time he commissioned Andrew Maitland in 1872[5] the 27 year old Captain Roderick Mackenzie with his 1,086 acres was only fourteenth among the largest Mackenzie landowners in the twin counties of Ross-shire and Cromartyshire.

The captain's inheritance included a mansion house, built around 1800, with wings at the rear, perhaps used as farm offices, close to each side but not attached. This is shown both in the first 25 inch to the mile Ordnance Survey map and in a photograph taken before the Maitland alterations.[6] To-day the original mansion house, given a steep crow-stepped gablet flanked by conical-roofed bartizans on the southern elevation, forms the central portion of the enlarged house. The additions include crow-stepped projecting wings at each side, a round tower with a conical roof at the south west corner and a gabled bay with a new main entrance in a hoodmoulded Tudor arch on the west elevation.

Improving his mansion house may have put some strain on Roderick Mackenzie's finances, and the situation seems to have been aggravated by the agricultural depression. The inventory on his death in 1889 suggests that he was on thin ice financially. His heritable estate was burdened by loans of £6,680, and his personal estate showed a deficiency of £2-13s-8d. He owed his tenants money for farm buildings, and shortly before the work on Kincraig House he had borrowed from the marriage settlement of his wife Georgina, known as Georgie. They had no children and the widowed Georgie became liferentrix. The

Maitlands were engaged during her occupancy to design farm buildings for the estate at Broomhill in 1890 and Tomich in 1896 and further additions and improvements to Kincraig House itself in 1901.

The estate passed in 1918 to Roderick's nephew William Martineau, a scion of a sugar refining dynasty. William (later Sir William) appears to have carried out further work to Kincraig House, said to have been completed in 1923. The *Dictionary of Scottish Architects* entry for the house suggests that he employed the leading Highland architect Alexander Ross and his son John Alistair Ross. But what the Rosses did for Martineau is uncertain - did it include the white harling? and did it include any part of the Scottish baronial features we see to-day? Whatever the answer it is likely that the bulk of the baronialisation is a result of the Maitlands' involvement.[7] One thing we do know is that when the Macleods of Cadboll, the largest land owners in the Invergordon area, disposed of their estates after the Great War Martineau bought the Invergordon Castle estate. He then demolished the castle, built in 1873 on a site occupied since the fifteenth century, in order, it was rumoured, to improve his view from Kincraig House.

It was not only young lairds who wanted more imposing residences. In 1877, following a fire at Allan House, near Fearn, five miles south east of Tain, the Maitlands sought tenders for building a new and imposing house.[8] David Munro, the 9th laird of Allan, had inherited his 965 acre estate 58 years before, and he was to live on it for a further 16 years. Munro was a noted agriculturalist, who had farmed the whole of his estate himself but now farmed only the farm of Balinroich, in the middle of which his new mansion house was built. A dominant central tower in the front elevation distinguished it from the ordinary run of farm houses. The Maitlands later designed cottages, still very visible, on the Allan estate for farm servants and ploughmen, both at Balinroich and at the more extensive Clay of Allan.

Another Easter Ross heritor who sought to replace his home was Donald Ross of Moorfarm, whose estate lay two miles south of Tain. Ross was a J.P., well respected and well connected, numbering among his close relations a bailie of Tain, three agents of the British Linen Bank in Tain and heirs to the chieftainship of the clan Ross. In 1880 he commissioned the Maitlands to design a new mansion house and in the following year alterations to the steading and cattle courts.[9] Stylistically the house bears a strong resemblance to a villa in Tain which James Maitland was to design in 1892 for his own use. Donald Ross seems to have been another of those affected by the agricultural depression. In 1882 his farming tenants, who were also meal dealers, became bankrupt. By 1888, after failing to let the farm he was advertising the sale by public roup of the 'compact, desirable estate of Moorfarm', extending to about 450 acres, with its 'new and commodious' mansion house, the following month re-advertising it at a reduced upset price of £6,000, and the next month advertising it to let. All of these efforts were clearly unsuccessful, as Donald Ross farmed the estate himself until his death in 1901. His own personal estate amounted to a modest £545-12s - though it no doubt helped that his wife was the beneficiary of a family trust.

Locheye House

But not all those who engaged the Maitlands to design country houses had inherited their property. Robert Hill was one who had worked his way up the social scale. Hill came from Somerset. but was said to be 'Scottish in most of his sympathies'. In 1843 he went to Golspie as lessee under the Duke of Sutherland of the Sutherland Arms Hotel, then a coaching inn. He managed it so successfully that some 20 years later he was in a position to retire, but instead took a lease from the duke of the sheep farm of Navidale, where he was again successful. In 1882 he bought the estate of Locheye.

The estate, picturesquely situated beside the fresh water Loch Eye, between Tain and Fearn, had been part of the Geanies estate. Kenneth Murray of Geanies, who was Provost of Tain, had died in 1876. The following year Locheye was offered for sale with a steading, farm cottages and 'an excellent site for a dwelling house'. John Innes, described as 'an extensive builder from the neighbourhood of Glasgow', bought it for £1,670 and started to build a new house well apart from the farm buildings. But the extensive builder over-extended himself. After he was declared bankrupt the 'small attractive estate … with right of sailing and shooting on [Loch Eye]' was again offered for sale. This time it was purchased by Robert Hill. In 1883 Hill engaged A. Maitland & Sons to design a new house at Locheye.[10] The result was a small but elegant country house, set above lawns sloping down to Loch Eye. Owning property, and thus being able to style himself Robert Hill of Locheye, was no doubt attractive, but the surprising thing is that Hill was 77 when he employed the Maitlands. Perhaps dynastic reasons entered into the his thoughts, as when he died in 1900 he left the Locheye estate to one son and the tenancy of Navidale to another.

Achany House

18.3 Achany House, with the Maitland additions of 1885.

In 1885 the Maitlands produced plans for additions to Achany House, near Lairg and overlooking the Shin gorge.[11] The occupant was Lady Matheson of the Lews and Achany. She was the daughter of a Canadian politician who was himself said to be the illegitimate son of Spencer Perceval (the only British Prime Minister to have been assassinated), and she was the widow of the prodigiously wealthy Sir James Matheson. Sir James had been a co-founder of Jardine Matheson, traders in opium, tea, silk, spices, sugar and other goods, ship owners, and the largest trading business in Asia. In the 1840s he had bought estates, including Achany, near his childhood home of Shinness, and the island of Lewis ('the Lews'). The Land Ownership Commission's report of 1872-73 shows him as owning 406,070 acres in Ross-shire (of which the Lews were then part) and 18,490 in Sutherland. He poured money into his estates and was widely praised as a kind laird. The 2,000 islanders for whose passage from Lewis to Canada he paid would, however, have felt differently. They were mostly in arrears with their rent, and if they could not pay up they had little choice but to emigrate. What were effectively clearances were pursued with ruthless vigour by Donald Munro, a Tain-born solicitor who served as Sir James's 'Chamberlain of the Lews' for over 20 years, and is excoriated as a 'Beast' in a compelling modern account by John Macleod.[12] Sir James died in 1878 and is buried in a graveyard overlooking Lairg under a grandiose Matheson family marble monument whose capitals are decorated, appropriately given Sir James's history, with opium poppy heads. Elizabeth Beaton describes this striking monument as 'the quintessence of architectural surprise in the Highlands'.[13]

At Achany there was a two-storey laird's house with three bays, built in about 1810.[14] After he acquired it Sir James had enlarged it with distinctive bowed bays at each side. After his death Lady Matheson, now the liferentrix, spent time there each year. The third stage in the development of the house took place during her occupation. Beaton describes and illustrates the Maitland additions of 1885 - a third storey with pedimented dormers and conical drum-tower roofs over the bowed bays, and also rear additions.[15] The names of Lady Matheson and of Achany frequently featured in newspapers of the period - but the reports were not of the architecture but of them as targets of crofter and land reform agitation.

Two gate lodges and the baronialisation of Delny

Landowners were now seeking not only new and improved mansion houses and farm buildings, but also ancillary buildings to adorn their estates. These included gate lodges. Elizabeth Beaton observes that 'the gate lodge is usually a cottage or a pair of cottages flanking a driveway entrance, accommodating the lodge keeper and his family. … They offer a statement about, and a prelude to, the mansion which comes into sight as the traveller proceeds through the policies. … Besides reflecting the architectural essence of the principal house, lodges can be fanciful creations, expressing the peculiar whims and tastes of the patron'.[16]

One such patron was Francis, second Earl of Cromartie, on whose behalf the Maitlands sought tenders in February, 1889.[17] This was at a time when he was beset by huge family and financial problems. His mother Anne Hay-Mackenzie, wife of the third Duke of Sutherland, had become Mistress of the Robes and a confidante of Queen Victoria. The grateful Queen had created her Countess of Cromartie in her own right, with the title entailed to her second son, thus reviving a peerage forfeited after the Jacobite Rising of 1745. In her later years Duchess Annie had lived as a semi-recluse and, it was said, 'spent much time lying on a sofa under a red silk eiderdown. She surrounded herself with mynah birds and parrots, which perched all over the room and on the head of her retriever'. When she died in November 1888 the duke was on the other side of the Atlantic aboard his yacht *Sans Peur* in the company of his mistress, Mary Caroline Blair. It was said that when he was contacted about what to do with his wife's body his reply was brusque: 'Bury it'.[18]

Francis, the second son of the ducal pair, thus inherited a title and also the Cromartie estates, including the fine eighteenth century Tarbat House near Kildary in Easter Ross. Since his mother's marriage the Cromartie estates had been under the general superintendence of the commissioners of the vast Sutherland empire. On her death this arrangement ceased, bringing to an end cross-subsidies which had kept the Cromartie estates afloat financially and had facilitated the expansion of Strathpeffer as a fashionable resort. The factor, William Gunn, reported on the dire state of the Cromartie finances. But the new earl appears to have been profligate, and Gunn's warnings do not seem to have had much effect. Only three months after Duchess Annie's death the Maitlands were planning the upgrading of one of the entrances to Tarbat House with a new gate lodge. The result, in an English-looking Arts and Crafts style, was a building of two storeys, the upper with distinctive dummy timber framing. A shield-shaped datestone has a large letter C, 1889 and an earl's coronet. A game-keeper lived in the lodge, and there were Maitland-designed kennels nearby.

Two and a half miles away another Maitland-designed gate lodge was built, this time for a local boy who 'made good'. Thomas Urquhart, from Logie Easter, was an engineer who had spent 24 years in Russia building and running railways and been decorated by the Tsar for his services. In 1895, two years after he had purchased the estate of Delny, he organised a ceremony at which the foundation-stone of a 'very handsome' gate lodge was laid at a new approach to Delny House. The lodge was 'designed by Messrs Maitland, Tain - which adds greatly to their well-known reputation as architects'.[19] The result was a picturesque two-storey cottage with decorative ridge tiles and a single-storey polygon-shaped wing and an entrance in the inner angle.

Today Tarbat House is a ruin. The modern A9 separates it from its former East Lodge, which now sits incongruously, and despite its listing,[20] in a shocking state of repair, amongst modern houses on what is now a side road. Further down the A9 the Delny gate lodge, in different ownership from the house, is visible from a stretch of road incorporated into the A9.

Both clients appear to have been sufficiently satisfied with their gate lodges to employ the Maitlands again for works on their estates. Work for the Cromartie estates ended, however, after the death in 1893 at only 41 of the earl, who contracted pleurisy after jumping off his yacht to save the life of a seaman. Thomas Urquhart commissioned the Maitlands to design alterations and additions to Delny House in 1898.[21] Contemporary accounts indicate that the house was almost doubled in size, and this is substantiated by map and photographic evidence. The result was the predominantly Scottish Baronial edifice that one sees to-day, with a four-storey crenellated tower, matching crenellations over bay windows on each side of it and crowstepped gables, looking as the *Ross-shire Journal* reported, 'like a first plan, whereas it has really been added to twice'.

Balconie Castle and Tulloch Castle

The early 1890s saw the Maitlands work on improvements to two of the grandest castles in Ross-shire, Balconie Castle and Tulloch Castle.[22]

Balconie Castle, near Evanton, had been bought in 1890 by George Hildyard Bankes. The Bankes family were landowners near Wigan (where they had prospered from the coal beneath their estate) and also at Gruinard and Letterewe in Wester Ross. The castle became the summer home of members of George Bankes's family, his mother Eleanor Starkie Letterewe Bankes being shown in the Valuation Rolls as the tenant. Balconie Castle was a substantial building, and it took a man two days to clean all the windows.[23] Map evidence suggests that the Maitland improvements were mainly in-filling to square off the castle and they probably included the baronial facade shown in old photographs. The castle, severely affected by dry rot, was demolished in 1965 and three years later its stones were used in the foundations of the aluminium smelter at Invergordon.

The Maitlands' work at Tulloch Castle was far more substantial.[24] This was a major restoration, carried out notwithstanding the depleted finances of the owner's family. All that remained of the ancient castle when the Maitlands drew up their plans was a sixteenth century tower and part of the keep. In 1845 the interior of the castle had been almost entirely destroyed by a fire started by a candle in a bedroom. Another fire in 1874 had destroyed the third floor of the residue and the front part of the keep.

Tulloch Castle from the East after the restoration of 1891.

18.4 Tulloch Castle, Dingwall, as rebuilt by the Maitlands.

The owner at the time of both fires had been one of the most vibrant characters of the nineteenth century Highlands, Duncan Davidson, 4th of Tulloch. He had fought a duel with Hugh Rose Ross, opposed the Great Reform Bill as M.P. for Cromartyshire, produced (on most accounts) 18 legitimate and some 30 illegitimate children. In 1879, at the age of 79, he became Lord Lieutenant of Ross-shire. When he died two years later 2,000 people, including Councillor Andrew Maitland in a delegation from Tain, braved drenching rain to attend an elaborate funeral. But, despite his social standing, his finances had been in a parlous state. Notwithstanding the sale (noted earlier) of the Braemore and Inverbroom estates to the railway engineer John Fowler in 1865-67, his residual estates of some 36,000 acres were burdened by debt, and at his death his personal assets of £4,768-6s-7d were marginally exceeded by debts of £4,768-10s-8½d. In his latter years he and his fifth wife had lived not in the castle but in the nearby 17 room Tulloch Cottage, with 11 servants under the same roof. Davidson's eldest son, another Duncan, survived him by only eight years. During this time he too was in considerable financial difficulties. A meeting of his creditors was called in 1887, at which they agreed to allow him to try to make a re-arrangement of his affairs. When he died in 1889 his personal estate amounted to only £5. His son, a third Duncan Davidson, seems to have been the most practical of the line. With the concurrence of his trustees he petitioned the court to allow him to disentail Tulloch and other parts of the Davidson estates so that they could be sold. Whilst his health permitted he pursued a career in the City of London, holding various directorships, including one in a company formed to operate railways and grow bananas in Costa Rica. Investment in the castle in order to maximise income perhaps formed part of the recovery plans, for within weeks of the completion of the rebuilding in the autumn of 1891 the trustees let the castle with its shootings to Mr and Mrs Leonard Marshall.

Newspaper reports commented favourably on the restoration. 'The castle has been built in the Scotch baronial style from designs by Mr Maitland, architect. ... There is a spacious entrance hall and staircase elaborately finished in pitch pine. The staircase is lighted by stained glass windows in old domestic lead quarries and has a very pleasing appearance. Other accommodations are a billiard room, a dining room, a drawing room, boudoir, gunroom, lavatories, &c. The walls of the castle are surmounted by a corbelled battlemented parapet, and a handsome stone porch adorns the main entrance.'[25]

After the death without issue of the last Duncan Davidson in 1917 his widow was recorded as proprietor of the castle, though it was occupied by the Vickers family, Douglas Vickers, of the aircraft company, having married a granddaughter of Duncan Davidson, 4th of Tulloch. A top floor with steep scroll-sided gablets was added to the Maitland east wing, to designs by Robert (later Sir Robert) Lorimer, in 1920-22.[26] Today the castle is a hotel. It is accessed not by a drive through what the *Ross-shire Journal* called 'sylvan grandeur almost unequalled in the north of Scotland' but through a housing estate. But go there for a cup of tea in front of the fire in the panelled entrance hall - the Maitland restoration is still very much in evidence and retains its charm.

Dalmore House

Andrew Mackenzie had been at Tain Royal Academy with Andrew Maitland Junior and he remained a friend of the Maitland brothers in later life. He was a highly successful distiller, and also grew large quantities of barley, besides breeding widely famed Aberdeen Angus polled cattle and pedigreed Clydesdale horses. He had, as we saw earlier, purchased the Dalmore estate, near Alness, from Sir Alexander Matheson's son and heir in 1891 preparatory to the building of the new Maitland-designed Dalmore distillery. Soon thereafter he sought a mansion house befitting his new status as a landed proprietor. The Maitlands were commissioned in 1895.[27] Elizabeth Beaton's description is evocative: a 'large crow-stepped gabled house, of rambling "butterfly plan" constructed in warm bull-faced sandstone ... [with] mullioned windows and tall chimney stacks'.[28] Alfred Barnard, the doyen of studies of the whisky industry, paid two visits to the Dalmore distillery. During his second visit he stayed with Andrew Mackenzie at Dalmore House. 'On the Estate', he noted, 'half a mile from the Distillery, Mr Mackenzie has erected on the heights overlooking the river a fine mansion house with tastefully laid out grounds, which commands splendid views at every point of the compass of loch, river, mountain, wood, and an extended level of rich fields and grazings'.[29]

Dalmore House, by then the property of Earl Temple of Stowe, was at the centre of sensational and widely reported events in 1933. The earl's butler, Francis Grey, gave the staff a day off, stole silver and jewellery (variously said to be worth £25,000 and £50,000) and used petrol to light a fire after which only the smouldering shell of the building remained. Grey was spotted burying his ill-gotten gains and was apprehended. He was sentenced to five years penal servitude for providing false references, stealing the silver and jewellery and setting fire to the house. He died in prison. The house was rebuilt, apparently incorporating the original Maitland fabric,[30] and in 1949 became a Church of Scotland Eventide Home.

Tarlogie and the Count de Serra Largo

Through most of the nineteenth century the estate of Tarlogie had been owned by the family of one of the more flamboyant characters in the history of Tain, Hugh Rose Ross of Glastullich and Cromarty, whom we met in an earlier chapter. Rose Ross had deployed a vast fortune acquired in the West Indies in buying great swathes of Easter Ross, including Tarlogie, one-and-a-half miles west of Tain, where he built a mansion house. He had a penchant for duelling and for litigation. The latter so weakened his finances that after his death in 1846 his son Hugh Munro St Vincent Rose had to sell all the estates he inherited in Easter Ross except Tarlogie and some small properties, mainly around Tain. Major Rose of Tarlogie, as the latter styled himself, lived mainly in Surrey, and when in Ross-shire at Tarlogie. After his death in 1876 his son Major Hugh Law Rose inherited the estate. Though the largest landowner in the parish, he played a relatively minor role in the public affairs of the area (as chairman of a dysfunctional Tain School Board and briefly as a burgh councillor). He spent several years in retirement in Nairn, where he died in 1892.

The estate of Tarlogie was bought in 1889 by James Neill, a farmer from near Dundee, who had first put it up for auction in October 1896, with an upset price of £27,000.[31] The estate of 2,290 acres included the mansion house of Tarlogie 'beautifully situated among fine old trees', a home farm 'mostly in Grass, and Feu to a Distillery' (Glenmorangie), and the farms of Morangie and Ardjachie, 370 acres of grouse moor with 'excellent shooting', mussel scalps and salmon fishing.

The estate was sold at the upset price to another flamboyant character, Peter Alexander Cameron Mackenzie, Count de Serra Largo.[32] The Count was a son of the postmaster of Kingussie in Inverness-shire. In his twenties he joined the Singer Manufacturing Company, an American company which had mass-produced sewing machines since the 1850s and had become one of the largest companies in the world. Under the presidency of another Kingussie born but unrelated Mackenzie, George Ross Mackenzie, Singer was expanding world wide. George, described as 'a pious and driven Scot', appears to have invited Peter, then a pupil-teacher at Kingussie School, where he himself had been educated, to join Singer. Promoted to being Singer's representative in South America Peter Mackenzie travelled extensively through that continent from 1883 onwards, making long journeys into the interior of Brazil.

In late 1891 or early 1892 he returned to Scotland at the age of 36, the possessor of a large fortune. He brought with him a wife - from what he described as 'a palatial home in the land of the southern seas' - and their three surviving sons. Two years later King Carlos I of Portugal raised him to the title of Visconde de Serra Largo. In 1896 the King elevated him to the higher rank of Conde, following which he received a Royal licence to use in Britain the title of Count. Clearly he had had a remunerative job promoting the sales of sewing machines, but there is a mystery as to what he had done to be awarded, after he had left South America, two titles from the King of Portugal.[33]

Before he moved in to Tarlogie House the Count engaged A. Maitland and Sons to design alterations and additions. In June 1898 it was reported that the Count and his family 'have now taken up their residence. The mansion-house has been partly rebuilt, refurnished in a thoroughly modern style, and fitted up with electric light, and it is now one of the finest residences in the North'.[34] Post-restoration photographs show a new frontage with a three-storey central tower, bay windows and balustrades.

The Count clearly took with relish to his new life as a Highland landowner, the largest in the parish of Tain. He had a half bottle of champagne at lunch every day. Surviving photographs show him wearing the kilt, always with spats and sometimes a plaid. Newspaper reports list him among the gentry at important functions, and sometimes the presence of his piper. He was a generous benefactor to local causes, not only in Easter Ross but also in Kingussie. He was President of the Tain Golf Club and the St. Duthus Football Club and, for 34 years, Chieftain of the Kingussie Shinty Club.

18.5 A group at Tarlogie.

The Maitland connection with the Count went beyond architectural services. James as Managing Director of the Glenmorangie Distillery Company would have been involved with negotiations in 1900 on the distillery's use of water from the Tarlogie Springs, owned by the Count. But there was also a social relationship. In August 1908 the Count's eldest son, styled Lieut. Percy M. Mackenzie, yr. of Tarlogie, came of age. The Count gave a party for 200 guests. It followed a pattern common amongst the landed classes in previous generations when an heir had come of age: there was a lavish seven course dinner, followed by speeches; a bonfire with fireworks; and a dance, with a buffet, in a large granary, at which a presentation of an illuminated address and a dirk with a *sgian dubh* to match and a shoulder brooch, all in solid silver, was made to the 'young laird'. There was, however, a difference from the past in that none of the landed gentry were present. The Count said it was 'not [our] intention to make any class or social distinction in the invitations'. Predominant among those invited, from Tain, Kingussie and elsewhere, was a wide spectrum of the middle classes - including lawyers (one of whom was the author's grandfather), ministers, shopkeepers, and several members of the Maitland family. The principal after-dinner speech, proposing the health of the young laird, was by Bailie James Maitland, and James was also chairman of a committee formed to organise the presentation.

Sadly, Percy was to die in the Great War. The Count survived until 1931, his finances apparently depleted. A substantial part of of Tarlogie House, including much of the work by the Maitlands, was demolished in 1966 when the house was owned by the Duchess of Westminster.

Farm buildings

The grander houses that the Maitlands were called upon to design or improve for landowners in the last three decades of the nineteenth century were the more spectacular part of their contribution to the rural scene, but they were massively outnumbered by new and improved farm houses, cottages for farm servants, and steadings of farm 'offices'.

The online *Dictionary of Scottish Architects* lists, mainly on the basis of invitations to tender appearing in the *Inverness Courier* in this period, well over a hundred commissions obtained by the Maitlands for these. The *Ross-shire Journal*, which first appeared in 1875, published numerous further ones, others appeared in the *Invergordon Times* and elsewhere, whilst others may not have been advertised. Among the Maitlands' clients were many estates for which Andrew Senior had worked in the 1850s and 1860s. Apart from those mentioned earlier in this chapter these included Balnagown and Novar (both on a considerable scale), Geanies, Foulis, Shandwick, Kindeace and Cromarty. New clients included the estates of Braelangwell, Allangrange and Poyntzfield in the Black Isle, and Conon and Brahan near Dingwall.

Generally speaking it was the landlords who paid for this work and engaged the architects. Tenants had to provide capital to finance crops, livestock and farm machinery and also to pay for repairs to buildings but not capital improvements. At the end of their leases (typically for 19 years) they sought to recover their outlay at 'displenish sales', well-attended all-day events, with lunch provided and many toasts drunk, at which their livestock and equipment were auctioned. Building and improvement work frequently took place at the expiry of leases, a time when the landlord needed to invest in better facilities in order to attract suitable tenants . It sometimes also took place during the currency of leases. On the Allangrange estate, where the Maitlands were responsible for several farm buildings, it was noted that 'building is chiefly executed by the proprietor, the tenant paying either an increased rent or a percentage on the outlay. When a tenant built at his own expense some special agreement is entered into'.[35]

Improving steadings

Numerically, far and away the greatest number of the Maitlands' advertisements for builders to tender related to steadings. Some of these were for new buildings, but increasingly, and particularly from 1880 onwards, the demand was for additions, alterations and improvements to existing ones to meet the evolving needs of the High Farming era. Manures, chemicals and animal feeds, brought in by the recently extended railway network, needed to be stored, as did the coal used to produce steam power.

At the same time the patterns of farming in the area in which the Maitlands operated changed as a result of the agricultural depression. The depression was very much in evidence in Easter Ross, though the area coped better than many others. Land reclamation in previous decades had increased the arable area of the twin counties of Ross-shire and Cromartyshire by some 32% in the 22 years up to 1876, with the bulk of the increase taking place in the eastern parishes. Dairying and fat-cattle production remained profitable even as grain prices tumbled, and livestock provision therefore increased. Local farmers found that mixing arable farming with livestock farming allowed a more profitable balance, particularly as good quality local beef could compete with imported beef. Easter Ross, moreover, produced two specialist crops. Potatoes were exported, particularly from Portmahomack, supplying markets as far away as the United States. And barley, where the price had declined less severely than that of wheat, found a ready market nearer home in the local distilleries, including the Maitland-designed ones. In order to facilitate livestock farming and more intensive fattening farmers needed more and better accommodation for cattle. Covered cattle courts therefore feature prominently among the commissions the Maitlands received.

Much of the resultant work by the Maitlands was thus for incremental changes - replacements or extensions to provide more spacious granaries, more cart sheds or threshing areas below, and increased accommodation for cattle. The changing outlines can often be seen, particularly in the case of covered cattle courts, by comparing the images shown in the first Ordnance Survey maps, surveyed in the early 1870s, with those in the second series, surveyed early in the twentieth century.

A rare description of the Maitlands' work on a new steading appears in relation to Arabella in the Easter Ross parish of Logie Easter. The estate of about 600 acres had formerly been part of the empire of Hugh Rose Ross, who had drained it and altered its name from 'The Bog' to that of his first wife. It was bought in 1875 for £23,500 by James Gordon, a noted agriculturist and tenant of Udale in the Black Isle. James Gordon not only grew cereals at Arabella, but also worked it as a winter farm for 2,000 to 3,000 sheep, and bred horses. Many Ross-shire farmers bought in cattle simply for fattening, but James Gordon was well known as a breeder of shorthorn cattle, and his bull Rosario, which he introduced as a stock sire, became widely celebrated. In 1877 the steading was totally destroyed by fire. Seventeen horses were lost (the newspapers providing, with great relish, gory descriptions of their demise), but the cattle were saved. The cause was unknown, but the *Ross-shire Journal* observed that 'there can be no doubt that the habit of smoking among farm servants is often most dangerous'. Within two months the Maitlands were advertising for tenders for restoration of the steading and two new farm cottages.[36]

The *Ross-shire Journal* described the new steading as probably the largest in Ross-shire. The author of two long articles, writing in a world very different to that of today, thought that 'a description of the buildings, as they now stand, will be of interest to the majority of our readers, and in case any of them should wish to pay a visit to the steading … we may mention in passing that it is hardly a mile distant from Nigg Station on the Ross-shire section of the Highland Railway'. The report described in great detail 'arrangements in advance of those ordinarily adopted'. A north block contained a water-powered thrashing machine, other 'elaborate' machinery and a variety of stores. A west block contained, inter alia, a coach house, with a granary above. An east block contained a stable for 15 cart-horses. The central block, entirely roofed in, in three spans, had accommodation for 114 cattle tied up and also two large covered courts for loose cattle. The works 'reflected the greatest credit on [the Maitlands'] professional ability'.[37]

When James Gordon gave up his tenancy of Udale to live full time at Arabella he commissioned the Maitlands to design substantial alterations and additions to Arabella House, built by Hugh Rose Ross the early nineteenth century.[38] These included a distinctive two-storey bowed bay and a crenellated wallhead in the south elevation.

18.6 Arabella House, modified by the Maitland firm in 1882.

Farm houses

John Gifford notes that 'Later in the C19 farm houses … were often enlarged or rebuilt, sometimes with architectural embellishments and usually with bay windows. Attics, formerly barrack rooms lit only from windows in the gables, were divided into small bedrooms, each with a dormer window'.[39] Other improvements included opening up windows and adding drawing room wings.

The Maitlands' work in this period included a wide variety of new farm houses. Substantial tenants, and also purchasers of parts

18.7 Balaphuile.

of estates that had been sold off, wanted larger farm houses, usually set well apart from the steading and reflecting their enhanced social status. The former farm house was either demolished, given over to a grieve, or put to agricultural use. On smaller farms the farmer's family constituted the main labour force, and the farm house remained near the steading.

Two contrasting examples from the Shandwick estate illustrate this diversity.

In 1884 the Maitlands were engaged to design two farm houses, at Wester Rarichie and the adjacent Balaphuile in Nigg, for the Shandwick estate.[40] Estates run by solicitors typically fell behind the curve in keeping facilities up to date, and Shandwick had been in the hands of solicitors for decades. Behind their involvement lay an extraordinary and long-running drama, worthy of Hollywood. This involved William Ross of Shandwick seducing Miss Reid of Tain who was a distant relative, a duel between her brother and Ross which ended in Ross's death, a will written prior to the duel by Ross entailing the Shandwick estate in an attempt to exclude Reid and his family from the succession, the estate later falling to the last heir of entail, Miss Christiana Ross, who was confined in a lunatic asylum for 23 years, claims following her death in 1872 by several potential heirs, ten years of protracted litigation leading to one of the claimants being exposed as an impostor (and later jailed for forging documents), and the estate being divided between two claimants, Captain Andrew Reid, whose family William Ross had sought to disinherit, and John Ross Duncan. Captain Reid died before the jury's verdict in his favour.

At the time of the Maitlands' advertisement the small arable farm of Balaphuile, apparently of 60 acres, was in the hands of Captain Reid's trustees. It was occupied by Robert Adams, the son of a carpenter. The first Ordnance Survey map surveyed in 1872 shows a corn mill and a mill dam, but no farm house or farm offices at Balaphuile. Adams and his family lived on a small farmstead on the Hill of Nigg belonging to the Balnagown estate. There, as related by the local historian Anne Gordon, he kept 'one of the finest flocks of grey-faced sheep possible' and may also have had an illicit whisky still.[41] He seems, however, to have persuaded the Shandwick trustees that he needed a more modern farm house at Balnaphuile and a steading beside it.

Wester Rarichie, consisting of 441 acres arable, was a grander farm. A 19 year lease was due to expire in 1884 and the solicitor for the trustees advertised for a new tenant 'with entry to the Houses at Whitsunday first'. The 'Houses' were, as Anne Gordon explains, an L-shaped block forming two sides of a square containing a steading, with the cottages facing inwards and the farm house on the corner facing outwards. A tenant was found in William Grant. Grant, a farmer's son from Elgin, was farming 400 acres at Killimster, near Wick. He seems to have been dissatisfied with the proposed living arrangements at Wester Rarichie, and, in order to attract him at a time of agricultural depression, the trustees probably had little option but to build a substantial new farm house.

At Balaphuile the Maitlands designed a modestly sized one-and-a-half-storey farm house with five rooms with windows. The steading they designed was built close to it, though today it has been beautifully converted to residential use. In sharp contrast, the farm house at Wester Rarichie was built on the other side of a farm road from the steading, with a lawn in front, and was more substantial - a two-storey building, with nine rooms with windows.

Housing for farm workers

The most visible sign today of the Maitlands' work in rural areas is the housing originally built for farm workers. Pairs or rows of cottages beside the public highway or estate roads are particularly prominent, but single cottages, often built for those of a higher station, such as the grieve (foreman), are also to be seen. These solidly built stone cottages have lent themselves to modernisation, to knocking two cottages into one, and to the sprouting of extensions, conservatories, box dormers and Sky dishes. Most of these were built in the latter part of the nineteenth century and the early twentieth century, a period which saw improvements in the quality of housing for the labour force.

In the northern counties married farm servants were hired annually by the tenant farmers and were housed in cottages, generally built in pairs or rows, owned by the estate and let to the farm tenant along with the farm. They brought with them wives and daughters, who sometimes had specific duties such as dairy work, and who also provided additional casual or part-time labour and undertook seasonal work such as binding and stacking corn. Single men were hired half-yearly and housed in bothies or sleeping chambers in or about the steading, except where their fathers were workers on the same farm ('double hinding'), in which case they lived in their father's cottage.

Since the age of Improvement, when the former small subsistence tenants had been relocated and employed as farm servants, the common type of farm cottage had been the 'but-and-ben'. This had two rooms, entered left and right from the front door - the 'but' being the kitchen and the 'ben' the bedroom - and a small closet or pantry between the two rooms. Conditions in the older cottages were frequently bad - they were over-crowded, often damp due to poor siting and the absence of under-floor ventilation, and lacking in basic facilities such as water-supply, washing and bathing facilities and lavatories.

In the 1850s and 1860s Andrew Maitland, and in the 1870s Andrew and his sons, received a trickle of commissions to improve, or more often to replace, farm servants' cottages. It was not until the 1880s that they received a regular flow of work, with the estates of Novar, Brahan and Munro of Allan all seeking their services several times. Old cottages were renovated by improving drainage, by under-floor ventilation, by obtaining more space by increasing the height of the walls and inserting dormer windows in the roof, and by replacing thatch with slate. New cottages were built with three or four rooms, following traditional rectangular and symmetrical patterns and typically still in rows of three or four.

18.8 Cottages, built by the roadside for the Allan estate, near Hill of Fearn.

Some landlords would have needed to attend to farm servants' cottages in order to be able to provide incoming tenants with housing of a quality to attract labourers as the rural population declined. Others were undoubtedly enlightened - and for politicians it paid to be seen to be enlightened. In the 1884 general election the 24 year old Ronald Munro-Ferguson of Novar, for whom the Maitlands designed numerous farm servants' cottages, stood as the Liberal candidate for the Ross & Cromarty constituency following the retirement of Sir Alexander Matheson. The election was called by Gladstone to get a mandate for a Franchise Bill which aimed to bring the franchise in rural areas into line with that in the burghs. The main change proposed was the inclusion of male rate-paying householders, which would give the vote to much of the male rural working class, including farm servants and crofters. When interrogated during the campaign on the management of his estates Munro-Ferguson was able to say 'I am under covenant to lay out sums which, by next year, will bring the cost of my improvements to over £50,000. ... I have built, rebuilt or improved one hundred and thirty labourers' and other houses'. Novar became so popular with the masses that when he arrived in his steam yacht to campaign at Fortrose he was thrust into a carriage 'by cheering crowds and drawn by willing hands to the Town Hall'. Months later, when he was an M.P. and the Bill had become the third great Reform Act, he was carried in a chair through the village of Evanton, 'the aged inhabitants hirpling to their door-steps to wave their congratulations'. Ironically, at a further general election in 1885 he lost his seat to Roderick Macdonald, the Crofters' Party candidate, a result ascribed by the *Ross-shire Journal* to intimidation of illiterate crofters, newly eligible to vote, in Lewis and the west coast.

References and Notes

1   Author's calculations based on the Report of the Land Ownership Commission 1872-3, NRS GD149/560.

2   *Tarbat, Easter Ross - A Historical Sketch*, Alexander Fraser and Finlay Munro of Rockfield (a descendant of the earlier Finlay), Ross & Cromarty Heritage Society, 1988.

3   *Inverness Courier*, 24th February, 1870.

4   Historic Environment Scotland LB15044, Highland HER MHG16341.

5   *Inverness Advertiser*, 2nd July, 1872.

6   The photograph is on a postcard marked Macpherson's Series 158, reproduced in the online Invergordon Archive. It is said to be dated 1907 (presumably from the date stamp on the back), but there is reason to believe that Macpherson's postcards sometimes showed historical rather than contemporary views.

7   Map evidence seems to be non-existent. The Ordnance Survey does not appear to have fully re-surveyed Kincraig House between the first 25" to the mile edition and the second half of the twentieth century.

8   *Inverness Courier*, 9th August, 1877.

9   *Inverness Courier*, 24th June, 1880 and 11th August, 1881. This was not the only contact between Ross and the Maitlands. A key issue in the established church in the 1880s was the introduction of instrumental music. Donald Ross led the opposition to a proposal by Andrew Maitland Junior that an organ should be introduced to the church in Tain (now the Duthac Centre) as 'an aid to the service of praise'. Ross lost the battle. He later joined the Episcopal Church, established in Tain in the 1880s by members of the local gentry, where he would inevitably have heard the organ.

10 *Inverness Courier*, 27th March, 1883.

11 *Inverness Courier*, 23rd April, 1885.

12 John Macleod, *None Dare Oppose - the Laird, the Beast and the People of Lewis*, Birlinn Ltd, 2010.

13 Beaton, *Sutherland*, p.25.

14 Historic Environment Scotland LB8016, Highland HER MHG16739.

15 Beaton, *Sutherland*, p.19.

16 Elizabeth Beaton, *Ancillary Estate Buildings,* chapter 9 in *Scotland's Buildings*, Tuckwell Press, 2003, at pp.191-92.

17 *Inverness Courier*, 22nd February, 1889. Historic Environment Scotland LB7770, Highland HER MHG16062.

18 Gilbert T. Bell, *A Prospect of Sutherland*, Birlinn Ltd, 1995, p.92.

19 *Ross-shire Journal*, 28th June, 1895.

20 Historic Environment Scotland LB7770.

21 *Ross-shire Journal*, 15th April, 1898.

22 *Ross-shire Journal*, 25th December, 1891 (Balconie) and *Inverness Courier*, 3rd March, 1891 (Tulloch).

23 *Evanton Oral History Project*, Booklet no. 5, Estate Notes, p.52.

24 Historic Environment Scotland LB24518.

25 *Dundee Evening Telegraph*, 2nd October, 1891.

26 Gifford, *Highlands and Islands*, p.408.

27 *Inverness Courier*, 7th May, 1895.

28 Beaton, *Ross & Cromarty*, p.61.

29 Alfred Barnard, *Dalmore - a Celebrated Highland Distillery*, reproduced in *The Whisky Distilleries of the United Kingdom*, reprinted by Birlinn Ltd, 2012, p.582.

30 Historic Environment Scotland LB45913.

31 *The Scotsman*, 10th October, 1896.

32 Lionel ('Donnaie') Mackenzie, a son of the Count's third son, wrote a ground-breaking article on the Count in the *Clan Mackenzie Society Magazine, 2002*, pp.12-14. Since then at least three other accounts (relating to the Count's connections with shinty, golf and football) have appeared and postings have been made on the Tain Image Library website. The author is particularly grateful to to Iona Evans, daughter of the Count's second son, who has made available the results of considerable research on her family and has helped by correcting errors in some previous accounts.

33 In Peter Mackenzie's day Portugal no longer had any colonies in South America. Until 1889, however, Brazil was an independent Empire ruled by the benevolent and popular Emperor Pedro II, a member of the Portuguese Royal House of Braganza. Pedro was removed from power by a military coup in 1889 and went into exile in Portugal. It is possible that Peter Mackenzie rendered some services to the Brazilian Emperor or his people that were rewarded by his Portuguese great nephew, Carlos I. Donnaie Mackenzie's article suggests that he may have facilitated loans from the British Government which helped the development of Brazil. Another account suggests that he helped 'Portuguese people living in trouble-torn Brazil'.

34 *Inverness Courier*, 7th June, 1898.

35 James Macdonald, *Transactions of the Highland and Agricultural Society of Scotland, On the Agriculture of the Counties of Ross and Cromarty*, 1876.

36 *Inverness Courier*, 2nd August, 1877.

37 *Ross-shire Journal*, 21st February and 14th March, 1879.

38 *Inverness Courier*, 6th July, 1882.

39 Gifford, *Highlands and Islands*, p.72.

40 *Inverness Courier*, 11th September, 1884.

41 Anne Gordon, *Nigg a Changing Parish*, in the Nigg & Shandwick section of the rossandcromartyheritage.org website.

19. BUILDING FOR THE VICTORIAN SPORTSMAN

From sheep farming to deer forests

In the decades before he was joined by his sons Andrew Maitland Senior had, as we saw earlier, been the architect of several new or re-built shooting lodges, including Loch Assynt Lodge and Lochmore Lodge, and he had worked with a London architect on the building of Braemore for the great engineer Sir John Fowler. The last three decades of the nineteenth century saw a considerable escalation in the building and renovation of shooting lodges, and the establishment by the Maitlands of a reputation as architects of shooting lodges.

A critical factor in the demand for shooting lodges was the increasing use of land for sporting purposes rather than for sheep. The middle decades of the century had been a golden age for sheep farming. Andrew Senior had obtained commissions as a result of landlords, particularly in the northern and western Highlands, seeking to enhance their income from land, often cleared of its inhabitants, by letting it out as large sheep farms. In the latter decades of the century, however, a number of factors combined to reduce the attraction of sheep farming to landlords and their tenants. Pasture land was deteriorating as a result of intensive use, sheep diseases were increasing, and a cold winter in 1879-80 hit sheep stocks. These problems were compounded by serious competition from imports of wool from Australia and elsewhere, which led to a collapse in wool prices. And the arrival in London of the *Dunedin* in 1882 presaged the dominance of New Zealand in the importation to Britain of frozen mutton and lamb.

At the same time something of a boom was taking place in the sporting market. Proprietors thus had the obvious alternative of putting land vacated by their sheep farming tenants to sporting use. Shooting deer and grouse and catching salmon had all of course had a long history in the Highlands. The Prince Consort's sporting activities at Balmoral had been admired by Queen Victoria and had been copied by those able to afford to do so. As the Highlands were opened up by the railways in the 1860s and 1870s wealthy beneficiaries of southern industrialisation were able to travel more easily to the Highlands. As one historian puts it: 'Unlike more modestly placed trippers, visitors of this type were not content to stay in hotels - however well appointed. What they wanted were holiday homes of the sort Victoria had pioneered: lavishly constructed mansions surrounded, ideally, by good deerstalking country. … Its appeal [that of stalking], for a time, was virtually irresistible. "As soon as a man has amassed a fortune in any way", it was noted in 1892, "his first desire seems to be to buy, or hire, a deer forest in Scotland".'[1] 'Deer forests' are estates where a stock of red deer is maintained for sporting purposes. They typically have few or no trees. By 1873 there were 79 deer forests in Scotland. This had risen to 130 by 1896, 105 of them in the northern Highlands, mainly in Ross-shire and Inverness-shire. The proportion of those let rather than occupied by the proprietor showed an increasing trend.

During the sporting season large house parties were held both in ancestral homes, suitably modified where appropriate, or in architect-designed shooting lodges. Highland architects like Alexander Ross, A.&W. Reid, John Rhind and the Maitlands thus received many commissions both for new and replacement shooting lodges and for incremental improvements. The ancillary buildings they designed typically included dog kennels, stables for ponies, ventilated larders for the deer and game birds shot and the fish caught, and cottages for game keepers, stalkers, ghillies and seasonal staff. Numerous Victorian and Edwardian shooting lodges have survived into the twenty first century. Descendants of the original owners and new owners, many of them using foreign-owned companies, continue to use them for shooting and fishing and to derive an income from letting their facilities.

The eccentric duke and Langwell House

On 7th October, 1873 Andrew Maitland Senior sat down to write a letter. In his best handwriting, and using the proper forms of address, he wrote: 'To His Grace the Duke of Portland. My Lord Duke, I was agreeably surprised last night by receiving a prime haunch of venison from Langwell Forest. It is now many years since Your Grace first honoured me with handsome gifts of game, and words fail me in which to express my heartfelt gratitude for your unfailing kindness, but while I live I will ever remember with pride and pleasure the many favours which you have unsparingly bestowed upon Your Grace's Most obedt & humble servt Andrew Maitland.' Three and a half weeks later he wrote again: 'The princely present of game which Your Grace has sent to me all the way from England - carriage paid - has just arrived in excellent condition, and I can assure Your Grace that any surprise at so soon receiving another token of your unbounded liberality is only exceeded by my heartfelt gratitude for the abundant favours you continue to bestow upon Your Grace's Most obedient & humble servant Andrew Maitland'.[2]

19.1 The 5th Duke of Portland.

William John Cavendish-Bentinck-Scott, 5th Duke of Portland, was the grandson of a Prime Minister and one of the most celebrated eccentrics of the Victorian age. Unmarried, he was a recluse and he shunned his social equals. At his principal seat, Welbeck Abbey in Nottinghamshire, he lived alone in a suite of four or five rooms, sparsely furnished and painted in pink, each with a lavatory in the corner. Using 'In' and 'Out' letterboxes at the entrance to his suite, he communicated with his staff in writing, and when one of them responded to a summons to enter he would disappear through a trapdoor in the floor. He wore up to three frock-coats at the same time, tailored to fit one over the other, and when it was cold outside he could add three matching overcoats. His trousers were tied up at the ankle, like those of a navvy.

Fortunately for architects like Andrew Maitland and for the hundreds of construction workers he employed, the duke had an obsessive love of building. At Welbeck Abbey he surrounded 22 acres of kitchen gardens with high walls with recesses for braziers used to speed up the ripening of fruit. He also built 15 miles of underground tunnels under the estate, in which he wandered at any hour of the day or night. These connected various subterranean and above-ground buildings, including gate lodges, a picture gallery and the largest indoor riding house in the world, illuminated by 4,000 gas jets.

In 1857 the duke acquired the Langwell estate, near Berriedale in Caithness for £90,000, and later bought other Caithness estates. There had been a mansion house at Langwell since the eighteenth century.

In July 1864 he paid his first visit to these estates. He took the train to the newly opened station at Tain. (He would later support an northward extension of the line - but only provided it did not go through his estates.) He then travelled in his private carriage, so designed that no-one could see inside, to the Meikle Ferry, where he was 'boated over, sitting in the carriage', stayed overnight at the hotel at Golspie and arrived without any prior warning at Langwell. He spent five weeks walking around the estate and making arrangements for extensive improvements. Andrew Maitland was clearly responsible for many of the building works that took place over the next few years. No plans of these have been found, but as they coincided with the creation of a deer forest on the Langwell estate they are likely to have included the conventional requirements of a shooting lodge.[3] The duke never visited Langwell again, and Langwell House and its deer forest were regularly let during his lifetime.

The duke became even more famous after his death. James Maitland, who was probably involved with the later stages of the work at Langwell House, would have read with astonishment newspaper accounts of a series of sensational legal actions between 1898 and 1908 involving relatives of T.C. Druce of the Baker Street Bazaar, a department store in London. They claimed that the duke had led a double life as the store owner and, tiring of the charade, had faked Druce's death in 1864 by using an empty coffin. Some of the claimants appear to have been deluded, and others were fraudsters. But the duke's eccentric life style made their claims plausible. It was not until the remains of T.C. Druce were disinterred that the last claim fell apart.[4]

Alladale, and another eccentric client

The first major sporting commission won after James and Andrew Junior had become partners was at Alladale, some 12 miles west of Ardgay in the parish of Kincardine. Alladale belonged to Sir Charles Ross of Balnagown. Sir Charles was the grandson of Admiral Sir John Lockhart Ross who had introduced hardy southern sheep into Ross-shire and had become an initiator of the Highland Clearances. On much of the Balnagown estates sheep grazing had now been replaced by sporting use. Alladale was an estate of about 25,000 acres with, according to a contemporary report, a deer forest where the stags were

19.2 Alladale Lodge.

considered remarkable for their size and quality, a capital grouse moor and some very fair trout fishing. The first shooting lodge on the estate was destroyed by a fire in September 1876. The fire was so severe that some of those staying there were injured jumping from the windows of the one-storey building.

Andrew Senior would have remembered from the time of his commission at Balnagown in 1842 (the precursor to his move to Tain) stories of Sir Charles's eccentric habits - not least spending hours perched in an oak tree, which gained him the nickname 'the Jackdaw'. Sir Charles's second wife, whom he married in a secret midnight ceremony in 1865, played some role in the administration of the estate and was able to control some of his more bizarre behaviour. Nevertheless when a son and heir was finally born in 1872, when he was 58, Sir Charles had promptly hidden the baby in Balnagown Castle and made the servants search for it. Although he played little part in the social activities associated with sporting activities in the Highlands, Sir Charles was passionate about shooting and fishing and he regularly migrated to the hills in the season.[5] He also derived a substantial income from letting Alladale and other deer forests. It is thus not surprising that he was quick to replace the original lodge. In December 1876 A. Maitland & Sons sought tenders,[6] and the present Alladale Lodge was built in 1877, 'prettily situated among clusters of weeping birch'. This was followed by considerable further work for the Balnagown estate, including alterations and additions to another shooting lodge on an adjacent deer forest, Dhianich or Deanich.[7]

After Sir Charles's death in 1883 his young son, another Sir Charles, used Alladale Lodge and the shootings, but they were more often let to tenants. A notable tenant was Sir Henry Meux who had inherited a brewing fortune. He secretly married Valerie Langdon, a flamboyant beauty, variously described as an actress, a barmaid or a prostitute, who was later the subject of sensuous portraits by James McNeil Whistler and was often seen travelling round London in a phaeton drawn by two zebras. They entertained at Alladale on a lavish scale until Sir Henry's death in 1900. A photograph taken at Alladale shows Sir Henry, gun in hand, sitting next to Valerie who is strumming on a banjo.

In recent years Alladale has attracted considerable publicity. The present owner has set it up as Alladale Wilderness Reserve, a nature reserve. His agenda has been reported to include restoration of tree cover and the re-introduction of several lost animal species - including, controversially, wolves. Alladale Lodge offers accommodation for visitors to the reserve.

Swordale and the ebullient Major Randle Jackson

Major Randle Jackson was a larger than life character who had assisted in quelling the Indian Mutiny, captained the Royal and Ancient Golf Club of St Andrews and married the daughter of a massively wealthy Dundee jute manufacturer. In April 1885 he bought from John Munro the 'fine sporting estate' of Swordale, some two miles west of Evanton. Its moors were reported to afford some of the best grouse shooting in Ross-shire. The purchase included about 4,000 acres and a 'good shooting lodge'. The major's intentions soon became very clear. Within a few weeks he was advertising that 'OWING to a REDUCTION in the STOCK of SHEEP to be kept on Swordale and Clare' seven lots of sheep, amounting to 2,012 in all, were to be sold at the Inverness Wool Market. Crofters who had lived on the estate for generations were employed by Jackson as servants and staff. Later Jackson became a Unionist politician and, at a time of agitation over crofters' land rights, advocated emigration as a means of limiting population growth. Controversy arose as to whether he had evicted the crofters from his estate. Evidence given to the Royal Commission (Highlands and Islands), 1892 (known as the Deer Forest Commission) suggested that Munro had removed them and that Jackson had sought a guarantee that 'no crofters or cottars have any claim to any part of the estate'.

In 1886 Jackson engaged A. Maitland & Sons to produce a substantial enlargement of the existing shooting lodge.[8] The result was a grand mansion house with the appearance of a baronial castle. Some years later Jackson and his wife Emily entertained the entire staff of the Unionist supporting *Ross-shire Journal* to a day's outing at Swordale. Their report of the occasion describes the beauty of the acacia trees and the benefits of a free and independent press - but not, unfortunately, the architecture of the Jacksons' house.

Jackson appears to have been what would nowadays be called a control freak, even beyond the grave. Thus in codicils to his will he left his properties, including Swordale to one daughter, Annie, requesting his wife to leave £50,000 to their other daughter, Dorothy. His 'dear daughters' should, he requested, not marry in a hurry or without the full approval of their fond mother. The husband of the one inheriting Swordale should add the name Jackson after his own name, and if the couple were blessed with a son he should be given the name Randle. The farm of Swordale should not be let because it was too near the house. On his death in 1902 his daughter Annie, an ornithologist, inherited Swordale. In 1921 Annie married Colonel Richard Meinertzhagen. Meinertzhagen failed to add the name Jackson to his own, though their second son was called Randle. Meinertzhagen was renowned as a war hero, a master spy and a leading ornithologist, but later writers have unmasked him as a fraud. Some also accuse him of murdering Annie out of fear that she would expose his ornithological deceptions. She was killed at Swordale in 1928, when alone with him, in a controversial shooting incident officially regarded as an accident.

Most of the Maitland additions to Swordale had been demolished by 1967, and only parts of the outer walls now remain.[9]

Kildermorie Lodge and the makers of fine furniture

Three of the projects undertaken by the Maitland partnership in the 1890s were on estates that had become sheep walks after notorious clearances but had now been converted to deer forests. The first of these was at Kildermorie.

Kildermorie, or Gildermorie, is famous in Highland history as the starting point of the 'Ross-shire Insurrection' of 1792, a year remembered as *Bliadhna Nan Caorach* or the Year of the Sheep. Kildermorie had been let by Sir Hector Munro of Novar as a sheep farm to two brothers, Allan and Alexander Cameron. Some small tenants had disappeared, probably as a result of eviction, and others lived in fear of the Cameron brothers. Disputes with them over grazing rights for cattle at Kildermorie escalated into widespread opposition to sheep farming. Plans were drawn up to expel all the sheep from Ross-shire and Sutherland, and flocks were seized from several estates. The heritors, mindful of what was happening in revolutionary France, had been determined to restore order. Sheriff Donald Macleod of Geanies sought military assistance, and three companies of the Black Watch were sent from Fort George. Macleod had led a party of armed gentlemen and the three companies of troops to Boath, where the rebels quickly dispersed.

In 1885 Walter Shoolbred bought from R.C. Munro-Ferguson of Novar the 24,000 acre deer forest of Wyvis, north west of Evanton, and erected a shooting lodge beside Loch Glass. In 1890 he added the neighbouring estate of Kildermorie extending to 26,000 acres, where the following year the then existing buildings were converted, to designs by A. Maitland and Sons,[10] to what the *Ross-shire Journal* described as 'one of the most comfortable and picturesque residences in the Highlands'. Shoolbred, it was reported, also did 'as much to make his servants comfortable … nowhere in Scotland are there better houses to be seen than those at Kildermorie'. Walter Shoolbred himself occupied the Wyvis estate during the shooting season, whilst his brother Frederick occupied Kildermorie Lodge and part of the deer forest. Frederick clearly devoted much of his life to sport, claiming to have 'grassed' 19 stags in 20 shots, erecting a salmon hatchery at Kildermorie, supporting the Surrey Staghounds and - for a change from blood sports - taking up residence at the Royal Hotel in Tain for a season's golf. He was President of the St Duthus Golf Club for some 20 years until his death in 1922.

The brothers were able to afford this lifestyle as descendants of the founder of James Shoolbred & Co. The business had begun as drapers in Tottenham Court Road in London in the 1820s and had become one of the first department stores. It was noted for its high quality furniture, much of it designed and made in-house, for which they obtained a royal warrant. Their catalogues were a huge success and became virtual pattern books for quality Victorian furniture. Kildermorie Lodge was furnished by the company. When Walter died in 1904, leaving £576,000, he left one tenth of his estate to Frederick and nine-tenths to his nephew Rupert Wilkin on condition that he adopted the arms and name of Shoolbred. During the twentieth century, under various owners, the condition of the lodge deteriorated and new owners replaced it in 1994.

Glencalvie and Gruinards

During the 1880s banners bearing the inscription 'Remember Glencalvie, Greenyards and Culrain' were being carried at events organised by the Highland Land League. The references, at a time of widespread protest, were to three of the most notorious Highland clearances earlier in the century, clearances which remained in the folk memory. With the spread of deer forests crofters were concerned about their lack of security of tenure and restricted access to land. The government responded by setting up the Napier Commission, but its report, published in 1884, did not meet all their demands. Many crofters joined the Highland Land League, and the General Election of 1885, with a widened franchise, saw the election of four Crofters' Party MPs for Highland constituencies, including Ross and Cromarty. The Crofters Holdings (Scotland) Act, 1886 brought some relief to crofters, granting security of tenure of existing crofts and establishing the Crofters Commission.

Glencalvie and Greenyards, both then part of the Strathcarron estate, had been cleared in the middle of the century in order to create sheep-walks. These clearances had received such adverse publicity that they marked the end of mass evictions in the Highlands. The principal instigators had been the owner, Major Charles Robertson of Kindeace, and James Falconer Gillanders, who was frequently employed to clear small tenants. Andrew Maitland would have recalled that he had received commissions from both Robertson and Gillanders.[11] Major Robertson died in 1868 and the Kindeace estates, including Glencalvie and Greenyards or Gruinards, were inherited by his son, another Charles Robertson.

In 1886, by which time the estate had been given over to deer rather than sheep, the younger Charles put up for auction the Glencalvie Deer Forest - 'eight miles long, two-and-a-half miles broad being in all about 4,632 acres'. It was currently let for £350 per year to Sir Alexander Matheson of Ardross, who himself owned some 220,000 acres in Ross-shire including the neighbouring deer forest of Dibiedale. Matheson's lease was due to expire in 1891. The sales brochure presented a picture that would have appealed to the Victorian sportsman: 'The ground is cleared of sheep and everything possible is done to encourage the deer to frequent the ground, ... the average being about 100 stags and 200 or 300 hinds. ... Salmon lie in large numbers. ... The Garvault Burn yields an abundance of trout. ... There are several admirable sites for a shooting lodge. ... If a shooting lodge were erected there would be no difficulty in getting a Rent of £700 or £800 a year for the Forest, which is an exceedingly good one'. Despite these attractions no acceptable offers were received either at this auction or at another one in 1890.

A retired surgeon, William Allis Smith, was thus able to make a private purchase of Glencalvie. Allis Smith commissioned A.

19.3 Glencalvie Lodge.

Maitland & Sons in 1890 to design a keeper's house and kennels, and in 1892 to design a new shooting lodge.[12] Glencalvie Lodge. 'pink-washed and gabled with angle turrets linked by a veranda dignifying the front elevation',[13] remains a fine example of a Victorian shooting lodge.

Allis Smith came to Glencalvie each year from Bournemouth, and his exploits with the gun and the rod were regularly reported in the press. In 1901 Allis Smith sold the estate to C.W. Dyson Perrins. Dyson Perrins was the son of the owner of Lea & Perrins, and the grandson of one of the originators of its famous Worcestershire Sauce. Dyson Perrins had recently purchased the Ardross estate, including Dibiedale which adjoined Glencalvie, and he was to go on to purchase the Kildermorie estate from Rupert Shoolbred in 1912.

Charles Robertson's other deer forest, Gruinards, was sold more quickly than Glencalvie, but the Maitlands' involvement was later. Gruinards was bought in 1885 or 1886 by Colin Ross, whose father Horatio Ross was a godson of Nelson and famed as the best shot in the country with rifle, pistol and fowling piece. Colin Ross, who was said to have inherited some of the shooting ability of his father, sold the estate in 1896 to R.T. Coupland of Cresswell Gardens, Kensington. Coupland, often staying at the Balnagown Arms Hotel in Ardgay, already featured prominently in the 'Angling Notes' of the newspapers of the day, as well as the 'Moors and Forest' reports. The chances of owning the Gruinards fishings on the River Carron clearly appealed to him.

Gruinards Lodge, Ardgay.

19.4 Gruinards Lodge.

In 1896, shortly after Coupland purchased Gruinards, the Maitlands sought tenders for work on a new sporting lodge.[14] This was to be on a grand scale. The lodge, still in use, is a substantial two-storey building with extensive Scottish Baronial detailing and more English-looking timber-decorated gables. Its central features are a four-storey rounded tower and an adjoining three-storey turret, both corbelled and crenellated, with a hoodmoulded entrance at ground level in the turret. The Historic Environment Scotland listing[15] notes that the Inverness architect W.L. Carruthers advertised for tenders in 1889 and suggests that the Maitlands may have overseen buildings to his design, or that details of his design were incorporated into those of the Maitlands, but it does not provide any evidence to support this theory.

The *Ross-shire Journal* of 29th May, 1903 reported that extensive improvements were being carried out at Gruinards House, 'the property of Mr Dyson Perrins', under the supervision of Mr [James] Maitland.

According to contemporary newspaper accounts, however, Gruinards had been purchased the previous month not by Dyson Perrins of Worcestershire Sauce fame but by Colonel Henry Platt, a member of a family who owned the world's largest manufacturer of textile machinery. The Valuation Rolls confirm Platt's ownership.

Shieldaig Lodge

We saw earlier how Sir Kenneth Mackenzie of Gairloch transformed the dire state of the finances of the estate he had inherited, particularly by increasing his income from sporting activities and also by the building or rebuilding, to Maitland designs, of the Loch Maree, Gairloch and Kinlochewe hotels. But the Maitlands' work for him was not confined to hotels. Sir Kenneth's sporting tenants included the 3rd Marquess of Bristol and James Bateson and for a time a Mr. A. Hamond, who together leased a 'pretty' lodge at Shieldaig, on the south side of the Gair Loch, and some four miles from the Gairloch Hotel. Following the expiry of the lease the Marquess sold the contents of the lodge, the dairy, farm and gardens in 1887.

Sir Kenneth commissioned the Maitland partnership to design a new shooting lodge, and they sought tenders in 1891.[16] A lease of the new Shieldaig Lodge was taken by the mining magnate Charles Rudd. Rudd was a friend and the main business associate of Cecil Rhodes, with whom he was involved in the formation of two vast companies, De Beers Mining Company and Consolidated Goldfields of South Africa Ltd. He paid rents of £580 for the Shieldaig shootings and £120 for the new lodge and its garden. But, whilst Rhodes pursued his imperial dreams in the political arena, Rudd settled in Britain, gave up his lease of Shieldaig and bought his own estate, Ardnamurchan in Argyll.

To-day Shieldaig Lodge is, like so many other buildings designed by the Maitlands for private use, a luxury hotel.

References and Notes

[1] James Hunter, *Last of the Few - A History of the Highlands and Islands of Scotland*, Mainstream Publishing, 1999, pp. 286-87.

[2] Manuscripts and Special Collections, The University of Nottingham, ref. no. Pw K 2431 and 2432.

[3] Thanks are due to Alexa MacAuslan of the Portland Estate Office for searching the records. Elucidation of what Andrew Maitland did to deserve the ducal favours is further complicated by additions, using concrete blocks, made to the house in the late 1870s to designs by a Mr Collingham of Nottinghamshire.

[4] For an entertaining account see Piu Marie Eatwell, *The Dead Duke, his Secret Wife and the Missing Corpse*, Head of Zeus Ltd, 2014.

[5] The stories of Sir Charles Ross's behaviour are taken from *Balnagown - Ancestral Home of the Clan Ross*, Brompton Press, 1997, pp.77 - 81.

[6] *Inverness Courier*, 28th December, 1876.

[7] *Ross-shire Journal*, 18th January, 1878.

[8] *Inverness Courier*, 26th February, 1886.

[9] Highland HER MHG22619.

[10] *Inverness Courier*, 13th January, 1891.

[11] See chapter 3.

[12] *Inverness Courier*, 22nd August, 1890 and 5th April, 1892.

[13] Beaton, *Sutherland*, p.14.

[14] *Ross-shire Journal*, 5th June (invitation to tender) and 12th June (article), 1896.

[15] Historic Environment Scotland LB7163.

[16] *Inverness Courier*, 3rd March, 1891.

[13] Beaton, *Sutherland*, p.14.

20. THE ERA OF THE VILLA

20.1 Lauderdale, built in 1884 by Andrew Maitland Junior for his own family.

Villas and suburbs

The years 1870 to 1905 are regarded as one of the boom periods for Scottish domestic architecture, a period characterised by growth in the building of suburban villas.[1] Suburbs had long been familiar features of the larger cities, but the last two decades of the nineteenth century and the first decade of the twentieth century saw extensive development of new, particularly middle-class, suburbs in the northern burghs and towns. Inverness, with attractive sites along the banks of the River Ness, was already seeing suburban development by 1870, but other Highland towns, including Tain and Dornoch, were behind the curve. Hence little of the domestic architectural work in these towns done by the Maitlands and their contemporaries pre-dates the 1880s.

A number of factors led to the demand for villas in this period. A key one was the emergence of a new breed of client - men sufficiently successful in their profession or business to be able to afford the services of an architect, and sometimes the widows or unmarried daughters of such men. Employing an architect to design a private house was no longer the exclusive preserve of the landed gentry. Some of the Maitlands' clients were thus people whom we have met in earlier chapters of this book as civic and commercial leaders. They were now able to have houses set in their own grounds, allowing them to have gardens, and sometimes summerhouses and croquet and tennis lawns. Other factors contributing to the demand for villas included a population shift from country to town; changes in social structure leading to reduced numbers of servants and hence the need for more compact and convenient house designs; and the attractions of moving to the Highlands, particularly to burghs like Tain and Dornoch with golf courses and opportunities for social life and cultural events.

Highland architects were able to meet this demand by designing villas which reflected a variety (and sometimes a mixture) of styles, including Scottish Baronial, Classical, Italianate, and Arts and Crafts. This variety was enhanced by study travel by architects as part of their training, and also by the increasing availability both of pattern books which architects could show to their clients and of architectural books and periodicals. Popular architectural features included decorative wooden barge boards on gable ends, roof lines decorated with ornate red terracotta ridge tiles, finials on ridge and gable ends, three-sided bay windows with their own roof, stained glass in doors and at the top of windows, glazed timber frame porches in front of the main door, fire places in each room (with decorative surrounds and mantelpieces in the principal rooms), cornices, floor tiles (often in geometric patterns) and ornamental woodwork, not least on staircases. Many of these period details are still observable on many Maitland villas, some being brilliantly captured in a DVD produced by the Tain & Easter Ross Civic Trust in 2007.[2]

Whilst there was some in-filling in the centre of towns, the main thrust of these developments was on the pastoral fringes, where landowners were often happy to sell or feu land. Sites beside the main arteries leading into towns were of particular interest to purchasers.

The Maitlands designed villas over a wide area of the Highlands. Newspapers of the period show them advertising for tenders to build Sheraton House at Fortrose for Major General Hugh Hodgson, formerly of the Bengal Staff Corps, in 1883; a villa in the spa resort of Strathpeffer in 1886; two semi-detached villas in Bridaig Park, Dingwall in 1892; a house at Lairg in 1896; Lorne Villa in Nairn also in 1896; and a house at Hill of Fearn in 1898.[3] Their most numerous commissions were, however, in their home town of Tain and in Dornoch.

Early Maitland villas in Tain

It was considered worthy of note in a report in January 1886 about building improvements in Tain that 'several villas have been erected within the last two or three years, notably Fern Villa, Lauderdale and a nice house in Moray Park for Mrs Matheson, late of Morangie. ... Messrs A. Maitland & Sons were the architects ... and the works were carried through with the taste and ability for which they are so widely and favourably known'.[4] These villas were all on the fringes of Tain.

The timing given for the first of them is probably not quite correct, as 'Fern Villa' is almost certainly Fearn Lodge in Knockbreck Road. Mary Middleton bought in 1876 part of the lands of Knockbreck known as Tain Park 'for the purpose of building a dwelling house and making a garden'. She was an unmarried member of a well-known farming family whose ancestors were 'improvers' who had come from Berwickshire to the Black Isle in 1790 and whose members were widely spread through the Black Isle and Easter Ross. Her house, less ornate than many of the later Maitland villas, was only the second to be built on the main road to the south between Tain and Knockbreck. (The first was the Free Church Manse, now a guest house, designed by Andrew Maitland Senior in 1852.) Mary Middleton lived at Fearn Lodge for over 30 years until her death in 1908, the censuses showing a lady companion and two servants also living there. She seems to have carved out a niche for herself in an overwhelmingly male dominated society. Newspaper reports show the range of her activities, including the presidency of the Young Women's Christian Association and the Nursing Association. On her death Fearn Lodge was exposed to roup, with an upset price of £900.

Lauderdale was built in 1884 for none other than Andrew Maitland Junior himself. By then he and Eliza had four surviving children, and the house he rented in Lamington Street was probably inconveniently small. Unlike his brother James and their father, he was unaffected by the disastrous collapse of the City of Glasgow Bank in 1878 and was thus able to acquire land in Morangie Road, an entrance to Tain from the north which was to become one of the main areas for development in this period. One of the attractions was that the site was only a few hundred yards away from his father's house in Esther Place, which still contained the Maitland partnership's main office. Another was the view of the Dornoch Firth and the Sutherland mountains from its slightly elevated position on the south west side of the road, a view preserved by his acquisition of land on the other side of the road. The new house, imposing but unostentatious, had three public rooms, four bedrooms, a dressing-room, a box room, a kitchen, a scullery, a servants' room, pantries and 'all modern conveniences'.[5] The DVD mentioned above dwells lovingly on the external architectural details.

In 1886 Lieutenant Colonel William H.E. Murray of Geanies, a scion of the family that had produced three nineteenth century Provosts of Tain, sold land at Murray Park in Manse Street, then on the southern edge of the burgh. The purchasers were Ann Matheson and her daughter Annie. Ann was the 71 year old widow of William Matheson, who had erected the first Glenmorangie distillery in 1849 and had died in 1862. She had recently sold the feu, water rights, buildings and plant to her son-in-law Duncan Cameron, who in turn had sold them on to The Glenmorangie Distillery Company, of which he and Andrew Maitland Junior were the principal promoters. Andrew Junior's fierce disputes with Duncan Cameron over the Tain quarries and on Cameron's involvement in the management of the distillery were then in the future. In late 1886 the Matheson ladies commissioned the Maitlands to design a villa, which they named Murrayfield. The Historic Environment Scotland listing calls it 'one of the more ambitious and intact of its scale, date and type within this part of Tain'.[6] The detailing, it adds, 'including ball finial and stone dentilled eaves cornice, metal work, porch and interior fittings add to the character of this building'. It particularly notes the unusually decorative porch (though this could be an Edwardian addition) and the boundary wall which is topped by spear-headed railings and an unusual wrought-iron overthrow, supporting a lamp-bracket, over the gate.

The following year Ann and Annie Matheson feued part of their recently acquired land to Jessie Ferguson for her to build a house next door. Jessie was the unmarried daughter of Fergus Ferguson, a well respected agriculturalist who had been the tenant of the farm of Tarlogie, one of only two large farms remaining in in the hands of the family of Hugh Rose Ross who had owned vast swathes of Easter Ross. In 1871, after Fergus had retired from farming, he was elected to Tain Burgh Council, where five years later he was joined by Andrew Maitland Junior. When he died in 1879 he left his house in Rose Place, Tain, together with cash and a portfolio of shares worth some £5,000 to Jessie. Jessie used some of her inheritance to build a villa to plans signed by Andrew Maitland Senior.[7] The house, whilst less ornate than Murrayfield, retains some pleasing period features. Originally called Ferguslea, its name was later changed to Drynoch Lodge and then to Glencoe.

The chemist, his wealthy wife, and houses in Scotsburn Road

Another fringe area of Tain to see late nineteenth century development was the Scotsburn Road, one of the main routes to the south west. Adjacent to it was East Mansfield, a small estate of some 60 acres partly within the southern boundary of the burgh. The estate was purchased in 1892 for £1,880-15s by Johanna Fowler. Johanna was one of two nieces of Joshua Taylor, an immensely rich tea planter. Early in the next century she and her sister were to commission two of the best known Maitland buildings in Tain. She was married to Donald Fowler, the immediate successor of Andrew Maitland Junior and predecessor of James Maitland as Provost of Tain. In 1892 her uncle still had five years to live, but he may already have passed money to his niece since Donald Fowler was able to own a property portfolio far greater than his earnings as a chemist and dentist could possibly have supported. Property investment was popular among the more prosperous members of the emerging middle classes in Tain, many of whom supplemented their income by investing in a house, or perhaps two or three houses. Fowler, however, leased out 19 houses in Tain in the mid 1890s, and after the death of his wife's uncle he was to extend this to 45 houses, 9 shops and 3 other properties, some being owned jointly with John Munro, a plasterer frequently successful in obtaining contracts advertised by the Maitlands.

Donald Fowler clearly spotted the potential not only for building a family home on the Mansfield estate but also for defraying part of the cost of purchasing the estate by selling feus of land on which villas could be built beside the road. The first feu was bought by James Maitland himself. In March 1891, before the purchase of the estate was complete, James Maitland advised the Commissioners of Police that he was erecting a dwelling and needed to make drainage arrangements for it. In July 1892, the very same week as Joanna signed the disposition, A. Maitland & Sons sent the Commissioners plans for a new house on the estate for Mr Fowler and also advertised for tenders for building a 'superior dwelling house'.[8]

The house the Maitlands designed for the Fowlers was almost certainly the symmetrical building in Georgian style which was incorporated in the next decade into the substantial Scottish Baronial Mansfield House (or 'Castle' Hotel) we see today - but this is a story for another chapter.

20.2 Scotsburn Lodge, the first of two houses built by James Maitland for his own use, photographed in 1907.

The other house was Scotsburn Lodge, the first of two houses James Maitland designed for his own use. He and Barbara with their son Henry lived in it until 1898. It was considerably larger than their previous house in Lamington Street, and it would have allowed them to have servants living in. Externally it has a simple elegance, achieved particularly through a decorative bargeboard and finial on a central gable and a simple portico at the entrance, the roof of which is an extension of those of the bay windows at each side of the door.

Soon afterwards another villa, Craigdarroch, was built on a plot next door to James Maitland's house. The new house was occupied in its early years by Elizabeth Ross, her four daughters and one son. Her husband, who died in 1894, had been manager of the Commercial Bank in Tain, following in the footsteps of the family's Murray relations, and then of a new branch in London. Their eldest daughter, another Elizabeth, became one of the few qualified women doctors of her day. She is commemorated in the Collegiate Church in Tain for her heroic work during the Great War as a military doctor in Serbia, where she died in 1915 whilst helping stricken Serbian soldiers during an outbreak of typhus fever.

The story of the building of Craigdarroch was handed down through the Ross family. A stonemason who had worked on Maitland villas decided that as he knew their plans so well he would build a house himself as a speculative development and sell it. This he did - though the house he built lacks the elegance of its neighbour. His action caused a huge rift with the Maitlands.[9] The story seems to be corroborated by an 1895 report in the *Ross-shire Journal* that Alexander Munro, contractor, Tain, had presented plans to the Dean of Guild Court for a large villa to be built in Scotsburn Road. He was not the first speculative builder to appear on the scene, as earlier in the same year a mason, Charles Macdonald, had presented plans for another house in Murrayfield.[10]

The attractions of Tain

The fact that speculative builders appear to have been active in Tain at this time suggests some confidence on their part in the growth of the local housing market.

All the indications are that the builders' confidence was not misplaced. Successful professional and commercial people were increasingly likely to be able to afford villas, and Tain was becoming attractive to incomers. The period was marked by a proliferation of social occasions where all sections of the middle classes met, often with the local gentry attending. Men frequently attended long dinners with innumerable toasts and speeches - though the Temperance movement was also active. Their wives and daughters played a prominent role in other events, particularly fund-raising bazaars and flower and vegetable shows. The intellectual life of the burgh also flourished, with music and drama playing a major role. There was a highly successful Literary Society, which had built up to 376 members by 1906, in which year it organised 21 nights of events at a cost of 2s 6d for the whole session. Many of the activities of the period took place in buildings designed by the Maitlands, particularly the Tain Public Hall, the Masonic Lodge and the Royal Hotel, and many of those who organised and attended them were Maitland clients.

There was also an increasing sense of the importance of physical activity. The Volunteer movement, a part-time citizen army, was popular in Tain, as in so many parts of the Highlands. Its members saw themselves as performing a social duty, and they gained status from their involvement and military rank. (But as volunteers had to pay for their own uniforms there was less incentive for the poor to join.) One of the the most notable features of the period was the growth of organised sport. Curling, long associated with the gentry, became more popular in the cold winters of the later nineteenth century, a Tain Curling Club dating from 1853. A Cricket Club was formed in 1870, a Tennis Club in 1884, and, after Tain players had flirted with the rival Rugby code, a Football Club playing under the Association code in 1885.[11] There were also a Cycling Club, a Shinty Club and a Rifle Club. The organisers of the Angling Club, the Bowling Club and the Golf Club all sought the support of the Burgh Council, which formed a Committee in 1897 for suggesting schemes to improve the amenity of the town. Bailie Andrew Maitland endorsed this with enthusiasm, but remarked that although he was willing to join all three of these clubs he was so busy that he might have to restrict his activities to bowls.

The St Duthus Golf Club was, however, the one recognised as having the best potential for attracting tourists and new residents. The hope was often expressed that Tain would become the premier golfing resort of the north. The club was formed in 1890. Its initial 15 hole course was laid out by one of golf's immortals, Old Tom Morris, and was made into an 18 hole course in 1894. It soon numbered among its members both the local gentry and a wide spectrum of the middle classes, many being Maitland clients.[12] A list of the 105 members' handicaps in 1898 shows several men we have met in earlier chapters, including the President, Major Randle Jackson of Swordale (handicap 6), the Count de Serra Largo of Tarlogie (10), Frederick Shoolbred of Kildermorie (10), and Roderick Finlayson of the Royal Hotel (18).

One of the lowest handicaps was that of the Hon. Secretary, Sydney Jennins, playing off 5, for whose family the Maitlands designed a villa in 1896.[13] Jennins lived with his parents. His father, Arthur C. Jennins, described as 'a gentleman of independent means' and 'one of an esteemed class of citizens very important in the social economy of Tain', was the son of a Hampshire landowner. He moved to the Meikle Ferry in the 1860s, attracted by the opportunities for field sports. The attraction of the golf course perhaps played a part in the family's decision to move into Tain, where he had a villa, Carrington House (also known as Carringtons and now Springfield Guest House), built in Morangie Road.

Several other villas were built in Tain in the last decades of the nineteenth century, mainly on what were then the fringes of the burgh. Some of these are generally regarded as Maitland buildings, but in the absence of Dean of Guild Court records the provenance of such buildings can only be authenticated by contemporary newspaper accounts and advertisements for tenders or by the preservation of original plans.[14]

Dornoch and 'Barrow's Castle'

A modern historian of Dornoch notes that 'the 1890s saw a wide range of developments that transformed and modernised the burgh ... an increasing number of inhabitants applying to the Dean of Guild for permission to extend existing properties or to construct new ones, and incomers to the town building their own holiday homes. ... Dornoch was now attracting families of considerable wealth and status.'[15] The result was the building of several architect designed houses mainly on what was then the periphery of the old burgh, notably in what are now known as Evelix Road and Cnoc-an-Lobht. Many of these were designed by the Maitlands, who advertised in 1888, 1891, 1894 and 1895 for tenders to build new houses, and in 1896 and 1900 to effect alterations and additions to Burnside.

Their most significant commission was in 1896, when the Maitlands advertised for tenders for building 'a large residence' in Dornoch for Mr J.J. Barrow.[16] John James Jerome Barrow, to give him his full name, came from Derbyshire. His family had owned the largest collieries in the county and had developed iron foundries. They had sold the business in 1863 to the Staveley Coal and Iron Company, in which they became substantial shareholders. John Barrow, born in 1829, was a director of various railway companies, but his Staveley dividends enabled him to lead the life of a gentleman with sporting interests. He had a London house in Hyde Park Gardens and an estate of 100 acres at Holmewood, near Tunbridge Wells in Kent. By 1891 he had taken a lease of Dornoch Castle from the Duke of Sutherland. The Castle, to-day a hotel, was then 'the only shooting lodge in the kingdom which can boast of being situated not only within a Royal burgh, but in the very heart of a County town ... the County Buildings are adjacent and a Sheriff Court is regularly held. The shootings in connection with it cover an area of 9,000 acres and there is much variety of game'.[17] Barrow and his family entered into the life of Dornoch. He became a J.P., and was known as a major benefactor, and his wife Dorothea was particularly associated with the Dornoch Golf Club, of which Barrow himself, a keen golfer, had been one of the promoters.

By 1896 Barrow wanted his own residence, and he chose to erect what became the most prominent building on the Dornoch skyline. The site he chose for Northfield - or 'Barrow's Castle' as the irreverent called it - was in an elevated position on Cnoc-an-Lobht, from which it was highly visible from the centre of the town. At the heart of the building was a conventional Victorian villa. It was made even more visible by a Scottish baronial square tower, surmounted by a round turret. The juxtaposition of these two elements looks odd. Gifford remarks that 'the unadventurous domesticity' of the building is 'badly jolted by a very martial tower'.[18] This must have been what their client wanted, but one wonders whether Barrow's architects were happy with the instructions he gave them.

20.3 Northfield (now Burghfield), Dornoch.

John Barrow died in 1903, and is commemorated in a stained-glass window on the south wall of the nave in Dornoch Cathedral. After his death Dorothea continued to spend time at Northfield. She sold it in 1921 to the immensely wealthy newspaper tycoon Lord Rothermere, who renamed it Burghfield House and used it to entertain the great and the good of the inter-war years. Rothermere also carried on an extensive correspondence with Adolf Hitler (who entertained him at the Berghof), Göring, Goebbels and Ribbentrop. Some of it must surely have emanated from Dornoch - though Rothermere did not return the Führer's hospitality at Burghfield House. Rothermere died in Bermuda in 1940, his reputation in tatters after his toadying letters to Nazi leaders had been exposed in a sensational court case.

The property has retained the name Burghfield in its subsequent history as a hotel and as an outpost of the University of the Highlands and Islands.

References and Notes

[1] For a useful discussion see Deborah Mays, 'Middle-Sized Detached Houses' in *Scotland's Buildings*, Tuckwell Press, 2003, pp.67-89.

[2] *The Maitland Legacy*, produced by the Tain & Easter Ross Civic Trust, copyright Mike Herd Films, 2007.

[3] *Inverness Courier*, 8th November, 1883 and 8th January, 1886, *Ross-shire Journal,* 18th November, 1892, *Inverness Courier*, 24th March and 13th November, 189, and *Ross-shire Journal*, 6th May, 1898 respectively.

[4] *Inverness Courier*, 22nd January, 1886.

[5] Mackenzie & Cormack advertisement for sale, *The Scotsman*, 21st April, 1920.

[6] Historic Environment Scotland LB49633.

7   Plans dated 29th July, 1887 in the possession of Jack and Vivianne Reid, the present owners. Advertisement for tenders in the *Inverness Courier* of the same date.

8   *Inverness Courier*, 5th July, 1892.

9   Information given to Douglas Reid by Edith Ross.

10 *Ross-shire Journal*, 4th October and 15th February, 1895 respectively.

11 Niall Harkiss, *Ross-shire Football's Pioneers*, K & N Publishing 2014, pp.10 - 22.

12 See Tony Watson, *Tain a Golfing History of People, Places and Past Times*, published by Tony Watson, 2014 for a well researched history of the club and those involved.

13 *Inverness Courier*, 26th June, 1896.

14 These include The Rowans in Moss Road, owned by William Ross, the jeweller for whom the Maitlands designed Victoria Buildings; Seaview in Academy Street; and St Duthus Villa in Chapel Road, which leads to the golf course.

15 Michael Hook, *A History of the Royal Burgh of Dornoch*, Historylinks Museum, Dornoch, 2005, p.108.

16 *Ross-shire Journal*, 24th January, 1896.

17 *Evening Telegraph*, 4th May, 1891.

18 Gifford, *Highlands and Islands*, p. 570.

21. THE PASSING OF AN EPOCH

21.1 Andrew Maitland Senior in his later years.

Andrew Maitland Senior in old age

Andrew Maitland Senior advanced serenely into old age. He is said to have been a bright and genial companion and to have enjoyed a chat with his friends about 'the good old days'. He remained in 'fair health' until the last week of his life. Though subject to 'fits of weakness' he possessed an extraordinary amount of vigour and vitality and was in full possession of his faculties until the day he died. The last major project in which he took a serious interest seems to have been Tain Free Church (now the Parish Church), opened two months before his 90th birthday in 1892, though he continued to take an interest in the business for another year. The two daughters of Andrew and Henrietta who survived to maturity, Christina and Henrietta Margaret, continued to live at Esther Row, or Esther Place as it was variously called, until Henrietta Margaret married Andrew MacDuff Ross, a draper in Tain, in her parents' house in December 1890.

Andrew's later years were, however, beset by sadness. From about 1882 his wife Henrietta suffered from heart disease, and by late 1886 she was 'debilitated'. She died on 4th November, 1887 aged 71. In August 1890 William, the sixth son of Andrew Senior and Henrietta, died in Sydney at the age of 49 'after completing a voyage in search of health'. Henry, the fifth son, also died before 1891, leaving children.

In November, 1891 Andrew Senior's daughter Henrietta Margaret died from blood poisoning only 11 months after her wedding and at only 32 years of age. She left a daughter, Henrietta Margaret Maitland

Ross. This was just the beginning of several misfortunes for Andrew MacDuff Ross and those connected with him. As we saw earlier, in 1895 fire destroyed the premises in which he carried on his drapery business. A second wife also predeceased him, and two of their children died in infancy. In 1910 at a meeting of the Tain School Board he wrongly accused a teacher at Tain Public School of flogging a girl in contravention of a policy that chastisement should only take place in the presence of the headmaster in a private room, and he was successfully sued for damages for slander. Soon after he was unable to pay his creditors and his estate was sequestrated. His daughter Henrietta Margaret Maitland Ross became a governess and in 1921 lost a legal action for a declarator of marriage to her employer, an Edinburgh lawyer - even though he had fathered a child by her and banns had been proclaimed.

With the death of Henrietta Margaret seven of Andrew Senior's eleven children had predeceased him. Only three of the four survivors, Christina (who lived with him for the rest of his life) and his two architect sons, were in Tain, and the other survivor, Alexander, in Sydney, had not long to live.

Only 24 days after Henrietta Margaret's death Andrew Senior's younger sister Helen, a retired housekeeper who had moved to Academy Street in Tain, died at the age of 84.

In the face of these losses Andrew Senior appears to have found spiritual consolation. The Minister of Tain Free Church, the Rev. Thomas Grant, recalled that 'owing to trouble in his family, it was my privilege to visit him, and busy as he was, and earnest in his work, I do not remember for the last thirty five years one occasion on which I visited that family that Mr Maitland was too busy to come and kneel with me in prayer, and even if I wished to go away without doing so, he would never permit it'. One wonders whether they also discussed politics: whilst Andrew Maitland had become a Liberal Unionist after Gladstone's conversion to Irish Home Rule, Grant was a Radical, describing himself as a follower of Gladstone, and the Unionist-supporting *Ross-shire Journal* complained in 1892 that his congregation 'have now been long enough dosed with his political opinions'. Or perhaps the old friends found something of common interest: before becoming a minister Grant had learnt to be a stonemason.

Andrew Senior contracted gastric catarrh in May 1894. Three days later, on 24th May, he died in the presence of his son James and probably also of James's siblings Andrew Junior and Christina. The Rev. Thomas Grant paid fulsome tribute to him at the close of the service the following Sunday in the recently built Free Church, which, as the Parish Church, remains to-day the most prominent memorial to the Maitland dynasty.

Andrew Senior left net moveable and personal estate of £2,170-13s-11d; in addition he used in his Will a valuation of £350 for his house. His estate would no doubt have been more substantial had he not suffered from the collapse of the City of Glasgow Bank. Notwithstanding this disaster his investments included shares in banks, as well as investments in Maitland projects - 6 mortgage debentures of £100 each in The Glenmorangie Distillery Co. Ltd and four £5 shares in the Tain Public Hall Company, the latter described as 'unsaleable' and valued at 1 shilling each.

Andrew Senior left possession and occupancy of his house in Esther Place to Christina so long as she remained unmarried. She never married, but she moved out of the house within months of her father's death. She went to Beechwood in Nairn and derived an income from letting Esther Place.

Andrew Junior and the freemasons

By the 1890s Andrew Junior was heavily involved with a variety of tasks and was widely respected.

In December 1890, still a very active freemason, he was elected Master of the Lodge St. Duthus, a position which he held until December, 1893. Until 1876 all Masters had been members of the landed gentry, but Andrew Junior was following in the footsteps of other professional men.

As we have seen, the original Masonic Hall, used for nearly a century, had been demolished in 1872 when the Royal Hotel had been built on the site, and the freemasons had met in the Tain Public Hall since it had been opened in 1876. Andrew Junior's successor as Master of the Lodge, Dr. Colin Mackenzie, revived interest in building a new Lodge.[1] Ground was purchased for £35 on the north side of Manse Street, from which it was well set back, and some existing buildings seem to have been demolished. The burgh acquired a strip beside the street to allow it, like so many other streets in nineteenth century Tain, to be widened and straightened.[2] Designs for a new Lodge were prepared by Bro. Bailie Andrew Maitland. An acceptable estimate of £595-5s-0d was obtained in March 1895. Half the funds required were raised from selling the feu of the Public Hall and from subscriptions. 'The brethren heavily took up the proposal' to subscribe, Bro. Andrew Maitland and Bro. James Maitland each subscribing 10 guineas.[3] Bro. Bailie William Ross (a baker in Tain, not to be confused with the jeweller of the same name who engaged the Maitlands to build Victoria Buildings in Tain) lent the other half at 4% *per annum* interest.

In December 1895 the new Masonic Hall was formally opened. In appreciation of the 'ability and enthusiasm he had brought to bear on the duties of the chair' Andrew Junior was presented - belatedly, owing to 'his pressure of work and absence from home' - with a masonic scarf ring with a jewel. The debt to William Ross was cleared in 1903 after a two day bazaar held in the newly renovated Town Hall and patronised by the great and the good of the county.

The Masonic Hall, which is still in use, is a fairly simple building, with its street frontage embellished with crow-step gables. It perhaps suffers in comparison to the Maitland-designed Parish Church further along Queen Street. But then the budget for the church was more than eight times that for the Hall.

Andrew Junior, councillor and Provost

Meanwhile Andrew Junior was playing an increasingly prominent role in local government. The Tain councillors are captured for posterity, with Andrew near the centre wearing a masonic sash and apron, in an evocative photograph of a tree planting in the Collegiate Churchyard to commemorate Queen Victoria's Golden Jubilee in 1887.

In 1889 the Local Government (Scotland) Act established a new system of elected county councils. Ross-shire and the enclaves that had constituted Cromartyshire were united as Ross & Cromarty 'for all purposes whatsoever'. The new county councils were given responsibility for matters previously dealt with by the heritors as Commissioners of Supply and county road trustees. They also took over some administrative powers, but not judicial or licensing matters, from the justices of the peace. They were, moreover, given authority outside burghs under the Public Health Acts, and police functions from burghs, like Tain, with less than 7,000 inhabitants were transferred to them. Police burghs such as Tain were regarded as electoral divisions, but their councillors were initially co-opted by the burgh councils rather than directly elected.

In January 1890, on the formation of the new Ross & Cromarty County Council, the question arose as to who should be selected as the county councillor for the burgh of Tain. The appointment was a prestigious one. The *Ross-shire Journal's* verbatim reports of the discussions show the delicacy with which the matter was approached. Provost Vass clearly had the best claim, was well respected and was apparently willing to do the job. Bailie Matheson was willing to propose him. But the view was gently put that new blood was required, and Councillor Andrew Maitland was elected amongst expressions of mutual goodwill.

In rural areas the establishment of county councils effected a significant transfer of powers from the heritors; but many heritors were elected to the councils and were thus able to exercise similar powers. Among the 55 members elected in Ross & Cromarty were 15 landlords and 4 estate factors, as well as

11 farmers. The work of the Maitland practice was predominantly rural, and mixing in these circles must have been helpful to Andrew Junior and his firm. Several previous and future clients of the Maitlands were elected, including Sir Kenneth Mackenzie of Gairloch (who became Convenor), Sir Hector Munro of Foulis, Ronald Munro-Ferguson of Novar, M.P. and Major Randle Jackson of Swordale, and William Gunn, factor for the Cromartie estates (though his employer, the young Earl of Cromartie, was humiliated by a Land League candidate in Coigach).

21.2 Tain councillors at a tree planting to commemorate Queen Victoria's Golden Jubilee, 1887. Left to right: Mr Dan Munro (chemist), Sergeant William Ross (caretaker of the Collegiate Church), Mr Gordbrand (Culnaha), Rev. Fraser (Fearn), Mr Edward Matheson (in Volunteer's uniform), Mr White (coal merchant), Mr John Mackenzie (Town Clerk and the author's grandfather), Mr Andrew Maitland Junior (architect), Rev. Colin Macnaughton (Tain Church of Scotland), Bailie Donald Duff, Mr W.J.Macdonald (Sheriff Clerk), Rev. Hutcheson, Provost Dr James Vass (planting tree), Sheriff T. MacKenzie, Dr Kennedy, Bailie William Ross, Mr Fraser (Mayfield), Mr Duncan Cameron (Commercial Bank agent).

Andrew Junior's election to the county council and his membership of its Easter Ross District Committee added to his already significant workload. In October 1890 there was a proposal to alter the time of Tain Burgh Council meetings from 6.30 P.M. to 11 A.M. in order to stave off the threatened retirement of Provost Vass who felt unable to manage evening meetings. Andrew Junior objected strongly on the grounds of his daytime workload.

In November that year Provost Vass and Bailie Wallace (who had been a councillor for 42 years, 32 as Bailie) did not stand for re-election. Edward Matheson was elected Provost and Andrew Junior Second Bailie. As a bailie Andrew became a magistrate, sitting in a variety of cases in the court house designed by his father.

Like his father, Andrew Junior became a Unionist in the wake of the split in the Liberal ranks over Irish Home Rule. In October 1895 a meeting was held to form a Unionist Association in Tain, and to study the more important points of modern electioneering. Provost Matheson and ex-Bailie Wallace were elected honorary presidents and Bailie Maitland became one of two vice-presidents.

Before the burgh elections of November 1897 candidates' attendance records for the previous year were published. Andrew's record was :-

	Total meetings	Attendance
Council	59	35
Police Commissioners	23	17
Gas Commissioners	19	9
Committee Meetings	61	39
TOTAL	162	100

These figures illustrate the extent to which local government was devolved in a burgh like Tain. But they also show the heavy demands it made on those involved. As much of the action required by the council was delegated to committees, moreover, there was much more to be done outside formal meetings.

Andrew Junior, aged 50, was returned at the top of the poll. The contest was 'conducted on purely political grounds' and the results were 'a decided victory to the Unionist party'.[4] Edward Matheson retired as Provost and Bailie Maitland was unanimously called to the Provostship.

All the evidence is that Andrew Junior was highly regarded by his contemporaries for his leadership qualities. As the *Ross-shire Journal* put it, 'a leader of thought, he was a leader of men with that fascination of presence essential to public success'. His tenure of the Provostship was, however, to be sadly brief. He presided only three times over monthly meetings of the burgh council.

A major shock

As 1897 drew to a close Andrew Junior was a family man with a wife and five children. Although he was no longer Master of the Lodge St Duthus, he had three business occupations - architect and partner in A. Maitland & Sons, Managing Director of The Glenmorangie Distillery Company, and proprietor of the Highland Ærated Water Company - as well as his responsibilities as Provost and county councillor.

Such a workload would have taxed a robust constitution, but Andrew Junior's constitution does not appear to have been sufficiently robust.

Towards the end of 1897 Andrew Junior showed signs of what was taken to be overwork, which developed into a loss of energy. A London specialist diagnosed heart disease and recommended a sea voyage. In February 1898 Andrew went to Las Palmas in the Canary Islands, contemplating a cruise round the world. He endured stormy seas en route, was 'a good deal upset' and was ordered to stay in bed for two weeks. His wife Eliza was sent for and joined him. He seemed to be showing sufficient signs of recovery by mid April for his doctors to allow them to travel home. Andrew and Eliza arrived in Plymouth, from where a telegram was sent to James saying that Andrew felt much better. Seeking warmer weather than that of Tain, Andrew decided to stay at Limpsfield in Surrey for a few weeks. From there another telegram was sent to James announcing a relapse in Andrew's condition. James set off south on 29th April, only to discover that Andrew had died early in the morning of 30th April.

There was an element of hyperbole in the *Ross-shire Journal*'s account: 'During its municipal history the burgh of Tain has not, perhaps, received a greater blow, nor any community a greater shock than was sustained on Saturday, when the intelligence of the death of Provost Andrew Maitland, architect, Tain, was received'.[5] But there is no doubt that his premature death, and the suddenness of it after news of his apparently improved health, caused consternation in Tain - or that the tributes paid to Andrew Junior in the then parish church and in the council chamber were genuine and heartfelt. The town council immediately decided to have a portrait painted (presumably from photographs) and hung, along with those of previous Provosts, in the council chamber.

21.3 The posthumous portrait of Andrew Maitland Junior as Provost.

The council and a 'large concourse of people' turned out at Tain station for the arrival of the train which conveyed the coffin in a van next to the engine, and Andrew's widow Eliza with her sons Arthur and Gordon (later to become a partner in A. Maitland & Sons) and her brother-in-law James in the after portion. On the day of the funeral all the shops in Tain were closed and 'from one o'clock to three o'clock the town presented a deathlike stillness'. The cortege was an immense one. Leading the procession from Lauderdale to the graveyard were the largest number of freemasons ever seen in Tain (the current Master being the Minister conducting the service), and following them the Provincial Grand Lodge of Freemasons, the children of the Tain schools, the St Duthus Lodge of Oddfellows, the Dingwall Town Council, the Tain Town Council, the mourning relatives and the general public. There was an 'exceptionally large assembly of the general public, representative of the whole of the northern counties'. The Rev. Colin Macnaughton of the established church conducted a service at the gates of Lauderdale and another at the St Duthus cemetery.

In the graveyard, close to the ruined chapel of St Duthus, and not far from the more modest tombstone of his parents and of his siblings who had died in childhood, Provost Andrew Maitland is commemorated by a large and imposing marble monument, on which the names of other members of his family were later engraved.

Andrew Junior left personal and moveable estate of £9,317-8s-7d. This included 300 £10 shares in The Glenmorangie Distillery Company, valued - notwithstanding the evidence given in the litigation only two years before - at £10 per share. The *Dictionary of Scottish Architects* notes the total as more than that of most leading Edinburgh and Glasgow architects. But then not many Edinburgh and Glasgow architects doubled as entrepreneurial distillers.

References and Notes

[1] The above account of the building of the Mason Hall is derived mainly from William T. Russell, *My Brothers Past*, vol.1, 1761-1899, Librario Publishing Ltd, 2000, pp,111-27.

[2] Plan of east end of Manse Street, showing ground added to street, 1894, Tain & District Museum.

[3] *Ross-shire Journal*, 11th May, 1894.

[4] *Aberdeen Journal*, 10th November, 1897.

[5] *Ross-shire Journal*, 6th May, 1898.

PART III

THE FINAL PHASE -
JAMES AND GORDON MAITLAND FROM 1898

22. UNCLE AND NEPHEW

In his brother's footsteps

James Maitland followed in his late younger brother's footsteps in a remarkable number of ways. These included his role at the Glenmorangie distillery, in the St Duthus Lodge of Freemasons and on the Tain Burgh and Ross & Cromarty County Councils. The first, however, was in his living arrangements.

In August 1898, four months after his brother's death, he sold the house he had designed for himself, Scotsburn Lodge in Scotsburn Road. The purchaser was Roderick Finlayson, for whom the Maitlands had designed the Royal Hotel in 1872. It was clearly an investment for Finlayson, who had retired to farming at Ardjachie, near Tain, since he proceeded to let it out to a bank agent. James then leased his late brother's house, Lauderdale in Morangie Road, from his sister-in-law, Eliza. Eliza herself returned permanently to Edinburgh, where she lived initially at 55, Morningside Road and later at 16, Merchiston Place. The 1901 census shows James and Barbara living, with a cook and a housemaid, at Lauderdale. Their 15 year old son Henry was a boarder at Fettes College in Edinburgh, a school increasingly popular with parents who could afford the fees or whose sons were gifted enough to gain scholarships.

One of the features of Lauderdale was a new telephone system which was installed whilst Andrew Junior had been convalescing in the Canaries, a system so advanced as to attract press coverage. There was already a telephone connection, the first in Tain, between the brothers' architectural office in Tain and the Glenmorangie distillery. The new 'Hunnings Desk pattern telephone' was portable and could be carried around the room. A 'three-way Miller Switch with a cow bell extension gong' now allowed communication from the house with either the office or the distillery.

James Maitland and the Glenmorangie distillery

James Maitland would have found this new-fangled gadgetry useful as he was immediately thrown into the deep end of the distillery's affairs. Andrew Junior had been Managing Director of The Glenmorangie Distillery Company, in which the Maitland family held 32% of the shares, and he had deployed an enormous amount of energy in managing and promoting its business. His death left a large void. This was quickly filled by the appointment of James as Managing Director. By October 1898 James was travelling, as his brother had done before him, to England to visit wholesalers. Much of the day-to-day management remained in the hands of James Stephen, the Company Secretary, who would have been at the distillery end of the telephone. Stephen, described in an obituary as manager of the distillery, died, however, in 1907. Thereafter Alexander Smart, referred to as Managing Brewer, seems to have assumed a more significant role in the distillery's affairs.

These were difficult times for the whisky industry and for Glenmorangie itself. The distillery building boom of the 1890s reached its peak in 1898, with production vastly exceeding demand. As we saw earlier, the collapse in December 1898 of the whisky blenders Pattisons Ltd precipitated a crisis. Whisky prices crashed, production fell by a third, some 30 distilleries closed, and many others were taken over by blenders. James Maitland's services were sought as a distillery valuator, and we find him reporting in the case of one Speyside distillery in 1905 that 'it would not be safe in present circumstances to calculate anything for goodwill, as it has now no marketable value'.

A decade after the depression started there were modest signs of recovery, but these were nipped in the bud by David Lloyd George's 1909 Budget. Whisky had been taxed at 10 shillings a gallon since 1860 and 11shillings from 1900, but the Chancellor, a silver-tongued Welshman who had a remarkable propensity to bed women but crusaded against the evils of drink, now raised this to 14s-9d. As a result consumption in the United Kingdom, the largest market for whisky, fell by a third. At a large protest meeting in Dingwall in May 1909 James Maitland moved a resolution, seconded by his friend and client Andrew Mackenzie of Dalmore, to be delivered to the Prime Minister and the Chancellor. The one manufacturing industry which had sprung up in the Highlands, he said, was the production of malt whisky. There were 96 distilleries in the Highlands, on which hundreds of thousands of pounds had been spent. They gave employment to large bodies of workmen of all classes. Much of the arable land was given over to barley. The tax 'affected not only the farmer, the distiller and the licensed trade, but the whole community, because merchants reaped the benefits when all classes were employed'.

Such protests were of no avail. The measures in Lloyd George's 'People's Budget' survived a constitutional crisis and a General Election. By 1914 the industry was in a poor way, and the Great War was to make it worse.

The Lodge St Duthus

Like his brother, James Maitland was an active member of the St Duthus Lodge of Freemasons. In December, 1898 he was elected Master of the Lodge, another position his brother had held before him. Between 1898 and 1920 he was to serve four terms as Master, for a period totalling eight years.[1]

The freemasons, who did not yet have the 'secret society' image often associated with them today, maintained a very visible profile. They continued to organise events, including processions round Tain with their Master at the head, though the scale of these seems to have been less elaborate than when they had celebrated the foundation of earlier Maitland buildings. Members' widows and orphans benefitted from their charity.

James Maitland and local government

James Maitland also followed his brother into local government. He was noted as a good public speaker, though his style was sometimes thought old-fashioned. His politics were staunchly Unionist and he played a leading role in local Unionist affairs.

When James began his career in local government the 'nightwatchman' state that had evolved during the nineteenth century was still in full flower. Central government played a fairly marginal role. It declared war and it levied taxes, but it seldom impinged directly on peoples' lives. Implementation of the Victorian reforms of the poor law, policing and education was devolved to local boards and councils, with bodies in Edinburgh (or London in the case of education) keeping a watching brief. The poorhouses, police stations and schools that Andrew Maitland and his sons designed were thus all commissioned locally. All this was to change as the modern centralised welfare state began to emerge. One of the major game-changers was the Lloyd George budget of 1909. The taxes it introduced on whisky, which devastated Glenmorangie and other distilleries, helped to pay for one of the pillars of the centralised welfare state, a system of national insurance.

James Maitland served on three different tiers of local government - at parish council, burgh council and county council level.

Parish councils replaced the parochial boards which had been had set up in 1845 to administer poor relief - and had led to one of Andrew Maitland Senior's first major commissions, the Easter Ross Union Poorhouse. The parochial boards' function was transferred by the Local Government Act, 1894 to newly formed parish councils, elected on a wider franchise. It was on the Tain Parish Council that James Maitland first cut his teeth in local government, becoming a member by December 1898. The parish council covered not just the burgh of Tain but also the rest of the civil parish, known as Landward Tain. James, using Glenmorangie as his address, represented Landward Tain.

The Tain Burgh Council had a far wider brief. Its members had long administered the assets of the Common Good Fund, including the Mussel Scalps, the quarries on the Hill of Tain, and from 1903 the Town Hall. A series of Burgh Police (Scotland) Acts and other legislation from 1833 to 1903 laid down duties which went far beyond what we would regard as policing. They in fact contained much of the social legislation of the period. The burgh council was responsible for distributing gas from the gas works (reconstructed in 1892 to James Maitland's designs); distributing water; paving, cleansing and lighting streets; preventing infectious diseases; regulating the infrastructure to improve sanitary standards (including ownership of the Maitland-designed Shambles or Slaughterhouse); issuing building warrants for permitted developments; and a variety of matters such as licensing under the Poisons Act. The advent of the motor car was now bringing with it further duties such as licensing petrol sales and storage, enforcing vehicle lighting and drawing up regulations for the restriction of speed (set at ten miles per hour in 1908).

The *Ross-shire Journal* noted in October 1905 that 'if there is one thing more than another that Tain has ever seemed to pride itself upon it has been the maintenance of a high standard of intelligence and public spiritedness in its bodies. ... This year, taking time by the forelock, Tain has been looking out for new blood. James Maitland, the well-known architect, on being approached by a deputation at first declined to come forward as a candidate for the Council. A second deputation, more persistent than the first, had the desired effect'. James thus stood in the burgh council election the following month. There was reported to be 'no burning question'. James, in London on distillery business, was unable to attend the annual "Hecklin' Meeting" at which candidates spoke and were heckled. There was a record poll with 343 people voting. James Maitland headed the poll with 275 votes, ousting two members seeking re-election, Roderick Finlayson, for whom his father had designed the Royal Hotel, and Alex Munro, a mason who had worked on many of the buildings designed by the Maitlands but also appears to have been competing with them.

As a councillor James was involved with a number of local issues, earning the reputation of being a strong 'Tainite'. One of these was trying to make Tain an attractive summer resort. The golf course was widely seen as one of the keys to this. To assist the club the burgh council purchased in 1907 from John Schofield of Balnagall the 500 acre estate of Wester, Mid and South Pithogarty, on part of which the golf course was situated. In 1907 James took the lead in reviving the Tain Highland Gathering, which had been in abeyance for twelve years. He was also involved in heated debates in 1907-08 about the 'Tain telephone scheme'. The Post Office was only willing to instal a 'trunk line' connecting an exchange in Tain with exchanges elsewhere if the council would provide a seven year guarantee against losses. The council was unwilling to provide such a guarantee unless it was backed by corresponding guarantees from local people. James was one of 16 who gave such guarantees, but only on condition that call-offices would be established at Fearn and Kildary. When a loss of £18-1s-6d was reported in 1911 both sets of guarantees were called upon.

In 1907 Bailie George Macleay, who had been a close personal friend of James Maitland for thirty years, died. James Maitland was then elected third Bailie, and thus a magistrate. Those speaking in support of his election, who included his brother-in-law the Treasurer Andrew MacDuff Ross, all stressed that in the ordinary course other older and longer-serving councillors, including themselves, might have a better claim, but that none of them was as well qualified.

Another death in 1907, that of James Stephen, the Company Secretary of the Glenmorangie Distillery Company, led to James Maitland joining the Ross & Cromarty County Council. Stephen had been the member for Tain (Landward), and in the elections that November James Maitland, was returned unopposed in his place. Membership involved attendance at full council meetings held four times a year and meetings of its Easter Ross District Committee. His main contribution to county affairs came three years later when the council's Road Board recommended on cost grounds that the main road to the north should take a 14 mile short cut across the Easter Ross peninsula by Aultnamain rather than run through Alness, Invergordon and Tain. James was able to defeat the proposal by 13 votes to 10.

In November 1910 Donald Fowler retired as Provost of Tain and James Maitland was unanimously chosen to succeed him. Traditionally lamps bearing the town's arms were placed opposite the residence of the chief magistrate, or Provost, of a city or royal burgh. Two such lamps outside Donald Fowler's house were quickly removed, and there were heated arguments as to whether one or two new lamps were required to restore the lighting in the Scotsburn Road. £10 was spent on a single new lamp erected outside James Maitland's house in Morangie Road.

22.1 James Maitland as Provost of Tain.

The new Provost quickly found himself in opposition to his predecessor on one of the biggest local issues of the day. Tain Royal Academy, where James had been educated, was a fee-paying school. It provided free education for pupils from the Tain Public School who passed its examination, and it got a grant from the Scotch Education Department to cover pupils from outwith the Tain area. The Tain School Board, which ran the public school, wanted to co-ordinate primary and secondary education under one management - their own - and its members had stood for election on this basis. The Governors of the Royal Academy, who were resolutely opposed to this, elected James Maitland as their Chairman in January 1911. They were in a weak position as the funds in their endowment were insufficient to provide free education on an appropriate scale, whereas the School Board had behind it the resources of the state. The Scotch Education Department held an enquiry in March 1912 into the 'transference' of Tain Royal Academy to the School Board. James Maitland, representing both the governors and the Ross & Cromarty County Council, asked that in order to allow an approach for subscriptions to be made to former pupils all over the world no immediate transfer should take place. James and the governors lost their battle. The Academy was taken over by the School Board in May 1912 - albeit not directly but by through a committee consisting of the members of the School Board and representatives of the Tain Burgh Council and the County Education Committees of Ross-shire and Sutherland. James Maitland, clearly upset, refused to take one of these places.

Another cause supported by James Maitland was that of women's suffrage. Women did not have the vote in parliamentary elections, though women who were ratepayers did have the vote in local government elections. Thus the Tain electorate in October 1908 was 416, of whom 301 were male and 115 female. James Maitland chaired a local meeting in 1911 of the Scottish Federation of Women's Suffrage Societies, who were suffragists and, unlike the better-remembered suffragettes, non-militant. He declared himself entirely in sympathy with their cause.

Another William Robertson

After the death of his brother in 1898 James Maitland, now sole survivor of the partners in A. Maitland & Sons, clearly had a heavy professional workload, even before he became involved with local government This was alleviated for a time by the employment of a young architect, William Robertson, in 1901.[2] Robertson, no relation of the Elgin-based architect of the same name for whom Andrew Maitland Senior had worked in the years up to 1841, was the eldest of four brothers. He had probably been destined to take over his father's thriving building business in the Glasgow area, but joined the Maitlands to gain experience. He is known to have been involved with the designs of Mansfield House and Morangie House, of which more later.

In 1904 he married a relation of the Rev. Gustavus Aird, who had preached at the opening of so many Maitland-designed churches. His best man was James Maitland's nephew Gordon.

Soon afterwards he returned for a short period to his family firm. In 1910 he went to British East Africa (now Kenya), where he was involved, possibly for the family firm, with the design of government buildings, apparently including the main post office and the railway station in Nairobi.

Gordon Maitland

Andrew Gordon Maitland, always known as Gordon, was born on 25th January, 1880. He was the second of the three sons of Andrew Junior and Eliza who survived to adulthood, and the only grandson of the first Andrew Maitland to become an architect. Gordon Maitland's use of his second Christian name has sometimes caused confusion, with 'Andrew Gordon Maitland' and 'Gordon Maitland' sometimes being separately identified and over-lapping entries being published.

Like his father and uncle, Gordon was educated at Tain Royal Academy. By 1899 he was working in the Maitland office and preparing designs for his first project. This was for the St Duthus Lodge of Oddfellows, a body similar to the freemasons but with membership particularly drawn from those lower in the social scale. It maintained funds to pay sickness benefits, doctors' fees and funeral expenses. Like the freemasons the Oddfellows enjoyed parading round the town, and crowds watched the debut of their brass band in

1897. They did not, however, have their own premises for their events and fortnightly meetings until in 1899 they obtained the feu of land in what is now Upper King Street. Gordon Maitland designed Oddfellows Hall for them, the Maitland firm making no charge. The hall was built by the tradesmen of the lodge, who provided their services free in their spare time. A cake and wine banquet was attended at the opening in July 1900 by over a hundred members and honorary members, the latter including James Maitland who formally opened the new hall. Gordon Maitland, still only 20, replied to a toast to the architect in a lengthy speech 'brimful of humour'.[3]

Whilst studying for the Royal Institute of British Architects exams, which he took in 1901 and 1902, Gordon worked in the office in New Bond Street, London, of William Flockhart. Flockhart, a Scot, is described as having a 'highly strung and very artistic temperament' and as being an inventive and scholarly designer prone to keep changing his designs. He had a number of very rich clients, and executed work mainly in London and the south of England. His best work, however, was probably at Rosehaugh in the Black Isle. There between 1898 and 1903 he produced one of the grandest mansion houses in the Highlands (since demolished) and numerous estate buildings. After leaving Flockhart's office Gordon was employed for a short time in the Government Office of Works.

In April 1903 James Maitland, who had been the sole partner in A. Maitland & Sons since the death of his brother in 1898, assumed Gordon as a partner. Thereafter Gordon took an increasingly significant role in the practice, particularly after James became more and more deeply involved in local government. He also joined his uncle in 1908 as a director of The Glenmorangie Company.

22.2 Gordon Maitland with Sheriff MacKenzie's daughter.

Surviving photographs of Gordon Maitland show a self-confident young man, clean-shaven, immaculately dressed, and perhaps something of a dandy. After his return to Tain he featured prominently in newspaper reports of the social and cultural life of Edwardian Tain - acting, singing, debating, presiding at events of the Tain Literary Society, the Tain Philharmonic Society and the Oddfellows, and helping to form an association determined to take practical steps to promote Tain as a summer resort. As early as 1907 he was described as 'a gentleman who takes a leading part in every movement for the advancement of the town'.

22.3 Tain Golf Club, 1911 - the opening of the new club house. James Maitland at right in the doorway.

Gordon was also keen on golf and when the town council acquired further land to extend the golf course, this time from the Kirksheaf trustees, he was the architect of a new club house opened in 1911. The club house, financed by public subscription, had a distinctive design, with a tower at one end and a large dining hall of circular design, with a domed roof at the other. In between these was the original small clubhouse, moved by sledge from its former position. The new clubhouse was on an earth mound, so that it could be more visible from passing trains. Provost Maitland in introducing Robert Allan, who performed the opening ceremony, emphasised the importance of the golf course in facilitating the growth of Tain as a resort. Two things were needed, he said, an hotel near the course and houses to let to families.[4] The club house has since been replaced by a larger building on the same site.

The census taken in 1911 shows Gordon Maitland as one of two boarders in a house in Esther Place, three doors away from where his grandfather had lived. But, as we shall see, his living arrangements were soon to take a very different turn.

In July of that year year, after an attack of asthma, Gordon consulted an Ear, Nose and Throat specialist, Mr Malcolm Farquharson, in Edinburgh. Farquharson advised that he should have a triple operation to remove his tonsils and adenoids and to perform a nasal resection on the septum - together in the days before antibiotics a dangerous procedure which necessitated proper attention afterwards. Farquharson carried out the combined operations at the house of Gordon's brother, Arthur, a solicitor in Edinburgh. Farquharson then said he was going on holiday the next day and that he was leaving Gordon in the sole charge of his assistant, 'Dr. Montgomery'. Painful and life-threatening complications then set in, which Montgomery failed to recognise. It then turned out that Montgomery was not a doctor but a medical student. Gordon consulted another specialist, who had to perform an emergency mastoidectomy. Gordon permanently lost the hearing in his right ear. With Arthur acting for him, Gordon successfully sued Farquharson and was awarded damages of £1,000.[5]

References and Notes

[1]   William T. Russell, *My Brothers Past*, Librario, 2002, Vol. I, p. 133 and Vol. II pp. 1,11, 30 and 44

[2]   The information on William Robertson has been provided by Ross Robertson, a grandson of William.

[3]   *Ross-shire Journal*, 20th July, 1900. The building was later demolished and flats built on the site.

[4]   *North Star and Farmers' Journal*, 24th August, 1911

[5]   National Records of Scotland CS256/61, Andrew Gordon Maitland v J. Malcolm Farquarson, 1912.

23. RURAL WORK BEFORE THE GREAT WAR

The rural economy

In the years in which James was sole partner and those in which he was joined by Gordon the Maitlands' core business continued to be related to the rural economy of Easter Ross and other parts of the eastern coastal plain. Further afield this was the golden age of the sporting lodge, and the Maitlands continued their involvement: the factors driving this were so different as to merit separate consideration later in this chapter.

At the turn of the twentieth century most of the Scottish countryside remained in the hands of landed proprietors. As we saw earlier, the latter years of the nineteenth century had witnessed some fragmentation of their estates (and so gave opportunities for architects like the Maitlands to build new mansion houses and farm houses), but owner occupation of farms was advancing only slowly. Nudged along by increases in the rates of death duty and, from 1907, by an unearned income surcharge payable on rental income, this process continued in the years leading up to the Great War. But it was still slow. By 1914 only 11% of Scottish farm land was owner occupied. The Maitlands' principal clients therefore remained the landed proprietors, though they also found some work from sitting tenants who bought their farms.

Farming in the Maitlands' area of operation, had survived the great agricultural depression of the mid 1870s to the mid 1890s better than in many other parts of Britain. This particularly reflected the prevalence of mixed farming and the ability it gave to adapt to changing market conditions. Members of the Easter Ross Farmers' Club, which boasted 161 members in 1900, prided themselves on being in the van of stock breeding, with prime positions in cattle and sheep breeding. Farming at the upper end of the livestock market gave them some protection against competition from imports. At the same time income from their arable crops benefitted from growing the barley required in local distilleries and from specialisation in potatoes.

But as a result of the depression farmers' selling prices for grain and fat cattle had declined from their earlier peaks. This had a significant impact on the level of rents landlords could seek from their tenants. The Valuation Rolls indicate that in 1905 the rents of nearly all the farms in Easter Ross were below those of 1885, some having fallen by a quarter and in at least one case one-third. Landlords thus had less incentive to build on the scale we saw in earlier chapters, and, as we will see, this affected the Maitlands' work.

Even the best agriculturalists were not immune from these pressures. Ian Wallace in his history of Arabella[1] gives an example which tellingly illustrates this. James Gordon, well-respected as a breeder of shorthorn cattle and blackfaced sheep, had bought the estate of Arabella for £23,600 in 1876. As we saw earlier, he had then engaged the Maitlands to design a very impressive steading and to extend his mansion house. He had borrowed £16,000, which he was due to repay in 1908. He could not meet the payment and put Arabella up for sale at an upset price of £18,000. There were no bidders. When it was re-offered for sale at £16,500 there were again no offers. His brother John Gordon, tenant of Cullisse in Nigg on the estate of Old Shandwick, came to an arrangement with the creditors and acquired Arabella, which was occupied by John's son. After John's death in 1915 debts on the estate required its sale, and it was offered at an upset price of £13,000. In 1918 it was sold for £12,500 to the Board of Agriculture for Scotland to be split into smallholdings for returning servicemen.

Mansion houses and farm houses

With much of the farming infrastructure already built, and with financial pressures affecting the sector, it is perhaps not surprising that newspapers of the pre-war period show only about a dozen invitations from the Maitlands to tender for work on mansion houses and farm houses. The majority of these were for alterations and additions. Most of the new buildings were for accommodation, often described as 'dwelling houses', on smaller farms, where new tenants seem to have had better leverage than hitherto.

One of the new farm houses was built in 1900 at Grantfield, near Tain, for Alexander Mackenzie, a native of Tain who had prospered in the drapery trade on both sides of the Atlantic and was known as the 'Button King'. When he died four years later at the age of only 41 it was reported that Mackenzie had used his wealth to purchase a lemon and orange orchard near Los Angeles, where he had a home 'embowered among heliotrope hedges and trailing vines, a veritable garden of the Hesperides'. After purchasing the 50 acre Grantfield he had engaged the Maitlands to build a 'commodious modern house and steading' near the site of the 'humble dwelling' which had been occupied by his father and grandfather.

Another farm house was built in 1901 at Balnaha on the Geanies estate in Tarbat.[2] But it was in the parish of Nigg that the Maitlands' services were most in demand. At Ankerville on the estate of Old Shandwick, where a tenant had been declared bankrupt, a new farm house was built for an incoming tenant.[3] 'Dwelling houses' were built on small farms on the Bayfield estate at Blackhill in 1910 and for a new tenant of the 28 acre Carse of Bayfield in 1912, and a small farm house was built, also in 1912, at Strath of Pitcalnie.[4] Another farm house was built on the Pitcalzean estate following the death of the tenant of the substantial Westfield Farm, the name of which was now changed to Pitcalzean.[5]

A rare example of a new mansion house being built for a landowner in this period occurred at Mounteagle in Fearn, some five miles from Tain. John Robertson was the only son of one of the founders of the Tain merchants later known as Wallace & Fraser. He inherited from his father the adjacent estates of Mounteagle and Rhynie. The estates, of some 500 and 600 acres respectively, bounded Loch Eye and the Tallich Loch, on both of which the wildfowl shooting was said to be unsurpassed in the north. Loch Eye froze over so regularly in the cold winters of the time that it was the venue for an annual 'bonspiel', in which the the North took on the South (the dividing line being the River Conon) at curling. In 1885 Robertson tried to sell, either together or separately, Rhynie, which had a 'commodious and comfortable' mansion house, and Mounteagle, which had merely a 'suitable dwelling house'. He succeeded in selling only Rhynic. He retained Mounteagle and lived in the suitable dwelling-house with his wife, who was the daughter of the Tain born architect and Clerk of Works for Scotland, Robert Matheson.

Their son William J. Robertson inherited Mounteagle on his father's death in 1902. He earned a reputation as a progressive farmer and he played a prominent role in local affairs, becoming a J.P., a county councillor, and for 30 years a member of the Volunteers and then the Territorials. He clearly found the suitable dwelling house insufficient, for in 1907 it was reported that 'a new and commodious residence' was to be erected at once to the plans of Messrs Maitland, Tain.[6] Presumably the rivalry between Robertson's grandfather, Robert Matheson and the Maitlands over the court houses at Tain and Stornoway (discussed in chapter 12) had been forgotten. The Maitland design for Mounteagle was for a three gabled front elevation with large bay windows at the sides carried up two storeys and an arched open porch in the middle. On the west was a conservatory communicating with the dining room. Sadly, Major Robertson did not live long to enjoy his new house. Although 46 when war broke out in August 1914, he joined the 4th Battalion of the Seaforth Highlanders and died seven months later of wounds received in action.

Meanwhile the estate of Rhynie was again sold in 1906, when the tenant, George A. Ross, paid £12,000 for it. Two years later the early nineteenth century mansion house (which is now listed) was extensively renovated and improved to plans by the Maitland firm.[7]

Steadings and farm cottages

In the years up to the Great War the Maitlands continued work on steadings for many estates in Easter Ross and beyond, albeit not at the rates seen between the 1840s and the 1880s. Understandably few of these steadings were new ones, though there were a surprising number of renovations and restorations after fires, often caused by steam mills going on fire. Some of the more frequent alterations, additions and improvements would have reflected the wish to accommodate labour-saving technical advances, such as the introduction of milking machines. Also observable in this period was the quest for cheaper building materials. Hence many of the Maitlands' advertisements sought tenders not just for the traditional trades but also for concrete works and galvanised corrugated iron works.

One area which saw a significant amount of work for architects in this period was the provision of cottages for farm workers. The report of a Royal Commission chaired by Sir Henry Ballantyne, which started work in 1912 and reported in 1917, with findings which revolutionised Scottish housing, addressed the issues head on.[8] Poor siting and the lack of damp-courses meant that 'dampness was so pronounced as to be injurious to health and a factor in the promotion of chronic rheumatism'. There were 'seldom to be found any of the conveniences that are necessary for the ordinary carrying on of family life, such as water-supply, scullery, washhouse, coal-shed, bath or water-closet'. One of the members of the commission was Leslie (later Sir Leslie) Mackenzie M.D., one of the leading experts on public health. He would have had personal knowledge of these conditions, having been born in 1862 at Shandwick Mains, near Kildary in Easter Ross, where his father was the grieve.

Structural repairs and improvements fell to the landlord, but the tenant farmer was generally bound by his lease to carry out minor repairs - a divided responsibility which was a serious deterrent to proper maintenance. This meant, moreover, that the question of major improvements to existing cottages or their replacement with new ones only came up at the commencement of a lease, and prospective new tenants negotiating a lease were often reluctant to ask too much, so the cottages were left out of account.

These problems were often discussed at meetings such as those of the Ross-shire Ploughman's Union. The Union had 350 members in 1898 and listened to some fiery oratory, but seems to have had little effective organisation. What appears to have made a more compelling case for Highland landlords to improve farm workers' housing was rural depopulation. The decline was particularly marked in the case of female workers. Part of the reason for depopulation was of course the lure of cities and towns in the Lowlands. Another was emigration. Farm workers could visit Sinclair's Emigration Office in Dingwall, which offered 'guaranteed situations', or the Office of Mr D. Macpherson, Emigration Agent, in Inverness, and they could respond to regular advertisements in the local newspapers such as those of the Canadian Provinces of Saskatchewan and Ontario and the Government of South Australia. In Tain MacPherson's Central Emporium acted as a shipping agency and had a poster outside saying 'Wanted … 20,000 men … Harvest Work … Canada'.

These pressures led to the employment on numerous estates of architects, sometimes to renovate old cottages, more often to plan new, improved ones. The bulk of such work in Easter Ross appears to have gone to the Maitlands.

An example of the Maitlands' work was at the 380 acre farm of Shandwick Mains.[9] The incoming tenant in 1908 was Alexander ('Alec') Cormack, a great uncle of the present author. The rent was increased from £301 to £387 (still below the 1885 level of £452), but the proprietor, Nevile Reid of Shandwick, paid for improvements to the steading and for four new farm workers' cottages. The solidly built one-and-a-half-storey cottages were clearly a huge improvement on the traditional type. The 1911 census shows a high level of occupancy. The farm grieve and his family of seven (two of whom were domestic servants) lived in a five-room cottage that must have been a considerable improvement on the accommodation half a century earlier of his predecessor, the father of Sir Leslie Mackenzie. A retired ploughman and his family of five (including his sons, who were the current foreman of the ploughmen, another ploughman and a farm labourer and his daughter who was a dressmaker) were in a four-room cottage. The second ploughman and his family of seven (including a son who was a farm labourer) were in another four-room cottage, and a groom boarded with them. A third four-room cottage was occupied a cattleman and his family of five. Altogether 28 people lived in the four cottages, whilst an old bothy housed two further ploughmen. Two farm students boarded at Shandwick Mains House with Alec Cormack and his two year old daughter, Tina, who had survived the death of her mother in childbirth.

23.1 Farm cottages built in 1908 at Shandwick Mains. Compare these with Image 18.8.

Within three years of this census Britain was at war. As we will see, this was to have a profound effect on the Maitlands' business, on Gordon Maitland personally, and on the rural economy of the Highlands. Many of the dozen or so men at Shandwick Mains of appropriate age would volunteer for, or be conscripted into, military service. Tina, who lived to the age of 101, would recall into the twenty-first century the names of the officers billeted at Shandwick Mains.

The golden age of the sporting lodge

The late Victorian years and those leading up to the Great War were the heyday of the Scottish sporting lodge, and they continued to offer opportunities for architects. The Maitland firm had, as we saw earlier, already established a reputation as one of the leading architects of sporting lodges, with Loch Assynt, Lochmore, Alladale, Swordale, Kildermorie, Glencalvie, Gruinards and Shieldaig among those to their credit. Further prestigious commissions for sporting lodges and the improvement of ancestral homes followed, one of which was to win the approval of King Edward VII.

Men who had made their fortunes in manufacturing, stockbroking and banking bought sporting estates, and they vied with each other and with the old aristocracy to create luxurious accommodation for their guests. People flocked to the Highlands from the central belt, from other parts of Britain and from overseas, and not least from America, to do the 'Highland Season'.

Deer stalking continued to be their main attraction in the northern Highlands, though further south grouse shooting predominated. The almost incredible propensity of salmon to return to their native river, even to the stretch where they had been born, was another attraction. Shooting and fishing were of course predominantly male activities, but the house parties were also calculated to appeal to the ladies, with walking, driving, boating and sketching in romantic scenery typically on the agenda. The highlight of the Highland Season in the northern counties was the Northern Meeting, held each September in Inverness. For two days Highland games and piping competitions were held on the Northern Meeting's own park. These were followed in the evenings by balls in the Meeting Rooms, attended by some 600 people, the men in Highland dress or uniform, the ladies usually in white with tartan sashes and not a few diamond tiaras.

Many of the leading architects of the day, including Sir Rowand Anderson, Sir Robert Lorimer, and Alexander Marshall Mackenzie, as well as Highland architects such as Ross & Macbeth, W.L. Carruthers, and the Maitlands, were involved in the creation of new shooting lodges and adapting older lodges and ancestral homes. The buildings, their drawing rooms, dining rooms, billiard rooms, and libraries and with extensive use of carved woodwork, stags' heads and marble, are nowhere better featured than in a recent lavishly illustrated book by Mary Miers.[10]

The owners of sporting lodges increasingly sought the benefit of developments in technology, and architects had to be able to accommodate their requirements. With the introduction of the motor car access became easier and motor houses, later known as garages, were required. Owners competed with each other to provide the comforts of modern life such as central heating, telephones, electric lifts, and refrigeration of the game shot and the fish caught. When he came to the throne King Edward himself introduced such developments at Balmoral. We have seen how he paid an unexpected visit to Andrew Carnegie at Skibo, and he was also to inspect a new lodge designed by the Maitlands that was at the forefront of technical progress.

More work for the Mackenzies of Gairloch

Sir Kenneth Smith Mackenzie of Gairloch, widely respected and considered a man of great ability, died unexpectedly of pneumonia in 1900, aged 68. He had been Convenor of the Commissioners of Supply for Ross-shire (who, as we saw, frequently engaged the Maitlands to design public buildings) and, when the Commissioners were replaced by county councils, Convenor of the Ross & Cromarty County Council for a combined total of 45 years. The Maitland partnership had also worked for him on three hotels and a shooting lodge in the parish of Gairloch.

His son, Captain Kenneth John Mackenzie, succeeded to the baronetcy and the vast Gairloch estates in Wester Ross and the Conan estate, near the (differently spelt) Conon Bridge in the east of the county. A few days before his father died the younger Kenneth had been appointed King's and Lord Treasurer's Remembrancer. The office was so-called as the holder had to 'remember' matters which were for the benefit of the Crown in Scotland. The department was located in Edinburgh, and the new Sir Kenneth and his wife, a sister of the Earl of Mansfield, lived for most of the year in one of the grandest streets in the New Town, Moray Place, whose residents were pillars of the Edinburgh social and legal hierarchies. Sir Kenneth's department was responsible for a variety of matters, including company registration, auditing the accounts of sheriff clerks and procurators fiscal, collecting fines imposed in courts, acting as Keeper of the *Edinburgh Gazette*, administering treasure trove and the estates of deceased persons falling to the Crown as *ultimus haeres,* and the custody in Edinburgh Castle of the Regalia of Scotland. These responsibilities have since been passed to a variety of officials. Nowadays not even the most senior of these officials are able to take an annual leave of two or three months. But newspapers in July and October in the early 1900s regularly reported the comings and goings 'for the season' of Sir Kenneth and Lady Marjory to and from their main seat, Conan House.

During the season they entertained on a large scale, which may explain the need for alterations and additions, organised by the Maitlands in 1904, to the back of Conan House.[11]

The three main contributions to the income of the Gairloch estate came from letting out three deer forests, with their shooting lodges at Shieldaig and Kinlochewe and the ancestral mansion house of Flowerdale, together with associated shootings and fishings. The Maitlands had, as related in chapter 19, already been involved with one of these, a new shooting lodge built at Shieldaig in 1891. They were now to be involved with the other two.

In 1902 they were employed by the new Sir Kenneth to carry out 'considerable alterations and additions' to Kinlochewe Shooting Lodge.[12] The deer forest and shootings of Kinlochewe, variously described as some 50,000 acres and 64,000 acres, were regularly rented by the Hon. William Peel M.P., a grandson of Sir Robert Peel. The movements of Peel and his wife, like those of the Mackenzies themselves, were regularly reported. For much of the nineteenth century the Parliamentary session had ended before the 'Glorious Twelfth' of August, the beginning of the grouse shooting season, but the increasing legislative programme of the Edwardian Parliament was now keeping politicians longer in London.

23.2 Flowerdale House, Gairloch. At right the original building of 1738, and at left the Maitland extension of 1904.

The Maitlands' most significant work for Sir Kenneth was at Flowerdale House. This had been built in 1738 for Sir Alexander Mackenzie, the 9th Laird and 2nd Baronet. In the words of Sir Kenneth's uncle, Osgood Mackenzie of Inverewe, 'it was not long after this that some English tourists, finding the lovely Baile Mor Glen peculiarly rich in wild-flowers, proposed to my ancestor that it should be named Flowerdale. ... The cause of the flowers being so plentiful in the good old times was that neither my grandfather nor his forbears would hear of a sheep coming near the place, except on a rope to the slaughter-house'.[13] Flowerdale had been the principal residence of the Mackenzies of Gairloch until Conan House was built later in the eighteenth century.

Flowerdale House and the Flowerdale shootings and deer forest were leased from 1874 by S.W. Clowes, a Derbyshire landlord, later an M.P., who derived a substantial income from estates around Manchester, and then by his son Captain (later Lieutenant Colonel) Henry Clowes until the latter's death on active service in Egypt in 1916.

In 1904, during the younger Clowes's tenancy, Flowerdale House was extended to the west and virtually doubled in size to the Maitlands' designs.[14] The symmetrical 1738 house, of two storeys and an attic, has six bays. The two centre bays are gabled and have a centre door at the first floor, approached by a T-shaped flight of steps. The principal rooms are on the first floor and have long round-headed windows. The building is two rooms deep and M-gabled. These gables and that at the front are crowstepped and capped by corniced string-coursed chimneys. The Maitland extension (which became a separate dwelling, Westerdale) was cleverly designed to avoid replicating the 1738 original, and at the same time to be sympathetic to it. Its distinctive features are a bowed bay and a broad gable, and its windows, crowsteps and chimneys match the original.

The Maitland family would have been interested to read in the newspapers in August 1921 that the Prime Minister had rented Flowerdale House. David Lloyd George had been advised by his doctor that he needed rest and recuperation, and he told his staff that Flowerdale would be the seat of government. He took with him not only his wife Margaret but also Frances Stevenson, who performed the dual function of secretary and mistress. Winston Churchill, Secretary of State for the Colonies, was housed in an attic bedroom. Events in Ireland, however, soon required a Cabinet meeting, and ministers were summoned to Inverness Town Hall, the first time a Cabinet meeting had been held outside London.

Speyside - and a royal visit

In 2016 the press reported that Scotland's most expensive sporting estate, with connections to King Edward VII and King George V, had been put on the market for more than £25 million, and the following year that it had been purchased by a Russian billionaire who owned a group producing and selling alcohol under 380 brands in 160 countries. This was the Tulchan Estate, near Advie in Morayshire, between Grantown-on-Spey and Aberlour. The estate of 21,000 acres contained, the sales particulars announced, fishing on one of the best salmon fishing rivers in the world, two grouse moors known as some of the best in Britain, and a lodge 'built to an impeccably high standard by Maitland and Sons of Tain in 1906'.

Following the deaths of her husband and their son in the 1880s the Dowager Countess of Seafield had become owner of the Seafield Estate, then extending to some 1,280,0000 acres and one of the largest estates in Scotland. Much of her income came from leasing out sporting facilities. These included the Tulchan Water on the River Spey, and the Tulchan and Cromdale grouse moors.

In 1905 these shootings and an earlier building, which was then known as Tulchan Lodge, were leased by Arthur D. Sassoon - not, as various accounts assert, by 'Sir Philip Sassoon, a close friend and financial adviser to King Edward VII' (the young Philip being in fact still a schoolboy at Eton).[15] King Edward VII, usually accompanied by his mistress Alice Keppel, was a frequent guest, both at Tulchan Lodge and in Hove, of Arthur Sassoon and his Italian wife Louise, 'a brilliant hostess, blessed with magnolia complexion and chestnut curls, magnificent diamonds and a French chef'.[16]

The Countess's fishing tenant was George F. McCorquodale. He was one of 12 children of another George McCorquodale, a Lancashire based entrepreneur who had founded a printing company whose factories in Newton-le-Willows, Glasgow, London and Leeds printed most of Britain's railway timetables, tickets and stationery. The factory staff worked a 54 hour week, with a half day on Saturdays. The younger George, however, had no such constraints on his time and was able to spend much of his life fishing. He was said to have caught nearly 9,000 salmon on the Spey, and his exploits were to earn him a whole chapter in a book on angling written in the present century.[17] When he took up the tenancy in about 1890 there was no fishing lodge associated with the Tulchan Water. He initially stayed nearby at Blacksboat and later at the then Tulchan Lodge, presumably by arrangement with the shooting tenant; but any such let would have had to end when the Sassoons arrived by the 'Glorious Twelfth' of August for the grouse shooting season. In March 1905 it was reported that he had arrived at Tulchan Lodge for salmon fishing, and that he had taken (i.e. leased) a small property from the Countess of Seafield, where he intended to build a house. It was probably then that he agreed plans with James Maitland, for in May the Maitland firm sought tenders for erecting a 'large residence at Advie, Strathspey'.[18] The *Aberdeen Journal* noted that a large wooden house was to be erected capable of housing 40 to 50 workmen during the construction period, and it estimated the cost of McCorquodale's new mansion house, 'the largest undertaking in Strathspey for a number of years', at £13,000 to £14,000. The *Ross-shire Journal*, estimated it at £10,000. Either way these were enormous sums: had he wished to do so McCorquodale could have bought a seven bedroom villa in Inverness for £1,100. A further Maitland advertisement in July 1906 sought tenders for an electrical power house, motor house and servants' rooms.[19] The new house, initially known as Dalchroy, was completed by June 1907. Its most distinctive features were a baronial four-storey rounded tower and an adjacent three-storey turret, reminiscent of those at the Maitland-designed Gruinards Lodge in Strathcarron.

That September, on a visit to the Sassoons at the then Tulchan Lodge, King Edward VII, accompanied as usual by Alice Keppel and also by Louise Sassoon and the Countess of Ilchester, motored over to Dalchroy to see the new house. He inspected all the principal rooms. The *Ross-shire Journal* reported enthusiastically that the King had seen 'an ideal fishing lodge unsurpassed in the north'. It was built, they noted, of the local whinstone found on the site, and a commanding tower was a prominent feature. It had a large and magnificent entrance hall panelled in oak, with a wide and stately staircase at the end, richly carved. The principal rooms were also very large and handsomely furnished, especially the library with old carved oak panelling. It was surprising to find in a country district such appliances as were to be found at Dalchroy. Electricity was used to light torches stuck out from the wall in the hall and Jacobean candelabra in the library. 'Equally as interesting as the house' were the Electrical Power House, the motor house with accommodation for five motors, the fish houses, ice stores, and quarters for motor men, ghillies, and other servants. There was a system of telephones throughout the house and between it and the outbuildings. 'A successful combination of art and science in a Scotch fishing lodge', the article concluded, 'is no easy matter, and the result at Dalchroy is eminently satisfactory. The architects are Messrs A. Maitland & Sons, Tain, Ross-shire'. The Historic Environment Scotland listing[20] also notes the McCorquodale coat of arms above the entrance.

George McCorquodale of Dalchroy died in 1936. His funeral at Advie was attended by eight nephews, among them the cousins Alexander McCorquodale, known as Sachie, and Hugh McCorquodale. In a sensational court case four years earlier in which the parties had been represented by Sir Patrick Hastings and Sir Norman Birkett, the leading King's Counsels of the day, Sachie's wife, the best-selling romantic novelist Barbara Cartland, had sought a divorce on the grounds of his adultery, and he had cross-petitioned on the grounds of her adultery with his cousin and best friend Hugh. Barbara Cartland is not recorded as having attended the funeral, nor is any conversation between the cousins. Seven months after the funeral Hugh became Barbara Cartland's second husband. In the same month George's daughter announced that she was selling Dalchroy. Meanwhile the original Tulchan Lodge had stood empty since the Great War (Arthur Sassoon having died in 1912), and it was demolished in 1937. Some time later the Maitland-designed Dalchroy was re-named Tulchan Lodge, the name it still bears.

Osgood Mackenzie and the Hanburys

We saw earlier how Osgood Hanbury Mackenzie, famous today for the garden he created at Inverewe, had had a grand sporting lodge built for him in the early 1860s by his mother, the Dowager Lady Mackenzie of Gairloch, and why this can be attributed with reasonable confidence to Andrew Maitland Senior. Osgood, a keen advocate of the Highland way of life and the Gaelic language, always regretted, according to his biographer Pauline Butler, that he had not been christened with a Gaelic name.[21] His Christian names came from his mother's family. She was the tenth child of Osgood Hanbury, several generations of whose family, many called Osgood, played a prominent role in the powerful English brewing firm of Truman, Hanbury & Buxton. Members of the Hanbury family and the Mackenzies of Gairloch seem to have often been romantically attracted to each other, as well as to sporting activities, and many of them feature in the Maitland story.

Charles Addington Hanbury was Osgood's first cousin on the Hanbury side and he married Osgood's first cousin on the Mackenzie side, the daughter of Osgood's uncle John Mackenzie of Eileanach. He bought the estate and deer forest of Strathgarve, some ten miles west of Dingwall, which included a 'beautiful and palatial' shooting lodge. Following Charles Hanbury's death Captain Alexander Stirling, a son of a Ross-shire landowning family, bought the estate. He carried out improvements, including a nine hole golf course, and fitted up the house so as to be practically new inside, with electric lighting powered by water from the hills above. In September 1905 he was entertaining a house party when a fire broke out in the middle of a night. Communications were such that the fire brigade did not arrive until 7 A.M. and the lodge was destroyed. Six months later A. Maitland & Sons were engaged to build a new, larger five-bay, three-storey Strathgarve Lodge, which came to be regarded as one of the finest shooting lodges in the Highlands.[22] It later became a hotel and is now a nursing home.

Osgood Mackenzie's own wealth could not compare with that of his Hanbury cousins, or that of his Mackenzie of Gairloch half-brother and nephew; and his marriage to Minna Moss, the daughter of an affluent English banker and merchant, had brought neither marital bliss nor the fortune he was said to have hoped for. After Minna had left him and gone to live in the nearby Pool House (suitably adapted by Andrew Maitland), Inverewe House was the nominal family home for Osgood, his mother and his daughter Mairi. But the need to maximise income led Osgood to let it out, along with 13,000 acres, half of which was deer forest. The smaller Tournaig House, two miles away, built by Osgood's mother for her own use, became the main residence of the family for much of the year. Until her death in 1901, Osgood's mother was the main carer for Mairi. On her death Osgood made Mairi life-rentrix of Tournaig. In 1907 there occurred another Mackenzie - Hanbury marriage, that of the 28 year old Mairi and her cousin Robert J. Hanbury. In the years leading up to the Great War Mr and Mrs Robert Hanbury of Tournaig led an active social life, in southern England and the Highlands, and they often entertained at Tournaig. They also travelled extensively, as did Osgood, who continued to seek plants for his gardens at both Inverewe and Tournaig.

Tournaig was much smaller than Inverewe and it was found necessary to extend it several times. Thus in January 1908 A. Maitland & Sons sought tenders for 'works of alterations and additions to Tournaig House' at a time when Mairi was expecting her first child.[23] The works appear to have included a conservatory, but sadly her son did not live long enough to play in it.

Inverewe House too needed to be substantially altered to meet the requirements of increasingly large shooting parties and to accommodate their servants. A. Maitland & Sons advertised in 1910 for tenders for work on 'considerable additions'.[24] The additions were almost certainly the rear extensions which the architect and heritage consultant Andrew Wright demonstrates must have been carried out between 1902 and 1914: 'the short wing to the rear of the lodge on the northwest side must have been taken down, and then rebuilt, so as to connect with the 1½ storey wing to the rear'. This allowed for a gunroom and kitchen larder on the ground floor, two high quality first floor bedrooms and three attic bedrooms.[25]

This was not the end of the Maitlands' work connected to Osgood Mackenzie's family. In 1911 they sought tenders for building a new 'parish council offices and nurses' home to be erected at Poolewe'.[26] Elizabeth Beaton calls it a 'pleasant design, with shaped hood-moulds and [a] panelled, pilastered entrance, generous windows and pretty, original decorative frosted glazing to [the] inner main door'.[27] Osgood, Robert Hanbury and Sir Kenneth Mackenzie were all members of Gairloch Parish Council, and they would have seen a plaque which records that the building was erected 'In memory of Mary, Lady Mackenzie, with money left for that purpose by Dr Charles Robertson, late of Achtercairn, Gairloch'. In the following year the Maitlands were engaged to renovate the steading at Inverewe Farm.

23.3 Inverewe House on fire, 1914.

In April, 1914 a party of sailors and marines from the King Edward VII class battleship *HMS Zealandia* were returning to their ship, on exercise in Loch Ewe, from the funeral of one of the crew when they saw that Inverewe House was on fire. Crew members and locals worked through the day to extinguish the fire and to save the contents, and 70 men watched the smouldering ruins through the night. Vice-Admiral Sir Lewis Bayly, commander of the 3rd Battle Squadron, directed operations. Despite their efforts much of the building was wrecked, though the 'New Wing' at the rear survived.

Four months later Britain was at war. The Victorian and Edwardian sporting lodges were quiet for some years. Shooting and fishing were largely suspended, many ghillies and other staff served in the armed forces, and a disproportionate number of the younger members of the sporting fraternity lost their lives. Admiral Bayly was no more successful in war than he had been with the fire at Inverewe. In 1915 he refused a destroyer escort when exercising his squadron in bright moonlight near Portland. The battleship *Formidable* was torpedoed, with the loss of 547 lives, and he was relieved of his command.

Robert Hanbury died in 1933, and in 1935 Mairi married Ronald Sawyer - yet another Mackenzie - Hanbury union, as Ronald Sawyer's mother was a Hanbury and the sister of Mairi's first husband. In the years 1935 to 1937 Mairi built a replacement Inverewe House on the site of the previous house - a large villa in a 1930s style, with steel-framed Crittall windows. She donated this and the garden to the National Trust for Scotland in 1952. The garden her father created remains one of the glories of Scotland.

References and Notes

1 Ian Wallace, *Arabella - A Community in the North East of Scotland*, privately printed, 2019.

2 *Ross-shire Journal*, 12th July,1901.

3 *North Star and Farmers' Chronicle*, 7th September, 1905.

4 *North Star and Farmers' Chronicle*, 26th May, 1910, 22nd August, 1912, and 6th December, 1912.

5 *North Star and Farmers' Chronicle*, 18th July, 1912.

6 *Ross-shire Journal*, 7th May (tenders) and 7th June (description), 1907.

7 *Ross-shire Journal*, 31st July, 1908.

8 *Report of the Royal Commission on the Housing of the Industrial Population of Scotland, Rural and Urban,* H.M.S.O.1917, pp..161-81.

9 *Ross-shire Journal*, 18th September, 1908.

10 Mary Miers, *Highland Retreats - The Architecture and Interiors of Scotland's Romantic North*, Rizzoli International Publications, Inc., 2017.

11 *Ross-shire Journal*, 25th March, 1904.

12 *Inverness Courier*, 17th January, 1902.

13 Osgood Hanbury Mackenzie of Inverewe, *A Hundred Years in the Highlands*, Edward Arnold and Co., 1921 (reprinted Birlinn Ltd., 1995), p.27.

14 *Inverness Courier*, 1st November, 1904. Historic Environment Scotland Listed Building 7910.

15 Philip Sassoon, a flamboyant socialite, later became Secretary to Field Marshal Haig, an M.P. and a friend of Edward VIII.

16 *Bertie, A Life of Edward VII*, Jane Ridley, Vintage Books, 2013, p.430.

17 *Great Salmon Rods of the Dee and Spey*, Iain D. Ogden, 2017.

18 *Inverness Courier*, 16th May, 1905.

19 *Ross-shire Journal*, 31st July, 1906.

20 Historic Environment Scotland LB346.

21 Pauline Butler, *Eighty Years in the Highlands - The Life and Times of Osgood H. Mackenzie of Inverewe, 1842-1922*, Librario Publishing Ltd, 2010 - an invaluable source of information on Osgood and his family.

22 *Ross-shire Journal* 5th April and 13th July, 1906.

23 *Ross-shire Journal*, 24th January, 1908.

24 *Ross-shire Journal*, 14th January, 1910.

25 Andrew P. K. Wright, *Inverewe House Conservation Plan*, produced for the National Trust for Scotland, March 2008, pp. 30-32.

26 *Ross-shire Journal*, 19th May, 1911.

27 Beaton, *Ross & Cromarty*, p.93.

24. MORE RELIGIOUS STRIFE AND MORE CHURCHES

More religious rivalry

Visitors often ask why so many small towns and villages in the Highlands have three (and sometimes more) churches. The answer lies in the recurring tendency of the Presbyterian churches in Scotland to fragment - a tendency particularly marked in the Highlands. Thus in this author's home village of Portmahomack the Tarbat Parish Church had existed from time immemorial. The majority of its members left the established Church of Scotland to join the Free Church at the Disruption of 1843. The Free Church quickly built a new religious infrastructure throughout Scotland, but many of its churches were built quickly and on the cheap. With rising prosperity in the 1870s, 1880s and 1890s many of the Free Church congregations sought replacement churches, which were often built on the same site. As we saw, this second wave of church building led to numerous commissions (including one at Portmahomack in 1892-93) for the Maitlands. A third wave of church building, particularly marked in the Highlands, was to come with a further split in the first decade of the twentieth century - a split which, paradoxically, resulted from attempts to unite the Presbyterian churches. James and Gordon Maitland were heavily involved in this third wave in many parts of Ross-shire.

At the turn of the twentieth century religious values remained central to the ethos of Scotland, as evidenced by church adherence (calculated to have peaked in 1905), strict Sabbath observance, the activities of a multiplicity of church-affiliated organisations, the evolution of social, welfare and educational policies, and extensive reporting of religious events in local newspapers. In the Highlands the Free Church had long played the principal role, but change was afoot. The Rev. Robert Rainy, Principal of the Free Church College from 1874, had become the most influential figure in the Free Church, steering it, as champion of a more liberal wing, through various doctrinal disputes. In the face of the threat to religion of contemporary scientific discoveries Rainy guided the church towards freedom of Biblical criticism. At the General Assembly of the Free Church in 1899 he successfully proposed a Union with the United Presbyterian Church, the third in size of the Scottish Presbyterian denominations. The 'U.P. Church' was itself a merger of two churches which had seceded from the Church of Scotland, and its doctrines were similar to those espoused by Principal Rainy and his supporters. Its strength lay in the south of Scotland and it was little represented in the Highlands. The parties to the Union shared a wish to maintain spiritual independence, which set them apart from the Church of Scotland which preferred to stay established.

But a minority within the Free Church remained resolutely opposed to the Union.

The U.F. Church versus the 'Wee Frees' - and work for the Maitlands

The Union took effect on 31st October, 1900, producing the United Free Church of Scotland, or 'U.F. Church'.

In the Tain Free Church, where James Maitland was elected a deacon in 1900, there were few dissenting voices to the Union. Principal Rainy himself had preached in Tain in 1898, when collections were made to reduce the debt on the Maitland-designed church of 1892-93. The Rev. Thomas Grant, Free Church Minister since 1858, was on the Union Committee of the Free Church and he and John Mackenzie, the Session Clerk, spoke both in Tain itself and at the regional Free Presbytery of Tain in favour of the Union. Their arguments were accepted by the vast majority of the Tain congregation, which made a transition, with little opposition, into becoming a U.F. congregation.

24.1 Logie Easter Church, built 1903-05 for a U. F. congregation who 'cherished the idea of a new church'.

The neighbouring parish of Logie Easter, south west of Tain, also favoured the Union. It was noted that the U.F. congregation at first worshipped 'in a church hallowed by Disruption memories, but altogether impractical for present use'. It was impractical not least because rain was coming through the roof. As so many Free Church congregations had done late in the previous century, they liked their comforts and thus 'cherished the idea of a new church'. Half the total cost of £2,000 was raised locally, and they obtained grants from the central funds of the U.F. Church. A. Maitland & Sons advertised for tenders in June and again in October 1903.[1] Built in red sandstone on a prominent site, and with lanceted windows, the church, opened in May 1905, has a distinctive pinnacled gable front topped by a Gothic bellcote.

Whilst easy transitions such as those in Tain and Logie Easter were taking place the remaining minority of the Free Church, who quickly became known as the 'Wee Frees', were defiant in many other parishes, particularly ones in its Highland stronghold. Discontent manifested itself in such ways as the burning of the U.F. Minister's haystacks in Tarbat. At national level the residual Free Church took to the law courts to assert its right to the property and endowment of the former Free Church. The litigation was conducted amongst scenes of astonishing acrimony. In 1904 the House of Lords determined that the Free Church was a closed financial trust, that this trust had been broken by the creation of the U.F. Church and that the U.F. Church had no 'right, title nor interest' in the properties, the right being vested solely in the Free Church. The question was raised, however, as to whether the Free Church was capable of discharging the obligations of the Trust. The Government therefore determined to appoint a Commission to report on the matter, and in 1905 it passed the Churches (Scotland) Act based on the Commission's recommendation to appoint an executive Commission to allocate the property in question. This latter Commission was to allocate property to the Free Church where, of those who were members or adherents of the Free Church in 1900 and were still in 1905 resident, at least one-third were members of the Free Church congregation. Whilst they awaited the Commission's verdicts many Free Church congregations secured interim interdicts which allowed them to evict U.F. ministers and congregations from manses and churches. In Scotland as a whole the great majority of the allocations were in favour of the U.F. Church. But in the Highlands many strong Free Church congregations received allocations. During 1906 in the Presbytery of Tain the Commission allocated congregational property in Croick, Fearn, Tarbat, Kilmuir Easter, Kincardine and Rosskeen to the Free Church and only in Tain, Logie Easter, Invergordon and Nigg to the U.F. Church. The Commission reported in its final report in 1910 that it had allocated 238 churches to the Free Church and 1,653 to the U.F. Church.

24.2 Religious strife: the eviction of the Rev. George Murray and family from the Free Church
manse in Portmahomack on 28th November, 1906.

24.3 Mr Murray's new church: Tarbat United Free Church, Portmahomack
(now the Parish Church), built 1908-09.

The new U.F. Church was well supplied with ministers, since only 27 chose to remain with the Free Church. But many U.F. congregations, not least in the Highlands, were left without churches and manses. Thus in Tarbat, where slightly over one-third of the congregation adhered to the Free Church, the Rev. George Murray, who had joined the U.F. Church, his wife and young children were evicted from the Free Church manse in Portmahomack. The eviction, at noon on 28th November, 1906 was recorded for posterity by a conveniently placed photographer. Murray's congregation had to worship in the Maitland-designed public school or the Carnegie Hall. Fund raising for the U.F. church began in earnest, locally and nationally. Members of the Tain U.F. Presbytery raised £2,926 in 1907 and £4,007 in 1908, when they contributed £1,228 to central funds and £1,223 to local building funds, members in the Tain parish being especially generous. After much discussion the Presbytery resolved in September 1907 to 'commit to Messrs Maitland, architects, Tain, the carrying out of the plans for new churches at Fearn, Tarbat and Kincardine and the new manse at Kilmuir [Easter]'. Rather different, and presumably cheaper, arrangements were made for the new U.F. church at Kilmuir Easter. Its construction was entrusted to Speirs & Co. of Glasgow, under the local superintendence of Messrs Maitland.[2] Speirs were specialists in the provision of partly pre-fabricated buildings, and the church at Kilmuir Easter was 'an iron structure on stone foundation, with inner wall of stained wood and open roof'.

New U.F. churches in the east - and one for the Free Church in the west

The Maitlands sought tenders in early 1908 for the new U.F. churches at Fearn, at Portmahomack for the Tarbat parish and at Ardgay for Kincardine and for the new manse at Kilmuir Easter.[3] The churches were all built in a simple but elegant style, described as minimal late Gothic. What is particularly striking is that the new churches were smaller than those in which the congregations had previously worshipped - lower in height and with no galleries inside - and with fewer architectural embellishments. Thus the new church built at Portmahomack in 1908-9, with seating for 290 (plus 50 more if a moveable partition dividing a hall from the church was folded back) was simpler than the Maitlands' Tarbat Free Church of the previous decade, which had seating for 900. Similarly, that at Fearn was dwarfed by the nearby tall and gaunt Free Church building designed by the Maitlands' competitor John Pond Macdonald, which had been opened in 1897. The low Maitland U.F. church at Ardgay (now Kincardine Parish Church) likewise was in stark contrast to the tall Kincardine Free Church of 1849-50. These differences clearly reflected a number of factors - the fragmentation of congregations, the capacity of the fund-raising to sustain a sudden heavy building programme, and perhaps also the beginning of a decline in numbers of worshippers. U.F. manses were also built to Maitland designs at Portmahomack[4], Kincardine[5] and Fearn - solid and respectable family homes, but less grand than the manses which the reverend gentlemen had vacated. The Fearn manse boasted 'modern sanitary arrangements, water [being] pumped from a draw-well into the cisterns by the aid of a small motor-engine'.[6]

The Maitlands' work was not confined to Easter Ross or to the new U.F. Church. At Ullapool in Wester Ross the church in Mill Street built soon after the Disruption (now the Parish Church) was claimed, and occupied for a time, by the Free Church. It was, however, awarded by the Commission to the U.F. Church. But the residual Free Church congregation was a strong one. Its members were upset that they had to worship in the Drill Hall, and in 1907 they even petitioned the King to have the allocation reversed. This did not happen, and the following year the Maitlands were engaged to design a new Lochbroom Free Church in Quay Street.[7] The design of the church, still in use by the Free Church, was remarkably similar to that of most of the Maitland U.F. churches of the period, and the gable front was embellished with three lancet windows.

Meanwhile the Maitlands and contractors, many from Tain, continued to be busy with U.F. churches in Easter Ross. The Nigg U.F. church was renovated in 1908-09 under the supervision of the Maitlands with new seating and heating and a vestry.[8] Matters were, however, more complicated in the parish of Rosskeen. At the Maitland-designed church at Achnagarron, commissioned by the Free Church congregation of Rosskeen and opened as recently as June 1900, over 500 people attended a U.F. service in April 1905 on the final Sunday before the Free Church took possession. In his sermon, after warning about the use of intemperate language, the Rev. John Ross asserted that law and justice had been separated and accused local Free Church members of 'audacious mendacity' in misrepresenting the facts. A new U.F. church for Rosskeen, designed and supervised by the Maitlands,[9] was built at Bridge of Alness on a site gifted by the Maitlands' client Andrew Mackenzie of Dalmore and was opened in 1910. The church was built to accommodate 400 persons, and the cost was about £1,300. Gifford notes with approval the ornamental metal ventilator flèche on the roof and the projecting wooden bellcote at the east gable.[10] A new Maitland-designed manse was built on a 'fine lofty site' nearby.[11]

At Edderton the early twentieth century was marked by declining attendances at all the churches, and by a dispute over the ownership of what is now known as Edderton Old Church.[12] This was the original eighteenth century parish church, which had been deemed unsafe and vacated by the Church of Scotland in 1841, but had been handed over to the Free Church after the Disruption. The Free Church, for which James Maitland had supervised extensive repairs in 1885-86, continued to occupy the old building after the Union. The Commission allocated it to them, notwithstanding the fact that the congregation had fallen from 400 in 1855 to only 34 in 1900. The Edderton U.F. congregation's needs led to the design by Gordon Maitland of one his firm's cheapest and most unusual churches. A newspaper account[13] of the church opening in 1911 noted that the church, with seating for 250 worshippers, was in a Gothic style, and in every detail, not least the pointed gables, gave a pleasing impression. It was built of stone foundations, cement walls and slated roof, and internally the walls and groined Gothic roof were in plaster. The young architect was clearly operating to a tight budget, saving particularly by using prefabricated concrete instead of stone. The cost was only £700. The building was demolished in 1963.

Work for the Church of Scotland

In the Highlands the established Church of Scotland played second fiddle to the Free Church before, and to the U.F. Church after, the Union of 1900. This reflected the Highlanders' attachment to evangelical Presbyterianism, and in some areas their recollection of the close relationship between the heritors and the Church of Scotland at the time of the Clearances. The established church had nevertheless begun to see something of a revival as the working class, particularly artisans, felt themselves alienated from the middle class ethos of the Free Church and excluded from its eldership and positions of influence.

The Church of Scotland's ancient buildings still had to be maintained and modernised, and the Maitlands received several commissions. Thus in 1903-04, when the new U.F. church at Logie Easter was being constructed to Maitland designs, the Church of Scotland, not to be outdone, also commissioned the Maitlands. The architect of their church, built in 1818-19, had been James Gillespie Graham, whose designs had inspired the young Andrew Maitland. In 1904 the Maitlands were responsible for extensive improvements, including 'new windows of antique British ruffled glass'.[14] The church is no longer used.

The Highland area was behind the south in the introduction of organs to churches. The inauguration in 1906 of a new pipe-organ in the then Tain Parish Church [now the Duthac Centre] was a major event. It was attended by the Provost and the burgh council (many of them stalwarts of the U.F. Church) and by the Freemasons and Oddfellows dressed in full regalia. They heard a sacred concert recital by Herr Stoltz of

Tain, and they admired the organ case of fumigated Austrian oak designed by Messrs Maitland and set in front of a new pulpit. Andrew Carnegie paid half the £400 cost of the organ.[15]

In Gairloch the Maitlands were responsible in 1909 for a major reconstruction of the parish church, which dated from 1790-93.[16] The pulpit was moved from the centre of the long side to the east end of the building and the pews re-arranged to run across the interior and face it rather than running from end to end. A small steeple was constructed on the west gable. Elizabeth Beaton remarks that the Maitland alterations effectively removed much of the building's original character.[17] The heritors, of whom the principal one was the Maitlands' client the second Sir Kenneth Mackenzie (the 7th Baronet), contributed £100 and the balance of £312-8s-6d was found by fund-raising.

The construction of a new church for the Church of Scotland was a rare event in the early twentieth century Highlands. The heritors of the parish of Creich, however, were concerned that the existing parish church at Dun Creich, most recently rebuilt in the early 1790s, was too expensive to keep in good repair, and the Presbytery of Dornoch were concerned that it was too far from the main centre of population, some three miles away at Bonar Bridge. In 1911 a joint meeting of the heritors and the Presbytery agreed to look for a new site in Bonar Bridge. An elevated site was found at the back of the village. A. Maitland & Sons designed a new Gothic church, with a 'sturdy buttressed tower, [with] inside its parapet, a small octagonal stone spire with lucarnes'.[18] The cost of the church, built to accommodate 300 to 400, was about £2,000. The heritors, the major one being Andrew Carnegie, contributed £800, with the balance being found from grants from the Church of Scotland and a bazaar. Carnegie's 16 year old daughter, Margaret, 'gracefully opened the church door' during an opening and dedication service in August 1913. This was the last Maitland-designed church and also the last Maitland building to achieve a Historic Environment Scotland listing.[19]

Aftermath

During the twentieth century many of the churches originally designed by the Maitlands for the Free Church or the U.F. Church became Church of Scotland churches.

In 1929 the majority of the U.F. Church merged with the Church of Scotland, bringing with them the Maitland churches mentioned above, and also those of the churches built for the Free Church discussed in chapter 17 that had been allocated to the U.F. Church in 1906.

This led to the Church of Scotland having more churches than it required. The situation was exacerbated by a decline in church attendance that had accelerated after the Great War, a war whose aims the churches had so firmly endorsed. Choices had frequently to be made, particularly when ministers retired, between two churches. The main criteria for choosing which church to close were frequently the on-going cost of maintenance and the availability of car-parking. The Maitland-built churches were invariably newer than the historic parish churches, so they tended to be the ones retained as the parish church.

References and Notes

[1] *Ross-shire Journal*, 19th June and 23rd October, 1903.

[2] *Ross-shire Journal*, 12th June 1908.

[3] *Ross-shire Journal*, 6th February, 17th April, 17th January, and 31st January, 1908 respectively.

[4] *Ross-shire Journal*, 10th June, 1909.

[5] *Ross-shire Journal*, 10th September, 1909.

[6] *North Star and Farmers' Chronicle*, 6th April, 1911.

7 *Ross-shire Journal*, 2nd October, 1908.

8 *Ross-shire Journal.* 15th May, 1908 and 16th April, 1909.

9 *North Star and Farmers' Chronicle*, 19th August, 1909.

10 Gifford, *Highlands and Islands*, p.381.

11 *Ross-shire Journal*, 3rd March, 1911.

12 See *Edderton Old Parish Church*, Edderton Old Parish Church Trust, 2007, particularly at pp.28-31.

13 *North Star and Farmers' Chronicle*, 28th September, 1911.

14 *Ross-shire Journal*, 29th July, 1904.

15 *North Star and Farmers' Chronicle*, 12th April, 1906.

16 *A Brief History of Gairloch Parish Church, 1255-1992*, bicentenary publication, December, 1991. Highland HER 16615, LB7885.

17 Elizabeth Beaton, *Building Traditions in Lochbroom and Gairloch Parishes*, p.160 in *Peoples & Settlements in North-West Ross*, The Scottish Society for Northern Studies, 1994.

18 *Ross-shire Journal*, 3rd May, 1912; Gifford, Highlands and Islands, p.558.

19 Highland HER MHG17111, LB 288.

25. URBAN WORK BEFORE THE GREAT WAR

25.1 The Carnegie Free Library, Tain.

Town centres and suburbs

During the Victorian age the Highlands had seen an unparalleled level of development of public buildings, churches, shops, hotels, banks and other commercial buildings. By the turn of the twentieth century the centres of towns and villages such as those on the Maitlands' home patch had most of the facilities they required. (An exception to this was Invergordon, where, as we will see in the next chapter, rapid development took place in the early twentieth century.) On the urban scene the amount of new building decreased. The most common role for Highland architects like Alexander Ross, W.C. Joass, Robert Macbeth and the Maitlands thus became the design of alterations and additions to existing buildings. Schools in particular needed more and better accommodation, and the Maitlands were responsible for further works at some of the schools which the firm had designed in the 1870s.

In two particular areas, however, there were increasing requirements for public buildings. One of these was public libraries, where the philanthropy of Andrew Carnegie ensured a plentiful provision. It is perhaps difficult for us, in an age when the role of libraries has been eclipsed by modern technology, to appreciate fully the cultural significance of libraries, free to all. A well stocked library now gave everyone free access to information and the literature of the world. The second area was post offices, where the General Post Office was in an expansionary phase. In both of these areas, as we will see, James and Gordon Maitland were involved.

Outside the centre of towns the years up to 1914, particularly the early years of the new century, saw the further growth of suburbs as the aspirational middle classes sought more spacious homes. The Maitlands continued to design villas in Easter Ross and elsewhere in the northern Highlands, including ones in Hill of Fearn, Dornoch, Ardgay, Bonar Bridge and Evanton. They did, however, face local competition from Mr Ogston, a Tain architect, and also from Alexander Munro, a mason contractor who became involved with speculative building. In Tain, nevertheless, the Maitlands were responsible for interesting developments in the Scotsburn Road and Morangie Road which included two of the most notable private residences, both now hotels, and an impressive house for James Maitland himself.

Andrew Carnegie, the richest man in the world

On 7th June, 1899 Andrew Carnegie, his wife Louise and their two year old daughter Margaret arrived at Skibo Castle, on the other side of the Dornoch Firth from Tain, for their second summer there, the first as its owners.[1] The following day Donald Fowler, the Provost of Tain, and John Mackenzie (this author's grandfather), who was the Town Clerk and a recent President of the Tain Literary Institute, travelled to Skibo to meet Carnegie. The Carnegies were living in one protected wing whilst all around them several hundred men were working on a major reconstruction of the castle in Scottish Baronial style, increasing its area from 16,000 to 60,000 square feet. Everything was the height of luxury, so much so that a few years later King Edward VII called unexpectedly to get ideas for the refurbishment of Sandringham.

Carnegie, born in Dunfermline, was the dominant force in the American steel industry, though he had retired from day-to-day management of the Carnegie Steel Corporation. The tactics that had led to his success were often hugely controversial. He believed, however, that a man who dies rich dies in disgrace. He had started to fund libraries, initially on a modest scale, and he was later to fund them in such quantities that his reputation as a philanthropist exceeded that as a robber baron.

Fowler and Mackenzie would have known that Carnegie had already promised to fund various libraries near to Skibo, and perhaps also that James Maitland was already designing ones in Lairg Road at Bonar Bridge and at Spinningdale, the latter overlooking the bay and the ruined mill which gave Spinningdale its name.[2]

They submitted 'as Directors of the Literary Institute and on behalf of the community' a proposal for the founding of a public library in Tain. They estimated that a three room building would require £1,000, fixtures and fittings and additional books £200, and an endowment £1,000 - a total of £2,200. Clearly mindful of Carnegie's principle that those whom he helped should help themselves, they indicated that local contributions of existing books and cash, the value of a free site and a public subscription would amount to half of this, leaving a requirement of £1,100. Carnegie immediately offered to bear the cost of the building, an offer later confirmed in a letter. Such an offer was in line with Carnegie's preference for funding buildings rather than books. This preference, his detractors claimed, was because he was 'Rameses II incarnate' and wanted to immortalise himself by having his name carved above every threshold.

The Tain Burgh Council held a Special Meeting on 9th June at which not only did they agree Carnegie's offer but also unanimously resolved to offer him the freedom of the burgh. On 5th July Tain was *en fête* for the presentation of the freedom. This took place in the Maitland-designed Town Hall. Carnegie was, however, not impressed by the internal state of the building, and he said to Provost Fowler that he would bear the cost of refurbishing it. Fowler had to to tell Carnegie that the council did not own the hall. But, appreciating Carnegie's offer, he soon set to work to remedy this.

Before work could proceed on the building of a library or the refurbishment of the Town Hall there were a number of hoops to go through. The majority of the shareholders in the Tain Public Hall company were persuaded to gift their shares to the burgh, and the council was thus enabled to acquire the hall on what were described as fair and reasonable terms. A site had to be bought for the library (one being found in

Stafford Street, where some old buildings had to be pulled down), and Tain had to adopt the Free Libraries Act. The *Ross-shire Journal* complained, however, of the project being hindered by some leading people 'indulging in sinister and significant objections, studiously interleaved with a recapitulation of its advantage'. It was not until 20th November, 1902 that James Maitland signed his plans for a single storey library with a baroque doorway (with 'Carnegie Free Library' inscribed above it) and ridge tiling.[3] Carnegie's secretaries, James Bertram and Robert Franks, reviewed all architectural plans for libraries to ensure that there was no unnecessary extravagance or waste, and James Maitland's plans must have passed their tests.

While all this was going on Andrew Carnegie negotiated the sale in 1901 of his steel interests to a consortium led by the financier John Pierpont Morgan at a price of $480,000,000. His personal share was $225,639,000. 'Mr Carnegie', said Morgan when they met to celebrate, 'I want to congratulate you on being the richest man in the world'. Carnegie now devoted his time to philanthropy and the pursuit of world peace. Tain did not lose touch with its new benefactor. He was invited to present prizes at the Academy, he paid for Tain's Papal Bull of 1492 (confirming the raising of St Duthac's church to collegiate status) to be framed in silver, and John Mackenzie corresponded with him on historical links between Tain and Dunfermline.

On 20th August, 1903 Dr (as he liked to be called) and Mrs Carnegie again visited Tain. The day, 'Carnegie Day', was held as a holiday and once again banners and flags flew. In the morning Mrs Carnegie laid the foundation stone of the new library. This was followed by a ceremonial re-opening of the Town Hall. The interior had been decorated under the general direction of A. Maitland & Sons, Carnegie contributing over £300 towards the costs. The most notable feature was artwork by P.C. Brown of Edinburgh. There were mural paintings illustrating the history of Tain from Malcolm Canmore to the opening of the Town Hall in 1875. Inside the apse was a central figure of St Duthus with the motto *Sanctus Beatus est Duthacus*, with bust portraits of Provost and Mrs Fowler beneath, and on either side portraits of past Provosts, including Andrew Maitland Junior. The panels at the side of the platform were filled with large portraits of Dr and Mrs Carnegie.

During the first three decades of the twentieth century the Town Hall was run by a committee of the burgh council. It was used for important events such as the granting of the freedom of the burgh and it was let out for a wide variety of purposes, including concerts, lectures, meetings, sales of work and entertainments. By the 1920s it was increasingly used for showing cinematographic films. In 1934 it was leased to Tain Picture House Ltd, which became a subsidiary of the Inverness-based Caledonian Cinemas Ltd, and bought the building for £4,000 in 1945-46. The Picture House was hugely popular during and after the Second World War. The advent of television and other forms of entertainment led, however, to a decline in cinema attendances and it was closed in 1964. Voluntary efforts sustained it for a further two years, following which it was in a deteriorating state. At the time of writing work, initiated by the Tain & Easter Ross Civic Trust and picked up by the community, is in hand to restore the building and to find profitable uses.

The Carnegie Free Library was opened on 4th August, 1904 by Sheriff Guthrie K.C. in an elaborate outdoor ceremony, which was followed by a cake and wine banquet in the Council Chambers.

Whilst the Tain project meandered on the Maitlands had been involved with two other Free Libraries, both small. One was at Rosehall.[4] The other was one of their more unusual commissions - a Carnegie Free Library on the island of Iona.[5] In 1899 the 8th Duke of Argyll, a veteran of the cabinets of Aberdeen, Palmerston and Gladstone, had made over the island's 'venerable pile of ruins' to the Iona Cathedral Trust. Restoration of the old abbey (associated with St Columba, who had converted the Picts to Christianity) soon began. In 1903 Dr Carnegie offered £250 for the provision of a library building. The Maitland plans were reported to be for a building 'of local grey granite, one storeyed, and with a steep roof to harmonise with its antique surroundings'. When completed it was noted that it was the smallest Carnegie Library in the world. 'It is less than 15 feet long and scarcely as wide. It is on a sea-swept spot and the walls are of granite and nearly two feet thick. It is used by fishermen.'[6]

The Temperance Hotel and Mock Tudor architecture

Mock Tudor architecture, based on a revival of vernacular styles of the Tudor period, was, and remains, a style popular in England. People have often wondered how and why on the north side of Tain High Street there looms for three storeys above what is now the Co-op supermarket at numbers 10 to 14 a very distinctive white harled, half-timbered building in a Mock Tudor style - seemingly out of kilter with the more typically Scottish styles of so much of the High Street, not least the nearby Maitland-designed Court House.

In the early twentieth century the upper part of the building in the High Street was Mackay's Temperance Hotel. Temperance hotels were of course usually run by supporters of the temperance movement. Some of Mrs Mackay's clientele would also have been of this persuasion, though if they were not they were within easy reach of numerous licensed premises where they could slake their thirst. (A solicitor appearing in the new Easter Ross Licensing Court in 1904 asserted that in the burgh of Tain there was 1 licence for every 147 of population.)

By 1900 Catherine Mackay had leased the upper part of the building, which was owned by James Urquhart, a painter who himself occupied one of the two shops on the ground floor. The following February Urquhart sought approval from the Dean of Guild Court for the Maitlands' plans.[7] These showed a projection in the upper storeys of about three feet over the pavement to give more room to the hotel bedrooms. Such projections were common in both genuine and mock Tudor buildings. The solicitor for William Ross, the jeweller for whom the Maitlands had designed the next door Victoria Buildings, moved that the burgh surveyor should be given an opportunity to examine the plans and see whether the projection interfered with the burgh's rights. Bailie John Gallie, who, along with Provost Fowler, was assisting the Dean of Guild, agreed and expressed doubts as to whether the foundations would be sufficient to carry the additional height of a third floor. James Maitland interrupted, saying that such a remark was a personal one. Provost Fowler said it was not, as there were two architects in court. (The other may have been James's assistant William Robertson or his own nephew Gordon.) Ultimately the Court approved the Maitland plans on the understanding that the roof projection would be reduced from twelve to six inches and that of the upper floors from two feet to fifteen inches beyond the roof. In March the Maitlands advertised for tenders.[8]

The 1901 census, probably taken before the building works had started, shows Catherine Mackay and her husband William as keepers of the fourteen room Temperance Hotel with their four children, along with a cook, a parlourmaid and a 'boots', and six boarders. One of the boarders was the 29 year old John R. Strachan, who leased a bakers' shop in the next building, with a bakehouse behind it, on the corner of High Street and Castle Brae. In 1903 Strachan purchased for £2,000 a block of buildings on this corner, which included not only the premises from which he operated but also shops let to a clothier and a draper. Meanwhile the Temperance Hotel seems to have prospered at a time when Tain was being promoted as a tourist resort. It featured in lists of guests staying in Tain regularly published by the *Ross-shire Journal*. Catherine Mackay further expanded her hotel by leasing the upper parts of adjacent buildings - on the one side from William Ross the jeweller (notwithstanding his opposition to her projecting upper floors) and on the other side, albeit temporarily, from her former boarder, John Strachan. The Temperance Hotel later became Fraser's Hotel, then the Kingsway Hotel, and later still housed a Co-op supermarket.

The temporary nature of Strachan's arrangement with Catherine Mackay may have been due to his wish to carry out extensive alterations to his own recently acquired property. For in August 1905 it was reported that extensive alterations were being carried out in the property belonging to Mr Strachan at the corner of Station Brae (as Castle Brae was sometimes called) and High Street and that Messrs Maitland were the architects.[9] Map evidence suggests that much of the work was on the Castle Brae side, and it is likely that it resulted in the present Mock Tudor building, half-timbered and with a projecting upper floor. This contained two shops, which Strachan let out. Today, along with what was formerly Strachan's bakehouse, it forms part of an art gallery.

James Urquhart and John Strachan were not the only people in Tain to have Mock Tudor work done, as the Railway Hotel further down Castle Brae has a gable end and Shandwick Place (or House) in Chapel Street, then owned by Dr Gillies, a rear extension, in this style. Whether the Maitlands were involved with either of these is not known.

Balcarres, Mansfield House, Morangie House and sibling rivalry

25.2 Balcarres (now St Mary's), the second of of two villas James Maitland built for himself.

A 1904 *Guide to the Royal Burgh of Tain and Surrounding District* highlighted three recently constructed or re-built private residences, with all of which James Maitland's firm was involved. One of these was designed by him for his own use. His firm's clients for the other two were Provost Fowler's wife and Fowler's wife's sister.

Soon after the death of his brother Andrew, James Maitland had taken a lease of his house, Lauderdale in Morangie Road from Andrew's widow Eliza. This arrangement may have been prompted by the presence in the house of the telephone system which, as we saw earlier, allowed contact with the Maitland office and with the Glenmorangie Distillery. It also allowed James to supervise the building of a new house for himself on the opposite side of the road. James's new house, Balcarres, is one of the most elegant of

Edwardian villas. The 1904 guide declared it 'worthy of special note as a model specimen of villa architecture, with its tastefully laid out grounds and conservatory'. It first appeared in the Valuation Rolls in 1901/02, and James and his family were to remain there until shortly before James's death. Balcarres is today known as St Mary's.

In 1892 Provost Fowler's wife Johanna had, as we saw earlier, purchased the 60 acre East Mansfield estate in Tain, on the Scotsburn Road and straddling the burgh boundary. The Fowlers had quickly engaged A. Maitland & Sons to build a Georgian style dwelling house on the estate. When Johanna's uncle, Joshua Taylor, died suddenly at Edderton in 1897 he left personal estate, accumulated from his activity as a tea planter in Bengal, amounting to the then enormous sum of £264,335-3s-9d. After substantial legacies, including ones of £10,000 each to Johanna and her sister Annie Gallie, the residue was to be divided into two equal parts, the income from which was to be paid to Johanna and Annie. The sisters used their wealth to build the two most substantial private residences in Tain.

A. Maitland & Sons advertised for tenders for work on 'alterations and additions to Mansfield House, the Residence of Provost Fowler', in October 1902. The work, which incorporated the existing building and increased the the number of rooms with windows from 11 to 20, was completed by January 1904.[10] The style adopted was a very assertive Scottish Baronial. The Historic Environment Scotland Listing notes a 'tall 3 stage Baronial tower with angle turrets and stair tower, decorative parapet and crenellations. Oriel at third stage; roundheaded entrance with hoodmould at base of tower; crow-stepped north gable with apex finialed aedicule'.[11]

The 1904 guide to Tain noted with approval that 'a fine asphalt path along the public road from Tain [to Mansfield House] is an improvement, which might elsewhere be imitated with much benefit to the general public'. Gas mains, water pipes and sewers followed. Thus were new suburbs connected with town centres.

Mansfield House remained in the hands of the Fowler family until 1947. Since then it has mainly been used as a hotel. One of the hoteliers tried to aggrandise it by renaming it Mansfield Castle, and others have claimed that the presence of the ghost of Johanna Fowler is often noticed. More tangible features that undoubtedly do remain are some fine woodwork, including pitched pine panelling, and ornate plaster ceilings.

Johanna's sister Annie also commissioned the Maitlands to design a large and imposing villa. In 1887 Annie had married Abner Gallie, who was a partner in the Tain ironmongers Wallace & Fraser and who also became a tenant farmer at Edderton Mains and later at Morangie. Like Johanna's husband he served on Tain Burgh Council, in his case from 1889 to 1897. Abner died suddenly of pneumonia, aged only 53, in 1899, two years after Annie had inherited a share of her uncle's fortune. Annie, left with four young children, was deeply shocked. From that moment, it was reported, 'she retired from public life, though her private beneficence was unabated'. But she nevertheless soon employed the Maitlands to design what the 1904 guide described as 'a very extensive mansion on the Morangie Road beyond the old Foundry, occupying over three acres of land. It is still in the hands of the contractors, but will, when finished, be one of the finest residences in the district'. The house had four public rooms, seven bedrooms and ample servants' accommodation.

The present owner's website refers to speculation that the building of Mansfield House and Morangie House was the manifestation of some ill feeling between the sisters. It adds that a local businessman who knew the sisters well suggests that, while there may have been some natural sibling rivalry between the sisters, rumours of a grand 'feud' were greatly exaggerated.[12] Nevertheless it appears to be well authenticated that James Maitland and his assistant William Robertson frequently had to alter the plans as the respective owners vied to build the more impressive house.[13] Those responsible for compiling the Valuation Rolls gave Mansfield House a Yearly Value of £60, and Morangie House £55, which perhaps put

Johanna one up. Sadly Annie enjoyed Morangie House for only four years before her own death in 1907. Her son sold it in 1962, and it later became a guesthouse and then a very fine hotel.

John Gifford, whose architectural guide was published in 1992, described Morangie House as 'low key Baronial, with a small tower over the entrance. In the main rooms, Glasgow-type stained glass in the windows' upper panes'.[14] Since this was written the success of the hotel has led to extensive additions which partly mask the original Maitland design, but some pleasing original features remain within the building.

25.3 Mansfield House, built for Johanna Fowler by the Maitlands in 1892 and enlarged and baronialised in 1902-04.

25.4 Morangie House, completed in 1904 for Johanna Fowler's sister Annie Gallie - sibling rivalry?

Upgrading schools

The Education (Scotland) Act of 1872, which laid the basis for the modern educational system, had made school compulsory for children in the age group five to thirteen. But it had allowed exemption for children over ten who could demonstrate proficiency in grade five of the curriculum. A further Act in 1908 eliminated the system of exemptions. At the same time more emphasis was being given to social welfare, and free meals for needy children and compulsory medical inspection were introduced.

Schools thus needed more and better accommodation. The Maitlands were thus responsible for works at the public schools at Logie Easter, Edderton and Hilton.

Significant additions were also made to the Tain Public School (now Knockbreck School), which had been designed by the Maitlands in 1877.[15] The main reason was the requirement of H.M. Inspector of Schools that the Infant Department, with 80 pupils, should be moved from the unsatisfactory premises in the United Free Church (now the Parish Church) Hall to the main site. This and other improvements led to a significant increase in size at a cost of some £3,000. The newly enlarged school was opened in August 1909 by the Countess de Serra Largo of Tarlogie, whose husband had in the words of the chairman of the School Board, the Rev. Colin Macnaughton, 'done more for the cause of education than all the landed proprietors of Easter Ross'. Bailie James Maitland presented the Countess with a silver key to open the building. Once inside the Count, whose mansion house at Tarlogie had been substantially rebuilt to the Maitlands' designs, replied on his wife's behalf. He thought his wife was wrong not to have replied herself when the suffragette element preponderated, and she should have replied eloquently or forcibly. 'But', he assured his audience, 'daisies of the suffragette kind do not bloom at Tarlogie, for we all believe, as good Highlanders, that it is best to see a wife attend to her household duties'. One of the few ladies present, in support of her terminally ill husband, who was a member of the School Board, was this author's grandmother. Her take on the Count's views is not recorded in the family history.

When secondary education was concentrated at Tain Royal Academy the Public School served as Tain's only primary school. It was renamed Knockbreck School in 1977 when a second primary school was opened. It was, however, almost lost in 1985, when a serious fire left only the external walls standing. It was carefully reconstructed at a cost of £420,000. It remains today an eloquent testimony to skills of its Victorian and Edwardian architects. At the time of writing, however, its future remains uncertain as plans are in hand to put both primary and secondary education in Tain on the same campus.

Post offices - and a Maitland initiative

The government-owned General Post Office became a formidable business in the late nineteenth and early twentieth centuries, and its political head, the Postmaster General, had a seat in the cabinet. With the advent of the railways mail coaches had been superseded by trains. The privately owned Highland Railway Company had a contract with the GPO to carry mail, and in 1864 it obtained an extension for carriage to Tain and Bonar Bridge (as what is now Ardgay station was then known). As new forms of communication developed the GPO claimed monopoly rights. It obtained responsibility for the 'electric telegraph' in 1870, and its business in telegrams required increasing numbers of telegraph offices in towns and at stations. Early telephones were, like those connecting the Maitlands with the Glenmorangie distillery, independently run networks, but the GPO obtained a court judgement in 1880 which allowed it to license all existing networks. In 1912 the telephone business was effectively nationalised. Meanwhile the GPO introduced a parcel business in 1880, and sending post cards attained a popularity only surpassed in our own age by the use of the internet and social media.

Not surprisingly, the early twentieth century saw a flurry in the building of bigger and better post offices. Elizabeth Beaton believes that the post office built in Dornoch around 1900, a 'delightful, asymmetrical building in red sandstone', was probably designed by the Maitland firm.[16] Although there seems to be a dearth of contemporary evidence, it is difficult to quarrel with this attribution. This very distinctive listed building,[17] in Arts and Crafts style, and prominently located on a corner site, has served a variety of purposes, having been used as a solicitor's office (by the author's Mackenzie and Cormack relations), a tourist office and a shop selling decorative products.

25.5 An Arts and Crafts building in Dornoch designed for the Post Office.

The main post office for the large parishes of Creich and Kincardine was at Ardgay. A new purpose built post office and sorting centre close to the railway station, with accommodation for the postmaster, was completed in June 1905.[18] Writing in 1995, Elizabeth Beaton noted that 'the plain post office, 1909 [sic], A. Maitland & Sons, retains the sorting office with all original fittings, which include desks equipped with pigeon holes and swivel stools, besides the post office with contemporary counter. There can be few other such post-office interiors surviving in Scotland.'[19]

In the early twentieth century the Tain Post Office was located in the Maitland-designed Tower Buildings beside the Tolbooth. By 1911 it had become apparent that the premises were too small. The burgh council minutes record how James and Gordon Maitland resolved the problem in an unusual way.[20]

In March 1911 the Postmaster General, Herbert Samuel, M.P., wrote to Robert Munro, the recently elected M.P. for the Northern Burghs. It was not practicable, he said, to extend the Tower Buildings lease, and it was therefore desirable to have a new Post Office by Whitsunday, 1912, when a break occurred in the lease. It was not their policy to purchase land and build but to obtain offers to adapt or build new premises which would be leased to the Postmaster General, usually on a 21 year lease. Only two offers had been received in response to their advertisements. One was for a site in Station Road (as Castle Brae was then known). The other was The Grove (set on the slope to the north of Lamington Street, a continuation of the High Street, with a U-shaped drive to and from the street). The owner of The Grove, the widow of a doctor who had died two years previously, wanted to sell the whole of the house and garden as they stood. The Postmaster General said that this would be too large and too expensive, and he therefore preferred the Station Road site. He noted, however, that the burgh council, reflecting public opinion, strongly objected to it, and that there was therefore deadlock.

The council looked at other sites, but continued to prefer The Grove. The deadlock was quickly resolved in favour of The Grove by Provost Maitland and his nephew. They bought the site and divided it into two, themselves having the Post Office built at the Lamington Street end and retaining The Grove, a substantial Georgian house built about 1793, as Gordon Maitland's residence. Gordon, who moved from lodgings near his grandfather's house in Esther Row, turned his new house around so that the front, with added bow windows, overlooked the Dornoch Firth rather than the street.[21] Plans and specifications for the Post Office were prepared by A. Maitland & Sons, who advertised for tenders in May 1912.[22] The building, 'small but authoritarian' in the words of John Gifford, was the last Maitland building in the main streets of the centre of Tain. The Valuation Rolls from 1913 onwards show Gordon as owner of The Grove and James and Gordon as joint owners of the Post Office, which they let to the Postmaster General at a rent of £130 per year.

At the time of writing The Grove, which suffered a serious fire in 2014, forms the centrepiece of a proposed new residential development. Only the sorting office function is carried out at the Post Office and the public area currently houses a hairdressing business. The building is now among Tain's many buildings at risk.

References and Notes

[1] Peter Krass, *Carnegie*, John Wiley & Sons, Inc., 2002 gives a useful account of Carnegie at Skibo and of his support for libraries.

[2] Bonar Bridge Library - *North Star and Farmers' Chronicle*, 22nd June, 1899. Spinningdale - *Inverness Courier*, 16th October, 1900.

[3] Highland HER MHG8686.

[4] *Ross-shire Journal*, 12th September, 1902.

[5] *Ross-shire Journal*, 20th May, 1904 and *Manchester Courier*, 16th April, 1904.

[6] *The World's Work Magazine*, April, 1905.

[7] *North Star and Farmers' Chronicle*, 14th February, 1901.

[8] *Ross-shire Journal*, 8th March, 1901.

[9] *North Star and Farmers' Chronicle*, 3rd August, 1905.

[10] *Inverness Courier*, 21st October, 1902 and *Ross-shire Journal* 29th January, 1904.

[11] Historic Environment Scotland LB41898.

[12] www.morangiehotel.com/history.

[13] Information from Ross Robertson, grandson of William Robertson.

[14] Gifford, *Highlands and Islands*, p. 462.

[15] *North Star and Farmers Journal*, 22nd October, 1908.

[16] Beaton, *Sutherland*, p.34.

[17] Historic Environment Scotland LB 24634.

[18] *Highland News*, 1st July, 1905.

[19] Beaton, *Sutherland*, p.11. (Ardgay was historically part of Ross-shire but was ceded to Sutherland in the 1974 re-organisation of local government.)

[20] Minutes of Tain Burgh Council, Highland Archive Centre, BTN 1/1/5.

[21] Article *The Grove, Tain*, in *Tain and Dornoch Picture Post* by Shona Arthur (a later owner), undated.

[22] *Ross-shire Journal* , 10th May, 1912.

26. THE END OF THE MAITLAND STORY

Invergordon and the build-up to war

The years immediately before the Great War were not kind to architects. David M. Walker in an introductory essay in the online *Dictionary of Scottish Architects* wrote that 'throughout the biographical notes for the Edwardian era will be found instances of architects closing their offices to practise from home; seeking employment from the Inland Revenue as valuators to administer the tax [a tax on incremental land values proposed in Lloyd George's 1909 Budget, but never implemented]; obtaining salaried employment with government departments, harbour boards and the railway companies; and even simply disappearing abroad'.

The surviving members of the Maitland firm did not follow this pattern until after the Great War, but in the year before it started they took what look like defensive measures. The *North Star & Farmers' Journal* reported in February 1913 that 'Messrs Maitland & Co., architects, are opening a branch office in Invergordon for the convenience of their ever-growing circle of clients in the district'. Readers were advised elsewhere in the same issue that 'We hear that new buildings, private residences and others, are to be erected in Invergordon in the near future. The town is now fairly booming, and Invergordon folks are looking forward to better times than ever before. … It is the sea that does it, and the prospects of the present summer, with the naval and other works, are decidedly promising for a prosperous future'.

It was indeed a case of 'the sea that does it'. Royal Navy fleets had made frequent visits to the Cromarty Firth in the second half of the nineteenth century. These visits facilitated growth, particularly of the infrastructure. Hence A. Maitland & Sons were engaged to design a new police station in 1900. James Maitland would have been flattered to hear H.M. Inspector of Constabulary for Scotland, Captain David Munro of Allan (who had inherited a mansion house designed by his firm), describe it as one of the very best police stations he had seen.[1] In April, 1909 the Maitlands sought tenders for alterations to the Post Office Buildings at Invergordon.[2] This seems to have been to allow the G.P.O. to occupy the whole of a building now known as the Old Post Office, of which they had previously rented only part.

As Marinell Ash explains in her fine history of the Cromarty Firth, rapid development of the Firth in the years leading up to the Great War was a direct consequence of the appointment of Admiral 'Jacky' Fisher as First Sea Lord in 1902.[3] Fisher believed that war with Germany was inevitable and initiated an urgent programme of shipbuilding. Fleet visits became more frequent, and business in Invergordon benefitted. Though Fisher retired (the first of two retirements) in 1910 his policies were enthusiastically continued by Winston Churchill, who became First Lord of the Admiralty in the following year. Churchill, like Fisher, was a proponent of fuelling the new Dreadnought class of battleships and battlecruisers with oil rather than coal, and oil storage tanks were constructed on land at Invergordon feued from Macleod of Cadboll. In March 1912, by which time there was a permanent and growing naval presence in Invergordon, Churchill announced plans for the Firth to become a 'floating second class naval base and war anchorage … fortified on a scale sufficient to deter enemy attack'. The North and South Sutors, twin headlands which mark the entrance to the Firth, were fortified against enemy attack. The Firth became, along with Scapa Flow and Rosyth, one of the great North Sea naval bases - bases from which the Grand Fleet was to sail to the all-important battle of Jutland.

The opening of the Maitlands' office in Invergordon probably reflected the reduced amount of work available in Tain. It certainly reflected opportunities expected to arise in Invergordon, opportunities enhanced by changes in the competitive situation for Highland architects. The Dingwall-based architect W.C. Joass had ceased to advertise for tenders after 1906. Robert Macbeth had died in 1912 (though a villa he designed in Invergordon was apparently completed posthumously). And although Alexander Ross, the leading Highland architect of the day, continued his prolific work, none of it seems to have been in Invergordon.

In early 1913 A. Maitland & Sons sought tenders for alterations and improvements to the Caledonian Hotel and for the renovation of the Victoria Hotel, both in Invergordon.[4] The 'renovation' was in fact the

construction of a new hotel, named the Royal Hotel, on the old site. Until it was burnt down in 1973 the 22 bedroom Royal Hotel, a distinctive feature of the High Street with something of the appearance of an old coaching inn, played a prominent role in Invergordon's affairs.

26.1 The Royal Hotel, Invergordon.

Following a visit to the Cromarty Firth by Winston Churchill it was decided to station a torpedo boat flotilla in the Firth. The officers of the flotilla formed a company to build a naval clubhouse on a commanding site with views of the Firth, and they engaged A. Maitland & Sons to design it.[5] They clearly liked their onshore comforts, as there were a smoking and meeting room, a billiards room and a card room, as well as bedrooms and bathrooms, whilst outside they could play tennis.

The start of the Great War

In late July and the start of August 1914, as an international crisis came to the boil, Scottish towns held meetings designed to demonstrate support for, or (less frequently) opposition to, war. A meeting was held in the Tain Parish Church (now the Duthac Centre) on Sunday 2nd August, at which Provost James Maitland presided. His client the Count de Serra Largo of Tarlogie moved a resolution: 'We, the inhabitants of Tain, in public meeting assembled, assure the Government of our united support at this time of national crisis in all measures they take for the safety of the country and to maintain its honour and interests'.

Two days later Britain was at war. The warrior hero Field Marshal Earl Kitchener of Khartoum was immediately appointed Secretary of State for War. At his first Cabinet meeting 'K. of K.' stunned his new politician colleagues, for whom he had little respect, by telling them that the war they had undertaken was likely to last not for months as they expected but for several years, to require huge new armies and to cause huge casualties. To be victorious, he declared, they must be prepared 'to put armies of millions into the field and maintain them for several years'. A massive recruitment campaign began, and towns everywhere responded to a request from the Prime Minister, H.H. Asquith, to organise recruitment meetings. Within days posters and newspaper advertisements sought volunteers. One of the most enduring images of the war was that of the handlebar-moustached Kitchener, his finger pointing imperiously at the reader and delivering the message 'Your Country needs **YOU**'.

The main theatre of war became the Western Front, and trench warfare became the predominant mode of life - and death - for those involved. From November 1914 until the *Kaiserschlacht* of March 1918 the positions of the Allied and the German troops rarely moved more than ten miles each way.

Gordon Maitland's war

Gordon Maitland was quick to enlist, and in October he received a commission in the 3rd Battalion of the Scottish Rifles (Cameronians). He was soon attached to the 2nd Battalion, which was posted to France. In February 1915 he was promoted to Lieutenant.

In July 1915 Gordon Maitland was in charge of a patrol party between the British and German trenches which encountered a German patrol. His patrol had the better of a skirmish, but another German patrol on their flank fired on them, wounding Gordon in the hand and eyes. Army medical records show that he spent two periods, aggregating 74 days, at Queen Alexandra's Military Hospital in Millbank, London, where he was treated for a fractured left wrist caused by gunshot wounds.

The next medical record is altogether more distressing. In March 1917, perhaps having served once more on the Western Front, he was again admitted to Queen Alexandra's Military Hospital. This time he was treated for 'Mania'. After being treated for 70 days he was discharged. His case notes were sent to Latchmere House, which suggests that he may also have been treated there. Latchmere House was a Victorian mansion on Ham Common, near Richmond in Surrey, which had been established as a mental hospital for officers.

In a way that no previous war had done the Great War, mechanised and waged on an industrial scale, produced vast numbers of mentally distressed soldiers. The British Army dealt with no less than 80,000 cases. At first what was called 'shell shock' was believed to be the result of physical injury to the nerves caused by such things as suffering heavy bombardment or being buried alive. Treatment included rest, massage, diet and electric shocks. As the war progressed, however, medical officers increasingly began to regard psychological factors as sufficient cause for breakdown, and more emphasis was placed on recovering the patient's will and self-control through suggestive power, on inculcating 'manliness', and on occupational training.

Even after discharge life could be difficult. A high proportion of soldiers with nervous disorders were unfit for further military service, and many suffered lifelong consequences and sometimes social stigma. The Ministry of Pensions was established in 1916 and its was given powers to make awards where disablement was due to, or aggravated by, military service. It was soon flooded with shell-shock cases. As late as 1939 some 40,000 war veterans were still receiving pensions, many of them pretty meagre, for nervous or mental disorders.

Gordon Maitland relinquished his commission in April 1917, and he received a military pension for the rest of his life. No records have been found relating to any further treatment that he received or to his adjustment to civilian life. As we will see, his post-war career was unsettled and peripatetic. We can only surmise that this was a result of his war-time experiences.

The war and its aftermath

The war had an unprecedented impact on the life of the civilian population. By late 1915, it was reported, more than 75% of men between the ages of 15 and 35 in the Easter Ross area were serving in the armed forces. Even though more women were employed than ever before in fields and towns. there was a skills shortage. Building stopped. The quarries whose stone had for generations been the main component of

Tain's buildings, and which had been operated by the Maitland brothers, closed in 1915 - permanently except for a temporary re-opening in the early 1950s.

Whilst more and more local men were sucked in to the horrors of trench warfare, James Maitland's role as Provost expanded to take involvement in the provision of comforts for the troops, organising 'patriotic meetings' aimed at securing more volunteers and, when conscription was introduced in 1916 (first for unmarried and later for married men), presiding over a Local Tribunal to which those seeking exemption for employment, business, personal or moral reasons had to apply.

Great celebrations marked the end of the war on 11th November, 1918. At a Special Meeting of Lodge St Duthus James Maitland, who was serving his fourth term as their Master, 'referred in glowing and eloquent terms to the glorious news that had been received that day that the German Empire had unconditionally surrendered, thus practically bringing to a close the greatest war that the world had ever seen'. But the abiding feeling was a sense of loss. The British Isles had suffered some three quarters of a million military deaths, and Scotland in general and the Highlands in particular had borne more than their proportionate shares.

Thoughts soon turned to war memorials. Some of the finest architects and sculptors of the day designed memorials. Alexander Ross was responsible for several in the Highlands, but there is no evidence that the Maitlands designed any. James Maitland presided over a public meeting convened by the Tain Burgh Council to consider memorial proposals. The retired schoolmaster and local historian William MacGill said that Tain was in a unique position of having an ancient and beautiful memorial church entirely devoted to monumental purposes, and moved that a worthy memorial tablet be placed there. An elegant brass plaque was placed in the Collegiate Church, 'In Grateful Memory of the Men of Tain who fell in the Great War', and it lists 122 names. One of the last surviving photographs of James Maitland shows him at a meeting organised by Mrs Littlejohn of Invercharron to remember the contribution of the men of Tain in the Great War.

26.2 Provost James Maitland (in the Courthouse doorway) at a meeting to remember the men of Tain in the Great War.

The sale of the Glenmorangie distillery

When the war began the Maitland family remained substantial shareholders in The Glenmorangie Distillery Company. James was still Managing Director and Gordon Maitland a director. It would appear, however, that James, aged 69 when war broke out, was not playing a very active role, whilst Gordon quickly became unavailable. Alexander Smart was the well-regarded day to day manager, and his son Gordon Smart became company secretary in 1915.

The war had a significant effect on Glenmorangie.[6] The distillery produced whisky on and off until 1917, though production was down because of a lack of barley (which was needed for food when imports were hit by U-boat activity) and a shortage of manpower. The maltbarns, not in use during the summer, were converted into makeshift barracks for recruits for the Argyll & Sutherland Highlanders. In early 1917 it appeared at first that things were returning to normal. But in March Gordon Smart joined the Royal Flying Corps and others left, presumably as a result of conscription. After the routine cleaning-up in June the workforce was cut to a skeleton of three men who ran the distillery on a care and maintenance basis until 1919. An increase in the excise duty from 14s. 9d. to 30 shillings per gallon in the 1918 Budget added further woes. At the same time the distillery had suffered for some years from reduced maintenance and new investment was badly needed.

Others saw Glenmorangie's problems as an opportunity. The company's largest customer was Macdonald & Muir, a Leith based firm operating as merchants and blenders, whose blended whiskies included the very popular Highland Queen ('HQ'). The partners in Macdonald & Muir, Roderick Macdonald and his brother-in-law Alexander ('Sandy') Muir, were approached by another whisky merchant, James Durham, with the proposition that the three of them together should acquire the stocks of whisky belonging to Glenmorangie. The three merchants negotiated with the Glenmorangie shareholders.[7] At the last minute the shareholders said that they would have to sell the company too in order to avoid having to pay Excess Profits Tax. (This was a wartime revenue raising levy set initially at 50%, then raised in 1917 to 80%, of profits above the normal pre-war level.) On 13th April, 1918 Macdonald, Muir and Durham paid £74,100 for the company.

Thus ended the Maitland family's connection with the company they had promoted and managed and whose distillery they had built. When Macdonald & Muir was incorporated as a limited company in 1936 it acquired all the shares in Glenmorangie. Macdonald & Muir was itself was acquired in 2004 by the French luxury goods conglomerate Moët Hennessy-Louis Vuitton, known as LVMH. Today Glenmorangie, still operating from mainly Maitland-designed buildings, rubs shoulders with iconic brands like Christian Dior, Veuve Cliquot, Guerlain, and Tiffany & Co.

The Maitland practice after the war

The name of Gordon Maitland crops up in many reports of the activities of A. Maitland & Sons in the years immediately following the Great War, but not that of his uncle James. It is unclear how far James was involved. He appears to have retired from the practice in 1921, leaving Gordon as the sole partner for a brief period. The practice was assisted by William Macdonald, a gardener's son born in 1894, who had been apprenticed to the firm in 1913. After war service from 1916 to 1919 Macdonald resumed his training and soon became Chief Draughtsman and then Principal Assistant.

Two factors had a significant impact on building in the post-war period, and thus on the work of architectural practices like those of the Maitlands - landowners selling off rural land, and the provision of 'Homes Fit for Heroes'.

The first of these factors had a negative effect on the demand for architects' services. During the war imports had dried up and farmers had enjoyed a secure market for the first time in four decades. Prices rose dramatically, and over the U.K as a whole farm incomes quadrupled during the war years. 'Many landowners however', as Glendinning and Wade Martins explain, 'looked upon the post-war prosperity with scepticism, and saw it chiefly as a good time to sell off much of their land. They feared a return to the pre-war depression, especially as they were feeling the effect of the new death-duties and super-taxes, and many had lost sons and heirs during the war. Nearly 40% of Scotland changed hands in the immediate post-war years, with most of the farms being purchased by their tenant-occupiers. ... This sea-change in tenure was to have an effect on the sort of farm buildings that were erected. Few tenants could afford expensive new buildings'.[8] Even before the war had ended the solicitors of the Cadboll estate rushed to inform readers of *The Scotsman* that farms in the vicinity of Tain, Fearn and Tarbat Ness with a total acreage of 9,400 acres would be sold by auction at an early date unless previously sold by treaty. They were followed over the next three or four years by advertisements for the sale of about a dozen agricultural estates in the Maitlands' area of operation. Whilst not all of these led to sales, many farms with farm houses and steadings built by the Maitlands for landlords in Victorian and Edwardian times were sold, usually to existing tenants. The new owners' finances were often stretched by their purchases. As a result buildings that had been constructed in the era of 'High Farming' were deemed adequate, and there was little building work of significance until, later in the twentieth century, the replacement of the horse by the tractor led to changes.

The second factor affecting building work in the post-war period was the emphasis given to the provision of houses for the 'working classes'.[9] We saw earlier that concerns about public health had led to the setting up in 1912 of the Royal Commission on the Housing of the Industrial Population of Scotland, Rural and Urban, chaired by Sir Henry Ballantyne. The commission published a very full report in 1917 which had a profound effect. It aimed to prescribe 'How to provide a healthy, comfortable dwelling for every family in the land', and it proposed state intervention on a massive scale. It estimated that 235,990 houses were required, with 121,430 needed immediately. It recommended that there should be explicit acceptance of the state's responsibility for housing the working classes and an obligation on local government to make the requisite provision, backed up by giving central government powers to compel them to meet this responsibility. This struck a chord with politicians, and as soldiers returned from the war they were promised 'homes fit for heroes'. Whereas central government's role on housing had hitherto been merely regulatory, Lloyd George's post-war Coalition Government adopted an interventionist policy. The Housing and Town Planning Act, 1919 set up a nationally co-ordinated programme of building houses for the working classes, with responsibility for its implementation given to local authorities under the supervision of the Scottish Board (later Department) of Health. The programme was financed by government subsidies, rates and rents.

Council houses were built on a massive scale, accounting for 253,000 out of 365,000 new housing units constructed in Scotland between the wars. They remain a distinctive feature of Scottish towns in the twenty-first century - typically semi-detached, low density (ideally 12 to the acre), and set back from the road. 128 council houses were built in Tain. The council found a site on Burgage Farm and borrowed £12,000 for the first scheme, known as Cromartie Gardens. Gordon Maitland was chosen as the architect (though he had to keep within official architectural guidelines) and William Macdonald as part-time clerk of works. In September 1920 the ceremony of laying the foundation stone of the first house was performed with full masonic ritual by James Maitland in his dual capacity as Provost and, for the fourth and last time, Right Worshipful Master of the St Duthus Lodge of Freemasons.[10]

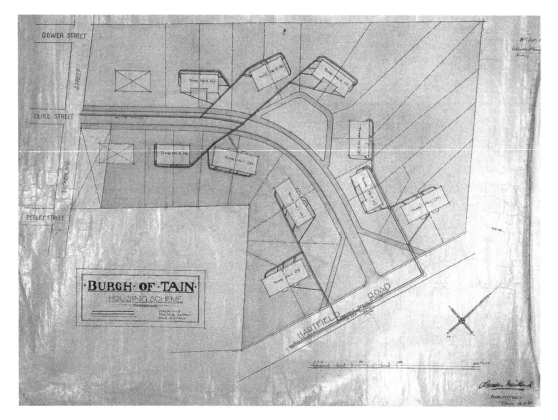

26.3 'Homes fit for heroes': Gordon Maitland's site plan for Cromartie Gardens, Tain, 1920.

This was the last significant building project with which the Maitland family were involved. Their connection with the firm ended when Gordon Maitland retired on 1st July, 1922. The practice was continued under the name A. Maitland & Sons by William Macdonald. Macdonald was involved in the building of further council houses, but otherwise his work seems to have been mainly additions and extensions to existing buildings. The 'Great Depression' that followed the Wall Street crash of 1929 had a devastating effect on the economy, and in the following year Macdonald closed the Maitland business and went to work for the Department of Agriculture for Scotland.

James Maitland in retirement

The end of James Maitland's involvement with the Glenmorangie distillery and his retirement from his architectural practice were soon followed by his withdrawal from local politics. At the burgh elections of November, 1921 James, now 76, did not seek re-election to the council and retired as Provost of Tain. In the same year he simplified his financial affairs by selling at auction feu duties which belonged jointly to himself and the trust estates of his brother Andrew Junior and his close friend George MacLeay. These investments had brought in an income of £136-13s-1d and were offered for a quick sale at an upset price of £1,800.

Thereafter he does not seem to have played any significant role in local affairs. In 1925, 'feel[ing] keenly the lack of appropriate civic insignia in a Royal Burgh which has had a Provost since 1066', he presented the council with an 18 carat gold chain of office for use by the Provost. This is now in the Tain Museum collection. From at least 1926 James and his wife Barbara took to spending their winters in Bournemouth, at Fairmount in Priory Road. This was a substantial house, now used as a hotel, within an easy walk of the beach and the pier.

In June 1928, whilst staying temporarily at the Balnagown Arms Hotel in Tain, James sold Balcarres, the house he had designed for himself in Morangie Road, Tain. The purchaser was the widowed Mrs Christabel Irwin Smart, described in an obituary as a 'rich and vigorous personality', a novelist, a poet, and a benefactor 'in a quiet way.' In her will of 1934 she requested that the house be offered for the benefit of Tain and the surrounding district (especially the Isle of Skye) as a convalescent home, home of rest or cottage hospital. Small fees were to be charged to those able to pay, and the very poor to be admitted free. It was to be called 'St Mary's Home', and her husband's picture and sword were to be left hanging over the mantelpiece. It was to be offered to a named committee of distinguished people, who were to be at liberty to refuse the offer. This liberty they appear to have taken, as the house is still in residential use - though the name St Mary's has replaced that of Balcarres.

James did not live long enough to hear of Mrs Irwin Smart's plans. He died in Bournemouth on 10th April, 1929 and was buried in the old cemetery in Tain. He left total moveable estate of £30,739-3s-2d, a substantial amount, comprised mainly of shareholdings in 62 companies.

Gordon Maitland's latter days

Mackenzie and Durham say that for Gordon Maitland 'architecture began to pall in the 1920s, and he left Tain to become a sculptor in Paris, where he died in 1933'. Whatever his intentions, however, his retirement seems to have been rather more complicated. Thus when he made his will in 1929 he described himself as 'without any fixed place of residence but temporarily residing at 57, Beaumont Street, London'. Four years later his executors deponed that he had been 'without any fixed or known domicile except that the same was in Scotland', and in presenting the Inventory of his estate (showing a healthy amount of £10,161-12s-5d) they stated that he had 'resided latterly in the South of France'.

Another account states that Gordon 'retired to Edinburgh where he was working for solicitors Morton, Smart, Macdonald & Prosser, W.S. at 19, York Place at the time of his admission as LRIBA in early 1925'. Many architects sought admission to the Licentiate class of the Royal Institute of British Architects on a professional merger in 1925, so it is possible that Gordon had not totally abandoned his career as an architect. But we can be certain that Gordon was not working for the Edinburgh solicitors. The firm had drawn up the wills of Gordon's father and grandfather, and his elder brother Arthur had worked for them before his death in 1920 at the age of only 42. After Arthur's death the firm continued to act as Gordon's solicitors, and also those of his uncle James, and throughout his travels Gordon, with no fixed place of residence, used their address for correspondence.

Nothing is known of Gordon's activities during his last years, but it is clear from the fleeting glimpses we have that his life was far from settled. This could well have been due to the shell-shock he sustained during the war. He died at the American Hospital of Paris in Neuilly-sur-Seine on 25th August, 1933.[11] His entry in the British Consulate Register of Deaths does not record the cause of death.

Marne Maitland - a coda to the family story

The death of Gordon Maitland marked the end of the Maitland dynasty of architects. But another member of the family, James Maitland's only grandson, was to achieve far wider fame in a different art form.

James's only child Henry Comyn Maitland joined the Indian Civil Service in 1907-08. 95% of the ICS officers, and all the top ranking ones, were British. Marriages with Indian women were unusual. But Henry Maitland nevertheless married an Indian, 'Dolly' Ray. Dolly died prematurely, but left a son, born in Calcutta in 1914, who was given the names James Marne Kumar Maitland. In 1932 Henry Maitland, now practising as a barrister in London and married to an English second wife, wrote to Magdalene College, Cambridge, his own former college.[12] He sought a place for his son, then boarding at the ultra-liberal Bedales School in Hampshire. 'I am not sure if you are aware', he wrote, 'that my wife was an Indian lady. I trust the fact that my boy is Indian on his mother's side will not prejudice this application in any way. For legal purposes he is of course a European British subject. ... His maternal grandfather was Principal of the Presidency College, Calcutta; his grandmother is now a member of the Senate of the University of Calcutta; one of his great uncles is a Judge of the Rangoon High Court; another, recently deceased, was Legal Member of the Viceroy's Executive Council; so his Indian lineage is much more distinguished than his Scots one'. His father's letter and his own performance in the entrance examination led to the young man's admission in 1933.

In his first term Marne Maitland performed with the Cambridge Amateur Dramatic Society and the following year on the 'National' radio programme. His father wrote to the college about his son's studies: he evidently favoured Marne's participation in theatrical performances rather than concentration on his studies. After service in the British army during the Second World War Marne joined the Old Vic company. In a film and television career lasting from 1950 to 1990 his sharp oriental features helped him to secure a variety of character parts, often as a sinister middle or far eastern villain. Among his best known roles were ones in the James Bond film *The Man with the Golden Gun* and the highly regarded television series *The Jewel in the Crown*.

The Maitland legacy - an inheritance we should not squander

Edmund Burke saw each generation as custodians of the past and trustees for future generations. 'Society', he wrote, 'is a partnership ... between those who are dead, those who are living and those who are to be born'. In his view we are 'temporary possessors or life renters of this world', with an obligation not to squander this inheritance lest 'we leave to those who come after a ruin rather than a habitation'.

In our generation many of the buildings that form part of our inheritance are at risk. The pressures, particularly on nineteenth and early twentieth century buildings such as those the Maitlands built, are enormous. Civic functions, policing and court services are increasingly consolidated as Scotland becomes what is sometimes said to be the most centralised country in Europe. Bank branches and post offices become redundant. Churches amalgamate their congregations. Local schools close when pupils are moved to larger central sites. Changing patterns of agriculture render steadings redundant. The protection offered by the listing of building, by their inclusion in Conservation Areas and by planning policies is useful but limited - particularly when, as so often, listing obligations and Conservation Areas are not properly policed. Conservationists and other experts make policy suggestions, such as those in report commissioned by the Scottish government on *The Conversion of Redundant Farm Steadings to Other Uses,*[13] but all too often these are ignored.

Fortunately, however, not all is doom and gloom. Villas such as those the Maitlands designed continue to be occupied and to be loved, as do manses - albeit usually by lay owners. Mansion houses, castles and sporting lodges built for heritors and sportsmen are frequently adapted for use as hotels. Private initiatives often lead to sensitive restorations and conversions. These are sometimes personal, as with the steading conversion at Balaphuile we saw in chapter 18. In other cases the initiatives are collective, and they often involve a search for new uses. Thus the Public Hall in Tain, vacant when it closed as a cinema, survived plans to demolish it for car parking, and this author is proud to have supported a promising restoration project.

The Victorian and Edwardian periods saw buildings which changed the face of the Highlands. On their patch, across the Northern Highlands, the Maitlands made a distinctive contribution.

Maitland-designed farm houses, steadings and farm cottages, often embellished with porches, conservatories and velux windows, remain one of the most prominent features of the landscape of Easter Ross and beyond - an enduring testament to the age of High Farming. The Maitlands were, as Mackenzie and Durham remark, 'employed by almost every family of consequence in the county [Ross-shire], and others beyond it'. The prosperity that agriculture brought to the heritors is still reflected not just in farm buildings but also in many mansion houses that the Maitlands built or altered, often in Scottish Baronial style. In more remote parts of the Highlands numerous Maitland sporting lodges are still used for their original purpose, and others have become hotels..

In towns and villages across the Northern Highlands there are public buildings - court houses, police stations, post offices, town halls and schools - built or extended by the Maitlands, some still in use, some converted to residential or commercial use. They reflect an age in which central government began to impinge on people's lives, but in which its functions were devolved to local level and the design of buildings remained a matter of local choice. Civic pride thrived throughout the period in which the Maitlands operated, and Andrew Maitland Junior and his brother James were able to nurture that pride through holding high civic office.

There are also numerous commercial buildings - shops, hotels, banks, the unusual Maitland office - built to serve the needs of a society in which the middle classes played an increasing role. On what were then the fringes of the larger towns, especially Tain and Dornoch, there are Maitland villas and substantial houses built to meet the aspirations of successful merchants, professional men and their womenfolk.

Maitland-designed churches, some converted to residential use, are to be found over a wide area of the Northern Highlands - witnesses to an age of faith but also of schism, sometimes acrimonious. Many are the legacy of middle class congregations who were increasingly able to finance churches that were not only more comfortable but also more impressive than those of the established church. Those in Tain and Nairn are particularly fine examples of their work.

Their contemporaries joked that the Maitlands were noted both as church architects and as distillery architects. In their day the production of malt whisky changed from being a farmhouse activity to becoming the most important manufacturing industry in the Highlands. Most of the Maitlands' work on distilleries has vanished, but at Dalmore and especially at Glenmorangie, where Andrew Maitland Junior was a key player, there remain distilleries that are largely Maitland-built.

The range of the Maitlands' activities was astonishing. Some of their work was routine, some was functional, reflecting the needs and the budgets of their clients. But they also produced buildings, in a variety of styles, of an extraordinarily high quality, a quality which makes them architects of note in the Highlands and renders their home town of Tain a place of rare charm and beauty. The Maitlands made an important contribution to the built environment of the Northern Highlands, and their legacy is an inheritance we should not squander.

References and Notes

[1] *Ross-shire Journal*, 19th January (submission of plans) and 31st May, 1901 (inspection of the new station).

[2] *North Star and Farmers' Chronicle*, 8th April, 1909.

[3] Marinell Ash, *This Noble Harbour - A History of the Cromarty Firth*, Cromarty Firth Port Authority, 1991, pp.175-205.

[4] *North Star & Farmers' Chronicle*, 23rd January and 6th February, 1913 respectively.

[5] *Aberdeen Journal*, 23rd June,1913.

6   Much of the information about Glenmorangie during the war is derived from Richard D. Oram, *Glenmorangie Research Project, Final Report*, 11th December, 1992, pp.33-35.

7   Information kindly supplied by Iain Russell, Brands Heritage Manager of The Glenmorangie Co. Ltd.

8   Miles Glendinning and Susanna Wade Martins, *Buildings of the Land, Scotland's Farms 1750-2000*, Royal Commission on the Ancient and Historical Monuments of Scotland, 2008, p.143.

9   For a useful account see the chapter on *Small Houses and Cottages* by Annette Carruthers and John Frew in *Scottish Life and Society, vol. 3, Scotland's Buildings*, Tuckwell Press, 2003, pp.97-101.

10   *Aberdeen Press and Journal*, 28th September, 1920.

11   One account states that he went to Madeira on medical advice but died en route in 1930. This is clearly incorrect.

12   Thanks are due to Dr Tilda Watson, Archivist of Magdalene College, Cambridge for her assistance in researching the early life of Marne Maitland.

13   Andy Davey, Simpson & Brown Architects, Scottish Executive Central Research Unit, 2001.

INDEX

OF PRINCIPAL BUILDINGS, PEOPLE AND THEMES

MODERN NAMES IN BRACKETS

Lightning Source UK Ltd.
Milton Keynes UK
UKHW021030071220
374691UK00005B/108